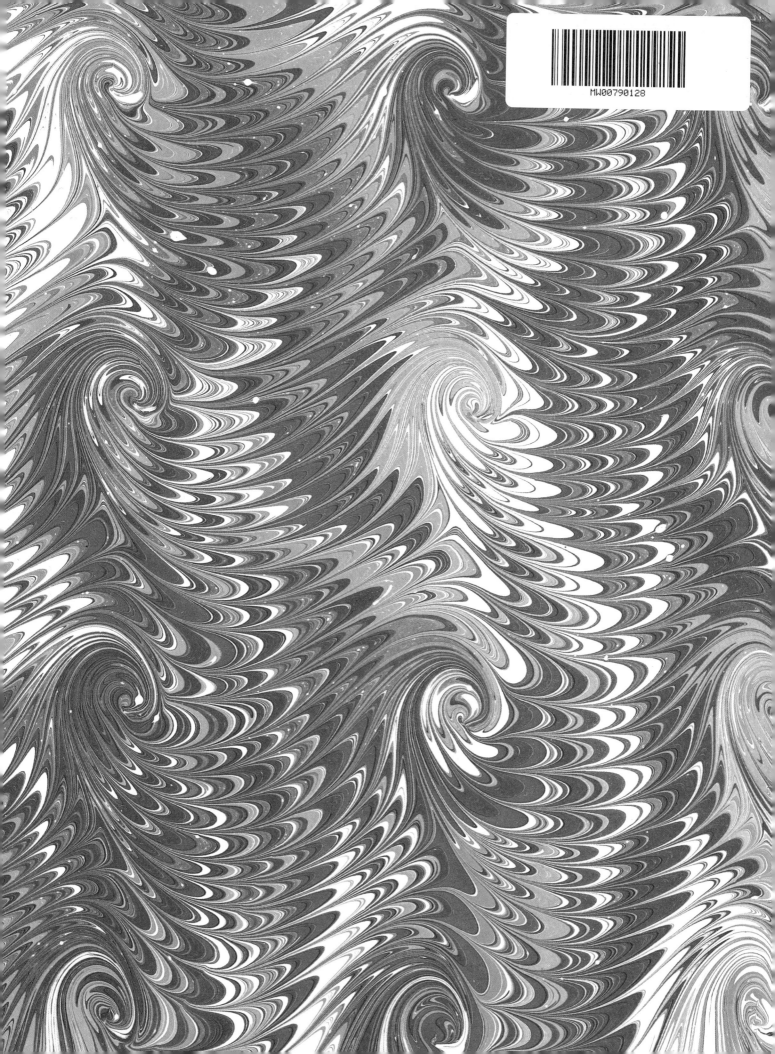

WARPATH

AIR APACHES

The Story Of The
345th Bombardment Group
In World War II

Schiffer Military History
Atglen, PA

Cover artwork by Steve Ferguson, Colorado Springs, CO.

FALCONS FEVER

The 345th Bombardment Group "Air Apaches" were at the forefront of every battle in the Southwest Pacific theatre. Their gaudily painted Falcon, Bat and Panther gunships struck at tree-top level, destroying any target that appeared along the path to victory. Neither fortress nor warship could provide safe haven for the soldiers and sailors of the Japanese Empire who retreated before the Mitchell bombers that pursued them to the very home waters of the Inland Sea. Depicted is a pair of 398th Squadron "Falcons" parafrag-bombing one of the many airfield targets on the north coast of New Guinea in the offensive of 1943. Coupled with the high altitude raids of B-24 units, the Air Apaches and their cohorts eliminated all threats of a sustained counter-offensive, first at Wewak in August, and at Hollandia in April of the following year when the enemy air forces were caught on the ground. Prisoners-of-war declared the Mitchell raiders were the most feared and respected of all the Allied air-crews.

Published by Schiffer Publishing Ltd.
77 Lower Valley Road
Atglen, PA 19310
Phone: (610) 593-1777
FAX: (610) 593-2002
Please write for a free catalog.
This book may be purchased from the publisher.
Please include $2.95 postage.
Try your bookstore first.

TABLE OF CONTENTS

To the men of the 345th Bombardment Group who gave their lives for Victory and Peace, this record is humbly dedicated by us who remained to see the fruition of their sacrifices.

July 14, 1946

TO THE MEN OF THE 345TH BOMBARDMENT GROUP

It is with great pleasure on my part that this book—your WARPATH—is presented to you men of the 345th. That part of our lives—from November 11, 1942 to November 11, 1945—is here set forth, written by you. The material contained herein has been approved by the War Department for publication.

The Staff of WARPATH consisted of the following: Max H. Mortensen, Business Manager; John C. Hanna, William R. Witherell, Jr., Co-Editors; Charles O. Metzel, Whitney T. Perkins, James E. McLaughlin, George K. Hansen, David A. Utley, Gabriel Farrell, Jr., John F. Dinges, Stanley Andrews and Donald T. Britton.

Acknowledgements: We tender grateful thanks to the many who either wrote down or told us of previously unrecorded indicents in our three years of war; the pilots and gunners who flipped the camera switches to take some of the war's best photographs, and the men who serviced these cameras and processed the films; the Air Apaches who gave us personal pictures to better depict our story. To all these men and many others, our thanks. We think this record is worth preserving and it could not have been done without them

The Staff
Max H. Mortensen
Lt. Col. A. C.
Champaign, Illinois

HEADQUARTERS FIFTH AIR FORCE
APO 710

29 September, 1945

TO: Officers and Men, 345th Bombardment Group (M).

The 345th Bombardment Group (M) will be forever honored and revered by freedom-loving peoples throughout the world. High esprit and pride of organization were always in evidence and contributed so much to the sustained driving power during its historic part in smashing the Japanese war machine. Strangulation of the Japanese empire by elements of the Fifth Air Force was a major factor in the defeat of Japan —and one of the brightest stars on the team was the great aggregation of Air Apaches.

All personnel of this Air Force are proud of your great war record.

(Signed) Ennis C. Whitehead
Lieutenant General, USA
Commanding

HEADQUARTERS FIFTH BOMBER COMMAND

The "Air Apaches" have truly earned superb recognition in their march along the "Warpath" from Australia to Japan. I have fond memories of my service in the Group, and of those fine men who lost their lives while serving there. Those who survived the many vigorous months of combat have further demonstrated their capabilities after relief from combat duty.

The 345th ground personnel have without exception proved their worth. Their fliers went out to combat with the knowledge that they were backed by the finest and most loyal men in the world.

The spirit of unity and esprit de corps of this Group cannot be "de-activated." It is a living thing which will again some day bring further honor to our United States.

(Signed) J. V. Crabb
Brigadier General, USA

COMBAT COMMENDATIONS
TO THE 345TH BOMB GROUP

At Port Moresby, November 11, 1943, celebrating our first anniversary, various literati wrote for a mimeographed paper edited by John Michalowski. The following is extracted from the publication, which was entitled "The Overseas Target."

General Blamey and General Herring extend their heartiest congratulations on the mignificent victory achieved August 16 and 17. Without the intense training and fine spirit of your organizations, the success of this decisive operation would not have been possible.

I want to add my personal sincere congratulations to all commands.

Maj. General E. C. Whitehead

My heartiest congratulations to all units of this command.

Major General Blamey

Again I commend your splendid mission performance. Your activities were highly successful.

Brig. General Ramey

General Whitehead and myself offer our congratulations on this morning's mission.

Brig. General Ramey

Congratulations on well planned and executed strike against the enemy by your four squadrons. V Bomber is proud of you!

V BomCom Headquarters

(The following commendation was received from the Commander-in-Chief of the Southwest Pacific and the Commanding General of the Fifth Air Force in regard to the recent operations over Rabaul.)

Quote, "To Lt. Gen. Kenney. Please accept my heartiest congratulations for yourself, General Whitehead and all forces involved in the superb double strike at Rabaul. It gives me a sense of great security to have such an indomitable unit in my command. Unquote. Never give a sucker a break. Keep it up!"

General Douglas MacArthur

In addition to the above, the undersigned desires to convey his heartiest congratulations to all ranks for these aggressive attacks against the enemy.

Maj. Gen. E. C. Whitehead

(Take a low deep bow boys 'cause these commendations are all yours)

The Staff

JARRED V. CRABB

CLINTON V. TRUE

CHESTER A. COLTHARP, JR.

GLENN A. DOOLITTLE

ACTIVATION OF THE 345TH
BOMBARDMENT GROUP

A bomb group consists of men and their planes. It also consists of typewriters and generators, hypo needles and cameras, radios and link trainers . . . a mobile city, with its own movie projectors and "coke" machines. These, and a multitude of other items make up a bomb group.

On paper, this incongruous mixture of machines and intangibles became the 345th Bombardment Group (Medium) by virtue of Third Air Force Order #275, paragraph one, September 6th, 1942. The backbone of the outfit was drawn from the 309th Bomb Group (M), a training unit at Columbia Army Air Base. Our activation date was November 11th, 1942.

Men began to pour in and were assigned to their duties. Under Group Commander, Col. Jarred V. Crabb, four Squadrons were established: the 498th under Capt. Bert S. Rosenbaum; the 499th led by Capt. Buell A. Bankston; the 500th with Lt. Charles M. Hagest; and the 501st whose C. O. was Lt. Robert S. Fain. By the end of the month, the first planes were parcelled out. The ships were B-25s, and though we picked up three types of Mitchells and made numerous modifications, the B-25 was

our weapon throughout the war.

Operations, Intelligence, and the Parachute Departments were in five buildings on the Columbia line. About a mile away the less functional part of the unit made its home. Off-duty, we were shoveling coal to keep warm in the barracks or BOQs. A few had quarters in the crowded South Carolina town. A bright spot on the field was Durham Hall, where the steaks were so big they hung over the edge of the plate. It was a cold winter, against a background of lukewarm war news from the Pacific, Europe and Africa.

The 345th thought it was headed for Europe. Our maps covered that area, we were briefed by RAF officers, and it was assumed that New York City was our POE. To strengthen the many ETO rumors, a super-secret detail took off with civilian clothes for Atlantic City.

The B-25s were far from idle, flying both day and night. We bombed targets at Lake Murray and held aerial gunnery practice at Myrtle Beach. On the ground, crewmen were busy with OTU lectures, link trainers and turret practice. Each squadron spent a week in rugged maneuvers at Aiken. Combat mission problems left "Tunis," better known as Birmingham, Alabama, a smoking ruin. Our pilots

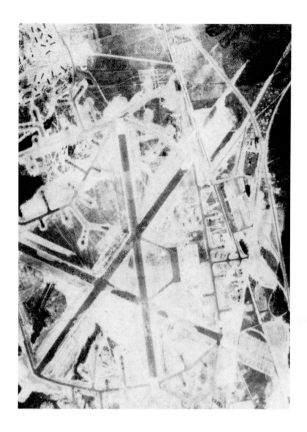

WALTERBORO

ish. Our destination was supposedly secret, but images of Fuzzy-Wuzzies and palm trees were well-fixed in our minds. The lucky contingent who were going to fly the planes departed on the 12th and the less fortunate started on a one week cross-country train trip four days later. The two trainloads ended up at Camp Stoneman, Pittsburg, California, where the 345th was one of the first Air Corps units to stage through. The fliers re-grouped at Sacramento, after an aerial jaunt from Columbia to Savannah, to Dallas and Tucson.

It was a long trip, no matter how you went. The planes hopped from map-dot to map-dot, touching Hawaii, Christmas Islands, Fiji, New Caledonia, and finally set their wheels down on Amberly Field, about 40 miles from Brisbane, Australia. A short rest, and off again and this time they ended up at several airfields near Townsville, Woodstock, Reid River and Charter's Towers. The SS *President Johnson* docked at Brisbane after nearly a month of crowded living, sub alerts, and two-meal days. The ship stayed in the harbor for three days, while troops went ashore to Cold Camp, Doomben, and then shoved off for New Guinea.

Debarking at Port Moresby, we climbed aboard mud-splattered Army trucks and set out on the dusty, confusing trip to our several camps. A large cloth banner stretched above

learned to handle their Mitchells in somewhat the same earnest manner that the ground men approached their machine-gun and rifle firing, and their calisthenics. It was strictly from the books. Even the Christmas dinner was very Army—from the fruit cocktail to the candied mints. The officers' New Year's Eve dance cost the Government one gymnasium! Despite the burning of the dance hall, we left an enviable training record at Columbia.

On March 5th, we packed our newly-acquired equipment and the next day we moved to Walterboro Army Air Field, a hospitable whistle-stop with runways. Ever eager, we drew up airdrome defense plans against possible enemy attack. April 1st, we started to prepare for our second move, only this, in the language of the day, was "it." Crating and marking and loading are not easy tasks, but we accomplished them with a Stateside flour-

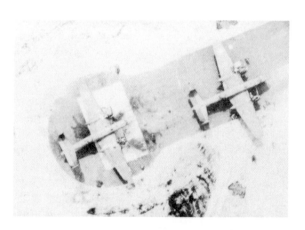

Two of our Mitchells on Walterboro hardstand bear early Air Force markings.

8

the road proclaimed that "Through these portals pass the best damn mosquito bait in the world."

To most people who had never been there, New Guinea in 1943 conjured up images of a small Pacific island covered with dense, inpenetrable jungle, palm trees, mud-filled fox holes, and camouflaged Jap snipers. We found, as we settled down for our first night, that this impression was not entirely correct. It was hot and the ground became muddy when rain fell, but dust was more of a problem than mud. There were plenty of mosquitoes and the grass rustled with the passage of large snakes and lizards. The land was swampy down near the strips, but large, rolling hills rimmed the camps. Rain was heavy and came un-

YANK photographer catches six smiling 345th men on crowded *President Johnson*.

expectedly, but it didn't fall continuously, except on movie nights. The Japs, pushed back quite recently, didn't take pot shots at us and we discovered that a helmet was more often used as a shaving bowl that for protection.

All in all, Port Moresby was far from the mental picture we had formed. Tall, slender trees cast a cool shade, and a refreshing evening breeze came from the harbor. New Guinea is the second largest island in the world. It has, undoubtedly, the hell-holes we had heard about but we never camped in one. It may also have its MGM paradises but we never camped in one of those either. It wasn't like the States, but it was livable and we acclimated ourselves. We settled down and prepared for action.

9

MISSIONS FROM MORESBY

By the 23rd of June the flight echelon had put the finishing touches on its training and modification and had flown up from Australia. They found the four Squadron areas at two strips and learned that we had experienced an air raid.

Our first missions dropped supplies to the Australian forces, then we swung into combat on June 30th, dropping bombs on the Nips at Logui strip, near Salamaua.

The month of July found us flying the treacherous "hump" to reach Salamaua. We helped to blast this odd-shaped neck of land into the pile of rubble that it is today. On the side, we escorted convoys, flew weather records and dropped more supplies. July 7th, 36 planes joined a flying rat-race dropping 1000 aerial burst bombs on suspected troop concentrations on Woody Island and Kitchen Creek. Toward the end of the

Our Biscuit Bombers service the Diggers at Guadagasal June 1943.

month, the higher-ups made a decision that changed our tactics considerably. Our B-25s, noisy, medium-altitude bombers were going to become low-level strafers. The Squadrons sent their planes back down to the mainland on varying time tables. At Townsville, the bombardier's greenhouse was replaced by a re-enforced nose with four lethal .50 calibre machine guns and two extra .50s were packaged on each side of the fuselage. Luxury-loving pilots also packed the planes with chairs, glasses, mirrors, lamps and various other comfort items which the Army somehow overlooked when planning our jungle stay.

The 500th Squadron, on August 25th, ran the first low-level combat mission. Instead of flying 6000 feet above the anti-aircraft positions at Hansa Bay, the planes went roaring in at a mean 60 feet. Although there was little change in actual speed, the baffled Jap gunners minutes before a large scale airborne invasion. We circled the area and had a good view of the proceedings. Five months later, we were to refer to Nadzab as "home," but we didn't know that as we observed the Americans and Aussies on the ground below us. Thirteen hundred men had been dropped in the first large scale use of paratroopers in the Pacific.

The Wewak and Boram dromes were 1050 miles round trip from our base. Three squadrons, led by Lt. Col. True, ran into our first aerial opposition—at least a half dozen enemy fighters. Two of our men were killed by ack ack.

Two veteran Pacific outfits, the 38th Group and the 3rd Attack Group, preceded us, but didn't steal all the gravy. Our bombs fell among the dispersal areas, our .50 calibers caught both trucks and planes. We destroyed at least ten enemy planes.

Lt. Magee in plane No. 041 crossed the strip on a 30-degree angle and dropped a dozen bomb clusters among the planes parked along the strip and in revetments. Capt. Coltharp saved his bombs for the densely-covered dispersal area, where palm fronds hid planes, vehicles and repair machinery.

Dagua, to the northwest, was hit by our 501st, which also ran into enemy fighters. All 345th planes returned, but not a few were holed.

On October 11, all four Squadrons sent planes to Horanda strip at Dobadura. Next morning, after a rather restless night, they took off at eight o'clock and went in with two Squadrons of the 38th Group to bomb and strafe Vunakanau airdrome, just outside of Rabaul.

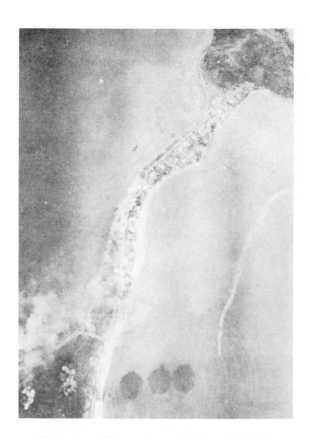

From June 30th to August 3rd we bombed Salamaua and adjoining area. On northern coast of New Guinea, we reached this target by flying over the hump.

hardly had time to see the planes, let alone track them. Everything worked out fine except the photographs. Not a plane was lost and we were satisfied that this new method of attack had its advantages. The only unhappy ones were the bombardiers. A bombsight doesn't work very well at 50 feet. The ex-bombardiers went along as navigators and enviously watched the co-pilot flip the switches as the plane chattered over the target.

We discovered, as we dumped our explosive loads along the island's north coast that paradoxical as it may sound, the lower the plane is, the safer it is, as long as it doesn't clip the trees.

Sometimes our targets were former plantations or Jap-occupied grass huts, with now and then an airdrome. Wherever we went, the most formidable enemy was weather. Storms were violent and sudden. The base that was bright and clear at take off was often socked in a few hours later. Bad weather over the Owen Stanley range cancelled many a mission.

September 5th saw us over the Markham Valley, exterminating the local Japanese,

One of the first successful low level missions was this September 1st attack on Alexishafen.

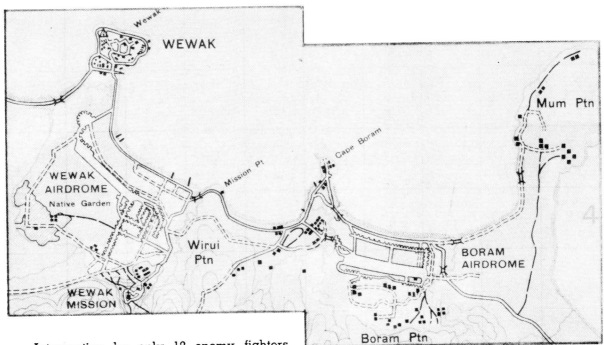

Interception by only 12 enemy fighters and generally inaccurate ack ack were far less opposition than was to be expected from such a stronghold as New Britain. This was the ideal surprise attack. A Jap fighter and a transport were trying to land during the raid;

Both sides of the Wewak runway and . . .

Lt. Moore in No. 094 dropped bombs on a Zero taxiing for take off; a bomber with engines running was hit and left burning. Capt. Manders in No. 089 dropped his bombs squarely on the wings of a "Betty" bomber, demolishing it completely.

The line-abreast formations swept over the drome, dropping cluster after cluster of bombs and strafing all the way. Nearly every revetment contained a plane. In aerial combat alone, we shot down at least three Jap fighters. Our crews saw a Zero going to work on a B-25 that was already crippled. The B-25 crashed into the water, but escorting P-38s shot down the enemy plane. Columns of smoke attested to our proficiency as we left the area after a neatly executed attack. This was the first of our ventures in this area . . . and there were even better ones to follow.

the Boram dispersal lanes were parafragged

Returning from Dobadura to home base, the four Squadrons sent three dozen Mitchells roaring over Wewak and Boram on October 16th, loaded with wire-wrapped 100 pounders. "Experienced and aggressive" enemy fighters, some 15 or 20, rose to oppose us. Some of them were still taking off from the Boram strip as our formation swept into view. Lt. Clark in No. 093, caught three Jap bombers with four American bombs. In addition to the many planes destroyed or damaged on the ground, nine were destroyed in aerial combat. One Squadron reported that in the midst of the running battle, one Zero dived too low, hit the water, only to come up fighting again with water dripping from his wings. The 500th lost Lt. Stookey in No. 561. He and

Three sitting ducks at Vunakanau

On the morning of October 18th we joined the 38th Group to execute an unescorted strike on Tobera and Rapopo airdromes and on shipping crowding Vunapope Harbor. Going in unescorted to an area where the enemy could muster 89 fighters and 107 other type planes was as much of a surprise to ourselves as it was to the Japs.

The weather was poor, but the fighter escort was seen above as the two groups hugged the water. After passing through some particularly bad weather, Col. True, leading the strike, discovered that the fighters had turned back. Realizing the importance of the mission he decided to go on as planned. Already airborne Nip fighters circled at high altitude, looking for the non-existent fighter cover. The 498th, 499th and 501st Squadrons completed their mission against the land objectives before interception occured. The 500th assigned to shipping in the harbor, sank a freighter transport and a corvette with 1000-

Three flying eagles on October 18th

his crew were last seen in a life raft three miles from shore, after ditching when hit by ack ack. Plane No. 071 of the 501st was well holed. A large chunk of shrapnel was found embedded in a spare parachute pack. The crew escaped injury.

A Falcon scorns the ack-ack at Boram, October 16th. Jap gunners hug the revetment walls.

Fire breaks out on a bomber, lower left

Transport at right was destroyed during October 18th attack on Rapopo. Plane at left had been ruined previously.

Anacker were shot down, the latter while escorting Lt. Wallace who had one engine shot out. Lt. Wallace flew on alone on his remaining engine, finally escaping after an hour and ten minute battle. Capt. Anacker's plane, on fire, made a water landing, with two survivors, Navigator Migliacci and Gunner Henderson, who spent five months in the jungles of New Britain. They were rescued and evacuated to the mainland on the 26th of March, 1944. There are many men today who recall the October 18th raid as the most heroic in the Group's history.

So they went, the Wewaks, the Daguas and the Rabauls. With every target, we won new respect from the Headquarters that had looked upon us as "that new bomb group from the States." The missions from Moresby were some of the roughest we've flown. The Japanese were a formidable foe. True, our air strength was growing daily . . . but we were routing out an enemy who had occupied an empire and established powerful military bases and who had every intention of remaining.

pounders, damaging and probably sinking another freighter transport of five to six thousand tons, another corvette, a small ferry boat and a patrol boat. Then, all hell broke loose. Nearly 50 fighters, the fastest and the hottest of the enemy's Southwest Pacific Air Force, swooped down from their fruitless search for our escorts.

The ensuing melee deserves a book of its own. Three dozen enemy planes were definitely destroyed. Our best protection against the Nip fighter cover was getting down on the deck and flying in compact formation. Several Jap fighters misjudged our altitude and cartwheeled into the sea. Lt. Peterson and Capt.

The meeting of a bomb and its target.

Debris flies high as direct hits obscure the small, but well-armed patrol craft.

Tenacles of an aerial phosphorus bomb reach into a 127mm dual purpose gun position, one of 83 along Sulphur Creek, Rabaul November 2nd. Our assignment was to knock out A/A so that 38th and 3rd Groups could get at shipping in Simpson Harbor. Three of our planes were downed.

Thirty-eight of our Mitchells staged through Dobo to get at Vunakanau October 24th. Enemy fighter opposition was weak and no one was lost. Revetments weren't quite as full as previously, but picture shows two of 26 planes on the drome claimed definitely destroyed.

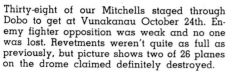

Some of 9,200 pounds of phosphorus bombs carried explodes over parked aircraft on Lakunai strip. Two of our planes were hit in bomb bays before load had been dropped. Lt. Krasnickas crashed over the target, but Capt. Mortensen brought his plane back, still smouldering.

There was ack-ack at Boram November 27th. Lt. Hyder of the 499th bombed and strafed 105mm six gun position at the tip of Cap Boram. Gun crews appear confused by low level attack.

We were good. Our pilots were the pick of the crop and our maintenance and administrative men were thorough and experienced. We were eager . . . in combat we were eager with a vengeance; on the ground we were eager with the grimness of efficiency experts. We had an exuberance of spirit that was more than esprit de corps.

Twenty enemy interceptors failed to stop four squadrons carrying out attacks on both ground and shipping targets at Wewak December 22nd. Nineteen-hundred-ton freighter was one of three vessels sunk by 498th.

Although we may not have consciously realized it, we felt as we began to prepare for our departure from Moresby, that a fighting team had been welded. We had left the States with the newness and arrogance of a "hot" outfit. We had done everything, but it was all in practice. Moresby gave us the chance to prove ourselves. To all the plus attributes we brought with us, we added the "know-how" of experience in combat.

Col. Crabb had relinquished his post as C. O. to Lt. Col. Clinton U. True on the 19th of September. From his new deck at V Bomber Command, Col. Crabb kept an expert eye on his old group throughout the remainder of the war. His occasional presence, whether official or informal, was a pleasant reminder of our early days.

One other item should not be neglected. The Moresby wreck, a battered pre-war hulk stranded near the harbor, was the practice target for our new experiments with skip bombing against shipping. Our ultimate unofficial classification as an anti-shipping unit stemmed from these tedious hours over the rapidly disintegrating vessel. There were other practice targets as we moved up the warpath, but the first, the Moresby wreck, is the best remembered.

Dobadura ceremonial dance in celebration of Allied victories.

Three of our 43 planes attacking Dagua drome February 3rd roar through dense smoke billowing up from some 35 of the 60 enemy aircraft parked on this important fighter and bomber base.

DOBADURA, NEW GUINEA

The move to Dobadura on the upper coast of New Guinea did not take place on any certain date. Like most moves of the 345th it was a slow, laborious process, complicated by heavy equipment echelons, flight echelons and ground echelons.

Dobo, as the jungle clearing was nicknamed, was not new to the pilots. Because of distance and the Hump, all the big strikes to Rabaul and other New Britain targets were staged from its strips. A staging is a miniature move in itself, and nearly every department of the Group had a small representation to handle the immediate details with the speed which is so important to an air unit. Not a few of the ground men were already familiar with its heat and humidity, its mud and its rain.

Heavy equipment is anything that weighs too much or is too bulky to get into our planes or transports. It includes big generators, photo trailers and link trainers. About the time we began to get our first big bundles of Christmas

Everything was lined up waiting for us February 3rd, even gas trucks in front of a camouflaged revetment.

19

An enemy tanker of 8,000 tons explodes in the background as its escorting corvette is under attack off New Hanover February 16th.

Forty-eight planes left Kavieng, New Ireland a mass of flames February 15th. Column of smoke at right is from medium size freighter.

mail, and, true to the Army's promise, we were celebrating Thanksgiving with real turkey and not long after we observed our first anniversary . . . about this time Lt. Holtzman and a handful of men started off on a water journey around the western hook of New Guinea with all the material that couldn't be flown to Dobo.

The 23rd of December, the flight echelon took off for the new base and ended once and for all the mass shuttling between Horanda and the Moresby strips. A move, for all its work and worry, is a step forward, a step toward the defeat of the enemy, and consequently a pace nearer home. The move to Dobo had another saving factor—there was no camp to construct. We were assigned to the old area of the 22nd Group.

No matter where we were, we managed to get through Christmas and New Year's Eve. Some were sad and many were very gay, while special meals made things seem a little better. We were at war, nevertheless, and both holidays saw our planes bombing and strafing the enemy.

Some time during all the holidays and confusion, our C. O. became a full colonel. From the 5th to the end of January, the Port Moresby contingent managed to cram what was left of our men and equipment into some 350 transport planes and fly the hump to the new base. To the C-47 pilots, the unsung moving men of the New Guinea campaign, go our thanks. They flew a difficult and dangerous route, often with overloaded planes, and all of them got there.

While the last part of the move was going on, the Japs staged one of their last big raids. We dug through the soot-like black dust, into the mud and climbed into foxholes. Fifty-one planes came over to bomb. Forty-nine of them were shot down over our heads and the remainder were caught at sea by the fighters. Other spectacles at Dobadura included the native ceremonial dances celebrating the recent Allied victories at nearby Buna and other New Guinea outposts, the Aussie races at Sana Namda track, where the horses ran the other way 'round. We were quite an exhibit ourselves, with practically everyone gaily daubed in all colors of the rainbow by the medics, who were inventing a technicolor cure for ear fungus.

The Kavieng Raid was an important part of the Dobadura chapter. Although there was no interception over Kavieng, February 15th, anti-aircraft fire downed four planes. Three of these planes made water landings close to the target. Maj. Coltharp, C. O. of the 498th circled the area for two and a half hours within range of enemy coastal defense guns and possible interception. He located the third crew downed after the rescuer Catalina had headed back for the base thinking its job over. He brought the Cat back to the scene of the ditching, observed the rescue. All members of Maj. Coltharp's crew had agreed to undertake the hazardous spotting assignment, but they were all sweating when the plane landed at Cape Gloucester. There were ten gallons of gas left in the tanks. All but one crew member of the three planes were rescued by the Cat which landed seven times around the target area to pick up the survivors.

Smoke, fire and debris are all that is left of the large tanker. Submarine alongside was also destroyed.

Corvette, no longer able to evade our attack, is on fire as a bomb drops towards the bridge.

The escort vessel is photographed on next day's raid to same area.

The 17th also added a freighter to our growing shipping score. Here vessel is on fire and sinking.

A small patrol craft trying to dodge the 345th, heads towards shore; gets caught on a reef; is bombed into oblivion.

Troop laden freighter was sunk by Captain Dougherty of the 500th. 501st, only other squadron on this February 19th mission to New Ireland sank three patrol craft and a small freighter.

NADZAB IN THE MARKHAM VALLEY

Starting the 16th of February, it took up a week to move nearly all of the Group up to our new base, Nadzab. For the first time the four Squadrons and Headquarters were together in a compact, but uncrowded area. Nadzab was some 20 miles inland from Lae. Much as we liked to claim that all New Guinea was unbearable, the sheer beauty of the soft hills rolling up and away from the Markham Valley was a contradiction in itself. Cool and green, it was perhaps the best area we'd been in. The view of the airstrips buzzing with activity during the day, the spectacular sunsets, the night time twinkle of lights, are not easily forgotten.

Our movie theatre seats were perched on the bank of a hill. You could see the screen without a head in the way. The officers had a club high on one of the slopes. Wet days and consequent mud made the road up the hill strictly a sporting proposition.

The aircrews with over 50 missions began to head back for home. New men came to replace them and gradually the faces that had been new and strange in the mess halls became part of the picture.

Every Group in the Air Force had a name to supplement its number. The 345 took a Jap's eye view and began calling itself the "Tree Top Terrors," often simplifying this phonetic foolishness to the T. T. T.'s.

We built up the area, installing wooden floors in our "shacks" as well as in our offices. There were the usual rumors that we weren't going to be there very long.

Lack of "big" missions, numerous medium altitude assignments made it a pretty routine period. We were busy, yes, but there was nothing electric about our operations. Constantly admonished to stay clear of all anti-aircraft, we were being saved for more important tasks ahead. The new crews had a chance to get combat experience the easy way—nothing really rough, nothing like the old days.

There was still Pacific weather to be reckoned with and we had a brutal reminder of that fact on the 16th, when 5th Air Force had scheduled another big Hollandia strike. A solid front was found north of Madang, forcing our formations to break up and seek haven at scattered bases. A few got back to Nadzab, others landed at Saidor, Finschaven and Cape Gloucester. Some of these messed up in landing, but all except one of our planes got through. Other groups didn't fare as well.

April 23rd, our enemy got its first glimpse of a new and terrifying addition to the firepower of the B-25. The B-25H, a new model acquired earlier in the month, had a 75mm cannon in the nose. We strafed, we bombed, and now we were flying artillery. The little bomber would buck and snort and fume, but we developed a flair for accuracy and wrought a lot of damage over the targets. The cannon was particularly effective against the Nips above Mokmer drome, who were turning their ack ack guns on advancing Allied troops below, near the end of May. We staged through Wakde at this time, and Wakde was no picnic. The boys logged a lot of fox hole time.

Gracious living at Nadzab was further enhanced by the Group PX. The building itself was decorated with a reasonable facsimile of the Sad Sack enjoying a tasty bite. Over its creaking counters came crackers for snacks, chocolate, a good part of it Aussie, and grapefruit juice. This last item was perhaps the most in demand, as it made a palatable mix for hard likker, gin in particular.

Some foresighted author wrote at the end of May: "We're all convinced that our stops from this point on will not be long enough for us ever again to indulge in the luxury of such a complete set-up."

For the first time since our arrival in combat some eleven months before, we had a formal presentation of awards May 13th. Gen. Whitehead, Fifth Air Force chief, decorated 19 men and officers in an impressive ceremony.

Proximity of squadron areas prompted a central utilities set-up. Joe Bitel was presiding genius of the generators.

Two of our planes, running the second of two missions completed March 19th, polish off an already damaged freighter transport.

Two small escorts were hit in the Wewak area also. We strafed the wreckage.

What was left of Hansa Bay was bombed from 7,000 feet March 1st. Medium altitude missions were frequent. Bombs were dropped "on" lead planes which carried bombardier and sight.

26

The tree-top terrors, 40 of them, took part on the "impossible" 5th Air Force strike on Hollandia April 3rd.

Sixty-one B-24's, 76 B-25's and 96 A-20's worked over the three strip base. Allied forces landed at Hollandia April 22nd and quickly secured the strips.

There was plenty of ack-ack. Seven of our planes were holed, but none was lost. One 498th ship was intercepted by a Zero and the gunner was slightly injured.

At Nadzab we observed our first overseas Easter Sunday. Catholic services were led by Father Kozlowski, Group Chaplain.

. . . smoke to 10,000 feet on April 5th.

Humboldt Bay was a storage area for enemy supplies going to Hollandia, a few miles inland. Large fuel fire sent . . .

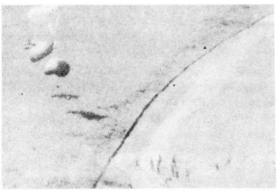

Wewak April 11th was one of several medium altitude missions flown during April. Three B-25's turn homeward as smoke drifts inland from the shorefront target.

Five days after Hollandia operation, we helped out our ground forces by dropping needed supplies.

April 28th attack on Sawar airdrome caught four enemy aircraft and eight motor trucks. Major Marston's plane was damaged by premature explosions of his own bombs, but he brought his plane safely to Cyclops drome at Hollandia.

Ominous shadow of a bomber and its bombs fall on bivouac area near Muschu Island. Nadzab period had many such missions—all effective but few spectacular.

One of 27 planes attacking Wakde reviews heavy damage caused by 345th mission May 11th. We started a fuel fire that was visible 30 miles away from the target.

Although most of June was spent supporting ground operations on Biak Island, we did manage to get in a good punch at Jefman and Samate airdromes. Eight enemy planes were destroyed, many fires started June 16th.

Col. True was awarded the Distinguished Service Cross and the Purple Heart, the former for his leadership of the Rabaul strike, October 18th.

The war was leaving us behind at Nadzab. To reach a worthwhile target it was necessary to stage through Hollandia or Wakde. It was evident that either a move or de-activation was in order, and the latter was very unlikely.

We tired of calling ourselves the "Tree Top Terror's," and set about renaming the 345th. A contest was held, both for a new name and a new insignia. As the votes were counted and the drawings inspected, it became apparent that the "Air Apaches" was winning out over less virile monickers. An Indian head had artistic possibilities, even though it ran the risk of becoming a flying ad for Pontiac. The Apaches were an extremely warlike tribe, noted for savagery and violence. Forgetting the Apaches that haunted the Eiffel Tower, the name seemed to fit our mission in this war. We came upon our enemy with sudden speed and without warning. Unlike many Air Corps units, we could see our foe as he trained his guns on us or ran for cover. We could see him fall as our strafing swept through his bivouacs. Our brand of warfare was somewhat akin to the Infantry and distinctly removed from the remoteness of bombing from 10,000 feet.

So it hapened that as our operations fell off, our buildings were dismantled and we prepared to move to a far more rugged base, we gave ourselves a new name, a name that was to become famous in the annals of the Pacific War.

Last week in June we stood formation to bid farewell to Col. True, who was returning to the States.

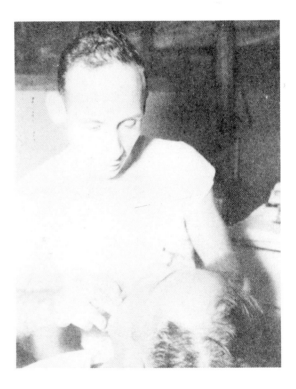

Molar maintenance of the 345th was performed by Doc Hoffman.

A good bomb group is versatile. Our planes could bomb like a bomber, strafe like a fighter, drop supplies like a C-47, carry kitchen stoves and refrigerators like a C-46. July 3rd, we laid a smoke screen at Kornasoren, near Biak.

BIAK, AN ISLAND

Once again, we completed a move by air. Our first island base, Biak, was little more than an overgrown chunk of coral with three airstrips on the southern side and one on Owi, the two mile isle where the VBC made its headquarters. For some reason or other, the Japs wanted to keep Biak. As we labored to fashion an area, the Infantry flushed Nips from the caves in the cliffs above our site. Tanks parked at the base of the cliffs and lobbed shells at the well-entrenched enemy. Unsuspecting souvenir hunters poked around in the positions until the word got around that some new casualties had been suffered.

A scrub forest, sharp coral underfoot and blistering daytime heat stood between us and a camp area. With a shortage of tools and men, we hacked out a spot to live and work. It wasn't just a detail of PFCs. There was plenty of rank with their shirts off, working the few native buldozers during the midnight hours. There was even a Jap bulldozer that would work once it was started. Somehow, by the end of July, we had a clearing and the dead Japs that had littered the ground had been buried. Before the mess halls were screened, eating was a battle. Hordes of oversize

flies had complete air superiority over the tables. They seemed to have a passion for that orange marmalade.

Water was a problem at Biak and the problem was licked with typical ingenuity. There are no statistics to prove it, but we estimate that about a tenth of the rain that fell over Biak never touched the ground. It was scooped up by tent flaps and helmets, stored in old Jap gas drums; converted into showers and shaves. Before showers were accessible to all, there was salt water a short distance across the road, even if you did have to wear sneakers or shoes to protect your feet from the coral.

Some ardent natators would hitchhike some eight miles up the road to a beach that had all the true tropical trimmings. Palm trees leaned over the water, there was grass and soft sand. To top it off there was a cold fresh water spring to rinse off the salt.

Brightest spot by far in the Biak existence was the camp theatre. Corrugated roofing and parachutes were the materials of the Apache Playhouse, but the ingenuity of John Michalowsky made it a theatre of which we could well be proud. The movies were good, but the stage shows were the highlights. Few will forget the

QM colored variety show, where two comics gleefully proffered "rolls" and coffee. Even the USO offerings were good. One hectic night, dinner dates were arranged with a man in each Squadron. The units outdid themselves in rival preparations for a civilian female was a thing of beauty. Despite the absence of any organized laundry facilities, everyone looked clean and scrubbed in spotless Class "A"s.

There were other shows, too, staged by the Nippon Raiders. Night attacks on both Biak and Owi were frequent and did us some damage. Despite the element of danger, the searchlights and our ack ack and an occasional burning raider were fascinating spectacles. After one particularly costly raid, September 1st, in which several of our personnel were killed and some planes put out of commission, the order came out to cover all fox holes. It was perhaps one of the most spontaneously obeyed orders to come out of Headquarters in many months. As our own combat activity increased, the Nip night raids fell off and we got a lot more untroubled sleep.

The last nail hadn't been driven in some of the organizational buildings before the details set to work dismantling them. In the midst of all this confusion, 16mm and 35mm movie

USO songstress added an attraction to the Apache Playhouse. Em's took gals to dinner.

Two QM comedians were out of uniform but in the groove.

flies had complete air superiority over the tables. They seemed to have a passion for that orange marmalade.

Water was a problem at Biak and the problem was licked with typical ingenuity. There are no statistics to prove it, but we estimate that about a tenth of the rain that fell over Biak never touched the ground. It was scooped up by tent flaps and helmets, stored in old Jap gas drums; converted into showers and shaves. Before showers were accessible to all, there was salt water a short distance across the road, even if you did have to wear sneakers or shoes to protect your feet from the coral.

Some ardent natators would hitchhike some eight miles up the road to a beach that had all the true tropical trimmings. Palm trees leaned over the water, there was grass and soft sand. To top it off there was a cold fresh

Strafing and bombing sets fire to fuel and stores piled up on the end of the Wasile Bay pier.

A freighter transport gets a direct hit while anchored in Wasile Bay, August 9th.

Another Halmahera waterfront target was attacked two days later. Four floatplanes bob in an inlet.

Six of the floatplanes on fire and one capsized.

As smoke rises from the shore, one of several Jap luggers settles to the bottom of Kaoe Bay.

Sixteen-hundred pounders dropped by the 499th crater the Nabire runway August 12th. Enemy night raids on our own base called for frequent neutralizations of nearby dromes on New Guinea and the Halmaheras.

Halmahera ports were primitive; could handle only small shipping, but were hotly defended. Over 50 Jap gunners cringe as Apache parafrags drift into their six gun, 75 millimeter position August 13th.

36

Formerly Dutch controlled, civilized Ternate
Island was suspected Jap transshipping port.
Fires were started during this August 15th
raid . . .
. . . and small craft were destroyed.

A near miss sprays the decks of a small freighter at Lembeh township August 24th. Later
photos proved sinking of this vessel. Large
minelayer in harbor put up anti-aircraft fire;
may have been damaged by attack.

Buayan airdrome, on the southern tip of Mindanao, was the scene of the Group's first con-
certed venture into the Philippines, September 6th. Eleven planes set fire to repair sheds
and heavily strafed and bombed the entire
area.

Staging from newly-won Middleburg, 14 Mitchells from three squadrons dropped demos and incendiaries on closely packed warehouses and other facilities at Gorontalo, N. E. Celebes. Jap flag flies from pole in circular court.

Photo interpreters, working from later pictures reported, "21 large warehouses and five smaller buildings . . . on west bank of river . . . destroyed in strike of 16 September."

Fourteen planes staged through Morotai to get at our first and only Borneo target, Sandakan Harbor. Captain Decker scores a direct hit on a freighter transport, one of five vessels obliterated during the 24th raid.

onto the *SS Loomis* and head for Lae with the Chemical Company. On the night of the 15th, troops from Headquarters and the two remaining echelons started to embark on the *Thomas Nelson*.

The *Nelson*, an old Liberty ship never designed to carry 650 men and officers, left Biak after a false start or two and anchored in Humboldt Bay on the night of the 18th. It was joined by the *Morrison R. Waite* now carrying the trans-shipped 500th, 501st and the Chemical Company.

At 1800 on the night of the 20th we received definite and final word of the Leyte landing, via the Philippine Hour, to which we had been listening regularly. There was little or no doubt about our destination after this broadcast and our many mathematicians estimated the distance between Hollandia and Leyte could be made by our ships in about six days. Three days later, the convoy pulled out.

crews from the 5th Combat Camera unit were shooting the last scenes of the historical film they were making to acclimate fresh troops to rugged living. The Headquarters building became a small MGM lot, with lights, and cameras, and stagehands walking through with slabs of plywood and sections of the building.

Culminating a hectic week's hard work for all members of the Group, we saw the ground echelons of the 500th and 501st load

Seventeen planes dropped parademos and firebombs on Koendang on N. E. Celebres October 11th. Flames swept through ten warehouses.

October 28th brought us to the threshhold of the Philippines. Never before had we followed so closely on the heels of the Navy and Infantry. We were intrigued by the thought of a civilized country again. We were pleased to be so close to what might be called American soil. Overshadowing all these thoughts was the fact that we were putting our heads into the jaws of the lion. The lion, enfeebled though he may have been, had bases to the south of us on Mindanao, on numerous islands to the west of us, and his powerful Luzon forces to the north of us. If he fought so suicidally for the small bases of Palau and Biak, how big a battle would he put up for the thousand islands that comprised the Philippines? This was the war as we had never seen it before, a far cry from the peace of the Markham Valley not so many months ago. Not a few envied the flight echelon, still operating at a slow tempo from Biak.

Enemy plane number 783-13, a twin engined bomber, responds warmly to strafing by the 499th's Lt. Mosser at Padada airdrome November 30th. Air Apaches definitely destroyed 260 Jap planes on the ground before war ended.

TACLOBAN

The Leyte landing took place October 20th. The 345th Bomb Group's water echelon pulled into the San Pedro harbor on "A" day-plus-nine. Dusk to dawn air attacks from then on kept us running.

We were the first Bomb Group to arrive in the Philippines in three years and proud to be so selected. We were anxious, however, to get ashore where we could dig foxholes. The troop commanders pleaded with the port director and finally, on November 10th, a small advance detail went in to build a camp area at San Pablo.

Four planes happened to be at Tacloban on courier-liaison missions on November 9th. The 308th Bomb Wing called these ships into service when an enemy convoy was spotted heading for Ormoc Bay. P-38s preceded the attack and dive-bombed six destroyers surrounding a large enemy troop transport that was busily unloading troops and supplies into barges a mile and a half offshore. Heavy ack ack forced our planes, led by Lt. Dick, behind the protection of a ridge and from there they swooped down on the transport at mast-height level.

Lt. Frazier concentrated his fire on the stern and guns there were silenced. Lt. Dick's plane was hit by a burst of heavy ack ack just before he was over the vessel. With his right vertical stabilizer completely blown off, he made a snap roll, skidded slightly to the left, and righted the plane in time to make a skip-bombing run on one of the destroyers. He was last seen feathering a prop and heading back to Tacloban. Maj. Doolittle dropped two 1000-pound bombs on the transport, scoring direct and effective hits. Capt. Decker maintained control of his aircraft, despite a badly damaged stabilizer and headed for base immediately after his run. Maj. Doolittle followed to offer protection for Capt. Decker, while Lt. Frazier in face of intense anti-aircraft fire circled in search of Lt. Dick but was unable to locate him. The tactical importance of this emergency four-plane strike was matched by the achievement and gallantry of the participants.

By the 11th of November, our second anniversary, the water echelon had clocked 74 red alerts since their arrival in the harbor.

On the 12th we suffered the greatest loss of personnel from any single event in our overseas history. With tragic accuracy two planes of the much-vaunted Japanese Special Attack Corps crashdived into both of our transports, filled with men waiting to land. The SS Nelson was hit aft of the midship housing at 1128 and the SS Waite on the port bow at 1818 that evening. Ninety-two men were killed and one hundred and fifty-six were wounded. Of these wounded, 15 died either en route to or in hospitals. Remaining personnel of the Nelson, excepting a few details, were evacuated that evening to the San Pablo area and the men on the Waite were brought ashore the next morning. During a catastrophe, some men arise as giants. The many men of this Group who, although wounded themselves, administered first aid or helped clear wreckage or lower stretchers over the side did not consider themselves heroes. They were doing their job and taking care of their comrades.

The effect upon the outfit's morale, as may well be imagined, was devastating. Not only the loss of close friends, but the shock of working amidst gear that was actually wet with blood, the herculean task of unloading the dead and wounded, made an unforgettable impression. The improvised camp area with its physical discomforts and shortage of blankets offered little rest.

We moved from San Pablo to an area south of Dulag with an intermediate stop that was soon a mudhole. At Rizal, we spent the remainder of the month, more comfortable, but practically isolated from the rest of the island by impassable roads. Somehow, we got fresh turkey the day after Thanksgiving.

The Filipinos and the Air Apaches, at first curiosities one to the other, got along very well. We enjoyed talking to natives of another country who understood our tongue and we were impressed by their comparative cleanliness and willingness to help. They in turn marvelled at our array of equipment and our foul language.

On the 28th of November, Jap transport planes landed nearby and successfully discharged troops. We were later informed that they were scheduled to land on the beach where we lived and take the road into Dulag. We were spared only by a beach that had been noticeably narrowed by formerly much-cursed carry-all scrapers that rumbled by our tents twenty-four hours a day. The next night, we established an elaborate and trigger-happy perimeter guard.

Our beachside area became quite livable. The absence of mud and the presence of the ocean made it very agreeable. If we had to sit and wait for our planes, this was the place to do it.

Soon the first loads of bags and baggage began to come off the ships and the unloading details continued working well into the night. Mail filtered in and was eagerly read by the glow of flashlights. Continued red alerts gave rise to many cries of "Turn off that —— —— light." Flight personnel on courier and mail missions from Biak kept us informed of the strikes that were run occasionally and the battle against the Japs that were coming out of the caves and stealing clothes, rations and, worst of all, gin.

The B-25Hs were being turned in. The cannon in the nose, despite the efforts of our ordnance and engineering departments, caused too much vibration. In their stead, we were getting planes with twelve fixed forward firing fifties.

As December began we were in the final throes of unloading the two Liberty ships. On the 2nd a brisk breeze levelled some of our hurriedly erected tentage, but did little damage. Most of our equipment was well used to water by this time. Unloading of the SS Morrison R. Waite was completed on the 3rd and on the next day the last LCT load from the SS Nelson was piled up in front of our camp.

At dusk on the 6th ack ack blazed from all points of the compass. This, we later learned, was a bold attempt at a paratroop landing. One of the transports was downed midway between our area and Dulag and a Nip strafer hit the dirt to the south of our camp.

The 11th added electricity to our night life. Red alerts kept the bulbs from receiving to much use, but long unused radios brought news and music. The PX opened and the next-afternoon everything from chocolate bars to pretzels was on sale. In addition to these luxuries, volleyball courts and horseshoe pitching alleys were in almost constant use. Off hours were spent in challenge matches usually attended by puzzled Filipinos.

A relatively quiet Christmas Eve was spent in anticipation of some typical dirty work, but the enemy disappointed us. Volunteer crews did a fine job of decorating the mess halls, with able assistance from the civilians.

In order to highlight the big event of December 25th, most Squadrons and Headquarters made arrangements for two meals . . . a late breakfast and the long-heralded Christmas dinner, our second overseas.

The proposed extensive operations from the Dulag strip were abandoned because of a sea of mud that made improvement of the airfield impossible. An enemy naval force was sighted heading towards Mindoro Island and orders came for our flight echelon to go into action from every available Leyte strip. Our planes came up from Biak as quickly as possible, but by the time they had arrived, the

Housing Problem at Tacloban. No matter what state you hailed from, you were an "Oakie" in this crowded area. Tent ropes actually crossed each other.

Jap force had ineffectively shelled the Island, turned for home and taken a terrific drubbing by other air units. Once our planes were on Leyte, VBC kept us running missions at a dizzy pace, both day and night. The B-25, versatile plane that it is, however, is not suited for night strafing because the pilots are blinded by the flash of the nose guns. The three dromes were overcrowded and all facilities were taxed to the utmost. Few of the new arrivals had a place to stay and meals were a hit-or-miss affair, as was sleep.

One of the three strips we had been using was at Tacloban. It was soon apparent that all our planes would soon be based there and gradually we established the group in an area as muddy as San Pablo and no bigger than the usual requirement for two of our Squadrons.

The early January missions were directed against enemy airdromes in the Philippines in an effort to destroy what aircraft might be on the islands and render the runways unserviceable for staging missions against us. Six different airdromes were hit on January 1st, with the first planes taking off before four o'clock in the morning.

The Air Apaches were the only B-25's in the 5th Air Force medium strike against the Clark Field Air Center January 7th, leading the first of two waves of 66 planes each.

Enemy planes were widely dispersed around the four Clark runways. A few of the 2,000 parafrags dropped glide towards a heavily camouflaged twin engine fighter.

This picture of a smoking plane at Clark was not taken on the ground. It was taken by a plane a very few feet above the ground during the attack.

The hangars and the few planes in them were demolished before the raid was half over. Jap fighters dropped aerial burst phosphorous bombs, one of which can be seen exploding above the rear hangar.

The day MacArthur's forces were landing at Lingayen, we helped prevent enemy troop movements by rail. Debris and explosions mark end of line for several trains at Tarlac, January 9th.

A roundelled bomber at Aparri that flew no more after an Apache attack January 14th.
Nearby fighter was probably damaged.

Rolling stock means anything that moves on wheels, as the Jap soldier discovered on his unlucky January 13th.

After five or six trips on the explosive express, there was talk of putting train whistles on our Mitchells. Up and down Luzon we left evidence that we'd been working on the railroads.

We haunted Subic Bay and historic Bataan peninsula towards the end of the month. Barracks on Grande Island get the treatment on the 24th.

Rescue of downed crews by Army or Navy Catalinas saved the lives of many men of the 345th. One of four such rescues during January, Lts. Daker, Jensen, Horwitz, T/Sgt. Dunn and S/Sgt. Wachtel are being helped aboard, January 21st.

February 1st at Puerta Princessa, Palawan. Scratch one Jap floatplane. Allied planes kept enemy runways unserviceable, forcing the Nips to rely on water-based aircraft. Because a near miss will capsize the fragile craft, floatplanes are extremely vulnerable.

Water transportation was continuously pounded to prevent troop movement or escape to adjacent islands. A jetty is demolished on the east coast of Luzon, February 6th.

Warfare isn't all bombs and bullets. News and propaganda was distributed to both the enemy and friendly natives. 345th was one of the first bomb groups used to drop leaflets; led all other SWPA units. January's total was well over two million.

SAN MARCELINO

February communiques stated that newly-won Clark Field was large enough to hold all Fifth Air Force units. While we were still musing over the possibilities of the swimming pool at Stotsenburg, we received rush orders to scrape the mud from our shoes and become operational by the 13th at little-known San Marcelino, some 60 miles west of Clark Field. The first few nights the men worked until dawn stuffing the high-hatched C-46, a more difficult taskmaster than the old reliable, but less efficient than the C-47 with which we had made almost every previous move. The situation was further complicated by a recent dose of shots in the arms. But we continued our work and were soon ready for our next move.

Against small hills that looked like a stepped-on Nadzab, a bumpy meadow was indicated by 309th Wing Engineers as our new home. The stay-over was billed as little more than a staging operation. Luckily we had plenty of room and spread ourselves out accordingly. Playful afternoon tornadoes and ever-present dust from the roads and the un-surfaced strip were overlooked by a Bomb Group that was glad to get out of the mud. Houses were rented in Manila for leave purposes and an advance echelon was sent on to Clark Field to prepare for our arrival . . . a matter of a few weeks, we thought.

On March 19th we put on our best uniforms and stood a one-hour formation while Gen. Crabb decorated 180 men in the first such ceremony since Nadzab.

Operational, San Marcelino marked the second peak of our career. In addition to close ground support missions on Luzon, we worked our lethal way over Formosa and other strong-ly defended land targets. We made our claim to fame, however, as we carried out, virtually unaided, the "Aerial Blockade of the China Sea." Every necessary ounce was removed from our Js in order to increase their range. The Pacific war had always been a battle of distance and it was a long haul from San Marc to the shores of China. As ship after ship poked its prow out of Jap ports, the Air Apaches swooped out of the skies and sent the ships to the bottom of the sea. To the chagrin of other air corps units we knew, newspapers spread our pictures across the front pages of the Nation; *Yank* Magazine devoted a center spread to our work; and correspondents snoop-ed around our briefing rooms. Civilians are denied a look at *Impact*, the *Life* Magazine of Army Intelligence circles, but if they could have seen the cover of the June issue or read such items as "The Mast-Height Marvels Do It Again" or "Here Are the Secrets of Apache Success" they would share our pride. Although our successes were not without cost, we felt

Twelve-hundred of the total 189,143 tons sunk by the 345th goes down to the bottom of the South China Sea off Swabu.

Palm fronds, excellent camouflage when vessel is near shore, didn't protect this small freighter. Bomb is about to enter port side.

a tremendous lift of our morale. Like an old and nearly forgotten actor who makes a sensational comeback, we revelled in our new acclaim. The tired 345th Bomb Group, entering its third year overseas, took a fresh breath and made tactical history.

Bomb and strafing splashes ring a 2300-ton freighter off Cape Hapoix. Eighteen Mitchells flew this 5 March strike. Forty-three quarter-tonners were traded for two freighter transports and two stack-aft freigthers.

Six Rogers of the 498th squadron turned their talents upon concrete Fort Drum, in Manila Bay. No visible damage was caused and Fort Drum is still there.

Unusual Bomber Photo shows one of 20 enemy interceptors air-borne. This plane slipped under our attacking formation and tried to land on well bombed Samah runway.

Nose guns still blazing, a Rough Raider pulls away from blasted Samah airfield March 6th. Two of our planes, hit by ack-ack collided and were lost over target. One ditched. 16 of our 34 planes were damaged. Several hangars and other large buildings, as well as many grounded enemy planes were destroyed. Twenty miles out to sea, our pilots could see at least 16 columns of smoke spiralling upward.

On March 10th, this heavily laden 2000-ton tanker suffered a direct hit amidships, Bottom photo, made several days later, shows results of bombing and subsequent inferno.

A ten thousand ton tanker, one of the largest encountered since Wewak days, was conviently anchored off the Indo China Coast on March 10th. Direct hit by the 500th caused towering flames, left ship smoking and sinking. Same day, another large freighter. Four Tojo's intercepted, but weakly.

Another tanker falls prey to the Apaches under the very noses of the Japs at Tourane Bay March 11th. Camera-wise pilots made extra runs to provide proof of vessel's doom, despite ack-ack which caused one plane to ditch.

Another escort for the March 21st convoy, already on fire near the ammo locker, is about to be decommissioned by 500 pounder ploughing towards stern.

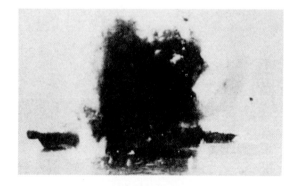

With Jap naval losses reaching a peak, this cablelayer was armed and pressed into convoy duty, but not for long. Note cable rigged bow. Five of our planes were holed, one shot down, same day.

One dozen Mitchells fought off interception by 10 enemy fighters, definitely blasting four of them out of the flak speckled skies. A 1900-ton freighter blossoms flame, March 21.

Large railroad shed at Phan Rang is illuminated by a bomb blast. Metal roofing buckles, flew sky high March 28th. Twenty-eight planes carried out destructive sweep of Indo China rolling stock.

First wave encountered two frigates, fast and well armed destroyer escorts.

Midway through the attacks, 1st frigate's decks are littered with debris and good Japs.

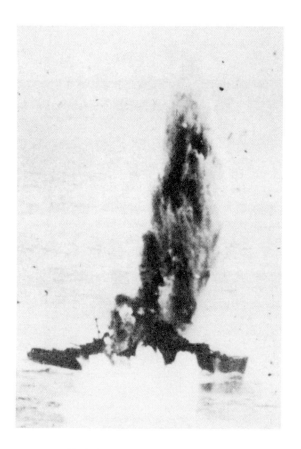

A direct hit finishes off the escort.

And she goes down, bow first.

A large convoy northbound off the French Indo-China coast was badly mauled by 31 of our B-25s between 11 and 12 o'clock on March 29th. From previous sightings, the convoy's composition was estimated to be six merchant vessels, including one tanker; and eleven naval vessels, consisting of five destroyers, four destroyer escorts (or frigates), and two patrol craft.

We had decided to send our strike force out in two waves, the first to track down the convoy, the second to follow 30 minutes later and proceed directly to the attack guided by radio instruments from the Group Commander, Lt. Col. Coltharp, co-pilot in the lead airplane of the first wave. The probable convoy position had been plotted, and an interception course laid. If the first wave reached the French Indo-China coast without having spotted the convoy, it was to search northward. But this was unnecessary as the plan worked perfectly, and two frigates were sighted. The eight planes

An Apache swoops in on second frigate.

of the 501st Squadron led by Capt. Jones and the seven 498th planes led by Capt. Cranford concentrated on the two vessels. Several good hits were scored; the ships burned and sank.

The two frigates had been bringing up the rear of the convoy. Up ahead in foul weather was the main body of vessels. Capt. Jones selected a merchant vessel and attacked. Lt. Steele, the wingman, out of bombs, made a strafing run. Meanwhile, Lt. Col. Coltharp, Strike Force Commander, had called the Squadrons of the second wave, the 499th and the 500th, giving them the position of the convoy. As they approached, the burning vessels guided them in. Fresh and ready for the attack, they turned north to hit the main body of the convoy. In the ensuing engagement, pilots were frequently on instruments going in and out of weather.

Bomb thuds into starboard side.

And second frigate burns and sinks.

Bad weather spoiled most pictures of the convoy proper, but this tanker is on fire as a bomb splashes into it amidships.

In spite of extremely adverse weather we sank a good proportion of the tonnage present. Final assessment by higher Headquarters credited our strike with destruction of four merchant and five naval vessels, for an estimated total in excess of 24,000 tons. We expended 26½ tons of 500 pounders, and 74,000 rounds of .50 caliber ammunition. The soupy weather which greatly hampered our attack by screening the enemy force (our crews saw but twelve of the seventeen vessels in the convoy), also reduced the effectiveness and quantity of the enemy fire. We lost no planes, although eleven were holed. With no casualties except for one crew member grazed by a bullet, we had scored impressively against the Jap's dwindling shipping.

Two squadrons flew to Mako Harbor in the Pescadores, a small island chain off southwest Formosa, on April 4th. Coming over the town, they bombed residences and administrative buildings in the small but important Jap port. One of four piers was completely demolished. The bow of a small freighter was lifted at least fifty feet out of the water. The pictures tell the rest of the story, except that it was later confirmed that the fire spread to small craft and stores lining the waterfront. Considering that only a dozen planes were committed, this was undoubtedly one of our most lucrative small-effort strikes of the year.

Culminating a series of successful strikes against Jap shipping, three naval vessels were destroyed on April 6th by 24 of our B-25Js in a mid-day mast-height attack off the China coast.

The first ships encountered were two

A one thousand tanker and a two thousand stack aft Naval Auxiliary (nearest vessel) on either side of the Mako Pier.

The 498th and 500th share the honors for this conflagration, which soon engulfed both ships.

Over and above havoc caused in the town, the Air Apaches are officially credited with the sinking of eight vessels on this strike.

Top frigate was missed on this run, but bulls-eye on nearest vessel, cleans off deck aft of bridge. Top escort was also sunk.

escort vessels, Frigate Class, PF-UN-1 (steam powered); and PF-UN-2 (Diesel) heading NNE. The 501st Squadron, leading, passed to their starboard, and then wheeled around and down to the attack. The nearest frigate received the full weight of a vicious attack by the 501st's six planes. In a very few minutes the ship went under. The two frigates had turned to starboard as we came in, enabling four planes of the 501st Squadron to carry their attack on to the second frigate. Although a

Another run, another bomb . . .

498th takes the air picture of the year as some 60 Nips are left scared, shipless.

good attack, featured by a direct hit and near misses, it was the 499th's second flight, next over, which got the fatal tallies. The vessel was sinking as the six planes of the 498th came in. Ack ack was still coming from it, however, and Lt. Myers' plane in the first flight was badly hit. Unable to continue attack, he made a successful three-hour single engine flight to a friendly base.

The 500th Squadron saw the two frigates ably disposed of and turned south to attack an Asashio Class destroyer with a temporary bow, which took violent evasive action and began throwing up intense fire. The Squadron leader, his co-pilot and navigator were wounded by en explosive shell. Also hit was the No. 3 plane on the Squadron leader's wing. Both, however, continued their runs over the ship. Lt. Schmidt, Squadron leader, managed to get back to base after scoring a bull's eye which

and another direct hit does the trick.

caused a huge explosion. Lt. Herick, his wing-man, crashed into the sea. Capt. Johnson, 498th Squadron leader, swung into the attack with five planes. He dropped his two remaining 500-pounders for a direct hit, but his plane was crippled and caught fire. He made a fair ditching about two miles further on with only one survivor sighted. As the last plane pulled away, the destroyer was burning fiercely.

The 499th and 501st flew to Palawan to hit Saigon, French Indo-China island shipping port, on April 28th. Other B-25 units were based nearer to the target, one on the airfield we staged through, but our reputation for sinking ships was becoming legendary. The low, flat country around Palawan made surprise virtually impossible and the enemy was ready for us with far more ack ack than had been plotted in higher Headquarters. The scheduled

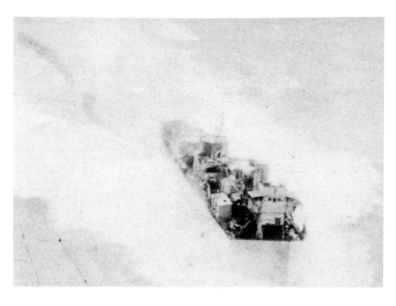

Heavily armed DD had been previously damaged, but, repaired with a jury bow, it was escorting important convoys. March 30th, it gave us trouble at Yulin Bay.

Hit by 500th's Lt. Schmidt causes large explosion aft.

Capt. Johnson of the 498th was shot down, but not before he had struck this telling blow. This was the only vessel of three attacked that we didn't see sink, but we are credited with its destruction.

Shipping began to disappear from the China Sea and more than once we had to turn to secondary targets. The Black Panthers sunk their claws into this former storage tank in the Karenko railroad yard. Smoke rose to 3,000 feet after the attack, 18 April.

Jap fuel supply, already whittled down by the aerial blockade, gets another blow at Woody Island, April 23rd.

friendly fighters did not appear, but Col. Coltharp took the 13 planes over without cover, opening his attack at 1115. Only one enemy plane intercepted, but anti-aircraft fire shot down Lt. Johnson's, Lt. Townley's and Lt. Espy's planes of the lead squadron, the 501st.

Lt. Harrah in No. 016 got an 18-inch hole in his left wing, destroying several left side control cables. He salvoed his bombs, strafed the target heavily and rejoined the formation. Three of the ten planes that returned were seriously damaged.

Lt. Blount got the prize target, a 5,800 ton freighter. Later Recco photos showed vessel way over on port side.

Assessment of the two squadron strike: 12,375 tons sunk; 3,750 damaged.

Thirty-nine planes from all four squadrons hit Mato, Formosa with napalm and demolition bombs on the 6th of May. Two pictures show refinery and storage sheds ablaze.

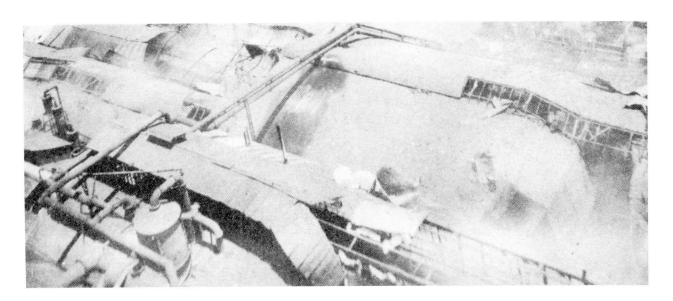

Twenty-three planes slugged Kari Town, Formosa two days before we moved to Clark Field. A large refinery is put out of action.

63

CLARK FIELD

The rains came, finally forcing an exit from spacious San Marcelino. Small showers became more regular and more intense as the days passed. On the 10th and 11th of May we began folding up the camp and trucking it through Zig-Zag Pass to the civilization that was Clark Field. On the morning of the 12th the Squadrons flew their planes over to the new base at half-hour intervals and we were ready to go again. The speed of the change was made possible by a large GI and civilian crew that had been building a war camp area since late February.

There was just one word for Clark Field—Fat-cat. Conditions were about as close to Stateside as any base in the Pacific could offer. A bombed-out Filipino barrio was converted into the Apaches' most unusual camp. House-boys, civilian work crews, friendly Filipino laundresses mingled in the area with Filipino guerrilla guards. Beer, steak, chicken, fresh eggs and butter became part of the regular daily fare. Two nearby barber shops offered reclining chairs, shampoos and massages. Nearby Fort Stotsenburg offered the facilities of tennis courts and swimming pools. In the officer's and enlisted mens' clubs, Army Nurses, WACS and Red Cross workers mixed with the dark-skinned Filipino girls in night-club atmosphere reminiscent of the States. All this, and Manila too! In the bombed-out city where feminine compaionship of every race and color was available, men from the Group spent their pass-time at the "rest-homes" staffed with Filipino personnel.

For the first time overseas, a sixty-mile jeep trip was not a day's excursion. The concrete roads between Clark and Manila were well travelled by Indian-headed jeeps and trucks and the ride was not too uncomfortable.

But all was not fun at Clark. Daily, guerrilla guards dragged into the area bedraggled and bowing Jap prisoners from the hills surrounding the camp. The assignment of planes equipped with rockets gave us the firepower of the cannon-mounted H, without its destructive vibration. Early rockets dropped far short of the strafing bullets, making accuracy difficult, but later, more highly-powered missiles accounted for much damage to the enemy. Apache bombers concentrated mainly on land targets during this period. Our mission was many sided—supporting ground operations on Luzon, and neutralizing Formosa by destroying its factories and transportation facilities and psychologically impressing the civilian population with the cost of the war. In addition to combat operations, an intensive training pro-

Locomotives were hidden in camouflaged revetments (center right) but strafing and bombing May 18th left little for the engine to pull.

Ground support missions preceded the infantry up the Cagayan Valley. These three houses in enemy-held Garit Norte will shelter no more Japs. Valley missions, like this of May 20th, were less difficult than ground support in the more mountainous area.

One of our planes failed to return from May 26th target, Byoritsu, Oil refinery there, like many Formosan targets was well defended. 498th's plane 192 has been hit, is trailing smoke.

Plane 192 crashes, explodes. The fine record of the 345th was not attained without cost. Losses were heavy, particularly during Moresby and Luzon periods.

gram was instituted to prepare the crews for the final attacks soon to follow on the Jap homeland itself.

The "point" system for returning men to the States had everyone figuring. No matter how you counted it, it wasn't enough just yet and only a very few men went home.

At Clark, Lt. Col. Glenn A. Doolittle, former Deputy Commander, assumed command of the Group from Col. Coltharp, 345th C.O. since Nadzab. Young, quiet and confident, Col. Doolittle brought the Group through that phase of operations that ended with final victory.

The interlude at Clark ended much too soon. Although it was expected that the Group's stay at this base would be a long one,

Sweep of Formosan oil and sugar refineries May 28th by two dozen Mitchells left plants like this one at Chikuto useless.

the speeding-up of Pacific operations was apparent since VE day and the momentum carried the Apaches forward closer to Japan. With the shots from the medics completed and the movement of equipment to Subic Bay, the 345th prepared for its trip to Ie Shima, a little-known island off the coast of Okinawa famed only for the death of correspondent Ernie Pyle there during its initial invasion.

Two group houses in Manila offered near-Stateside solidarity and hilarity. For five months, Apache personnel were able to get away from tents to enjoy "city life".

Crews test fire LST's guns on way to still contested Okinawa.

67

IE SHIMA AND OUR LAST MISSION

The water echelon's LST's slowly moved into the waterway separating small Ie Shima island from Okinawa on July 25th. From the harbor, the flat surface of the island, broken only by the peak that jutted from the center, gave the impression of a huge, unsinkable aircraft carrier. Once ashore we were introduced to Ie's soggy mud and lashing rains as we slithered towards our home for one night, a partially submerged camp. Both the Navy and the Army were anxious to get us ashore, lest there be a duplication of what happened in Leyte harbor. The next day, we went to

First big Kyushu target was the Japan Nitrogen Plant at Marushima. Ninety-six five hundred pounders started large fires and explosions. Two bursts of ack-ack downed Lt. Burg's plane.

Planes out on strike of August 1st to Makurazaki got "hurry home" message, reached Ie before typhoon struck.

Fighters and heavies and the 345th demolished Tarumiza, Kyushu, August 5th. Industries and workers' homes were the assigned targets.

Small engines-aft freighters, nicknamed sugar dogs, were carrying burden of Jap cargos. Four such vessels were sunk August 6th. Two larger ships were sunk same day.

Another sugar dog, with Jap flags painted on hull and bridge will sink in a few seconds, was photographed August 10th.

A small destroyer escort attempts to lay a smoke screen off Tsu Shima, August 8th.

But debris flies from starboard quarter as Apache bombs tear into hull. Three Japs man forward gun. Nine planes were holed.

what was going to be our camp area and started the back-breaking task of unloading the LST's. The trucks rumbled up the coral roads from the shore and then into our soggy area, where their cargo was dumped on any dry spot available.

The air echelon arrived on the 28th and went into action the next day. Weather prevented 18 Apaches from making their first shipping sweep of the Inland Sea, but we hit targets of opportunity on the very southern tip of Kyushu. The first raid on the home islands of Japan had become history. From this most forward Apache base, the Group's planes concentrated on enemy radio and radar installations, factories and shipping off Korea, Kyushu, in the Sea of Japan and the Inland Sea. The intensive training program of Clark Field paid off with dividends in the enemy's home waters.

71

The Japs didn't see our jeeps and trucks, but they saw too much of the Indian Head on the vertical stabilizers of the 345th.

In August, the feeling of imminent victory was in the air. The Soviet Union's sudden entry into the war, followed shortly by the miracle of the atomic bomb proved the final blows. Even these did not stop the nightly red alerts, the searchlights scanning the skies and the flashes of bombs and Kamikazes hitting ships in the harbor. Our Group suffered no casualties from these raids, but a lot of needed sleep was lost.

10th of August shipping sweep between Korean, Honshu and Tsu Shima netted nine vessels definitely sunk. 498th snapped off bow of this 6000 ton freighter with two well-placed bombs. Two planes were lost and five holed. Lt. Wright logged near- record 11 hours and 45 minutes while escorting and circling one plane that ditched.

Demonstrating the perfect anti-shipping run, the 501st's 062 drops a bomb amidst most vulnerable portion of this 1500 ton converted freighter, which was sunk.

Our mission of 15th August was half in the air when word came through that offensive operations had ceased. Two of our Squadrons, the only bomber command units scheduled for combat missions, landed and at last we knew. During the last 15 days of the war, although we knew full well that negotiations were under way and there was not much doubt about the outcome, we had flown 11 completed missions and had sunk 29,600 tons of enemy shipping. August combat operations during that same 15 days had cost us 12 planes.

We counted up the kills, found that the Group had sunk some 260 enemy vessels, damaged 275 more. In our 28 months overseas, we had destroyed 107 planes in combat and flown more than 10,100 sorties. We had participated in eight campaigns: New Guinea, Bismarck Archipelago, Northern Solomons, Southern Philippines, Luzon, Western Pacific, China De-

At Aburatsu, secondary target 11th August, direct hits destroy a railroad "choke point" and several component buildings at an unidentified plant.

Last big mission: Apaches McClure and Decker pick up Jap planes south of Kyushu and escort them over Ie strip.

fensive, China Offensive and the Air Offensive against Japan.

August 19th, six of our planes loaded with the great and near great of the group searched three assigned areas in pairs for the plane loads of Jap peace emissaries that had left Kyushu in the early morning. The 345th had been honored and those on the ground were either at the strip with a camera or listening

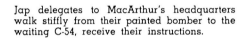

Jap delegates to MacArthur's headquarters walk stiffly from their painted bomber to the waiting C-54, receive their instructions.

The Manila conference over, the homeward bound Japs once again peered through thick-lensed spectacles at the familiar Indian Head insignia of their escorts. Captains Naas, Tatelman, Bannister, and T/Sgts. Le Blanc and Gaylor flew in this 499th ship on August 21st.

to the Jap planes on the radio. Maj. McClure had to land on Moko Strip to show the Japs the way in, much to the consternation of the P-38s also escorting. We had performed our last mission.

Four hundred and twenty-four men were started Stateside before the end of August. The 19th of September, 59 officers and 462 enlisted men staged through the 380th Bomb Group on Okinawa, departing for home about ten days later.

Earlier plans for the group to be part of the occupational air force in southern Korea were definitely cancelled and the final job of turning in equipment was all that was left to do. Two typhoons, the one in early October especially, all but levelled what was left of our camp area and made rations and tentage a serious problem. We were set up to go home as a complete unit, with 50 per cent over strength being supplied by men from other parts of the 5th Air Force. We fell under the control of the 7th Air Force and were finally sent home. The Group was de-activated Nov. 11, 1945—after exactly three years of service.

This is our combat story. The 345th arrived in the Pacific in time to count cadence with its bombs and bullets for the great aerial march north from New Guinea, through the Philippines and onto the very soil of the enemy. We lost both fliers and ground men; many of them We made our camps in some of the world's most rugged terrain. We bargained for eggs and smuggled lumber. We were the "soft" Americans on a warpath that had led to the Emperor's Palace. Despite committments that were often over-ambitious, the sheer force and power of our spirit and weapons had made a record of which we can be justly proud. And we are proud.

Story Of The Air Apaches

FALCON SQUADRON 498 TH.

This section of the chronology of the Air Apaches is dedicated to all the men of the "Falcon" Squadron, but particularly it is dedicated to those who are no longed present to enjoy the peace that their deeds and sacrifices made possible. Their exploits will be forever a brilliant part of the air history of World War II.

FOREWORD

In one way or another, each of us has come to know that there is no glory in war. Every experience eventually falls into the same dull pattern of blood, sweat and tears. But there are some things each of us will want to remember. Perhaps it was that last forlorn look at San Francisco's Golden Gate—like having a door closed in your face—or maybe the time you tried to buy Sydney on a thirty-dollar-a-day installment plan. If Columbia or Castellijos hold a special niche in your "Falcon" memories, they are here to help you remember some of the little things that happened.

BERT S. ROSENBAUM

CHESTER A. COLTHARP

MELFORD M. MAGEE

THEODORE R. WRIGHT

JACK C. McCLURE, JR.

OLLIE E. HATCHER

SQUADRON COMMANDING OFFICERS

JOHNSON CRAIG

JOHN J. SCOTT

EDWARD T. AUGUSTINE

ROBERT P. CORNWELL

SQUADRON EXECUTIVE OFFICERS

84

ANTHONY CHIAPPE

FREDERICK FAIR

ROBERT W. TUFTO

CLIFFORD W. FAIRCLOTH

ALBERT W. GRUER

SQUADRON OPERATIONS OFFICERS

Life began for the 498th Bombardment Squadron on the 11th day of November, 1942, when the original cadre of ninety-six men and seven officers was assembled at the Army Air Base, Columbia, South Carolina, and Capt. Bert S. Rosenbaum assigned as the commanding officer.

through." The flimsy siding and loose-fitting doors, however, didn't contribute any to our comfort during the frigid Carolina winter. Several times a night we had to forsake the warm covers to pad about on the icy floor and cram the little stove with coal to keep a semblance of heat in the building. Then, of course,

For a couple of weeks it was an existence on paper only since the planes had not yet arrived. After living in the old 340th Bomb Group area for a time, we moved to the 376th area near the gate. Our barracks were poorly built and typical of the kind thrown together in the early days of the war when quantity was more vital than quality. They may not have been as bad as one sergeant put it: "Those walls had holes you could throw a cat

there were little things like the showers which featured icicles hanging from the pipes, and the rickety mess hall which would make a cow barn seem luxurious.

During the earlier days of our organization we had to put up with some of the "chicken" always associated with Stateside Army life. There were the occasional Saturday morning parades, the shoe inspections, the standby inspections, and some of the other features we thought we'd seen the last of during our basic training. It was during one of these routine inspections that the Group C. O. halted in front of a man to inquire his name.

"M-m-moore, sir," stammered the flustered soldier.

"Maj. Moore?" archly queried the Colonel.

"No, Corp. Moore, sir," he answered miserably.

Haircuts of a reasonable length were another "must" and more than one who lacked the foresight to visit a barber shop in time spent a chilly night in a pup tent. Occasional dances at the Casino gave us a little taste of our pre-war social life and the big turkey feasts, complete with all the usual extras right down to after-dinner cigarettes, on Thanksgiving Day and Christmas, helped to keep the 498th morale up where it had always been. New Year's Eve was another occasion, but the refreshments were a different kind and morale was even higher—at least until morning.

It was late in November before we received our first airplanes. They weren't the clean, trim jobs just off the assembly line, but much used and somewhat battered B-25C's and D's which had been discarded by another Group whose training had been completed. T h e y were welcome sights in our eyes, however, and we immediately pitched into the job of learning how to maintain and fly them. A good many training missions were flown and scores upon scores of practice hundred-pounders were dropped on Myrtle Beach in the next few weeks before we felt really capable of tackling the enemy. Crew chiefs and A. M.'s got their first real experience in keeping the airplanes in the air, the Communications Section had its little problems with the radio equipment and the armorers, most of whom had trained for work on fighters, learned the

hard way how a bomber's weapons of war must be kept up. The training was not without loss. Plane No. 071 cracked up on take off one day, killing the pilot, Flight Officer Mason, and his entire crew.

The ground forces have their maneuvers and the Air Corps have theirs also. At least we did. We spent four days at an old C.C.C. camp near Aiken, South Carolina, in weather that would make a polar bear shiver. Every few hours (we had 18 separate alerts during that time)—the A. M.'s and crew chiefs would be routed out and rushed to the strip to prepare the planes for take off while other ground men hastened to repel imaginary enemy ground attacks. The oil would be half-congealed, the engines stiff, and many a run down battery and frayed temper would result. Alerts were no respectors of mealtime either, and on more than one occasion the boys had just seated themselves before some hot chow only to be hustled off to the cold hard stands to perform a pre-flight. Needless to say, the food was no longer hot—or even warm—when they returned. A good many of the line men lived in their mechanic's sheep-lined suits during the whole time; otherwise they'd have spent too much of their time dressing and undressing. If you were caught abed during an alert you were poorer by fifty cents; and if you disobeyed the orders against shaving you could expect a fine of two bits.

All bad and good things come to an end, and our stay at Aiken was closed with a rousing blowout where beer flowed freely and troubles were forgotten. Back to Columbia we went to continue with out training—more practice missions, more pre-flightting, gun cleaning, bomb loading, etc. We had been issued various items of our overseas equipment by this time, had enjoyed three-day passes to Greenville and Savannah, and now it seemed that we certainly must move out soon. One day we got

orders to pack up. "This is it," we thought as we crammed things into our A and B bags, but it turned out to be nothing more than another overnight camping drill. We marched to that little grove behind the hospital and set up the pup tents, which the enlisted men occupied dutifully and which most of the officers furtively forsook for a comfortable sleep back in the barracks.

It was along about this time that the officers had their big party at the Columbia Woman's Club. Once again glasses tinkled, spirits soared, and the war was relegated to a position of only passing importance. It was generally agreed that the affair set an all-time record in Columbia for something-or-other.

On March 3rd a small advance detail went to Walterboro and three days later after the barracks, mess hall, latrines and other buildings were cleaned up

for use, the rest of the Squadron followed in trucks. The line area was built up, tents erected and the Squadron geared for continuance of the training program in the new location. We kept up our hard work, but in spite of the practice missions, the calisthenics, and trips over the obstacle course, there was still time for some friendly little games on the line and for sessions of skeet on the new range.

Late that month we got our first of the new airplanes, which were to go with us overseas. Since the plane was a winterized job, rumors were common that we were headed for the ETO. Our shipping number was issued but it was changed several times before finally being settled at 2960B. Then when the new planes' equipment was supplemented with jungle kits even the rumor-mongers were baffled. We didn't know where we were going.

More new ships continued to arrive, additional men were being assigned all the time, and the outfit was definitely taking on the proportions of a real bombardment Squadron.

Finally the great day arrived—the seventh of April. Sixteen ships roared off the Walterboro runway that morning and flew to Savannah.

Here they remained three days while new equipment was installed after which they continued to El Paso where they stayed the night (or what was left of it after they paid a call across the border at Juarez in the interests of international goodwill, of course.)

On April 11th the crews arrived at Sacramento and although inwardly chafing to be off for the rest of their journey they found interesting things to occupy their attention in California's capital. All but a few moved right into town for their final fling at Stateside pleasures, and lived in hotels for the full fifteen days. One revelry spot—Donovan's by name—was patronized so consistently by our group that a nightly roll call would hardly ever have turned up a 498th A.W.O.L. Late that month they left for Hamilton and after three days of final processing, checking, etc., the

Mitchells took off for the first and longest hop on their trip to the Pacific war zone. The engineers went to Hawaii by water and finished their trip in C-87's, while the crew chiefs traveled to Hickam in a converted B-24, there to be picked up by our own planes for the rest of the oversea junket. On they flew to Christmas Island, Canton, Fiji, New Caledonia and at last they skimmed down on to the Amberly Field runway near Brisbane on May 8th.

Meanwhile the ground personnel had had other things to do. After the planes left, the line men busied themselves largely with packing the equipment in overseas crates and then in rebuilding the crates when they didn't meet with the approval of the super-critical inspecting engineer. There was always time, of course, for full and complete attention to all rumors and few were the inhabited spots on the globe which were not at

one or another of those times mentioned with positiveness as the Sqaudron's destination. Latrine intelligence had us going to Africa, the

Aleutians, Hawaii, England, Iceland, Guadalcanal and Australia, not to mention India and Panama.

We didn't know for which coast we were headed until the train, which we boarded on the night of the 16th, puffed out toward the west. Through Macon, Memphis and Little Rock we went, stopping once a day for calisthenics in some railroad yard, eating from a mess kitchen which had been established in a baggage car, dozing, reading and playing cards throughout the day and sleeping in the berths at night. We passed the smoking mills of Pueblo and chugged up into the breath-taking scenery of the Royal Gorge country in the Rockies. Salt Lake City, Feather River Canyon, and then one night we were in Pittsburg, California, shuffling wearily off the train and looking forward to our first good wash and night's sleep in a long seven days. Army plans, however, didn't exactly coincide with ours at the moment and we were herded together for one of those brief and extremely localized physical inspections before being permitted to collapse on our sacks.

Then followed several days of final processing . . . getting new carbines . . . having

the same records which had been rechecked a dozen times earlier gone over a few more times . . . issue of impregnated clothing . . .

allotments . . . wills . . . bonds . . . power of attorney . . . censorship instruction. As the day for our departure approached we were impressed with the need for secrecy and cautioned against any attempt to circumvent the censorship and let our folks know where we were and where we might be going. Then, as a climax, we moved out from Stoneman in the broad light of day and struggled through the town of Pittsburg causing more notice and public attention than a mile-long procession of Godivas.

At Oakland we clambered off the river boat and staggered under the weight of our A bags along the entire length of what seemed an extra long dock before we reached the gang plank of the SS *President Johnson*. It was early on the morning of May 1st when we finally stowed ourselves aboard and examined the quarters which were to be ours for more than a month

to come. The first-three-graders had been assured that comfy little staterooms had been set aside for them so their jaws dropped when they learned they were to occupy the same cramped three-tiered bunks in the same stuffy hold to which all the other enlisted men were assigned. The head, which is Navy language for relief station, c o u l d b e reached only by a route which led up and across the weather deck. Since smoking was prohibited below deck, the Navy—with all its shrewd attention to detail—calculated that some men might use this trip as an excuse to sneak in a few furtive puffs. And the gold braid also had figured out a preventive measure—any man who wasn't a non-com and who had to leave the compartment in accordance with the demands of nature must be escorted to and from his destination by a non-commissioned officer. There were just six men in the outfit who weren't non-coms so the whole thing worked perfectly.

Promptly at noon the following day, May

4th, the big gray craft with its load of 345th men and some engineers—about 3000 in all—backed out into the bay and swung around

for her 7000-mile trip across the Pacific. Still we were ignorant of our destination but since a good deal of the action was concentrated on land and waters near Australia it seemed most reasonable that we should be heading there.

A last glance at the receding Frisco skyline, a witsful look at the majestic Golden Gate bridge, and we turned our thoughts to the months that lay ahead and the adventures they were to bring. Was this to be our last glimpse of America? Would it fall to us to be one of those who were to make the toatl sacrifice? For some of us it did and while we all were outwardly confident, we still had that sobering thought that we were going into war and of the inevitable casualties which must follow. Thus, there was fairly good attendance at the weekly church services all the way across.

It was only shortly after our leaving the

harbor that some of our heads grew dizzy and our stomachs developed that peculiar unrest described in polite circles as *mal de mer*. Many were the fish that didn't have to hunt far for their dinner that afternoon as the *SS President Johnson* reared and plunged across the rough Japanese current. Some, of course, never did get seasick and their exuberant spirits and lusty appetites made the rest of us feel even worse, if possible.

The *Johnson* wasn't a bad ship, though it was commissioned a dozen years before the First World War (there was one passenger aboard who swore he sailed on her to France in 1917 when she bore the name, *SS Manchester*.) She foamed along at a steady 12 knots and didn't treat us too roughly after the first couple of days. The troop quarters were the worst feature ——crowded, hot, very poor ventilation (not enhanced at all by the practice of a few of the

fellows who paid a visit to the kitchen and came back to munch large quantities of garlic), but we endured them as cheerfully as we could. After all, we reasoned, we had lights. They didn't have any in the Black Hole in Calcutta.

Our Chow wasn't exactly calculated to help us put on weight. We never saw so many hard-boiled eggs in our lives. If the outside instead of the inside had been colored that same yellowish-purple hue we'd have thought sure as hell there was a squadron of Easter bunnies aboard because we had hard-boiled eggs every single morning for breakfast during the whole voyage. Our noon meal was lunch in the very narrowest sense of the word. Usually it consisted of an apple, and a couple of slices of dry bread enclosing a slab of questionable something. At night we fared some better. Chow lines were long and slow and the mess hall was the temperature of a boiler room. The only ones who were fortunate in this regard were the armorers who had been assigned to duty in the guntubs and were thus entitled to crash the mess lines.

Recreation on shipboard was understand-ably limited but there were the old standbys— reading the paper-backed books and playing cards. Then we had a boxing match or so, a program of calisthenics which fizzled out in short order, and a little detail. There were drills, drills and more drills — fire drills, air raid drills, submarine drills, abandon ship drills and drills for any and everything.

There was once when we thought that abandon ship business might come in handy. Our lone escort, a Free French corvette, had disappeared in a storm about a week out of Frisco. It was shortly afterward during a sub alert that she reappeared and then we saw great mushrooming columns of water rise up behind her boiling stern and seconds later we'd get the concussion of the depth charges. While we were worrying about whether the sub would be sunk or break loose and sink us, the report came over that the valiant little corvette had destroyed

her under-sea enemy. Meanwhile the SS John-son almost had a casualty of another sort. The fascinated GI's had all rushed over to one rail to better watch the excitement and the old craft heeled over to an alarming degree, threatening to capsize. The Captain barked some quick

orders and the crisis was averted.

Another incident that disturbed our peace of mind happened one bright moonlight night when the ship suddenly developed trouble with its boilers or engines or something. Belching fire and dense black smoke from her stack and seemingly doing all possible to invite attack by any submarines within a score of miles, she lay motionless in the water, a sitting duck, for more than eight hours, until repairs were effected and she got under way once more.

On May 12th the *Johnson* plodded across t h e equator amid all the ceremony that had been attached to this event for centuries past. King Neptune and his shellback associates (veterans of a previous equatorial crossing) officiated in administering the proper initiation rites upon the pollywogs (anyone who couldn't prove he had been over the equator before—and some who could). Officers fared especial-

ly badly and emerged with grotesque haircuts, bilge-water shampoos, grease-smeared clothing, and with liberal gobs of thick yellow paint on unmentionable regions of their anatomy. Of course there wasn't time for the same individual treatment of all the men so the shellbacks contented themselves with thoroughly soaking the unwary spectators at intervals with sudden squirts of the fire hoses when they least expected it.

The International Date Line lay across our path on May 19th and we skipped from Tuesday to Thursday, missing Wednesday altogether. S i x days later, on May 25th, an airplane hove into view. Nerves were tense until it was identified as an Aussie patrol plane and our feeling of relief increased when a destroyer appeared and escorted us into the Brisane anchorage which we reached the same day.

Unhappily we learned that we weren't to

be allowed off the ship for the time being but we soon made contact with some friendly Aussies and talked them into doing some marketing for us. In spite of the intricacies of turning dollars into pounds and trying to calculate in terms of shillings and florins, we made deals involving large sacks of pineapples, bananas, vegetables and pretty nearly anything edible we could get out hands on. Fresh food surely tasted good after those twenty-five days without.

May 27th we felt the first solid ground under our feet for almost a month when we disembarked and marched about five miles through Brisbane to Camp Doomban, carrying full field equipment. Passes to town were forbidden since we were under quarantine but there was a loose board in the fence surround-

ing the post and . . . need we say more. The girls were entertaining and the beer and fresh chow most satisfying. We had our own beer blowout the next evening and a snappy "Digger" stage show at the same time. The The Squadron "wheels" got to feeling so gay they forgot all about being "wheels" and threw their dignity to the winds. But even an alcoholic glow couldn't keep off that winter nip in the air. We practically emptied our barracks bags over us in an effort to stay warm at night. The showers we had anticipated with a great relish after washing in salt water for four weeks must have been equipped with its own freezing unit because we almost congealed under its frigid spray.

After two days in the race track camp we climbed into trucks and returned to the ship, setting out the same day on a pleasant coastwise cruise to Townsville. Here we stopped briefly for orders on June 2nd and then, under the watchful eyes of patrolling planes and a destroyer, we nosed out from the Coral Sea and headed for Port Moresby. Three days later the green peaks of the Owen Stanley Range crept into view and we steamed into the anchorage of what in pre-war days had been a sleepy little trading center and now was one of the most important military bases of the Southwest Pacific.

The sight of Papuan natives or "Fuzzy Wuzzies" as they were aptly called, working at the dock with their big flat feet, great bushy hair and primitive costumes, left no doubt in our minds that we were at last in the tropical wildernesses of the South Pacific we'd read so much about. At last we had come to our destination. The months of training and the journey of almost 11,000 miles by land and sea were over and now we could pitch in and do the job for which we'd been sent.

We lost no time in disembarking and piling into trucks which took us several miles away to the point near Jackson strip where we were to establish camp. Of course there were the patronizing "old timers" on hand to chant the worn-out phrase "You'll be sorry," and to cheer us with the information that the place had been nicknamed "Death Valley" because of the frequent damaging enemy raids. A one hundred-plane raid just before our arrival had destroyed much of Moresby, they pointed out. But we didn't borrow trouble. We proceeded with the setting up of our pup tents—they were scattered so widely through the tall kunai grass that the "wheels" had a heck of a time finding us for details—and the digging of our first fox holes.

Our first experience with New Guinea rain came that same night. A good many of us got wet too, all except those who chose to sleep in the 500th mess hall. This was the first of a great deal of wet weather to come and it was just as well we got accustomed to it at the start. C rations, supplemented with purchases at Moresby and at the nearby Aussie camp, constituted our chow for the first several meals while we worked busily at unloading the ship, re-sorting the jumbled equipment which had become thoroughly mixed up among the four Squadrons and setting up our line and living areas. In the meantime we had acquired pyramidal tents along with canvas cots and after sleeping on the ground for several nights these made it seem as if we were living in the lap of luxury. Water was a problem for a time. There was but a single shower and only one trailer with which to haul water for all purposes. Mosquitoes weren't too thick though they did pack a malarial wallop and we slept under our nets and tried to take our atabrine fatihfully.

Our first air raid came on the night of June 13th when the red alert sounded and three Jap planes droned over the valley. No bombs fell near us but ack ack fragments pierced the mess hall. That was but one of several times the yellow so-and sos interfered with our sleep, but they never caused much damage that we could see and never attempted to send over large forces of aircraft. Something which startled us more than any Nip bombers was the 90 millimeter ack-ack gun which had been set up behind our area without our knowledge, and which suddenly opened up with a thunderous roar during one of the raids. The heavy shells whistled over our tents like so many skyrockets and it was a little while before we could stop ducking.

On June 20th we were rejoined by the flight echelon and after the two months' separation there were many hearty backslappings and swapping of stories about experiences. The first crews had arrived at Amberly on May 9th, as noted before and the rest had come through the following day. One crash marred our brief stay there. A plane being piloted by Lt. Melvin Best mushed in on takeoff and was destroyed. All the crew including Lt. Best escaped serious injuries.

Leaving Brisbane the next stop had been Woodstock near Townsville where they remained for more than a month training with the 22nd Bomb Group. Here another accident caused the loss of a second aircraft. A blown tire on takeoff thoroughly wrecked the plane but once more the occupants including Lt. William Gerber, the pilot, were not badly hurt. The short training period in Australia enabled some of the 498th boys to inspect the "Down Under" country at first hand. Many visited

Townsville and like immensely what they found there though they probably didn't appreciate it as much as they did after spending

several months in New Guinea's no woman's land. One of the novel features at Woodstock was the nearness of a cattle ranch and the disturbing habit of the cows to consider the runways as a definite part of their g r a z i n g ground. Quite often it was necessary to shoo away the placid bovines before planes could land or take off.

The air crews arrived at Jackson to find the Squadron getting well-established. T h e mess hall was in operation, the administration quarters set up, tents ready to receive them, plans advanced for a nice EM club and there were even outdoor movies though we had to go to a nearby Aussie camp to see these Saturday night double features. All the pyramidal tents had dirt floors, of course. Until we got a few overseas service months chalked up on our calendar we couldn't be expected to know the intracacies of getting floor lumber by means

of—er—ahem—acquisition.

Fifth Bomber Command didn't wait long before putting us to work and on June 27th eight Falcon ships took on their first combat zone mission. However, the load was not bombs but supplies which were intended for Australian troops fighting in the tangled jungle where other means of transportation were not practicable. Our first real combat mission came four days later on July 1st. Nine airplanes deposited almost ten tons of explosives on Logui Village No. 2.

In the next month we worked quite hard. Our airplanes flew almost daily missions, nine ships each most of the time, and did a lot of damage at Bobdubi, Salamaua, Madang, Komistum a n d other places with all sorts of unpronounceable names. Our first aerial interception was encountered July 11th when a couple of Zekes made passes at one flight near Old Bobdub.

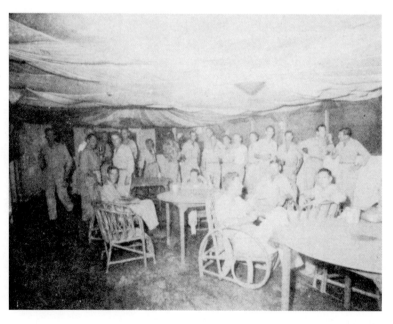

Ridge while ten others lurked just out of range waiting for a good chance to pounce. P-38s put in an appearance, however, and drove the enemy off before any damage was caused to the bombers.

July 15th we were ordered to provide

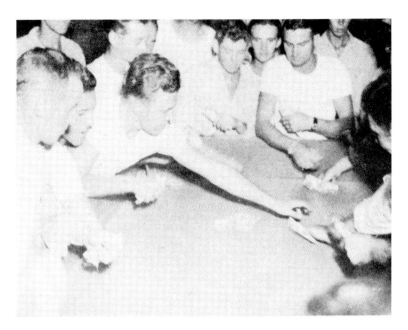

anti-sub cover for three small ships putting out from Moresby. Lt. Victor Brooksby, piloting No. 293 with the following crew members, Lt. Frank Gerber, Lt. Robert Gagen, Cpl. Ephraim Poole, T/Sgt. Paul Drinkard and S/Sgt. Adam Domijan, took off on the mission and were never seen again. An undecipherable radio message sent 90 minutes after takeoff was the last heard from them.

Late in July the men with the stars and bars decided that the outfit would be more effective in combat if our planes were sent in at low instead of medium altitude bombing attacks, so all but two of our ships plus some ground men to take care of them were flown to Townsville for conversion to strafers. Here they remained at the depot for three weeks, affording the personnel an excellent chance to get re-acquainted with civilization. Some were content with Townsville, but others discovered

the town of Ingham, a spot not too far away where American GIs were still a novelty and treated accordingly. It was here too that we saw the Australian aborigines for the first time.

When we returned to Moresby on August 20th we found that in the meantime the men had been busy building strafing and bombing targets, flying incessant recco missions, eating bananas which they purchased from the natives at the Thirty Mile strip and brought back by the bomb bay load, and enjoying the new officers' and EM clubs which were then in full operation. The bottled refreshments hauled back from Townsville helped admirably to make the two institutions the rousing successes they were. Due credit should be given also to Lt. K. C. Dean who procured for us the "coke" machine which served faithfully throughout our career in the Pacific. The Squadron laundry was also in full swing.

Ingeniously made from the illimitably useful gasoline drums and a stray motor, it helped to ease an irksome burden.

The first big medium bombing raid on Wewak probably would have fallen to us had it not been staged just a couple of days before our converted planes returned from Australia. As it was, the 3rd Attack Group planes used our camp facilities and the men of the Squadron serviced the craft for the raid.

September 5th we helped make history again when we supported the paratroop landing at Nadzab. The strike, however, cost us a plane when No. 043, its strut and tire damaged in the air, cracked up on landing. Another was lost on a Lae mission when an aileron was shot off No. 031 and Lt. Magee crash-landed at Dobodura. Sgt. J. A. Murphy, wounded in the leg by the same burst of shrapnel, had the unwelcome distinction of being the first 498th man injured in combat operations. The first airman killed was Sgt. Ochsner, engineer-gunner on No. 047, which was struck by anti-aircraft on the September 27th raid at Wewak and irreparably damaged on landing. Lt. Donald O. Landsness, bombardier, was killed September 21st on a practice bombing and strafing mission, and impressive military services were conducted for each.

Meanwhile our C. O., Maj. Rosenbaum, was transferred to FATF at Dobodura and replaced by Capt. Chester A. Coltharp, former commanding officer of the 376th Bomb Squadron. First Sgt. Cameme received an appointment to attend OCS about this time and his job was taken over by Sgt. C. D. Carrington. Another change was the assignment to the Squadron of Lt. Johnson Craig as executive officer.

The next two months saw some rough missions. On October 11th, while planes were being loaded with parafrags for the following day's strike at the big Vunakanau airdrome at Rabaul, PFC O'Neill was killed and S/Sgt. Chard wounded as the former tried to dispose of an accidentally armed bomb. Twelve ships, taking off from Dobadura, participated in the mission with outstanding success. Three airborne Bettys were shot down by the Falcon's strafing guns, two Zekes destroyed by the gunners, and many craft shot up on the ground. Other raids on Rabaul in the following few

weeks met with excellent results and the last one, on November 2nd earned us the Presidential Citation. We also kept hammering at other targets along the New Britain coast with now and then a swing up towards Madang, Hansa Bay or Wewak. It was late in November when Capt. William Kizzire, flying No. 046, had to crash-land his flak-damaged ship just off the Sepik River mouth. Five men were seen to survive the landing, and supplies and a life raft were dropped to them. Rescue efforts were unsuccessful, however, and the crew, listed below, was carried as missing in action: Lt. Charles Reynolds, Lt. Joe Carroll, S/Sgt. Wilfred Paquette, S/Sgt. Fred Nightwine and S/Sgt. Roy Showers.

In November a trip by the flight echelon and maintenance men to Kiriwina Island was made in readiness for a raid that never was ordered. Three days later, after getting acquainted with real jungle country that featured saucer-sized spiders and other fearsome wild life, they returned.

As Thanksgiving Day drew near we dispatched planes to Australia on a purchasing mission and they returned in time for us to have an excellent feast which included not only the traditional turkey and garden vegetables, but milk, frish ice cream and gin punch as well. It's not hard to see why we arranged for regular "fat-cat" trips after that and the result was a marked improvement in the chow

situation. Christmas dinner too was a great success—lots of turkey and the other things that helped to keep the spirits high.

December 23rd the planes and maintenance crews flew to Dobadura to begin operations from a base nearer to our targets and removed from the hazards of the Owen Stanley peaks. The balance of the Squadron followed about two weeks later and proceeded with the job of establishing themselves. The ambitious ones built tent floors from poles cut in the jungle and lived high and dry above the ground while those less concerned with their personal comfort contented themselves with the natural earth. Lumber was still scarce. There was no shower at Dobadura but something ever better—a river. A cooling swim after several hot hours on the line was very pleasant and so was the fishing we indulged in occasionally. This was the big reason we disliked moving from Dobadura.

Our new location was not far from the scene of the bloody campaign at Buna and the Sananada trail and we got our first chance to examine some fresh battlefields. The area was a good source of battle souvenirs and the sight of a well-filled Jap cemetery was cheering.

Furloughs were other important items in our lives those days. The luckier ones got to Sydney and Coolangatta and the others had to be content with Mackay but wherever we

we went it was nice to get back and enjoy the things that only civilization can offer. We generally returned thoroughly busted, but we had memories that were worth all they cost—ice cream, fresh milk, vegetables, lots of beer, dances, dates, etc. Then it was the usual thing to bring back a B-4 bag well loaded with

bottles—not empty ones either.

Trinket-making was a hobby that almost all of us took part in at some time or other in our overseas careers, and at Dobadura we spent many long hours turning out a variety of things. Aussie florins, we discovered, could be hammered into handsome rings and the little "cat's eyes" made excellent settings. Shells and bits of wire could be fashioned into attractive necklaces and bracelets; strips of stainless steel could be turned into long-lasting watch straps; novel salt and pepper shakers emerged from 20 mm. shell cases; picture frames and dozens of other things from the versatile plexiglas; "spangly" hula skirts from parachute shroud lines. Some worked

industriously at their newly found trades and sold enough of their products to earn very substantial sums; others contented themselves with sending the stuff home as gifts. All in all it helped us to kill time and keep other things off our minds.

During our Dobadura stay we continued to wallop targets in New Guinea—mostly between Wewak and Saidor—with occasional trips to New Britain and the Admiralties. There were no losses until the big Kavieng raid on February 15th, one of the most successful in the Group's history. Capt. Coltharp and his crew distinguished themselves by being in a large way responsible for the rescue of three downed crews, all shot into the sea within a short distance of Jap guns. One of these, the only 498th ship lost, was No. 041,

piloted by Lt. Edgar Cavin.

Early in January the advance echelon was dispatched to Nadzab where the men helped to set up installations ready for our arrival on February 24th. The mess hall was on a fair way to being completed by then but we had to put up the shower, administration building, and supply department besides a few other odds and ends before we could consider ourselves established. This was our first experience with the portable buildings and we considered them a decided improvement over the squad and hospital tents we'd been using at Dobo and Moresby. Our enlisted men's club was a primitive affair with little more than a "coke" bar, dice table and a few seats. We used the mess hall on the one or two occasions when a few Red Cross girls came over to entertain us with an evening of eats, a little danc-

ing and chatting. The officers had their club up on the hill and threw a few successful parties, complete with pretty nurses.

Some lumber from the dismantled mess hall at Dobo was brought to Nadzab in our B-25s (boards were even protruding from the tails of some ships) and part of it found its way into tent floors. The nearby sawmill also proved a source of floor lumber and those who were unsuccessful in making a deal there found that a bottle of liquor placed in the hands of engineers could produce a load of

boards in an amazingly short time. The tents were all arranged in symmetrical rows, giving the camp a much more orderly appearance.

Our line area was set up by strip No. 4 on the edge of the jungle, about four miles of very dusty road from where we lived. Because there were reports of Japs still in the vicinity we had to carry carbines or .45s with us when we left the Squadron area. We never did see any Nips, however. A few red alerts in mid-March were the only hints of enemy activity.

In March we continued to strike against targets in the same neighborhoods — Los Negros, Boram, a convoy off Wewak, Dagua, Kairiru Island, etc., and we suffered our only loss on March 30th when No. 040 was declared missing in action on the Dagua raid along with its crew: Lt. Bernard Foley, pilot; Lt. Wade Westfall, Lt. Richard Hochadel, S/Sgt. William Branstad, T/Sgt. Orville Diedrichs, S/Sgt. Leon Monteith and S/Sgt. James Beattie.

Early in April we received a full comple-

ment of new Hs equipped with the 75 mm. cannon, the only Squadron in the Group to be so honored. There followed a week of transition flying and on April 23rd we tried the new weapon in a raid on Wewak. The .75s could do a lot of damage, it was agreed, but the concussion sheered skin rivets and caused instrument trouble and the ships were not entirely satisfactory. We lost one of them when Lt. Stapleton, out of fuel upon returning from the Hansa Bay strike on April 24th, had to crash-land just off Yule Island. Two more planes went down in May. Lt. Cutinelle and his crew; Lt. Charles Knight, Lt. James Quesenberry, T/Sgt. Leon Hupp, S/Sgt. August Card and Sgt. Frank Leach were listed as missing in action when they failed to return from a weather recco in No. 393. The other crew—Lt. Elmer Kirkland, Lt. Robert Jackson, S/Sgt. Cecil Barnes, S/Sgt. Charles Jones and Sgt. Claud

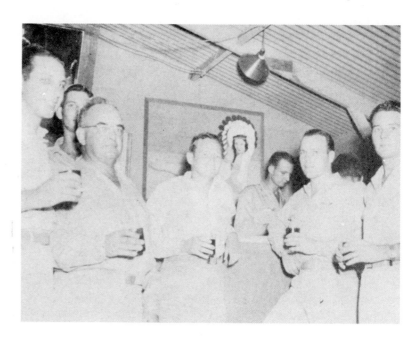

Hill, were shot down by ack ack in ship No. 344 over Biak and one of the several raids staged out of Wadke Island during the last

days of May.

Maj. Colthrap who had proved himself one of the outstanding executives and pilots of the

Group was advanced from Squadron to Group C. O. in June, receiving a promotion to lieutenant colonel soon after. His place was filled by Capt. Milford M. Magee. Also Capt. Merton K i l g o r e, flight leader, was appointed C. O., Headquarters Squadron of Fifth Bomber, and another original officer, Lt. Walter Barnes, left us as Personnel Officer and Assistant Adjutant and became Adjutant of the 499th Squadron. Sixteen new combat crews, all trained in the use of the BO25H5 radar-controlled planes, were assigned to us along with the full complement of ships which replaced our old B-25Ds. The increase in strength was partly offset by veteran combat men going home, leaving our Squadron with 457 men as of the end of June. The personnel included 380 enlisted men and 77 officers.

More raids staged from Wakde and Hollandia netted additional damage to juicy Nip targets further up the coast—especially at

Manckwari where a June 10th strike co-ordinated with the 501st Squadron, destroyed buildings, ack ack positions and a dozen luggers.

Then orders came to move and after hurried preparations most of the personnel was flown to Biak on the 12th, 13th and 14th of July.

The island of Biak had not long been in Allied hands so we were not greatly surprised to learn that Japs were still there in abundance. The little yellow devils would perch in the mouths of their coral caves in the cliffs behind our camp and make t h e entire night miserable for us with their howling and moaning. Every now and then during our entire six months there a Jap would come down out of the hills, most often in search of food, sometimes armed, sometimes seeking only to surrender. Once Sherman tanks were trundled right up into our area and fired their .75s point blank at the dozens of

caves in the ridge. But they never completely succeeded in driving the Japs out. The area on the hill around and beyond the caves was rich with less valuable kinds of battle souvenirs and almost everyone in the Squadron made a trip up there at some time.

Setting up camp on a coral island can be a mighty hard job as we soon learned. The wooden pegs splintered and broke as we tried to set up our tents, the flinty rock stubbornly resisted our efforts to excavate for posts and fox holes, the knee-deep mud in the area and along the "road" to the strip, the absence of our trucks which were still at Nadzab, and the frequent heavy rains all contributed to our general disgust, and brought us to conclude that the Allied war effort would profit by returning the darned island to the Japs. But we finally got our tents established in orderly rows, built the mess hall and administration buildings, EM club and supply department, blasted a latrine pit and were ready to settle down to business. The shower was something that never did materialize. Though we got a small building set up for the purpose, the water supply was so restricted that we had to be content with rainwater helmet baths or else rig up an individual shower from gasoline drums as several of the men did, showing marked ingenuity in the process.

Our first issue of beer, something we had waited for ever since getting overseas, helped our morale at Biak as did the improved chow.

Our "fat-cats" continued to make regular trips to Australia returning with the eggs, fresh vegetables and meat which tasted like nectar

from the gods after a few months of bully beef and canned beets. Liquor in some quantity found its way up to us also but returning furloughees learned that the demand still exceeded the supply and those that were so inclined had no trouble selling a quart of gin for ten pounds ($32.00).

Three airplanes were lost, ten officers and men were killed and several others injured during the last week in July. After sinking a "Sugar Charlie" off the Halmaheras on July 22nd, Lt. George McCullough and his entire crew were lost when No. 452 plunged into the sea. The casualties included Lt. William Shack, S/Sgt. Francis Macone and Sgts. Louis Medina, Thomas Monahan and John Henwood. Machine gun fire from the target ship struck the plane causing it to veer into Lt. Neblett's craft almost resulting in a second crash. T/Sgt. Charles Becker was badly wounded by ack ack in a strike on Utarom on July

27th, and died three days later. Lt. Espevik and S/Sgts. Holloway Pittman and Andrew Delgado did not survive a forced water landing made during an attack on shipping at Utarom on the 29th of July. The pilot, Lt. Robert Best, and two other crewmen, T/Sgt. Robert Dow and Pvt. Harold Neal, suffered slight injuries but were rescued a few hours later by a Catalina.

Though the H models had proved themselves valuable in shipping strikes, a number of malfunctions had made themselves evident during our four months' experience with them. So in August they were flown south and traded for Js. The flight and maintenance echelons spent most of the month at Nadzab and Townsville working with the new ships and there was not much in the way of activity for the Squadron. A number of weather reccos were flown and some missions to the Halmaheras pulled in the early part of

the month. On August 1st we lost another crew when Lt. John Miller's plane, No. 332, struck a coconut tree on Geboken Island as it made a second pass over a sinking lugger. The crew included: Lt. Stanley Stickler, S/Sgt. Jack Flinton and Sgts. Howard Johnson, James Rodgers

and Harry Szalanski.

Unfavorable weather began to interfere with our missions but we succeeded nevertheless in carrying out several effective strikes on the Celebes. It meant ten and sometimes eleven hours in the air but the new Gs and few Js which were in use by that time proved rugged ships capable of taking it. With one exception the attacks were executed without loss. Lt. Walter Garrison's ship was hit by ack ack over Namlea township and crashed with the loss of all on board; Lt. Milton Green, Lt. Donald Friese, S/Sgt. Paul Sawyer, and Sgts. John Healy and Harry Shubley.

The Jap air raids which had been a source of annoyance and worry to us off and on since our arrival slacked off during late August, but on September 1st the Nips came over with a pretty good-sized force and dropped some bombs in our line area just to remind us that there were

still two sides in the war. Red alerts came with decreasing frequency until they ceased altogether.

Once again the moving fever struck us and we began to pack for a trip we knew not where. Some rumors had us headed for the Philippines and others were just as insistent that we were to participate in an invasion of the China coast. After several days of loading the ship, we in the water echelon boarded her late on the night of October 15th and crowded, along with most of the 499th Squadron, into her hot holds.

Next morning the SS *Thomas Nelson* pulled away from the jetty and we were on our way. Two days later we arrived at Hollandia and after laying at anchor while other ships of the convoy steamed to the rendezvous we set out again on October 20th, and in the company of about thirty other Liberty ships and LST's

with an escort of several DE's we set a northward course. The same day an announcement was made that the island of Leyte had just been invaded and that was to be our destination.

It was first-come-first-served as to sleeping space on deck and because of the suffocating atmosphere in the dark and unventilated holds every available square foot of deck space soon was occupied by a cot. No possibility was overlooked and some beds were perched up on the life raft platforms where even a steeplejack would get dizzy. Canvas was rigged to protect the sleepers from rain and sun with the result that practically all parts of the ship except the superstructure were hidden under a motley assortment of ponchos, raincoats, shelter halves, tarpaulins, pyramidal tents, and anything else that would shed water. Fortunately we didn't have any heavy rainstorms enroute so we all stayed reasonably dry. The mild showers we did run through were seized upon as means of taking fresh water baths.

Chow was a two-meal-a-day proposition and most of us had to draw our belts pretty tight until a PX opened on board with a stock

of cookies and candy. It was the same lazy life we'd led on the SS *President Johnson* 18 months before—dozing, playing cards and

reading, with a little detail thrown in—mostly standing watch to prevent smoking in the holds and to enforce the blackout. Some of the armorers were placed on duty in the gun-tubs again. There was the usual fraternizing with the merchant seamen and sailors, and several of the men blossomed out in swapped Navy clothes.

On D-day-plus-nine we sailed into the Gulf of Leyte and anchored just off Tacloban, giving us our first glimpse of the Philippine Islands. That night also brought us our initial experience with typhoons. The wind began rising about dusk, moaning through the rigging and rippling our canvas shelters. It kept mounting in strength until it reached typhoon proportions, whipping the sea into a creamy froth, driving the rain before it in horizontal sheets, screaming past the lofty booms and cables and snapping the heavy canvas tarps like cracking whips.

Nearly everyone who was brave enough to stay on deck was soaked and many were the blankets, cots, air mattresses and tents which soared overboard at the height of the blow. Later it was reported that the wind's velocity had reached sixty-five miles per hour.

The Army "wheels" ashore weren't nearly as anxious to have us land as we were to do so, it seemed, for we remained aboard day after day. A very few men were sent in to locate and lay out our area. Duck loads of 10-in-1 rations were hoisted aboard and the grub underwent an improvement. During calm weather the ship's captain allowed us to go swimming over the side, a pleasant diversion especially during the real hot days. Then we had frequent visits from sampan loads of natives who were interested in trading for GI clothes, rations and blankets. A number of them came aboard and answered our questions about the Jap occupation, sang songs in their shrill voices, and accepted our gifts of candy, cookies and cigarettes.

There were more than 200 air alerts in the two weeks we were aboard. At the first alert we headed for the holds according to instruc-

tions but as alert after alert passed with no evidence that the planes were interested in attacking shipping, we became bolder. Only a few would retire below decks with their helmets and life preservers when the whistle sounded and the rest would either roll over in their sacks and go back to sleep or line the port rail to watch the ack ack over the airdromes ashore. All the alerts went by in this manner and then one day it happened.

It was about 11:30 A. M. on Sunday, November 12th. There was no alert at the time and the men were lounging about as usual. Suddenly three Zekes, coming seemingly from nowhere, dove from the sky. The first struck and exploded on the bow of the SS *Leonidas Merritt* some 800 yards in front of us, another veered in an unsuccessful effort to crash a second neighboring craft and the third came at us. The zing of machine gun slugs and the explosion of

20 mm. cannon shells from the Jap's strafing guns gave a second or two warning and some men succeeded in diving to places of safety before the plane tore into No. 5 hatch and exploded.

The giant cargo boom with its massive block was blown completely overboard; fires were started in vehicles chained to the deck nearby and among other pieces of equipment; and the entire after portion of the deck was suddenly transformed into a twisted, smoldering mass. Quickly the unharmed men ran to lay hoses to fight the fire, help men from No. 4 and 5 holds, carry the injured to the front of the ship, administer first aid where possible, and do their best to meet the situation. A "duck" which happened to be in the vicinity picked up a load of injured who had been blown into the water and an LCVP rescued the others, taking them and many of the injured still aboard to the hospital ashore.

A number of the victims were transported to a nearby hospital ship for treatment. It was days later before a final count determined that

the 498th had suffered 68 casualties—33 killed and 35 wounded. The 499th Squadron's losses were even heavier.

Falcon fatalities were: M/Sgt. Lloyd Cleary, T/Sgts. James Brown and Peppino Flaminio; S/Sgts. Robert Andrews, Leroy Carlton, James Crose, William Davis, Jr., Edward Dibbern, Fred Rainey, Jr., Leo Brown, August Apelt and Bryant Roberts; Sgts. John Dudas, Alfred Codorecci, Charles L e n t i n e, John McCann, Jr., Verley Tate, Lawrence Davis, N o r m a n Thompson and Odis Sullivan; Cpls. Kenneth Austin, Charles Daprato, Theodore Eiseman, Cyril Little, John Scholl, Edwin Neimeyer and Perry Harris; PFCs Sam Cribaro, Rogert Hoffman, Frank Golden and Thom-

as Henson, Jr.; and Pvts. Merritt Smith, Jr., and Arthur King.

But the Japanese Special Attack Corps(suicide pilots exclusively) wasn't ready to call it a day and twice more in the afternoon the fanatic airmen broke through the protecting P-38s and screamed down on the anchored ships. Six vessels in all were hit amidst the thickest hail of ack ack we ever expected to see. Many m o r e Zekes missed their targets and struck the water. One of the ships hit was the *SS Morrison Waite* which bore the other two Squadrons of our Group. A huge triangular hole was blown in its port bow but fatalities were less than twenty-five percent of the *Nelson's*.

While the later attacks were

in progress, all of the *Nelson's* personnel except about a dozen who exhibited more courage than the rest and volunteered to remain

and help clear away the debris, were on the way ashore. We reached it safely and proceeded to a transient camp in a lonely section of the island several miles inland, and not far from the Jap lines. Occasionally strafing attacks by Zekes, frequent dog fights over our camp area and a threatened break through by the Jap ground troops didn't help our peace of mind any and we were pleased when our own camp site was finally decided upon a few days later and we moved in.

The area was one of the nicest we had. Located in a cool, coconut grove (though it was near a mosquito-breeding swamp) it was also close to an excellent beach. With a good deal of hard work we got ourselves established — orderly room, supply and mail tents up, mess hall and the EM club erected, shower well and fox holes dug and the other innumerable items which go into setting up a camp.

Air raid alerts came several times each day and night in those first weeks and although only one bomb was dropped in our area, the enemy planes often came far too close for comfort. One night the Japs crash-landed two transport loads of airborne infantry troops on the beach just below our area. A few evenings later on December 6th a large force of transports came over and dropped paratroopers, some of them landing only a short distance from us. The move was timed with an offensive by the Nip ground troops and together they regained and held part of the San Pablo strip for several days, threatening to drive farther in our direction. We stood guard those nights and slept with our weapons close at hand (there were some who dragged their cots right down into their oversized fox holes), but nothing developed and the threat was soon eliminated. We'll bet there is more

than one Leyte caribou with a carbine bullet in his thick hide as a souvenir of those jittery hours on guard. The lumbering beasts could always be found prowling about in the most suspicious places on the darkest nights and it's not much wonder they sustained a few casualties.

We were well pleased to find ourselves in a country where the natives bore some resemblance in speech, dress and customs, to ourselves. A majority of the Filipinos spoke understandable English and they didn't hide their joy at the Americans' return. Very early in the game they learned of the GI's generosity in spending, and quickly figured out ways to place themselves in the path of this golden tide. All day long at the Dulag camp the Filipino women—and quite often men, too—would circulate among the tents, peering under the eaves and saying timidly: "Sir, you have dirty clothes to be wash?" Their laundry service was good too, though we couldn't understand how they could get the clothes so clean with only cold water, soap and their primitive pounding method of washing.

They also recognized our liking for the fresh foods unobtainable through GI channels and made daily trips from their gardens with cucumbers, camotes, sweet potatoes, bananas, coconuts, etc. Though there were coconut trees all about us we couldn't skin up the lofty, swaying trunks like the smallest of native boys could and we were unable to match their ability to lay open the toughest-hulled nuts with only a few skillful strokes of a sharp-edged machete.

Thanksgiving and Christmas dinners at Dulag featured the traditional turkey menus. In the absence of Christmas trees, the mess hall was decorated for the occasion with enough palm fronds to make the place look like a greenhouse. They lent an air of festivity to the occasion, and anyhow a good many of us—all our cares lost in the gin punch which the EM club was serving—couldn't then have told the difference between a fully-decorated Christmas tree and a green onion.

Now that we had become comfortably established, were able to enjoy a little leisure, and had a rousing volleyball tournament under way it suddenly became time to move. A Jap task force had been sighted off Mindoro December 27th and since our planes couldn't operate from the boggy strip as originally

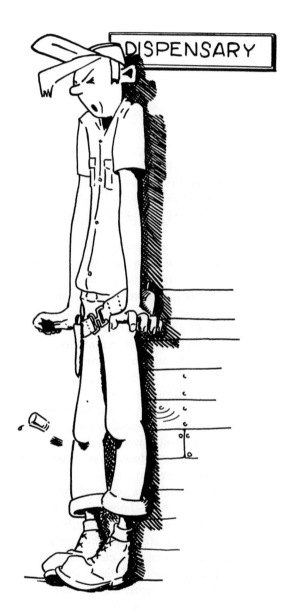

intended, we had to move to Tacloban. We made the 30-mile move by truck the last week in December and there joined the flight echelon which was now equipped with sixteen new Js.

Maj. Magee completed his tour of overseas duty before the flight crews left Biak, and our Squadron commanding officer became Capt. Theodore Wright, widely recognized as one of the Squadron's best pilots and universally respected as a man. Both Capt. Craig, executive officer and Capt. Bloomenthal, flight surgeon, were transferred to Group Headquarters. Capt. Stott was advanced from Adjutant to Executive Officer and Lt. Augustine was assigned from the 499th as a Squadron Adjutant. Lt. Boing, supply officer was also transferred to Group and was replaced by Lt. Finn. Our new flight surgeon was to be Capt. Fabian though he did not join the outfit until three months later.

Our living area at Tacloban was one of the least desirable in our overseas career. The entire Group was sandwiched onto a slender peninsula bordered by two swamps, each of which bred thick clouds of mosquitoes with voracious appetites for the 345th blood. However, we made the best of the insects (centipedes included), mud and rain, and went through the usual process of setting up our buildings and tents. Wooden floors were almost a must for most of the tents because of the soggy ground. It was here that the frag bomb boxes procured from the ordnance dump came in so handy. Fox holes were a problem, too, since the underground water level was only a foot or so below the surface in the lowest areas but we got by somehow and didn't get hit by any bombs. That wasn't because there were none dropped, however. The Nips were fairly active in the early part of that month and came over many times.

The city of Tacloban, capital of Leyte, was only a couple of miles from our living area and most of us found time to get in and look around at least once. In fact some of the fellows took quite a liking to the place and could be found in there several times each week. It was the most civilized community we'd seen since leaving Australia and we enjoyed the novelty of seeing streets, homes, churches and clothed people again.

Three crews went down during January. Capt. Edgar Girdler; Lts. Leslie Schreiber and Henry Muster; T/Sgt. Robert Harris; S/Sgts. Russell Sweet and Mike Pitek were killed in a Cebu raid on January 3rd. Lts. Wallace Chalifoux, Neil Davis and August Bauer, Jr.; T/Sgt. John O'Donnell; and S/Sgts. John Orloff and Paul Panciocco were listed as missing in action after a January 10th mission. Lts. Bertram Welch, Robert Hochgesang and John Wilkinson; Sgts. Lachlan McArthur, Harold Gregory and Walter Hahn croshed fatally at Manila on January 13th.

This heavy loss was partly offset by a very great amount of damage to the Jap war effort. Targets were confined to the Philippines area, mostly Luzon, where raids on rolling stock during the month netted the destruction of 11 locomotives, 63 railroad cars, 25 airplanes, 4 buildings and one truck, besides many other installations damaged. The highlight of the month was our participation in a raid on Clark Field when 64 planes roared abreast from one end of the field to the other, causing widespread havoc. We now had many of the latest J models equipped with 12 forward-firing machine guns, which were particularly effective in strafing operations.

Another move by the Jap Navy, this time a report of heavy enemy ships steaming north along the coast of the continent, resulted in orders for the 345th to move up to San Marcelino in Luzon on February 12th. The air and maintenance echelons flew up immediately, but in spite of repeated search and strike missions into the South China Sea and vicinity, no contact was established. A good deal of damage was done to miscellaneous shipping and ground targets on Luzon and other Philippine islands during February.

The weather at our new location was in direct contrast to that we'd just left. In place of the rain and mud at Tacloban, we now had aridity and dust. Where we were cramped and squeezed onto a patch of swampland, we now could spread out on the dry, grassy plain as far as we wanted. Mosquitoes were rare and all in all it was a most pleasant change. Air alerts were practically non-existent and although we did stand regular guard duty we never saw a Jap in the vicinity. Days were hot but the nights were very refreshingly cool and sometimes we were surprised to discover that one blanket wasn't enough to keep us warm.

We ate with the 499th until the Filipinos finished building a bamboo frame for our own mess hall. The native motif was also carried out in the other Squadron installations—bamboo frames, railings, counters, etc., for the orderly room, supply, operations, parachute, radio and mail buildings. In conjunction with the 499th we also dug a well for our shower water but in spite of its 30-foot dept it soon dried up and we had to use water hauled in by the engineers.

The natives' laundry service continued at the new station, but on a less satisfactory level. Where one peso had been considered a fair price, they now wanted two or three pesos. The Squadron dealt with this situation fairly successfully when it established a clearing station for all laundresses and enforced the price ceilings set by the Philippine Government. Bananas, small striped watermellons, mangoes, onions, camotes and tomatoes were sold through the camp every day and here again the prices asked were all out of relation to the average GI pay envelopes. But that didn't stop the buying.

Our line area was within a 15-minute walk of our tents, a handy factor when transportation wasn't available and a decided convenience for those who liked to "goof off" a little early now and then. The dust was a great annoyance, however. Revving propellers would stir up immense clouds of the fine, sandy soil and it would cling to a sweaty torso until its owner looked as if he had been mining coal. Occasional rains would settle the dust for

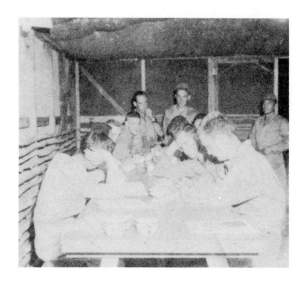

shipping along the China coast continued to feel the Falcon claws during April but the month cost us heavily in casualties and aircraft, leaving us with but nine planes at the month's end. Near Swatow on April 6th Capt. Albin Johnson went in alone to bomb an enemy destroyer in spite of the fact that his strafing guns would not fire. Intense ack ack fire met the plane, the aircraft burst into flames and crashed into the sea two miles away. In addition to Capt. Johnson, the victims were: Lt. Robert Snyder; F/O Kenneth Bridges; T/Sgts. James Robinson and Wilbert Yorke; S/Sgts. Marion Collier and Frederick Gladych. Anti-aircraft from another vessel knocked out an engine on Lt. Myers' plane and it was only by skillful flying that he brought it back to a crash-landing on Laoag, Luzon.

Plane No. 034 piloted by Lt. Ranger was struck by 20mm. fire on a locomotive raid at Formosa April 18th and the hydraulic system was shot out in addition to considerable damage inflicted on the right engine. After flying nearly two hours on a single engine, the plane was crash-landed at Laoag without injury to the crew. The loss of Capt. Elmo Cranford, mortally injured by an exploding bomb on a practice mission April 18th, saddened the entire Squadron.

Since early March an advance echelon had been busy preparing a place for us at Clark Field and when we arrived there by truck in late April and early May we found much of our work had been done for us. The mess hall and administration buildings were well along, the showers were up and operating, and some preliminary work had been done short periods but the dust problem remained there as long as we did.

San Marcelino, Castellijos and Subic, all small native towns, were within traveling distance of our camp and many of us used to drive or hitchhike there for an evening of entertainment. Then, after Manila was fully occupied by American troops, the Group leased two large Filipino homes—one for officers and one for enlisted men—so we could enjoy three-day passes looking over the city. All who so desired visited a rest house at least once.

March was a busy month for our planes. Except for a raid or two on Formosa we concentrated on the shipping blockade of the China Sea, flying almost daily missions to sink the cargo craft which sought to keep the Jap supply lines open. They were long missions, too, nine and ten hours in the air, and waist guns as well as four of the fixed nose guns were removed to save weight. Interception was encountered on the raids at Hainan Island and Mencheong Village but the attacks were not pressed. It was on the March 10th shipping strike off Indo-China that one engine on Lt. Benjamin Chambers' plane quit and forced him to crash-land in the sea. Other Squadron aircraft circled the raft and its survivors but could offer no more help at the time. Subsequent search missions failed to locate the raft and it was not until 23 days later that Sgt. Baudy R. Grier, by then the only survivor, was rescued by a submarine. Besides Lt. Chambers, three others were lost—Lt. Charley Raney, Sgt. Amedeo Vincenti, and Sgt. James Lane.

Targets on Formosa, western Luzon, and

on the Squadron laundry which was to be manned by Filipinos. Many tent floors had already been built from Squadron lumber and the rest of us managed by hook or crook to scrounge enough material for wooden floors. We were to remain here for several months, according to rumors from the "most reliable" sources. After all, wasn't Clark Field the original home of the Fifth Air Force?

Consistent with our plans to stay here for some time we fixed up a few luxuries for ourselves. We got a brand new icebox for our mess hall and built up as fancy an EM club as you'd see in the Western Pacific. The officers dined in their own wing of the mess hall where they sat down to tables with tablecloths and were served by white-jacketed Filipino boys. Filipinos did the KP detail, too, as they had ever since we hit Leyte. We could even go into town—San Fernando—for an evening (if we had a pass) to while away a few hours. It was all very civilized.

At our line area also we prepared for a long stay with a portable building instead of a tent for engineering and tech supply, and sapacious squad tents for the other sections. We even had electric lights. Our parking area was a low section without hard stands right next to a rice field and hard rains would send a good-sized stream coursing past the tents to form puddles throughout the area. However, a few hours of hot Luzon sunshine would dry up the mud and before we knew it there was the old familiar dust blowing in our eyes again.

The newly-announced point system came in for a good deal of discussion these days. Those whom the May 12 count disclosed had more than the required 85 points conjured up visions of an early return to the States and of taking up civilian life again while others who fell short of the critical score chewed their pencil stubs as they sought to figure how many more months and battle stars it would take to make them eligible. Some of those with long army careers behind them did place high enough on the list to be sent home from Clark, but the quotas were low and hardly met with popular approval.

Over a period of weeks nine new ships were assigned to the Squadron, bringing our plane strength up to normal. The outstanding feature of these latest model Js was the rocket racks—four mounted under each wing. There was much interest in this newest weapon especially after viewing the Navy training film which showed the effectiveness of these projectiles. However, the trials were disappointing. The rockets would fall far short of the .50 caliber tracers and make accurate aiming almost impossible. Later, however, we were provided with rockets using the newer type motor and the range and effectiveness were greatly improved.

Continuance of the destruction of targets on Formosa and parts of Luzon featured the Falcon activities during May and June. Sugar refineries, rolling stock, oil plants and other ground installations on Formosa were struck crippling blows by our aircraft, not without cost, however. Lt. Robert Kanuf, flying one of his first missions as first pilot, crashed May 26th during an attack on an oil storage area at Byoritsu, Formosa. Other members of the crew killed in action were: Lt. Lloyd Bodell, Lt. Martin Mulner, Jr., Sgt. Tennyson Horrell and Cpl. Harold Montville.

A demonstration of particularly skillful piloting was given by Lt. Erickson on May 30th when his ship, No. 262, was struck by an ack ack shell at Shinei, Formosa. Although the entire left rudder and all but a foot-long section of the left horizontal stabilizer were shot away, he made his run over the enemy target and dropped his bombs before setting a course for the nearest emergency landing field on Luzon. The reduced control surface made the plane unmanageable at speeds less than 170 miles per hour and the use of landing flaps was impossible, but with the aid of a parachute dropped from the rear hatch at the strategic moment he made a power-on landing and stopped in time. One crew member was injured by the ack ack but he recovered after hospital treatment. Both the crew and the airplane were saved to fight again.

Maj. Theodore Wright, his combat missions in and an excellent record as Squadron Commanding Officer behind him, went home while we were stationed at Clark. His final unofficial gesture was a buzz job so low it had us all hitting the ground. Maj. Jack C. McClure was assigned to succeed him.

Many practice bombing runs, training missions and formation flying in addition to our usual assortment of strikes were keeping our planes in the air during those weeks. Rumors were beginning to circulate that soon we'd be moved to a new position where all this training would pay dividends and early in July they came true. Details were assigned to tear down both the administration building and the EM club, and to begin the packing of equipment. One loading detail was sent to Subic where the men camped for a week and a half unloading the trucks of equipment in a massive pile on the beach while they awaited arrival of our ship. By this time it was generally understood that we were bound for Ie Shima, a tiny five-mile-long island just west of central Okinawa.

Presently our LST did come in, old "863," and with the help of the rest of the water echelon we loaded our scores of tons of baggage, rations, lumber, tents and miscellaneous Squadron equipment into the cavernous hold. Of course there was an almost unceasing rain during the entire operation and most of us lived in soaking clothes and went without sleep for forty-eight hours until the job was finished. Finally the last jeep was driven aboard. As the great iron ramp was hoisted into the bow, the big ship started to back out into the harbor. She started, that was all. She was stuck and though her engines strained and her screws thrashed the water to foam there she stayed with her bow well up on the sand. Finally with the help of a couple of towing vessels she broke free and followed the others out of the bay to begin our journey north.

We soon discovered that an LST, with its shalow draft, is a lot less stable than a Liberty ship and the resultant pitching and tossing even on mild swells, disconcerted some of our stomachs for a day or two. And it was little short of a catastrophe not to be able to eat the chow that was being served. Instead of existing on our 10-in-1 rations as expected we were fed the ship crew's own food—fresh meat, eggs, celery, apples, oranges, all crisp and cold just out of the cold storage locker. Then there was the good Navy bread and fresh butter— all we could eat! We'll have a soft spot in our heart for "863" and her crew for a long time to come.

The quarters problem was resolved about the same as on the Biak-Leyte voyage. Some slept in the hold on bunks provided in the troop quarters, and others improvised beds on the weather deck. We slept, read, played cards—the same old stuff—and the four-day journey came to an end soon enough when we cast out the anchor in front of our new island home on July 25th. There was no sign of the Kamikaze raiders which had been so active in the Okinawa sector and which we had been considerably concerned about. The Navy crew told us that the suicide attacks were becoming rare and that the targets were mostly warships anyhow.

Our first sight of the new Squadron area brought expressions of dismay to our lips. It was just one big field of mud with here and there some patches of weeds. The mud was of a peculiar quality with which we'd had no experience before, overseas at least. It was at the same time as slippery as grease and as sticky as warm tar. It would cling to your shoes and build up layer after layer until you felt, and probably were, six inches higher and twenty pounds heavier. We had steady rain for the first several days in our new location and before long there was no one who wasn't wet and muddy from top to bottom. The problem was made worse by the lack of water and some of us had to go several days without even so much as a good face washing.

We pitched in as we always do and with shifts of work both night and day we made steady progress at the job of setting up camp. We hauled and shoveled hundreds of loads of coral rock and sand for roads through the area and as a foundation for some of the buildings; we put up a dispensary and a utility shack for generators; we erected the supply building and the parachute headquarters; we

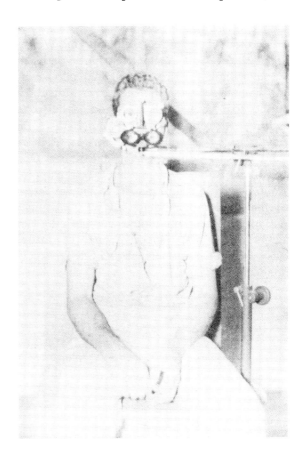

blasted two latrine pits, put up a shower, constructed a mess hall, dug grease traps, strung telephone and electric lines, and assembled the tropical barracks building used for administrative offices. And besides all the community effort we were working privately on our own tents, building floors with the lumber which whiskey had bought from the Negro truck drivers and putting in shelves, cabinets, racks, washstands and the dozens of little improvements which each individual likes for his own convenience.

Meanwhile the flight echelon had come up from Clark Field and our targets were shifted for the first time to the home islands of Japan. An immense amount of damage was inflicted on the enemy during late July and early August; more than 8000 tons of shipping sunk and nearly 2000 tons partially destroyed in addition to extensive wrecking of buildings, factories, bridges and airdrome facilities. The rockets were proving their worth as aerial weapons and were credited with damaging many of the targets.

Three of our airplanes went down during this period. Lt. Robert Green, piloting No. 207 on the radar station raid at Teurmi-Sake July 30th, crashed into a hill and the whole crew was killed: Lt. Curtis Middleton, Lt. Wayne Hendricks, S/Sgt. Walter Kingsbury and Sgt. Sammy Shaber. Aircraft No. 300 piloted by Lt. Robert Neal was last seen over Matsubase during the August 7th raid and is listed as missing in action. The other members of the crew were: Lt. Louis Winiecki, Lt. Richard Land, S/Sgts. William Cohen and Robert Goelet. On the August 12th mission to raid shipping in the Sea of Japan plane No. 567 never reached the rendezvous point and was presumed lost. Lt. Wallace Pennington was the pilot and others were: F/O Robert Brand, Lt. Joseph Lurix, S/Sgt. George Langer and Sgt. Lawrence Henderson.

It was shortly after our C. O., Maj. McClure, was made 345th Operations Officer and was replaced by Capt. Ollie Hatcher from Group that we heard the almost-too-good-to-be-true rumor that the Japs had made a surrender offer. Breathless days of waiting followed. That the long war might soon be over seemed a hope almost too remote to take seriously, but we hoped anyway and finally it came to pass. There was celebrating over our beer bottles the night after President Truman's announcement and a slightly more boisterous time a few evenings later when the club doled out some of its more potent stock, but for the most part there was no wild exultation. We were saving that for the time when we'd get home.

Aside from some shipping searches and a few couriers, the Falcon's last dramatic gesture of the war came on the historic date of August 19th when one of our planes held a rendezvous with the two Jap Betty bombers, Bataan 1 and 2, and escorted them and their peace envoys back to Ie Shima on the first leg of their trip to receive the surrender instructions at Manila. It was most fitting that the 498th, which had played an important part in bringing the treacherous enemy to his knees after a three-and-one-half-year war should be included in the scene when Japan sued for peace.

The war is over, the 498th Bomb Squadron is no more and once again we're back with our sweethearts, wives and families enjoying the things we've dreamed about during all those long months overseas. Our fighting is done and we have put it and all thoughts of it behind us. But the passage of years will never cause us to forget the deep and lasting friendships we formed in the Squadron nor take from us the satisfied feeling that, as an integral part of the 498th Bomb Squadron, we made a direct and individual contribution toward victory for our country.

One of our men has given us the following exciting story of the adventure of "A Falcon Crew."

Biak, September 11th, 1944: Today was maintenance and training day, which meant no combat missions for the Squadron. Our ship, assigned a routine flight to Nadzab, carried five passengers besides its regular crew of five.

The ship checked out and we had a dandy take-off. As we gained altitude and set our course all relaxed. Suddenly the usual steady roar of the engines was interrupted by a concert of roars, groans, and whines. The ship lurched forward. As rapidly as she went erratic she returned to normal. Dull, dense gray smoke was pouring from the left engine. Instinctively Lt. Fabale, the pilot, cut the switches on the bad engine, hit the feathering button, kicked the right rudder, and trimmed her up. We were at 3000 feet and losing altitude. The laughing, relaxed crew were suddenly awake and sober faced. Many tense, unrelated thoughts were expressed on every face.

Like an oasis, there appeared a clearing in the jungle. An angel must have placed it there just for us. Johnnie calmly called over the inter-com and told the men to brace themselves for a crash landing. Other than those words, not another was spoken. Just before we hit the ground all switches were cut. Then it happened—a thud, a crash, and all hell broke loose. A second or two (but what seemed an infinity of time) passed before the mind once more began functioning. Then every man fought frantically to get out of the battered plane, driven by the fear of fire. After making sure that there was no fire, we returned to the ship and surveyed the situation. Fortunately no one suffered more than a scratch or two.

We didn't spare words in congratulating each other, and Capt. Putoff, being senior officer, was placed in command.

The time was 1340 and the first question was, where do we go from here? After talking it over, we decided to stay at the plane that night. The possibility of a passing plane seeing us was our main hope. We ripped open parachutes and displayed all the bright material we had to make our position more noticeable from the air. Lts. Kuechler and Prentice took an inventory of our supplies. We were better off than we had thought. The jungle kits were intact; we had the radio; two .45s and ammunition, plus two carbines, and a Very pistol and flares. While Sgt. Lopez, the radio man, attempted to send out distress signals, the rest of us removed or destroyed all vital equipment on the plane. Because the dingy radio was found to be inoperative, and the radio could receive but not transmit, radio aid was abandoned as a means of rescue. The food rations were not sufficient for ten men, so we decided not to eat that day but wait until late the next. Medical supplies were plentiful. Our water supply was low, but we had halozone to purify enough for our needs. We checked the bomb bay and found our luggage intact and decided to remove it the next day.

During the afternoon, several planes were sighted, but most of them were too distant for us to attract their attention. Our hopes were lifted when a C-47 headed straight in our direction at 5000 feet. We immediately got out the Very pistol, filled the sky with red flares and then hoped for the best. From all indications they were unseen. The turret was still operative so we fired about 250 rounds high into the air, hoping the tracers would be seen. This too failed. Our hopes were dampened, but our morale was still high. And besides, our thoughts were arrested by the quickly falling shadows of night.

As we had no idea how far we were from enemy territory, each man was scheduled for one hour guard during the night. All except Sgt. Simmons, who stood first guard, climbed up on the plane's wing to lay down for a fitful sleep. The mosquitoes were fierce. It wasn't a matter of swatting—we just wiped off a coating of them. The jungle was hot and damp. None of us slept except for a few winks.

September 12, Tuesday: As first light showed on the distant horizon, everyone was up and ready to start our unknown trek out of the bush. We hadn't eaten since early the previous day, so the first subject was that of food and water. None of us admitted to be too hungry, so we decided to save the rations

came into view. Japs had been in this territory and the natives showed signs of fear. The scouting party worked fast and shouted several times, "Americano." After friendly gestures and signs, the natives were finally convinced they weren't Japs.

The rescue party of fourteen natives in one large and two smaller canoes returned to us by mid-morning. The usual handshakes were exchanged all around, and cigarettes were passed out to them. Using pidgin English we convinced them that they would be amply rewarded if they took us to the nearest white men. We even generously promised them the whole plane of they helped us. They are probably the first natives in New Guinea to

until evening when they would be most needed. A scouting party of F/O Beardsley, Sgt. Collier and Sgt. Kelley set out to look over the possibilities of replenishing our food and water supply. One of those "Fuzzy Wuzzies" would surely come in handy now.

While they were gone, the rest of us salvaged as much as we could. Sgt. Simmons chopped a hole through the bomb bay and one bag was extracted, the contents of which offered a change of clothes for all of us. Ten pairs of sox, one camera and ten rolls of film, one .45 caliber pistol, three clips of ammunition, three cartons of cigarettes and miscellaneous items were added to our stores. If we found natives we at least had something with which to bargain for their help. We then destroyed all vital equipment in the ship in case it should be discovered by Japs.

At 1005 we were most happy to see the scouts return with friendly natives. They had discovered a small stream, and while bathing heard native voices. Soon a group of natives

own an airplane. The number one boy motioned to the village by which we understood him to mean we were going there first. After a mutual understanding had been reached we started down stream to the village. After this novel experience the situation took on a more cheerful light. The nervous tension we had been under soon relaxed to a considerable degree. We were finally started on our way.

The village soon appeared on the bank of the stream. The situation looked better all the time. We were treated to a royal native feast of bananas, coconuts, yams and papayas which was served with hushed excitement. The surprise came when they laid ten large boiled eggs in front of us, and although we couldn't quite figure out what kind of eggs they were, we ate what we could. Some of them were already in the process of hatching. We later learned that they were crocodile eggs! With the completion of the meal, we again talked business. "Tremili," the most friendly and intelligent native, was chosen as number one boy. He told us we were to stay in the village that night and get an early start in the morning.

The clothes and equipment were brought up from the canoes. A make-shift tent was made of parachutes, and palm fronds were brought to us in armfuls to sleep on. One man was to be on guard. We again worked it in hourly shifts. The mosquitoes were bad, and rain added to our discomfort. During the night crocodiles could be heard splashing in a creek about twenty feet from us.

September 13th, Wednesday: At 0450 we made preparations to start for "Annaway." We thought Tremili meant the Aussie outpost at Annenberg, so we repeated the name several times. Even though we could get nothing but "Annaway" out of him we had to place our trust and confidence in him, as we had no idea how close we were to the Nips. We made it clear to Tremili that the marking we had made on the plane was to be left there. This marking was made with ammunition belts on a parachute spelling, "All O. K." and an arrow pointing in the direction of the village. With Tremili and ten native bearers, we loaded our belongings in two canoes, started up stream and traveled three hours before going ashore for food. The natives disappeared into the bush and returned shortly with yams and sugar cane. This was indeed a treat. Having consumed all we could, we were again on our way up stream, only to stop twenty minutes later at another small village. The canoes were left there since the remainder of the journey was to be made on foot. The native boys constructed litters to carry the equipment, and food was again obtained in the form of papayas and coconut milk. We hit the trail again at 1130 and an hour and a quarter later we arrived at the village where we were to spend the night. This seemed a short day's travel to us, but realizing the natives knew best we just kept silent. We were given a hut to ourselves and spent the afternoon relaxing as much as possible and discussing further plans with the number one boy. Tremili still insisted "Annaway" was not Annenberg. We were greatly encouraged, however, when he spoke of "Cap Engle, nine Annaway." With some use of imagination we interpreted this as meaning nine Aussie soldiers were at Annenberg.

September 14th, Thursday: Dawn found all up and ready to be on the move. We had a breakfast of hot chocolate which was prepared from the "D" rations. Before changing bearers, Tremili and the number two boy were paid off with one razor blade apiece. Everyone seemed happy and satisfied and we were then introduced to our new bearers and number one boy, "Imibogue." Once again we were on the trail. Despite mud and sore feet, everything was going well. Soon we came upon a large river and another village.

The natives brought us food and gave us a private hut. A box of "K" rations was added to our meal and everyone seemed quite satisfied. There were no streams nearby so the natives brought us water in bark containers. This we used sparingly in washing our faces and hands, and with the remainder bathed our sore feet. We felt like new men, refreshed and clean.

The natives had an innocent child-like curiosity about them. It was quite obvious that they had had very little contact with white men. They sat around and gazed at us with somewhat of an air of amazement. They were always polite and willing to help so their watchful eyes were ignored, although at times it proved to be a little embarrassing.

A talk with the number one boy about the journey for the following day indicated that things were amiss. We were sure they understood that they were to be paid the next morning when new carriers would arrive. We retired for the night quite confident that things would straighten out all right and at 2100 we were awakened by Imibogui, the number one boy. He had a sad tale to tell. "Boy no likum, him cross much," he said. This and other unintelligible phrases indicated that we were without native boys. At first he too seemed none too eager about continuing. Promises of more pay induced him to stay, but he could only convince two other boys to help carry. We later learned that the seven others had returned to their village, or bush home, thinking we were not going to pay them. We retired feeling none too sure that when morning came we would find ourselves doing the carrying and navigating.

September 15th, Friday: At 0445 we arose and prepared to move on. We gave Imibogui clothes for the boys that left us the previous afternoon, and for those that remained. Native smiles of delight and satisfaction indicated our troubles were over. We now had all the native boys we needed. There were plenty of clothes for barter, and a good supply of razor blades and fish hooks which the natives highly prized, but we were determined not to become too generous in case "Annaway" was further than we expected. Everything being settled, we were on the trail at dawn. At 0900 we stopped to rest and also viewed a most amusing and interesting scene. There seemed to be a bit of excitement among the natives and soon Imibogui approached us. He wanted "waswas." This we understood to mean he wanted soap. When he returned there wasn't much evidence he had used it. Now he wanted a razor blade. When we presented it to him and showed how strong it was, his anxiety and pleasure was like that of a child being given a new toy.

There, deep in the jungle, a first-class native barber shop was opened. We settled down to watch an amazing performance of shaving. With ease and comfort, one native would sit on the ground while the barber, without the aid of the soap we had given him, made long, merciless strokes. It was impossible to understand how a small blade, held

123

in the hand could be wielded with such skill on a long, dry beard. Oddly enough, not a scratch or the least bit of pain was shown. Next came the eyebrows. In one clean stroke they too disappeared. When the barber shop closed, they all stood around and with childish delight, admired each other's appearance. They were more than happy when we promised each one a razor that night.

Paying off the natives at the next village was another entertaining session which boosted our spirit and morale. They were given razor blades, fish hooks and articles of clothing for which we had no need. They even accepted the empty ration and medical supply containers as part payment. Imibogui made a striking and comical appearance with a 2nd

Once again on the trail we came to another river where we met the most heartening sight we had seen up to this point. Two native soldiers, with rifles slung over their shoulders, stood on the opposite bank. Ferrying across the river on two canoes tied together we were greeted by the soldiers who immediately set off at a very rapid pace. As tired as we were, we managed to keep up and never once did anyone ask to slow down. This, we all knew, was the last lap of our trip.

As the sun lowered in the west we reached the Ramu River. There high on a little hill on the opposite shore was Annenberg. It was a beautiful sight. Six Aussie soldiers appeared from a large native building, waving and yelling words of welcome. They came across

Lt. bar on his cap to show that he was number one boy. He was very proud. The pants we gave him had a fly zipper. After a little instruction he joyfully demonstrated the art to the other native boys. They continued to talk in pidgin all night, seemingly for our benefit, and before Imibogui left, he assured us that we would reach Annaway the next day.

September 16th, Saturday: Tropical dawn found Imibogui strutting around like a peacock, in his new clothes. Because we were hopeful of reaching Annenberg late that afternoon, the first rays of the morning sun found us again plodding along the trail. We hadn't traveled more than two hours when we came upon another village. It was quite a thrill to all of us to hear the natives beat their drums, telling the next village of our approach.

After having traveled for some time, we approached another river, where we met several new natives. Their Laluai, or chief, was a colorfully dressed native named "Guyguy." Around his neck he wore rosary beads. At Guyguy's village the natives brought us green bananas which we baked in a small fire. Capt. Putoff played the role of doctor by applying sulfa-powder and bandages to four natives with bad tropical ulcers. We knew this would be of little help but it was better than nothing.

the river in a motor boat to pick us up, and thirty minutes later we were at the outpost of Annenberg. The Aussies told us they would pay the natives, but I'm sure the natives didn't get as much as they would have if we had paid them. In a few minutes we were enjoying our first real meal in almost a week.

Fatigue and exhaustion made us weak as kittens. We did get a message through to the 25th Liaison Squadron, and relayed to Biak, which was acknowledged by the promise that L-5s would pick us up the following morning. We were given every possible aid, and spent the night in the first sound sleep of a week.

We awoke greatly refreshed. The first thing we did was form a procession to the river to bathe while the natives cheerfully washed our clothes. Shortly after our bath we ate a wonderful breakfast of bully beef, tea, rolls and jam. We spent the time after breakfast in a liesurely fashion. After having our feet treated at the dispensary, we loafed around talking to the Aussies. Four of the boys went down to the river to try their luck at fishing.

Shortly after 1100 we heard the drone of the little planes. While they circled for a landing, we ran out into the clearing waving wildly. The little planes dipped their wings in return.

ENGINEEING

R. Kimball, V. O. Elam, H. P. Quinn, L. V. Hall, G. R. Graves, J. Morr, Boeheneman, E. Beausoleil, Huffman.

J. Elder, J. B. Dudas, A. W. Arklander, N. Paden, H. B. Garland, Leverock, E. Cicci, R. J. Miller.

R. E. Hull, O. L. Sullivan, P. Schreiner, C. Brass, W. W. Smith, H. A. Thompson, R. Forenza.

J. Keown, D. Janovee, E. A. Marcusson, C. Pushetonequa, E. Frawley, S. J. Wozlek.

Huffman, R. Kimball, L. V. Hall, G. R. Graves, G. Halvorson, G. L. Smith, H. P. Quinn, J. B. Dudas, Lester Howard, E. F. Cicci, N. Paden, D. Janovee, W. A. Burns, L. Rishel, H. Cote, V. O. Elam.

A. W. Arklander, H. A. Thompson, C. Pushetonequa, G. R. Smith, E. O. Brimer, Capt. W. P. Farmer, Maj. S. D. Katz, Capt. R. Forsyth, M. B. King, M. Coloff, E. L. Bowen, J. Elder, L. M. Radke, A. C. Rubel, H. P. Rone.

S. J. Wozlek, R. E. Hull, R. Forenza, D. J. Russell, H. H. Ponder, G. Womble, Leverock, H. B. Garland, P. Schreiner, E. Frawley, P. H. Aloia, J. W. Sullivan, W. C. Gott.

W. W. Smith, R. Folkerth, J. F. Williams, C. E. MacDowell, T. N. Rustin, R. N. Runnels, E. J. Wardle, D. J. McCarthy, R. J. Miller, W. Bird, C. E. Brass, Rousseau.

R. Folkerth, P. H. Aloia, C. E. MacDowell, L. Howard, G. R. Smith, E. J. Wardle, M. B. King, E. L. Bowen.

M. Coloff, G. Halvorson, J. F. Williams, H. H. Ponder, Capt. W. P. Farmer, Seguin, G. S. Farrabaugh, S. J. Wozlek.

E. O. Brimer, D. J. Russell, G. L. Womble, M. G. Wooden, Cote, L. M. Radke, T. N. Rustin.

W. C. Gott, G. L. Smith, H. P. Rone, R. N. Runnels, Rousseau, D. J. McCarthy, L. Rishel, A. C. Rubal.

127

ARMAMENT

Niemeyer, R. Pedelty, C. E. Blevins, P. Steele, R. L. Montney, Gegetski, Nass, Clary.

St. Julien, E. J. Dibbern, Davison, Capt. D. A. Geer, L. G. Cleary, E. A. Pospisil, A. V. Cole.

T. R. Morris, C. A. Marlin, G. Doggett, S. A. Dewar, G. Ballirano, F. DiSalvo, Rustad, Simon-son, Thayer, Golden, E. S. Zimmerman, Wilderson, P. C. Thomas.

COMMUNICATIONS

G. M. Sullivan, C. R. Redwine, J. Carley, E. L. Herbst, F. P. Breen, Lentine (deceased), B. A. Slausson, H. P. Mitchell.

J. W. Jones, W. A. Robinson, Sandler, J. C. Witlock, T. D. Paxton, R. J. Fegusoa, W. Melieste, K. Haller.

D. Morrett, L. Curtis, D. F. Brown, G. Scott, L. V. Smith, J. Lane, L. E. Smith, H. D. Benson.

E. H. Taylor, R. H. Schexnayder, R. Collins, C. L. Rettich, R. L. Simpson, E. H. Lankheit, T. C. Nuendorf.

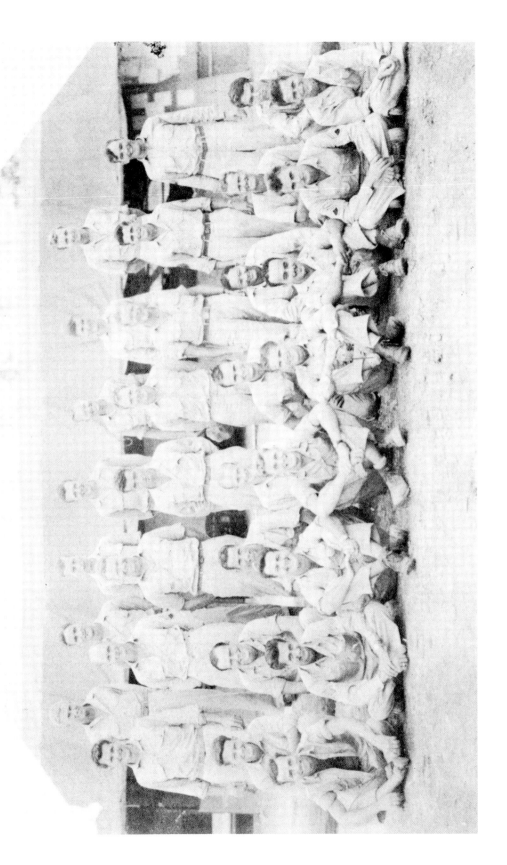

129

ORDNANCE

N. Thompson, T. Eiseman, P. Minor, A. R. Cheek, C. DuPrato.

J. Brvenik, B. Solomon, Lt. J. T. Halferty, F. Gucciardo, J. B. Nailey.

M. Mutchler, S. Cribaro, J. Cavorti, T. Calabro, S. Adams.

130

BATS OUTA' HELL

499th

TO THE OFFICERS AND MEN OF THE 499TH SQUADRON THIS STORY
OF THE VALIANT AND VICTORIOUS STRUGGLE FOR FREEDOM IS
DEDICATED

Captain Bankston

SQUADRON

Major Walters

Major Decker

Major Baird

Major Reinbolt

COMMANDERS

The 499th Bombardment Squadron (M), 345th Bombardment Group (M), was formed on November 11th, 1942, at the Columbia Air Base, Columbia, S. C. The original cadre of eight officers and seventy-one enlisted men were commanded by Capt. Buell A. Bankston, their former C. O. in the 377th Bombardment Squadron of the 309th Bombardment Group. During the next few days the Squadron was employed in the various details of organization and in re-

Briefing at Columbia, S. C.

ceiving a stream of personnel to bring the unit up to strength.

The First four B-25s were assigned to the Squadron on November 30th, and training flights were begun. Col. J. F. Crabb, the Group C. O. conducted weekly inspections and on two occasions, reviewed the Group in parade.

Christmas Day will long be remembered for the gastronomic wonders which our mess personnel prepared and the New Year was ushered in with the usual celebrations.

During January the briefings on various theatres of war, presented by the Intelligence Officer, gave rise to widespread speculation as to our overseas destination.

On one of the many cross country training flights our well-beloved Capt. Bankston and his

Colonel Crabb reviews Squadron at Columbia

crew were lost when bad weather forced their plane down. Under Capt. E. K. Walters, the new Commanding Officer, the Squadron moved to Aiken, S. C., where four-day maneuvers under simulated combat conditions were held. The low-level bombing and strafing missions were conducted under conditions as near to

actual combat as possible. From start to finish each mission was carried out with the now familiar routine: receipt of teletyped orders, briefing, pre-flights, loading bombs, early take offs, dodging flak, destroying the objective, driving off enemy fighters, returning to base, interrogation, and reports. The entire flight was "on the deck" and the orders were carried out to the letter. Under the direction of the Operations Officer, the combat crews began to function as a team and became proficient in flight performance. Finally the allotted training period was ended and the Group returned to Columbia.

On March 6th, after extensive practice in bombing, gunnery, navigation, formation, and other phases of training, the Group moved permanently to Walterboro, S. C., for the final phase before embarking for overseas duty.

Wild parties at Walterboro inspired Capt. Julian B. Baird to suggest "Bats Outa' Hell' as the Squadron name. Cpl. John Michalowski designed the insignia and in due time the War Department approved both.

On March 16th, our 14 new B-25's were ferried from Savannah to Walterboro. Crews were assigned to each plane and the planes were flown to Columbia and Greenville for modification. The flight echelon set out on April 13th for Savannah on the first leg of its overseas flight. The 46 officers and 63 enlisted men remained in Savannah for two days checking the planes and drawing personal equipment.

On April 16th the ground echelon boarded a train and set out on the transcontinental journey which progressed through Georgia, Arkansas, Oklahoma, Kansas, Colorado, Utah, and California, to Camp Stoneman. At Stoneman the last minute details of drawing equipment and checking records occupied several days. Off the record activities included trips to San Francisco which gave rise to many of the legends of the 499th. The "Top of the Mark," "Slapsie Maxie's," "The Sir Francis Drake," and many other places knew the "Bats" well. Meanwhile, the flight echelon was making a reputation of its own in Sacramento, having arrived there after stopping at Hensley Field, Texas, and Tucson, Arizona. During the ten day lay over planes underwent final modification and the crews were thoroughly briefed on the overseas route. On Easter Sunday the bombardiers, gunners and engineers departed by boat in order to cut down on weight, a critical item on a long hop. In the pre-dawn hours of May 1st, sixteen "Bats Outa' Hell" roared off McClellan Field. Sunrise found the planes well on the 2100-mile flight to Hawaii.

Somewhere along the long overwater hop to Hawaii, one of the planes was lost and despite all efforts of search planes, no clue to its disappearance was discovered. With the exception of this instance, all the planes and crews reached Hickam Field in good order. Modifications required several days and this time was used to the best advantage in sight-seeing tours. Each day saw fewer and fewer planes on the line at the field, for the crews flew them to the next destination, Christmas Island, as soon as the modifications were complete. Individually, and in twos and threes, the planes came to rest on Christmas Island to find the early arrivals in the midst of a "beer bust." From Christmas Island some crews flew to Canton Island while others took the southern route to the Samoa Islands. In the Fiji Islands, our men had their first glimpse of the bare-bosomed native belles. From there the planes bore steadily on to Plains des Gaiacs, New Caledonia, and from there to Brisbane, Australia before proceeding to Reed River some 700 miles to the north. Group Headquarters was set up at Woodstock, five miles north of Reed River, and the remainder of the flight echelon was bivouaced with the 22nd Bomb Group, a veteran outfit back from New Guinea for a rest period.

The ground echelon had boarded the *President Johnson* in San Francisco Bay, and at noon on May 1st tugs nursed the liner under the Oakland Bridge, past Devil's Island and under the Golden Gate Bridge. Thus the "Bats Outa' Hell" took leave of American shores without any of the traditional ceremony and fanfare. While the flight echelon was making its crossing, the old *President Johnson*, escorted by a tiny corvette and an old Liberty ship, was wallowing along at seldom more than 14 knots. At any hour of the day the decks were covered by men playing poker, reading, sunning, taking calisthenics, or holding boxing matches. According to custom, rites (administered in the name of Neptune Rex) on May 12th left many individuals with parts of their anatomy bruised and sore. Only once during our several alarms did our escorting corvette track down a sub. The undersea vessel was sunk by depth charges from the corvette. No land was sighted during our 26-day cruise, nor had we any idea of our position. On the 25th day of May the eastern short of Australia broke the horizon. We proceeded slowly along the coast and on the following day steamed into Brisbane Harbor.

On the next day, after a five-mile march, we established quarters at Camp Doomben. During the next few days only a lucky few were allowed passes to town but those who remained behind were consoled by a terrific binge which Col. Crabb had arranged. Those who visited the city were entirely captivated by the foreign customs and habits.

May 31st found us again aboard the *President Johnson* and in the dark morning of June 1st, the ship nosed out of Brisbane Harbor with lights dimmed. For the better part of two days we took a northerly course for Port Moresby,

our new base. On the fifth day the rugged mountains of New Guinea were sighted and a welcoming committee consisting of B-25's of the 38th Bomb Group made several friendly passes at the ship.

Our first look at the town of Port Moresby quickly dispelled any illusions we may have had about romantic New Guinea. Thick, choking dust arose in clouds, covering entire towns with a blanket of dirty brown. The port was the very picture of bustling activity. Aussie, Papuan, and Yank drivers kept trucks shuttling back and forth in endless streams over the dock area while harbor boats and native canoes plied from ship to shore. To further confirm our impression of a vital military port, shore batteries and AA guns could be seen through camouflage nets.

After a weary wait, personnel marched down the gangplank, boarded trucks, and set out for our assigned camp area 17 miles back in the hills. We began a downhill ride which carried us across Jackson Drome. Finally, just at dusk we arrived at the most forlorn area we could have imagined and were told that this was to be the New Guinea home of the " Bats Outa' Hell." Darkness came on quickly and after a hasty meal of "C" rations and coffee we settled down to a hot, restless night, broken only by low voices and the buzzing of hordes of mosquitoes.

While the flight echelon was at Reed River, the ground echelon set to work building a tent city, centered around the orderly room and

Port Moresby S-2

mess hall. The carpenters worked like slaves on mess hall, showers and latrines. The area for the sections on Durand Strip (also called Seventeen Mile Strip) were set up by Engineering, Armament, Operations and Intelligence.

In the midst of this we experienced our first air raid. The red alert signal caught most of us in the "sack" after a hard day's wrok, but there was no sign of fatigue as we rushed pell mell to our fox holes. In various stages of undress, we dived headlong and lay there quivering from head to foot, while we hugged the ground for dear life. We lived in sheer terror for what seemed an eternity while the whine of shells and thunder of gunfire rent

the air with a fortissimo of ear-splitting sounds. At last the enemy planes passed out of range and one by one the guns became silent. Slowly and prayerfully we emerged from our trenches and gathered in small groups. Our baptism of fire was over. Before we had time to relax another raid followed and this time we had the satisfaction of seeing one of the planes suddenly burst into flame and drop rapidly out of formation.

Back at Reed River the flight echelon was busily engaged in the usual training activities. The help extended by the 22nd Bomb Group left us with a very high regard for this veteran outfit. It was here that the "Bats" founded their reputation of being a bunch of "hot rocks." Take offs were made at incredibly short intervals and buzzing was the order of the day. On the 20th of June the move started and continued until all the "Bats" had arrived at Seventeen Mile Strip.

Seventeen Mile was a 5000-foot steel mat laid over a strip which had been bulldozed out of a swampy jungle some three miles from our camp area. It was home to one Squadron of P-38s, two B-25 Squadrons of the 38th Group, and two B-25 Squadrons of the 345th. The marshy shore of a small lake to the west was the stronghold of millions of misquitoes which, even during the heat of the day, made life on the strip miserable. Probably the hardest fought battle in New Guinea was waged there on Seventeen Mile between the varmints and the "Bats Outa' Hell."

On the 24th of June, "A" flight flew the Squadron's first combat mission. Although unexciting and uneventful, it represented a great deal more than just a routine escort mission. Our entry into the New Guinea campaign came when the Aussies began their first offensive in the Salamaua sector south of Lae. On several important supply-dropping operations in the mountains our planes flew down tortuous valleys, dodging and turning to avoid crashing into the mountain sides, in order to dump their supplies.

While the battle for Salamaua raged, the Squadron flew daily, continued building up the camp, and nightly attended movies or listened to "Tokyo Rose." During this period the Aussie Ground Forces expressed sincere appreciation for our excellent support. On one occasion, after advancing into one of our targets, they reported some 300 Nips dead as a result of our attack. Our first casualties were sustained when an unusually accurate heavy AA position on Salamaua Peninsula scored a direct hit on one of our planes.

For some time rumors had been circulating that the 345th was to be converted to "strafer-bombers." With the exception of the Squadron bombardiers every man was eager for the conversion. At last the day came when the flight echelon was ordered to Townsville, Australia, for modification of the Squadron's B-25s. Modification consisted of installing four .50 caliber machine guns in the nose and two more on each side of the fuselage. A secondary

modification placed camera, gun, and bomb release switches in the cockpit. The change-over was to require the better part of a month and as a result most of the personnel were granted leaves in Sydney, Australia. One of the men has given us the following nostalgic picture of "The Battle of Sydney," which shows how that Air Corps playground was taken by storm.

After angling around to get your name on orders (any old orders will do), the next thing was to sweat out getting on a manifest for the long ride down. If you were a "wheel" and wangled aboard a fat-cat, this sweating was not necessary, but we'll assume you're just one of the eager Sydney-bound birdmen.

As we moved north, it meant more transient camps (used to be only Townsville and Brisbane to worry about), but after we'd left Moresby, it too, became a stopover. Much later there were Biak and Moratai to fumble with. Draw your blankets and pad, messkit your way through those transient camp meals, get up in the middle of the night and wait under the wing of a C-47 for hours to take off. Eventually you landed at Sydney and the big contest started—the bus, groaning with its load of B-4 bags and birdmen, hauls up to David Jones,

Early model B-25 Strafer

and later *Mark Foy's*, then sign up in the Leave Bureau, draw the liquor card and ration tickets and then off to line up a flat at King's Cross or Bondi or Rose Bay.

S. O. P. says to get that room at the Bernley or Cheverells or No. 4 Elizabeth Bay Road first and then go after a flat. The all-night access to the kitchen with its eggs, milk, tomatoes, ice-cream, etc., always made having a room at the Bernley or Cheverells a good idea —so everyone did it.

Camera installation on Strafer Model B-25

142

No time lost calling the old gals or chasing down some new ones—meet me at the *Australia*—or I'll be around to get you at so and so—did any city ever have gals like Sydney? Well, we take off for *Prince's* or *Romano's* or the all-Yank *Roosevelt* in King's Cross. They say some of the boys even went to the Gilbert and Sullivan shows but we can't prove it. Favorite pastime: the steak and salad dinner the gals would cook in your flat, with the culinary extras and otherwise. Always those fun-loving Rovers and their Sydney gals—the Battle is on. Blackmarket chicken, or steak, or grog to make that "rest leave" really restfful. And those Sydney gals!   •

Every day started with beer—call at the *Australia*, remember? Tossing beer down and pennies up at the big glass chandeliers. Every-

body was there until the beer ran out, then over to 40 York, or No. 4 Elizabeth Bay or *Mark Foy's* for the daily liquor ration and the day is off to a good start. A dip at Bondi, beer at the flat, maybe the Tivoli to s e e t h e *Tivoli Girls' Revue*, or one of a dozen other pastimes which may have been sailing, a trip across on

the ferry to see the Zoo, or just logging the old sack-time for the after dark campaign.

Pick up a small gasoline stove, some folding charts, get your films developed and printed at Kodak, shoes half-soled—lots to do in those few days. Watch out for the trams and traffic going up and down the wrong side of the road—drop a fortune in cab fares—but who cares—it's the Battle. The time went fast in Sydney. Lug that B-4 full of bottles carefully, brother, that's all I've got—store your clothes until the next trip down—the Battle is over.

While the men were "resting in Sydney and various other towns, work progressed

Orderly room and operations at Nadzab

Nadzab enlisted men's club

144

499th Ships returning from New Guinea strike

Nadzab enlisted men's club bar

Kitchen at Nadzab

146

New Guinea natives at Nadzab

slowly back at Townsville because of the enormous volume of modification being accomplished at that time. Gradually the planes began coming off the line, and one by one they were flown back to Port Moresby. As the planes arrived they were checked by engineering personnel. Using the results of daily practice missions and bore-sighting operations as a guide, the armament section obtained the correct alignment for the guns and the group started missions as strafers. These missions included the targets of Madang, Salamaua, Lae Nadzab, Wewak, and Rabaul. Rabaul was probably the most heavily defended target attacked by our Squadron at any time. Besides doing great damage to ground installations, the Squadron accounted for five Zeros in flight and many others on the ground during one mission there.

While the combat crews were pounding the Japs in the air, the ground personnel were working on the camp to make things more comfortable. Mess halls and office buildings were constructed and clubs for both enlisted men and officers were erected. The clubs, well stocked with Aussie beer and whiskey, provided places for relaxation during off duty hours. The many parties kept everyone in good spirits and all were sorry when the move to Dobadura came.

On December 23rd, 1943, the Group was to stage out of Dobadura. Upon reaching Dobo strip, however, it was learned that the mission had been canceled and that the Group had been ordered to remain there. The rest of the planes were soon brought up, and the heavy equipment loaded on boats for the long trip around the end of New Guinea. The Squadron moved into the area left by the 408th Squadron of the 22nd Bomb Group, where they found mess halls and office buildings already con-

20mm ack-ack damage

structed. When the water echelon arrived, it was necessary to build an addition onto the mess hall to accomodate our men; with that one exception, no construction work was necessary. The combat crews flew missions over Cape Gloucester and for some daring missions over the Admiralty Islands the Squadron received a Presidential Citation. The stay at Dobo was a short one and the middle of February found the ground echelon packing to leave for their new station.

The move from Dobadura to Nadzab was accomplished almost completely by air on the 23rd and 24th of February, 1944. Squadron vehicles were moved by water whereas the rest of the outfit traveled via C-47 transports, which lived up to their name of "Work-horse of the Air Corps." Loading of the planes was so organized that only 30 minutes elapsed between landing and take off.

The Squadron area at Nadzab was spacious and extended to the base of the foothills on the north side of the Markham Valley. The sometimes beautiful valley was never without a breeze, especially at night. This made sleeping more comfortable in the tropical heat. Some of the Squadron officers built shacks on the small hills and knolls overlooking the valley. A Group Officers' Club and Mess were combined and built on one of the many hills overlooking the area. Many the drunk who fell down the hill during an exceptionally riotous party!

Food was the best since arriving overseas. At the slightest need a "fat-cat" would go to Australia for fresh eggs, green vegetables, butter and the wherewithal to make parties complete.

Biak Natives

Wheels up landing at Biak

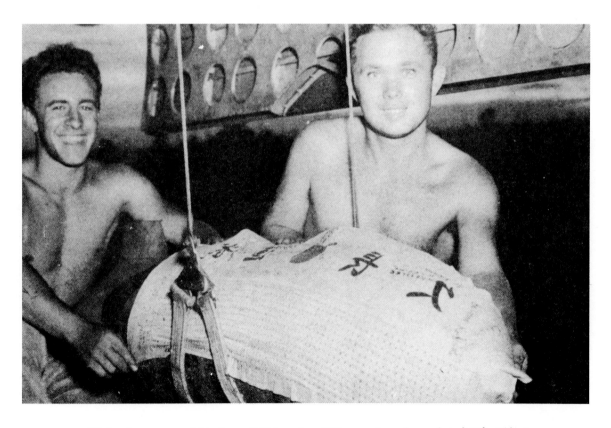

Air Apaches repay a debt when a B-25 from the 499th squadron dropped a bomb with a message from New York War Bonds Subscribers. The message was a captured Jap "Belt of Thousand Stitches" signed by the bond buyers.

Damage due to enemy Bombing at Biak

Enemy ack-ack damage

A homemade Squadron laundry provided a solution to the dirty shirt problem, which had really became catastrophic to the "sack-hounds." The laundry saved many toilsome hours of scrubbing muddy and oil-splashed clothes.

There were some incidents which many will long remember, one of these being when the flight surgeon's kerosene refrigerator set the "Majority Hill" shack on fire at nine o'clock one night. Most of the officer personnel at that time happened to be attending a party at the "Casbah," an adjacent hill where they lived. Suddenly some one noticed the fire and spread the news. A few minutes later a half-inebriated bucket-brigade was on the spot. The fire was put out but the drunken firemen threw as much water on each other as they did on the fire.

In general, Nadzab was a comfortable place. The camp was well planned and far from being crowded. The lack of air raids and frequent leaves to Australia also added tremendously to the morale and made our stay as enjoyable as possible under the circcumstances.

July 25, 1944 found four B-25s on the strip at Nadzab ready to leave for Biak with the men of the advanced echelon of the 499th. For the first time in the history of the Squadron it was to move into an area which was not already cleared of Japs, and rumors ran wild as to the nightly visits paid by our new Nipponese neighbors.

Our new area appeared to be little more than a mass of tropical plants, vines and small trees rooted in almost solid coral rock. By evening of the first day, however, enough space was cleared for twenty tents and a guard detail was posted. The first night passed comparatively uneventfully, notwithstanding the fact that one of the guards took a shot at the O. D. as he was making one of the night's inspections.

The lack of proper equipment considerably handicapped progress for a few days, but with the help of confiscated Jap gasoline and the local natives a larger area was soon cleared. The 499th encampment was located on a small plateau which extended several hundred yards from a tall rugged cliff down to the steep shore line. Both sides of the area were surrounded by a thick green, almost inpenetrable tangle of tropical vegetation.

During the second week of our stay, natives reported large numbers of Japanese infiltrating into the caves at the rear of the camp, and subsequently an infantry company and several tanks were called in. The "Bat Men" for the first time were afforded a front row seat in ground force operations. Many of the men merely reclined on as their back porches and looked on as tanks and mortars shelled the caves and infantry men moved up through the jungle to finish off the remaining Japs.

Water for washing purposes became a considerable problem and in an attempt to reach fresh water a thirty-foot well was dug

through the coral, but to the utter dismay of the laborers word was received that a pipe line was already begun. Not wishing to see their efforts end in vain, the well diggers converted the hole to a latrine and placed this appropriate sign in a position where it could be read and appreciated by all patrons: "This is the Deepest Damn Outhouse in the World." It was said that this latrine was used by the men of the 498th and 499th Squadrons from six in the morning until six in the evening and by the Japanese the remainder of the time.

Stories of individual Jap forays into the area were numerous, and a favorite pastime of the more adventuresome "Bat Men" was Jap hunting in the nearby cliffs and caves. Many of the Japanese soldiers became so desperate for food that they stole nightly into the area in search of anything edible. One even went so far as to walk boldly into the area and give himself up. An officer insisted on laying the loss of his belt to his tentmate who pleaded innocent and suggested the possibility of a Jap theif. It was not, however, until a Jap was captured wearing the stolen belt that the accused was exonerated in the eyes of the officer.

During the entire stay at Biak with its many Jap scares, only on one occasion did a "Bat Man" fall the victim of a bullet. On this occasion one of the enlisted men at two o'lcock in the morning staggered from his sack to the nearby underbrush to relieve himself. Hearing a commotion in the vicinity, another man awoke and fearing an invading Jap, called, and upon hearing no reply, opened up with his .45 wounding his unsuspecting mate in the shoulder. Prompt medical attention, however, soon repaired the victim and he was shortly evacuated.

,Despite the initial hardships encountered by the "Bat Men" during the first days at Biak, the area gradually underwent improvement. Those who remained at Biak after the planes and combat crews had departed for Leyte, were left in the rear echelon, and enjoyed a comfortable and almost restful period from October to December. As the result of the decreased number of men remaining at Biak and their proximity to Australia, fresh food was never lacking and the Post Exchange supplies were plentiful.

Combat operations from Biak were relatively limited, and what few missions were flown during the stay there were against Baguio and the Celebes Islands. These strikes were flown from advanced staging areas at Sansapor and Moratai. In the meantime, activities in the early campaigns in the Philippines were reaching a climax.

October 14th found the men and equipment of the 499th in a turmoil of rush and confusion as the ship Thomas Nelson, one of the original Liberty ships, loaded in preparation for the trip from Biak to Leyte. At one point, due to the lassitude of the Negro dock hands it was thought that all Squadron tentage and baggage would be left behind. Only after considerable fast talking was the ship's master convinced that the Air Apache personnel would completely load the ship by the deadline, six o'clock in the morning of the 15th.

Aboard the ship the ground echelon of the 498th, Group Headquarters and the 499th Squadrons were crowded into the hold, jammed into and under deck loaded vehicles, scattered under makeshift rigs of canvas, and some even in the life rafts. Only a few of the fortunate and high ranking Squadron officers found quarters with the ship's officers. On the 18th of the month the ship pulled into the harbor of Hollandia where, together with the Morrison Waite, another Liberty ship carrying the 500th and 501st Squadrons, awaited the formation of the convoy.

The trip to Leyte was uneventful with the possible exception of the anxiety which was caused by the reports of the great naval engagements which were taking place in Leyte Gulf and off the coast of Luzon. All aboard were relieved when word was received that our Navy had licked the enemy completely by the 24th of the month. On the evening of the 29th, nine days after the initial Leyte landings, amidst the beginning of a typhoon the ship dropped anchor off Tacloban. The typhoon struck with full force about nine o'clock that night throwing the ship into a complete uproar; canvas was torn from the deck, bunks were blown overboard and considerable personal equipment was lost. The following morning, however, dawned bright and clear over the calm sea. Shortly after breakfast many Filipinos congregated about the Nelson in their outrigger canoes selling souvenirs of doubtful origin. One officer noticed too late that the fine straw hat he had purchased had a USA label inside.

The first night, we were soon to learn, was spent in comparative ease, for the succeeding nights were rendered sleepless by continuous air attacks against our ships and nearby shore installations. Although many of the men had been overseas for a year and one half, this was their first real taste of war. The officers in charge did all in their power in an effort to move the men ashore, but to no avail, since there were other and more pressing needs for the limited unloading facilities. A few days after arrival an advance echelon with a small amount of equipment went ashore to make what preparations were possible on the area.

The first camp-site was located just outside the perimeter of a marine battery of "long toms," and the men soon realized that an

elaborate system of guards would be necessary as the enemy controlled the immediate vicinity. No improvements at this site were feasable for the air engineer had chosen a new area. It was, however, impossible to move into the new camp-site as the mud was too deep to allow the passage of the heavy Squadron vehicles.

On shore the air raids were found to be far worse than on ship, as the majority of the troops were camped within several hundred yards of San Pablo Air Strip.

In the meantime the remainder of the men stayed aboard the Liberty ship passing away the hours by playing cards and watching the tracer and ack ack filled sky during the air attacks. The enemy raids were frequent and men soon became accustomed to the dangers and remained on deck.

At approximately 1125 on November 22nd, 1944 the men were as usual lolling around the deck in the warm sunshine or playing cards. Ships cooks were cleaning up after the morning meal. The scene was typical of a morning aboard ship. Suddenly two red streaks of tracers flashed parallel to the starboard rail. Two Jap suicide planes had come in low and unnoticed and were making a strafing run on the ship. There had been no warning, and the men were caught unprepared. One of the planes peeled off and crashed into the stern of a nearby LST. The second plane continued parallel to the ship and suddenly banked sharply and struck the Liberty ship at the number five hatch where the majority of the enlisted men were quartered in makeshift

tents. The ship shuddered from deck plates to keel, and a violent explosion almost knocked flat those men who were left standing. No sooner had the second plane hit, when a third screamed at the stern completely spraying the afterdeck with machine gun fire. The afterdeck became a raging inferno and most of the men rushed back to assist the ship's crew in keeping the flames away from the gasoline and bombs stowed below.

During those first hectic moments no one could be certain as to whether or not the ship would go up in one gigantic explosion. Those men who were not engaged in fighting the fire carried the dead and wounded men to the forward part of the ship. The Squadron ambulances and medical suplies were completely destroyed by the fire and the ship's emergency equipment was pitifully inadequate, but the remaining uninjured men improvised bandages of anything at hand and worked valiantly throughout the remaining air attacks until outside aid came one hour later. By 1500 the wounded men were transferred ashore or to a hospital ship which came alongside, and at 1800 an LST pulled alongside and took the remainder of the personnel to the comparative safety of the beach.

The men who climbed from the LST to the beaches of Leyte thanked God for letting them get safely ashore. It had been an experience they would never forget. After a couple of hours of tense waiting, the trucks arrived to take the men to the temporary camp. It was near midnight when they arrived at the muddy, mosquito-infested site. Every available

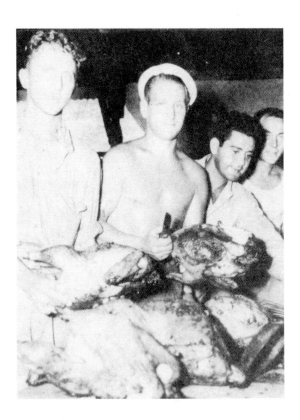

Dulag Christmas Turkey

the next morning a Jap plane strafed the area without warning. Men slithered in the mud and dove for their water-filled fox holes. It was not comfortable, but it was safety. That afternoon tents and cots were found for all the men so they could be sure of a place to rest. Except for an occasional bomb and the constant roar of the anti-aircraft guns, the night was spent in uneasy slumber.

Three days later, everyone was given a hurried warning to pack their belongings as the move to the new area was soon ot start. The new area appeared to be dry and solid, but after a short rain it quickly turned into a quagmire. Tents and available mess facilities were quickly set up and K rations, the only food available, were issued to all. The nearby anti-aircraft guns made a good night's sleep only wishful thinking, as there was a constant floundering to and from the fox holes. Six days later, good spirits were again found in the camp as a new location was found a few miles away on White Beach.

With the help of borrowed transportation the men and equipment were moved during the day and by nightfall a new camp had been set up. In the folowing weeks, life on the beach proved to be very eventful. Every day the water was filled with men enjoying the rolling surf, the best relaxation available. Nights were spent watching the red tracers flash across the sky in a never-ending stream directed at the enemy planes overhead. It was always a welcome event to see a P-38 or P-47 shoot down an attacking plane. Suicide attacks in Leyte Gulf were numerous. The sky was filled with

tent was set up to give the men shelter from the rain, but all could not be accomodated. Some slept under trees, others under trucks or any place that would offer a little shelter. Early

"I FOUND TWO JEEPS, ONE TRUCK AND THE BOW OF ADMIRAL DEWEY'S FLAGSHIP!"

Ditching survivors

black puffs of ack ack from land and ship batteries. Most of the enemy planes were shot down but others came through to add to the toll of American shipping sunk. In November the men were hastily loading their guns and setting up guards to protect against Jap infiltration. A Jap transport plane had crash-landed a few hundred yards down the beach and the troops on board had started guerrilla action. There was little sleep that night, but the vigil was relaxed in the morning when most of the Japs were rounded up.

Christmas Day found the men in high spirits with the usual desire to celebrate. Carefully hoarded liquor was brought out and a good time was had by all. Very few Christmas packages had arrived from home, but the fresh turkey dinner made everyone forget his disappointment. The word finally came that all had been waiting so long to hear. Our planes could now start operating from Tacloban. The ball really started rolling then. On December 30th the ground echelon joined the flight echelon at the new area— only a short distance from Tacloban strip. The following morning pilots and crews were in their planes, ready to take off on another mission. The many missions run during our stay at Tacloban included the Clark Field raid on January 7th. This co-ordinated raid of heavy, medium and attack planes on the Jap's major air base in the Philippines accounted for many of the Nip planes on the ground and in the air and caused a sharp decline in the number of air raids at Tacloban. Other missions consisted of strafing runs up the valleys of Luzon where railroads were the chief target.

Tacloban, the first civilized town seen by the Squadron since Australia, became the

gathering place for the "Bats" during off-duty hours. Many native shops sold gifts and restaurants specialized in fried chicken. Filipinos came through the area gathering laundry and selling cigars and chicken on the hoof. It soon became necessary to forbid the keeping of chickens in the area because the chicken population had become larger than the population of the Squadron.

As has been mentioned before the battle of Leyte was one of mud and Tacloban was no exception. While the Squadron area was fairly dry, the road leading to the area was a different story. The mud was about the consistency of thick pea soup and ranged from two to three feet deep. It has been rumored that two of the jeeps that were reported missing there were not stolen, but simply sank into the ground in the motor pool area during a heavy rain. The next most important problem was that of fighting mosquitoes.

February 12th, the group was scheduled to go on a mission staging out of San Marcelino, Luzon, an airfield on the northern end of Bataan Peninsula which had just been captured from the Japs. As in a previous move, the mission was called off and the men already at San Marcelino were ordered to remain there. A few days later, the rest of the personnel and most of the equipment were ferried up by air and the Group moved into a large green valley at the foot of some wooded hills. Thus those magic words "Bring enough clothes for three days" had materialized into another move as at Dobadura.

Tent after San Marceleno Wind Storm

The Leyte campaign had been anything but a pleasant one, and for the most part the men eagerly awaited a move away from the mud, constant

General Crabb decorates men of his old group at San Marceleno, Philippine Is.

155

Wheels up landing at San Marceleno Air Drome, Philippine Is.

Ship hits strip

Wrecking crew takes over

rain and continuous air attacks. Roads, although far better than the ones previously encountered, were unable to withstand the constant pounding by heavy vehicles, and clouds of dust filled the air clogging our equipment.

The surrounding countryside was densely populated and Philippine villages or barrios could be found in almost any direction from the area. Many a "Bat Man" found a break in the routine monotony of combat by wandering about talking to the natives, hunting souvenirs, both Filipino and Japanese, and taking in the cock fights which climaxed the festivities of a Philippine Sunday. Some made friends of the Filipinos and Chinese inhabitants of nearby barrios, and many were the tales of strange household customs and stranger meals.

As time went on the engineers finished the landing strip and were able to spare some of their men and equipment for the roads, which were by this time badly in need of repair. For the most part the Squadron area was a temporary installation as plans were being made to move to Clark Field at some early date. In place of the usual type of lumber tent frames, bamboo was used. Practically no finished lumber was used in the entire Group area, for the Filipinos quickly displayed their indigenous ability to build structures and furniture of bamboo.

The occupants of each tent soon acquired the services of a houseboy, who not only kept the tent area clean, but acted as a shrewd bargainer for food and souvenirs. Many of the "Bat Men" were put to shame by the dexterity of the alert young houseboys in bamboo construction. No job seemed too much for them and their pleasant temperament under all circumstances was a source of wonder to all. To the officers of the 499th one of these

Philippino cart in Manila

Building tent frames at Clark Field

Clark Field "Wheel House"

young Filipinos, Johnny Corpus, stands out above all others. His sincere friendship, and helpful assistance will be remembered by all who knew him.

In bargaining for chickens, fresh eggs, vegetables, and laundry the houseboys were invaluable. Often were the times when, after a long and noisy conference, he would succeed in making a suitable price. Upon arrival at Luzon almost any native item could be traded for an undershirt, but as time went on the once much prized item bought less and less. Despite the efforts of our houseboys the Philippine OPA continued to function as prices were steadily rising.

Combat activities during the first days at San Marcelino consisted of ground support missions. Later, the Group began a long and adventuresome series of shipping strikes along the China coast. These later activities were soon to bring noted recognition to the men of the 345th Bomb Group.

On February 18th, 1945 the Apaches were called on for a twelve-hour pounding of the Bagac Road, north of Bataan, in support of our infantry in retaking the famous peninsula. The "Bats Outa' Hell" flew two missions over the same target during that day. The entire length of the Bagac Road was sprayed with "fifties" and cratered with 500-pound bombs. The next day came a commendation from the Commanding General of the Infantry forces for the great support the Apaches had given them. It was stated that a total of 4,400 Jap dead were found in the target area; they had only to walk through and count the mangled bodies of the Japanese. The men of the 499th took pride in the fact that no infantrymen were lost in taking this objective. The operation was truly a magnificent tribute to air power.

With the campaign in southern Luzon in its final stage the men of the 345th turned their attention to enemy shipping along the China coast. These missions were the longest flown in Group history, and in order to increase the range of our aircraft, further modifications were required. The four forward firing package guns and the two flexible waist guns were removed and the crew of six was reduced to five by the elimination of the armorer-gunner. The tail guns were manned by the radio operator, who crawled back to the turret as the target was sighted. These changes in the B-25 made possible flights of ten-hour duration; on one later occasion one of the planes was flown eleven hours and forty-five minutes, a Group record.

Squadron sign at Clark Field, Philippine Is.

The long planned move to Clark Field was postponed several weeks and the prospect of being caught at San Marcelino in the rainy season became the subject of considerable worry. Without warning at six o'clock in the evening of May 12th, the tents were torn down, the Squadron equipment was loaded on trucks and the sixty-mile ride to Clark Field was begun.

Upon arrival at Clark Field, the "Bat Men" found what were perhaps the most permanent Squadron buildings since the days at Nadzab.

The various types of tents, huts, and shacks which had served as orderly rooms, operations offices, and mess halls during the early days of the Philippines campaign, were now replaced with screened-in, tin-roofed houses. The new mess hall complete with tables and cooking facilities was a far cry from the seatless tents of San Marcelino. Running water was the order of the day, and both the officers' and enlisted men's area were complete with an inexhaustable supply of water for the showers. Roads had already been constructed, and for the men there remained only the problem of satisfying their personal needs and living accommodations.

Clark Field and the surrounding installations offered the most fruitful pickings yet encountered by the Squadron operators. During the first few days trading operations were hindered because of the shortage of transportation, but the second week found men of the entire 499th covering every source of lumber and building material. Most of the men slept by day and worked by night. Trucks ranged from Lingayan Gulf to Clark and from Subic Bay to Manila. Manila's harbor area and the Pandican engineer's dump proved an inex-

158

Squadron engineering section on Jap bomber at Clark Field

haustable supply for all who could make a deal. So successful were the results of "acquiring" that no dirt floors were to be allowed in the officers' area. In several weeks' time the 499th area displayed as fine an array of shacks as could be found, other than at Fort Stotsenburg.

As was the case during the first days at San Marcelino, the Squadron area was filled with an endless procession of Filipinos. Young boys went from house to house offering their services as houseboys, and women in their usual colorful garb walked in stately fashion between the tents carrying their wares of fruit, bananas, and pineapples upon their heads. The laundry workers too were ever present, and their characteristic cry of "any durty clothes, sirs" filled the area.

The new home in the Philippines found us almost five thousand miles from Sydney, and as a result Sydney leaves were cancelled; in its place a rest house in Manila was rented by the Group. Two of the better houses remaining in the almost totally destroyed city were the cause of many an envirous eye cast at the men of the Air Apaches. A system of rotation was set up whereby each man spent four days out of each sixty in the newly acquired houses.

During the early days of our re-occupation of the Philippine Capital the men spent their time wandering among the ruins and searching for souvenirs or what little merchandise had been left in the few remaining stores. As time went on nurses and WACs arrived in ever increasing numbers. As might well be expected this fact met with the full approval of the Air Apaches, and soon the houses with bars and facilities were holding dances nightly. The "Bat Men," with an abundance of vehicles, combat stories, and the leave house, soon became the favorite of the new female arrivals.

The last days at San Marcelino had seen the end of Jap shipping off the China and Indo-China coasts and efforts were now directed towards knocking out all military installations on the Japanese island bastion of Formosa. Also during the stay at Clark the Air Apaches were called upon to give ground support in northern Luzon where they were of valuable assistance in routing the enemy from the heavily-defended positions in the Cagayan Valley and Belete Pass areas.

Towards the end of June with Formosa no longer an important military target and the campiagns of Luzon and Okinawa in their final stages, the Air Apaches temporarily suspended combat operations and turned toward a training program in preparation for new targets on the Japanese home land. Several new bombing techniques were developed, new crews were checked out and in general the Squadron was made ready for the final stage of its combat career.

On July 18th plans for the move to Ie Shima began to take form. Squadron buildings were hurriedly disassembled, shacks in the officers' area were torn down in an effort to salvage as much lumber as possible. The last vestige of the already shrunken mess hall, once pride of the 499th, was torn down. Little did we realize that Ie Shima, which we considered a foremost outpost on the road to Tokyo, was to offer much in the way of needed materials.

The following day found the enlisted men at Subic Bay with the intent of loading the LST which was to take us to our new home. Work at first progressed rapidly, but due to a last minute beer ration, men began to fall by the wayside—the result of over indulgence. Loading efforts were, however, continued through the remainder of the day and on through the night. At three o'clock in the morning, in true G. I. movement fashion, those who were destined for the water echelon were awakened, and in the midst of a torrential downpour, loaded themselves, their belongings, and little lumber onto a semi-trailer in preparation for the first and none-too-comfortable leg of their journey. A few moments later, the ever-gracious commanding officer, Maj. Wendel D. Decker, wished us best of luck and God speed, and then fell exhausted into his warm dry sack. We proceeded wet, cursing, and miserable over the treacherous Zig Zag Pass to Subic Bay and our waiting LST. Upon arrival in the loading area it was learned that loading had been delayed and would not be completed until late that morning. During the intervening hours the officers roamed about the ship, bump-

ing their heads and skinning their knees in the unfamiliar, crowded passages of what was for the majority the first experience on an ocean-going craft. About mid-morning the first and perhaps only catastrophe of the move occured when the Coca Cola machine, the faithful little Squadron refresher, slipped from a loading truck and fell into the Bay, where it pitifully reclined amidst the sand and pieces of its broken parts.

In the early hours of the afternoon the LST pulled away from the beach and out into the bay to await the formation of the convoy which consisted of twelve LST's and three escorting destroyers. Early morning of the following day found the convoy on its way up the west coast of Luzon. After the first day the novelty of the ship lessened and the enlisted men occupied their time on the foredeck playing cards and sleeping in the warm tropic sun, while the officers gatehered in groups in the various wardrooms for poker or bridge.

The Flight Surgeon and his corpsmen in conjunction with the ship's pharmacist-mate, set up a dispensary where the usual sick call was held each morning.

On the second day the convoy passed through the U. S. Navy gunnery range on the northeast coast of Luzon. Accordingly, two Navy TBF's towing targets flew passes over the ships of the convoy, affording the ship's crew an opportunity at gunnery practice. The Army personnel got a chance to observe the fire power of an LST and the accuracy of our Naval gunners. The men were particularly

impressed by the display of the five-inch guns of a destroyer escort which, after two warm-up shots, knocked the target out of the sky.

For the most part the passengers were very favorably impressed with the quality of the food served on board. This impression and the remarks about it were met by crew men's statements that the good food was being withheld until the ship was free of passengers!

The remaining days of the voyage passed by with few mishaps and a minimum of activity save a few hours spent in relashing the Squadron vehicles which were pulled loose by the unusually heavy roll of the ship. This roll, we were only too soon to learn, was the cause of the temporary indisposition of many a good man, and for some the excellent Navy food became only an undesirable necessity.

On July 23rd, six days after departure from the Philippine Islands the men of the Air Apaches got their first look at Okinawa and the Ryukyus, when the convoy steamed into Buckner Bay. Here the ships lay at anchor until the following day when the remainder of the trip to Ie Shima was to be made.

For the most part men of the 499th were greatly surprised and somewhat encouraged by their first sight of Ie. We had been led to believe it was merely a barren outpost. Actually, it turned out to be a hub of activity not only for the air forces but ground units and Navy as well.

The first few days prior to the selection of a permanent area were spent in the island transient camp. Recent rains had left it a mass of deep ruts and a veritable sea of mud. The menu during these first days consisted solely of K rations as no cooking facilities were available.

On July 29th, two days after the arrival at Ie Shima, work on the new area swung into high gear. Permanent Squadron buildings were constructed of lumber salvaged from the Clark Field area. For the first time in its history the Squadron was issued a portable hut to be used as a mess hall.

As always during such a period of construction the Air Apaches' vehicles began to appear in ever increasing numbers throughout the island's various engineers' dumps and lumber yards. The night's silence was broken by the sounds of unloading as the contraband material arrived in the area. Plywood, the invaluable build-all material, rolled in at an ever increasing rate and many an enterprising truck driver found himself with the means for a good drunk. In short, the Air Apaches were at work again. At this time it was suggested that the Squadron should set aside one truck painted black and void of all Squadron and Group identification. This procedure would eliminate the chance of recognition and also do away with the careful scrutinization of all Squadron trucks on legitimate business in the island supply dumps.

Regardless of the fact that the Group was soon banned from most supply sources, the area grew at a rapid rate and soon those ambitious members of the Squadron were enjoying quarters as comfortable as their liquor supply and the island building materials could afford.

The planes which arrived on the 30th were now in condition, operations and line maintainence facilities were set up, and thoughts turned once again to air operations against Japan. After the several weeks of non-operational activities the prospect of stepped-up combat was met with considerable anticipation. The Squadron and Group, however, were soon to learn that this period was to be perhaps the most intensified one, and after several weeks of ceaseless combat and rather heavy losses, any let up would have been a welcomed change.

On August 9th, news of the new and extremely powerful atomic bomb crept into the Squadron. The majority of the men, however, met the story with considerable scepticism and only the most prolific of rumor mongers continued to spread stories of its devastating effects on Japan.

Two days later, however, with the new bomb a confirmed and potent reality, and the entry of Russia into the war against Japan, the thought arose that, perhaps, the end, if not in the immediate offing, would come sooner than was previously expected.

Combat operations, however, continued at an accelerated rate and what seemed to be premature ideas of an early peace were soon forgotten. Just eleven days after the entry of Russia into the war, men of the 499th received what undoubtedly was the most significant and welcome news of the entire war: Japan had actually accepted her fate. Contrary to any preconceived ideas, there was little celebration. Men accepted the news as a possible beginning of the long dreamed of end and went on with lightened spirits. Activities in the area were centered about those tents equipped with radios. Men waited and listened to news, almost breathlessly, for just the faintest hint that a satisfactory proposal would be offered by Japan.

Rumors ran wild, stories that a majority of the civilians back home spurned a treaty and wanted a continuation of the war until Japan was in ruins, infuriated those who were foolish enough to believe them. Combat operations continued, and the Air Apaches continued to lose aircraft. Combat crews merely existed between news broadcasts and flight schedules hoping against hope that the war would end before another mission was flown. Impossible as it may seem, the mental strain and tension which had always accompanied combat operations, became even more intense. Always in the background was a constant thought that perhaps no suitable terms could be reached and the war would continue. For those of the 499th something must happen. It did, for on August 14th the U. S. Government received word of acceptance by the Japanese Government of our last proposal. All hostilities and combat operations for the Air Apaches had ceased.

The last lines of a great story which was started just two years, eight months, and twelve days ago back in Columbia, South Carolina, U. S. A. were about to be written. A story of courage and bravery, of laughs and fond memories, of hardships and death, was closed as Air Apache planes proudly escorted humble and defeated Japanese peace envoys to Ie Shima Island on August 19th.

OUR mission was "to destroy the enemy." Our actual weapons were .50 caliber bullets and bombs, but supporting them were our airplanes, their crews, and the men who worked to keep them flying month after month.

Final success of the mission depended upon the crew members who flew their planes to the target, fired the guns and released the bombs. That was the pay-off, the published result—but behind those few seconds over the targets is another story and one we hope to include in our picture of the 500th.

It is the story of the hours spent on the ground between missions, of the long, hot and dusty hours working on the Line, the briefings and interrogations, the games, the shacks, the rest leaves, the chow, the weather, the songs, and all of the dust and mud, humor and sadness and dying and living that blended into the war for the 500th.

How well the mission was accomplished is immortalized in the Squadron's battle record and in the pride which each member has in the organization. We hope this chapter will help keep bright the memories of the Fighting 500th.

IN any combat organization there is bound to be a feeling of difference between the "old man" and the "new man." The 500th was no exception; two week's seniority in the outfit was almost enough to enable one to offer advice to new comers, and to have been at the previous base gave one a chance to speak of the "good ole days." So here at the beginning of our narrative we must state that much of this story has, by necessity, been prepared by Squadron members whom some readers would consider mere recruits and others would feel were quite venerable. We do hope, however, that the real "old boys" feel that we have done our best under the current circumstances of rapid and sudden departure of tradition-filled-old-timers. We have listened to their tales of the old days, asked questions, delved into reams of carbon copies of records, and tried to preserve for all the traditions of the 500th as they were passed to us.

The Editors, September 21st, 1945

Our history starts with activation at Columbia, S. C., in November 1942. We learned that the sunny south could get just cold as any other place in the States. All of the nice pinks, O. D.'s and winter flying clothes weren't too much to wear there, especially while practicing medium bombardment. There was no Officer's Mess in the Club at the time, and it was plenty of meals of milk shakes and sandwiches at the fountain that fortified crewmen back in those early days. Of course, one could always refuel at one of the numerous unofficial PX's set up in Operations down on the Line.

Things weren't so tough in town; there were such hangouts as the Wade Hampton Hotel, the Chatterbox ballroom at the Jefferson and the Elks' Club. Another good place was the old Rexall drugstore, good for picking up both dates and rumors. The Ship Ahoy restaurant served the best food in town, such as it was, and more than made up for any culinary deficiencies by its cute waitresses. Speaking of food, we might add that grits were obtainable at any reliable local eating place. In season, a really good diversion was the local high school football games which exhibited some classy open-style playing.

High spots of the Columbia stay were: the short bivouac at Aiken in February which featured barracks, red alerts, air raids by Squadrons with the Group, a PX, a big beer bust and Cavoti's Spaghetti House; the EM's big Squadron party in their club at the Base and the officers' party at the Wade Hampton; and finally the staging for the ETO out of Walterboro in March and then the trip to Stoneman in April.

The flight echelon left for Savannah on April 12th. It was at this point that the 500th, which had had no losses in training, lost its first crew, Lt. Shepherd's, who crashed while flying through weather. Our route was to Hensley Field, Dallas to Tucson to Sacramento, but "Rip" Anacker managed to get weathered in (?) at Hollywood for three days enroute. The flight echelon spent about two weeks in Sacramento before going to Hamilton doing what people generally did there at that time, topping it off with a group formation and close order drill at 0900 every morning—ugh! Finally, near the end of April four man crews started leaving for Hawaii.

Meanwhile the ground echelon went with

all the standard impediments to meet its troop train on April 16th and waited until late afternoon for a train due to leave in the morning. Once under way, however, things proved comfortable enough with berths or compartments for all. The week's stay at Stoneman followed the usual pattern of final overseas indoctrination training and quick trips to Frisco and a last Stateside view from the "Top of the Mark" for a few fortunate ones. Then came the boarding of the troop ship SS *President Johnson* on April 30, 1943.

Meanwhile the flight echelon was on its way. At Hickam the crews were reunited, ships gone over and small bomb bay tanks installed for the rest of the trip and they were once again

RAIDERS

on their way. Next stop was Christmas Island—a place devoid of women and where liquor was bringing $75.00 per quart. Tutuila was an interesting stop. Some Marines tipped the crews off to a native dance featuring good looking tan native girls in beautiful formals and barefooted—and the gals could jitter-bug! About half of the men had dates and the rest checked out on the local liquor. Some of the boys also saw some of the native dances held in observance of some religious occasion; the dances lasted all night and were said to excel any Hollywood production.

Nandi was next and here the boys of the flight echelon tasted their first Aussie beer—'nuff said! They went from Nandi to Amberly

the same day—by virtue of the International Date Line. It was on this leg of the trip that Lt. McLean crashed (no one killed), and Lt. Poe was seriously injured in a jeep accident. Amberly was reached about 1700 and instead of the expected rest the crews were told to fly north to Reid River the next day, May 17th. There they moved in with the 408th Squadron and started training—bombing from 7-8000" with D-8 sights, and bombardiers started training navigators who were to lead flights in combat.

There was one sub scare near Brisbane—shortly after the Nips had sunk a large Aussie hospital ship. Life aboard ship was of the standard variety featuring a home talent show and the customary ceremony marking the crossing of the Equator—the full significance of which was probably not impressed upon the flight echelon. The troops were able to leave the ship for three days when they reached Brisbane on May 26th and were quartered at Camp Doomban, a former race track. It was then that the boat echelon first tasted their Aussie beer and the event was celebrated appropriately. It was also their initiation into the mysteries of foreign exchange. At first the problem was solved by merely holding out a handful of currency and inviting the creditor to take his due, but the Yanks soon learned it was cheaper to take a little time out and study the Aussie system of finance. All in all, the first taste of Australia was pleasant, especially the reasonable prices for food. The climate was a bit of a shock with hot days and cold (nine blanket) nights.

On May 29th the Squadron reboarded the *President Johnson* and embarked for Port Moresby, New Guinea, where they arrived on June 5th. As the ship entered the harbor at Moresby, many a man was wondering why the Nips didn't come over the ship and attack us since we were now in "combat." An advance echelon from Group had arrived earlier to prepare the area for the troops. The Squadron area itself was on a wooded hillside—and now the overseas troubles began.

We might briefly outline at this time the Squadron staff organization as it began its overseas life. The C. O. was Charles M. Hagest; Adjutant was Alexander T. McCurdie, Jr.; the Personnel Officer was Curtis R. Erspamer; Intelligence, John C. Hanna; Operations, William J. Caroli; Supply, Martin Holtzman; Medical Officer, George J. Fleury; Communi-

Hardships at Columbia, bivouac style

Shindig at EM club in Columbia.
You name 'em.

Deuces Wild: Dougherty, Levy, Geer, O'Brien.

Operations and S-2 at Welterboro

cations, Irwin Levy; Engineering, Farnham H. Hessel; Armament, John O'Brien; Ordnance, Harold DeWeil.

It was these officers and their men who faced New Guinea back in the early days when we will all admit it was "rough;" they were short of materials, tools and experience but somehow they made it. It rained all the first night and then the mosquitoes came. The 43rd Group sent over some hot coffee which did much to restore our faith in mankind and somehow about three weeks later the area was liveable. On June 21st the flight echelon arrived and began flying missions from Jackson Drome.

At first the missions consisted chiefly of dropping supplies to bands of Aussie troops isolated in the rugged Owen Stanley range. It was on one of these runs on June 27th near Salamaua that the 500th lost its first crew in combat when Lt. Ow crashed into a peak while flying through weather.

To make the Group more effective it was decided that the planes be modified into strafers and they were flown to Townsville for this purpose. This was also the Squadron's introduction to Sydney for while awaiting completion of the modification, Lts. Mortensen, "Chief" Howard, Stepp and Stine managed to discover its wonders and brought back appropriate reports. This episode also had its very tragic side when, while the modification was underway, 20 of our combat and ground personnel bound for leave in Sydney were lost in a C-47 which crashed into the Bay.

As a bit of sauce for the memory for some of the men who flew back in those days, some of the pilots and ship numbers went something as follows: Lt. Peterson, 061; Lt. Mortensen, 055; Lt. Van Auddell, 068; Lt. C. W. Howard, 079; Lt. McLean, 312; and Lt. Anacker, 048.

On September 17th the 500th got the first Nip plane downed by the Group. It was credited to Sgt. C. W. Brown who was flying with Lt. Howard on a single plane pamplet-dropping mission over the Finschafen area.

It was during this time that we learned further news of Lt. Stookey's crew which had been shot down at Wewak, October 16th and was last seen in their raft off Cape Moem. Word was received through a missionary that some airmen, quite possibly our crew, were beheaded by the Japanese in the Wewak area.

Two days after this strike, the 500th, flew one of the most heroic, breath-taking and daring missions of the Pacific War. Nine of our A/P's were scheduled to bomb shipping in Vunapope Harbor in the Rabaul area as part of a very large coordinated strike. Our nine planes staged out of Dobadura; three A/P's turned back because of mechanical failure. The

Moving in at Moresby: left to right, Cullitan, Carro, McLean, Frye, Bobker, Brasko.

scheduled fighter cover and eight squadrons of heavies had turned back because of weather.

Capt. Anacker's flight dropped five one-thousand pounders on a freight transport, lifting it out of the water. Then things got rough, enemy fighters dove to the attack, hitting Lt. Wallace's right engine which he had to feather. Anacker and Peterson then flew as escort for the cripple until Peterson was hit and forced to ditch and seven or eight Nips strafed him. Capt. Anacker and Lt. Wallace, flying Tondelayo, continued on and headed for home. At Cape Gazelle, however, 40 or 50 Nips were waiting. Lt. Mortensen's flight was able to defend itself pretty well but Capt. Anacker and Lt. Wallace, in his crippled ship, bore the brunt of the attack which ran for approximately an hour and ten minutes at wave-top level. During the engagement, from Cape Gazelle to several miles below Cape Dampier on the New Britain south coast, five Zeeks were claimed shot down by Lt. Wallace's gunner and two by Capt. Anacker's gunner which were seen by Lt. Wallace's crew.

One nervy Jap eased into formation between the two Mitchells and flew for more than a minute not over fifty feet from either of them. Our gunners dared not fire for fear of hitting the other plane; the Nip was described as a "mean looking bastard."

The activity inside our planes during this wild chase can well be imagined; in Tondelayo gas was leaking and fumes filled the aft part of the plane causing the radio man to pass out for a while. More ammo had to be passed over the bomb bay to the busy turret gunner. Even the co-pilot, Lt. Hicko, got some good licks in by firing at the Zekes with his .45 until a fighter's bullet went through his stomach, seriously wounding him.

In the vicinity of Cape Kwoi on the south coast of New Britain, Capt. Anacker's plane was apparently damaged by fighters and headed for shore when about 12 miles out. He

was last seen near the coast losing altitude and still under attack. More about him later . . .

Meanwhile, Lt. Wallace continued on alone, finally heading for Kiriwina with the Japs becoming more frenzied all the time. They became so daring that four crashed into the water as they wheeled low to attack Tondelayo which was flying at 30 feet. Despite having his ship crippled by the loss of one engine and by more than 41 gaping holes, Lt. Wallace met head-on attacks four times by climbing into them and then turning into his dead engine to get down to his former level. The attacks dwindled, the Japs appeared to be less eager and soon all but one had turned back. The remaining Zeke, apparently out of ammunition, did several rolls, finally waggled his wings and headed for home. Lt. Wallace landed Tondelayo at Kiriwina where Lt. Hicko was successfully operated on. Counting the four Nips who "augered in" trying to get at Tondelayo, 14 fighters were claimed by the Squadron as a result of that one mission. In recognition of the Squadron's fine work, the men received the Distinguished Unit Citation and numerous Silver Stars and DFC's.

To return briefly to Capt. Anacker who was last seen losing altitude and heading for shore—he ditched successfully and all but the radio man got out of the plane. The navigator, Lt. Migliacci, got out safely and supported S/Sgt. Hardy, the engineer-gunner, for an hour, before he died in his arms. Lt. Migliacci made his way safely to shore. Capt. Anacker was seen afloat in the water but nothing has been heard of him since. Sgt. Henderson made his way to shore by himself near Cape Kwoi where both he and Lt. Migliacci, through native contacts, independently reached an Aussie spotter station some 20 miles west of Rabaul. They remained there from October until March when they were picked up by a Catalina and flown to Finschafen and eventually returned to the States. While they were on New Britain,

The first overseas orderly room. Port Moresby

the Squadron ran numerous supply missions to their camp dropping food, clothing, papers, ammo and letters.

The story isn't quite complete. Valiant Tondelayo was fitted with a new engine, a new blade for the prop of the good engine, a new wing, new radio equipment and many other repairs. She flew a little more combat and then was assigned to fat-cat duty and renamed "Chow Hound" with an appropriate picture replacing the seductive lass formerly gracing the fuselage. "Chow Hound" brought home the bacon faithfully until San Marcelino days when he got lost in weather south of the Philippines, ditched successfully—and that was the end of Tondelayo.

Such was the combat flown from Moresby and the staging from Dobadura. But as rough as the missions were then, it wasn't all fighting; chow was fairly good, what with fat-cats bringing fresh food, even ice cream in dry ice from Australia ever so often. There were some good times too, in the officers' and enlisted men's clubs. The enlisted men decided to build a combination club, PX and day room. It was a product of Stateside energy and feeling of comradeship created by the introduction of combat into their lives. The thought may also have been in the back of some minds that on the few occasions when liquor was available, competition might be offered to the din and clamor which emanated nightly from the officers' club.

Under President Jimmy Walker and Manager Gene Tubbs and with the help of numerous others, a series of parties were held which made the fire-breathing horse of the Raiders a suitable mascot for our men. Typical incidents that will long be remembered were the rise and fall of our line chief, the "shoot a hundred quid" nights, the Schryver-Baker table-tennis matches, the abuse nightly heaped upon the head of the C. Q. when he turned off the lights at 2400, the obstacle of the big ditch

in front of the club, which never failed to trap numerous slightly loaded merry-makers trying to find the way back to their tents, the piggy-back ride given to "crippled" Guetgemann by Werner, Baker and Dornan, and the Houdeshell belligerancy. The move north to Dobadura meant the end of the club house and, unfortunately, the end of the club, for it was at Dobo that it was dissolved, not to be resurrected until we were stationed at Clark Field, many, many months later. In the meantime many hours were logged reminiscing about the times and characters the mention of club brought to mind.

We mentioned an officers' club—there was one that kept the tin roof of the place ringing. It was a tropical structure made of plywood, tin and local building materials and constructed by the officers themselves. An important feature of the club was the bar at one end, well stocked with Aussie liquor which added much to the spirit of the club. Many gala parties were held there, especially one big one opening the place. These clubs, both officers' and enlisted men's, served a real function in bringing together men whose daily duties might not have given them such a chance to make each other's acquaintance. Red Cross girls and Aussie enlisted women also provided added attractions to an otherwise womanless base.

Moresby was also the site of some early engineering feats, particularly by two members of the S-2 section, Lts. Carter and Bomberger. Lt. Carter organized a marvelous laundry set-up, ingeniously devised from gas drums, a salvaged truck motor and heaven knows what all else. It is readily understandable what a boon this really efficient laundry was in the Guinea jungles. Lt. Bomberger supervised the construction of a streamlined incinerator that, despite its lowly function, was a showplace and a work of art. About six weeks were spent constructing it and we've wondered ever since

Tondelayo — Before

Tondelayo — After

how we got along without one just like it. Speaking of engineering it's too bad that the Engineers who constructed our mess hall at Moresby didn't do something about those cascades of rain water that rushed through the hillside building. Remember how the mess hall stoves used to blow up ever so often? But those were trials soon to be over.

After staging out of Dobadura for some time, the flight echelon finally moved there permanently and was soon followed by the ground echelon in late December. The new area had formerly been occupied by the 22nd Group. The latter left their buildings intact, which saved us considerable work. It was not, however, much of an area, being located in low, swampy country. There was no provision for showers; bathing was done in the nearby river—liver flukes or no liver flukes.

By the way in case anyone was wondering, the submarine painted on the Rough Raider's scoreboard was chalked up on Feb. 17th by Lt. Shirreffs while flying a shipping strike in the New Hanover area. He dropped two 1000-pounders in quick succession, one less than 50 feet from the sub. As he racked his plane up sharply, his crew saw the sub lifted bodily above the surface where amidst violent upheaval of water, it appeared to bounce a few times. A sheet of flame obscured the vessel and the claim for destruction appears justifiable.

It was while flying out of Dobo that the C. O., Maj. Hagest, really sweated on a mission. While releasing bombs, the co-pilot accidentally cut the master switch and everything went "out" on the plane for no apparent reason. Just in time the Major discovered the trouble and fortunately was able to restart his engines.

We had a very nice native-built nipa officers' club with a veranda and garden at Dobo, another heritage left by the 10th Bomb Squadron. There was a nearby Coast Artillery band to liven it up occasionally. What with an adequate supply of Aussie liquor available and a good number of Army nurses not too far away, the set-up wasn't bad at all. The club was also used by the enlisted men for their parties.

Some of the things the boys who were there will especially recall were the big birds with the plaintive wail who rocked us asleep at night and awakened us in the morning with the weirdest sounds this side of the Styx; the rats which played in the tents and slid down the roofs during the night; the Squadron's own little movie run by Sgts. Guetgemann and Bynum which caught its share of sarcasm as every light in the area had to be turned off to get enough electricity to run the speaker and

Bomberger's Folly

projector at the same time. "Turn 'em out or we'll shoot 'em out!" At best everyone had to huddle around the speaker to hear what was going on. Every man in the Squadron was on the look-out for films for we wanted a movie every night—and usually had it too.

Chow at Dobo wasn't bad but the fat-cats were doing much to relieve its standard GI overseas monotony. We all gratefully recall Sgt. Murphy's "Open House" kitchen. Coffee and sandwiches were available any hour of the day or night. Murphy was there practically all the time—later he transferred to combat flying and was killed on a flight from Nadzab.

In mid-January, Capt. McCurdie and an advance echelon left for our next base, Nadzab, and by late February we were flying missions from there. The Nadzab period was difficult for many of us in our stay overseas. Morale was not too high. The Squadron was flying missions regularly and only a few crews had gone on leave. Missions were more or less routine ground support strikes along the New Guinea coast, hitting troops and air installations with an occasional shipping strike thrown in for good measure. On one of these,

"Mort" and Aussies Timms, and Connors, soberly discussing International problems at Dobo.

171

however, a co-pilot temporarily lost his mind in the cockpit and took things into his own hands. He was subdued at the point of a gun held by the pilot while the engineer flew the plane back to the base.

In May we celebrated, if that is the proper word, one year since we left the States. Many of us weren't so happy about it; nearly all the original combat men had gone home. We were glad to see this good fortune come their way, but their glowing letters upon return only made us long for Home all the more. That is, when we received their letters. The mail service became very poor. There were weeks when we did not receive any mail and then, at times, it took three to four weeks for a letter to arrive when it formerly reached us in two. Mail was a thing of utmost importance to us overseas and its absence or delay was keenly felt, we might say, resented. Remember how a decrease in mail delivery was enough to start rumors of final preparations for an impending major operation? "All the C-47s are being used to fly stuff up to——."

On the 17th of May a blow causing great indignation was struck the Squadron—the Group C. O. banned Sgt. Eddy Ison from pitching in certain of the league softball games. It was really fair enough though, considering that Eddy had pitched the team to a perfect record. The only games he was to be permitted to pitch were against teams thought to have fair chance against him. After the first bursts of protest by the Rough Raiders subsided the team settled down and carried on its unblemished record under the pitching of Pfc. H. E. Burton.

Then there was the tent furling order from V Bomber, tents were to be furled once a month to permit the ground to dry inside, so shortly after we were set up at Nadzab we received the order—"furl your tents." In typical "Maypole Dance" style they were wrapped around the center pole—several were burned up when

Work starts on the orderly room at Nadzab

shorts were caused in the wiring—some were ripped in the process and of course once we had them furled it rained in torrents. That was the last of the tent furling.

It was while we were staging at Hollandia from Nadzab that the tragic bomb explosion on the Hollandia strip occured. One of our pilots opened his bomb bay doors after taxiing into the space alloted our Squadron and two parademos fell out to the ground. Evidently he believed he had dropped all his bombs over the target but these two had hung temporarily. In the ensuing explosion, 12 men of the 500th were killed and several others wounded, including four of the six crew members. Other members of the Squadron exhibited great heroism in aiding wounded men and taxiing nearby planes to safety.

The engineers out on the Line solved a little personal problem in their own way at Nadzab. One of their fellows, Sgt. Sire, had established for himself, in all innocence, and as his idea of fun, a reputation as a fighter, giving off with pugnacious stances and remarks, until the line began to get a little tiring to his buddies. M/Sgt. Schulz "stopped his clock" with this little bit of drama: couple of

Nadzab

EM area in the garden spot of New Guinea

Schulz's Aussie friends jeeped over to see him. Sire and some of the other engineers were about and Schulz walked over to the jeep to talk with them. When he returned he told Sire that he had just matched him in some fights the Aussies were known to be holding weekly.

The realism was too much for Sire who immediately offered numerous excuses for not being able to go through with the arrangements. Of course the other fellows witnessing the scene all added their "two-bits" worth to the discussion. Finally Schulz's ruse was revealed but Sire, who was really a good fellow, was cured and peace reigned once again over the Engineering Section.

In early July out of a mass of rumors and a bit of official confusion came the fact that we were to move to Biak, where we had flown support missions during the invasion of that island. Our advance echelon was dispatched to that newly-won base on July 23rd.

On August 28th Capt. Mortensen took over the Squadron as C. O. moving up from his operations post. Lt. Frederick W. Dick was our new S-3. Many of our old men had gone back to the States and we were flying an average of six combat missions a week. Not only were we short of combat men but we could have used more men on the Line too. That coral strip was one of the hottest places in the Pacific . . . Remember the transition from Aussie money to Dutch? Those fifty-three cent guilders did make things a little easier—but there wasn't much to buy on Biak. We were close enough to Nip strongholds here to get in on the receiving end of some raids. Once, three bombs landed in our dispersal area resulting in minor damage to three planes. There was the two-hour-and-forty minute raid by eight Nips on little Owi, not so far from our area. We'll bet more fellows were scared the night

the C. Q. came around warning us of the gas alert. The Allies took Paris in August. Remember the lift it gave us and the speculation it caused as to when we would get some more help over here?

One of the 500th's many "firsts" was scored on the night of September 2nd and 3rd when Lt. Whitsell was the only one of the four planes on a night shiping mission to Davao Gulf to complete his assignment. This was the Group's first strike to the Philippines in its advance northward—hence the "first" for the 500th.

On the 4th of September T/Sgt. Neal Ryan had completed his hundredth mission, a strike to the southwest coast of Moratai. The mission turned back due to weather, but here we might say a bit more about this man Ryan. He was with the outfit since activation, previous to joining the 500th he had completed a bombardier's course and was carried as a Bombardier-Navagitor in the Squadron until these ratings for enlisted personnel were disallowed. He then flew as a gunner. In April of 1944 the Squadron was short of Bombardier-Navigators and his training was recalled. With

Tragedy at Hollandia

173

Biak

a little refresher course and his native enthusiasm for flying he proved very capable in his new role. He chalked up the Group Record for both the number of missions flown and combat hours. Our little "Iron Man" finished up with 113 missions and 658:12 hours and went home from Clark Field. He had won promotions to Flight Officer, then 2nd Lt. and finally 1st Lt. and had served as Squadron Navigator.

Having thrown so much at the Japs up until now, the Rough Raiders decided to add the traditional "Kitchen Sink." The idea originated with T/Sgt. Fred Guetgemann, S-2 Section Chief. The sheet-metal men rigged up a good likeness, installed two faucets and painted it a gleaming white. The names of the crew who were to drop in were painted alongside the names of the men who built it. It was dropped on Sidate Drome, northwest Celebes on September 19th.

We didn't know it then, but our stay at Biak was drawing to a close so we will briefly review some of the final memories of such things as: the red alerts and the Group order for covered fox holes. Well and good but we had insufficient tools (five picks and three shovels) for 300 men to cope with the coral of Biak, so dynamite was found and used to dig our fox holes quickly.

On September 10th the movement orders came and after some hurried activity we left Biak on the SS *Charles Lumis* which was quite comfortably fitted for troops. The trip to Lae was uneventful but there we were transferred to a Liberty Ship the SS *Morrison R. Waite* which was almost completely unequipped for troop duty. There were no bunks, no mess hall, no latrines and no means of securing water for washing or drinking purposes. Sleeping arrangements were on deck (taking a chance on the weather), or in the stuffy, dark holds. After the first feeling of disgust had subsided the 500th settled down to make the best of the

situation, a latrine system was set up, cots were broken out. Shortly after leaving Lae to join our convoy at Hollandia a portable mess hall was set up on deck; the food turned out to be the best we had enjoyed overseas but even then, it took hours to finish a meal from the time you first got in line until you washed your mess kit—oh, well, what else was there to do on a ship like this? On the 20th of October, Lt. "Ike" Baker, 501st Assistant S-2, in one of his daily news casts gave us word of the Leyte landings. Now the whole pattern began to take more definite shape and we heard we were due to arrive at D day-plus 9.

On October 21st we reached Hollandia and were all impressed by the shipping in the Harbor, about 50 vessels of various types. The next day when we were at anchor some of us swam near the ship. Then we had a real surprise—mail sent down to us by the flight echelon and nearly every man had at least one letter. We left Hollandia on the 23rd with about 31 ships in our convoy. The voyage north was fairly uneventful. We were glad to cross the Equator though, because we felt we were on our way home then. Of course the ships were all blacked out which made things stuffy and uncomfortable but the continued excellence of the chow kept morale fairly good. We were always eager for news of the campaign on Leyte.

We sighted Leyte at 1630 on the 29th, and quite a spectacle it was, with the harbor filled with ships. We had a red alert the first night but nothing happened.

The night of October 30th will be long remembered by those on the *Waite;* it was the night of the typhoon. There was quite a commotion on deck as we had men sleeping there under tarpaulins and shelter halves. The wind tore most of these loose and flung them about. Blankets, cots, air mattresses, clothing, etc., were scattered about the boat and some blown over the side. Meanwhile the men in the hold

174

were fairly comfortable. About 0100 there was a terrific explosion. A ship a short distance from us blew up in the harbor. All the ships turned their lights on and we could see men floating around in the water. The wind was so high though that it was almost impossible for anything to pick them up. Cause of the explosion was unknown. Another Liberty ship came close to ramming us. The wind was so strong that it was necessary to run the engines to keep from dragging anchor.

Meanwhile we were encouraged by the good news of our Navy's victory over the Nip fleet and another landing on the southeast shore of Leyte. From our ship in the harbor we could hear the guns on shore fire and see the smoke from their muzzles and from where the shells were landing. At night it was almost beautiful. The gun flashes and tracer patterns were an unusual sight and the moon was so bright we could play cards by its light.

This was also our first contact with the Filipinos. They came out in their canoes offering to trade Japanese money and other souvenirs for clothes and food. They appeared fairly

Everything including the kitchen sink: Roma,

Jones, Ryerson, Ostroot

intelligent and were sharp traders. The women were very cleanly dressed in American style clothes; the majority of the men were also clean but their clothes were of a more make-shift variety.

It was not until the fifth of November that some men for detail were taken off the boat and brought to the proposed Squadron area by Duck; things had been fairly quite on the ship until then and continued so until November, 12th when tragedy struck us.

Two Kamikazes attacked the SS *Thomas Nelson* which carried the 498th, 499th and most of Group Headquarters plus 26 men from the 500th at 1128/I. Eighty-nine men were killed and 50 to 100 injured.

That same day our own ship, the SS *Morrison R. Waite* became the victim of another

such suicide attack. The red alert sounded at 1818/I. Two enemy planes were seen approaching from the port side off the stern of the ship. As the two planes came even with the stern, one of them peeled off to make a pass at the *Waite*. The ship's guns had opened fire and scored several hits but they did not cause the enemy's plane to veer away from his course. As the Nip came abreast of the ship he made a deliberate suicidal dive into the hull of the vessel. The force of the impact was so great that the enemy aircraft was carried through the hull into the bowels of the ship.

When the alert had been sounded, all personnel were ordered into the hold. The men didn't particularly care for the idea as there were only two wooden staircases for exits. They were aware of what might happen if the ship were hit. They also realized that their presence on deck during an air alert would offer a luscious target, but they would have been content to take their chances. At least they would be able to jump overboard. Nonetheless, they were ordered into the hold and there they remained.

There were approximately 120 men below decks at the time of the attack. The enemy plane plunged into the hold and immediately burst into flames. Apparently there was a bomb in the aircraft's rack as a terrific explosion followed. The concussion blew the hatch covers from the main deck causing them and the shattered bits of aircraft to fall into the lower hold. The vehicles that were stored on the top deck were jounced around but luckily enough they did not fall into the hold.

The 500th, surprisingly enough, came through with the lowest number of casualties. Previously our Squadron had been the "hard luck" outfit. We had lost the most airplanes and crews of any Squadron, but all that we suffered in this ordeal were three men with minor wounds. A goodly number of our men, however, suffered from shock and were fairly jumpy for some time afterwards.

The men who had been taken off the ship for detail, meanwhile, were landed in a fairly nice area near a river and also near several batteries of 155's which, unfortunately, worked the night shift. A few of the little incidents they should recall were: how they alerted the Infantry when they started some carbine target practice . . . The fifty bags of Jap and American cement found at Burauen, two or three miles from camp. This we used to floor all of our buildings. Then they will remember the young typhoon that hit the night of the ninth and how Group took over our truck and lumber when it came off the boat. Then there was November 11th, the second anniversary of the activation of the 500th . . . the miserable rains that kept on while we were waiting for a definite area to be assigned us. Finally on November 16th we moved to our new area at Dulag, fifty yards from the ocean.

Now to get back to the flight echelon which had stayed back at Biak. For the most part life was uneventful. Our Squadron was the last to receive the new B-25Js, and considerable time was spent on acceptance checks, making minor modifications and testing them, so there were not many days when sufficient planes were available for a combat mission. Since we had received quite a few new crews, and because we realized our missions in the near future would be much like those former ones to Rabaul and Wewak, Capt. Mortensen flew our crews on many training missions, stressing particularly close formation flying, approach, breakaway and proper spacing on take-off and landing. Even radio operators and engineers were given additional training in their duties. It was evident that there would be definite need for talents such as the Air Apaches' in our new sphere of operations. None of the October missions were unusual—except for the time Lt. Rasmussen came home so low on gas that he didn't have enough to taxi his plane to the hardstand. For the most part days of maintenance and training and occasional couriers slipped by. Japs sneaking into the Squadron area provided a little excitement; Capt. Cole of our Squadron shot one near his shack; the Nip was dressed in officer's khaki with a 1st Lt.'s bar and was carrying a bottle of gin.

Other than this, life back at Biak was fairly easy with November being high-lighted by such things as Lt. Bissel returning from a courier to Leyte with shrapnel-wounded Col. "Pappy" Gunn. When staging out of Moratai on November 7th there was a red alert at 0345/I. Our boys were pre-flighting the planes at Pitoe strip when a Jap plane swooped in, strafing down the runway. There were no casualties but it surely did scare our men. Lt. Symington was put on Squadron Orders as the new Operations Officer on November 14th, after Lt. Dick was shot down in Ormoc Bay.

Meanwhile, how has the ground echelon been getting along up at Dulag? The area was cleaned up without too much difficulty. For a while there were the LCT's to unload; those our Squadron unloaded seemed to come in either at chow time, red alert time or in the rain. Speaking of rain, along about the 23rd of November it had rained so much the ground could take no more and a ditch had to be dug to drain surface water off to the sea.

December was the month Behymer joined the Communications Section. He surprised many by flying a box kite as soon as he had disposed of his gear and provided several interesting moments for us since. By the 21st we were nine days without mail except for a handful of letters and a few beat-up packages. On the 24th some went to nearby Christmas services, lounged around on the free afternoon. On Christmas Day, Mansueto's men gave one of the most elaborate meals overseas: fruit cocktail, ice cold tomato juice, roast turkey, giblet gravy, mashed potatoes, bread stuffing, golden corn, jam and peanut butter, bread, cinnamon rolls, sugar twists, pumpkin and chocolate pie and coffee. After a reasonable breathing spell there was a volley ball game. An officer's team challenged the enlisted men but weren't quite good enough and were beaten two out of three. The Filipinos, too, took advantage of Christmas. They roamed through the area stopping at almost every tent with the greeting: "Merry Christmas—what you give me for Christmas? Give me some soap." If they received a negative reply they would ask for powder, gum or candy. Every one that came around already had a box full of odds and ends picked up from the easy-going Yanks. Some mail did come in for Christmas delivery, but not as much as should have arrived. Near the end of the month big events were a welcome beer issue, the transfer of Capt. McCurdie to the 309th Bomb Wing with Capt. Erspamer advancing to the Executive post, and our first fresh meat since arriving on Leyte. That certainly was a treat. All future leaves to Sydney were cancelled. The flying personnel were coming up from Biak to our new base.

During the first ten days of January the ground echelon moved from Dulag to Tacloban where the flight echelon was also assembling. Thus for the first time in many months the whole Squadron was together.

On January 9th on a rolling stock mission on Luzon, Lt. Buffington was hit by enemy fire and had to crash-land his plane in the vicinity of Clark Field. Three members of the crew were killed in the crash and two were murdered by the Japs. T/Sgt. Walter J. Nelson, the radio-gunner, was the only crew member who escaped and was rescued by friendly Filipinos. When the Filipinos returned to the scene of the crash they found the rest of the crew sprawled in and out of the plane—their throats cut by Jap soldiers.

Our heaviest casualties were suffered by the Squadron during January. In that month alone we lost five airplanes and 15 men.

Meanwhile on the ground the first few days of January were marked by much rain, occasional red alerts (including bombing not so far from our area), and preparations for

the move from Dulag to Tacloban. It was during this period that Lt. Munro joined our Squadron as Adjutant. He had been with the Group originally in the States, was transferred out before it left, but was able to rejoin it when he came overseas as a casual. He had been Group I and E Officer before coming to the 500th.

Near mid-January some of the communications boys made preparations for a dance which was to feature local girls. The girls came in their Sunday best with lipstick and powder. The Yanks exhibited their best manners and all in all it was a gala affair. T/Sgts. Guetchman and Hugh D. Smith were the first two men to go home on the 30-day furlough plan, an encouraging sign to all of us.

Along about the 10th of February we sent a plane and crew to Hawaii; they were to navigate some fighters back from there to the Philippines—what a lucky break it was for that crew!

On February 11th came orders for eleven planes and crews to go to San Marcelino. This was a prelude to a move to this area by the whole Group. Maj. Mortensen and Lt. Reheis flew to our new area, by way of Manila, where the Major's plane picked up two ack ack holes in the stabilizer. Men were gradually going up to Marcelino to set up the new area along about the middle of February which was also the time a fat-cat from Cairns came in. Stories about our new area were coming back from those who had seen it; it was in a dry level plain' with mountains or hills on three sides; hot during the day, cool at night and apt to be windy and dusty. Water was a bit of a problem but a well was being dug. We were to stay there about a month and then move to Clark Field; hence no permanent buildings could be set up, just tents. A day or two after the Executive Officer arrived at Marcelino, a man was sent to look over our new area at Clark Field.

An unusual incident occured during the ground support mission to Bataan on February 16th when Lt. Herrick was unable to release a hung-up 1,000-pounder. All crew members parachuted to safety. A P-47 shot our plane down near the San Marcelino area.

In the meantime, more personnel were moving up to our new area at San Marcelino and on the afternoon of the 19th of February we learned that our C. O., Maj. Mortensen had been moved to the post of Group Operations Officer and our new C. O. was Capt. Bazzel. A few days later our First Sergeant was evacuated to the hospital at Biak and T/Sgt. Oskea from Communications was named acting First Sergeant. Things came along normally in our Squadron, the showers were installed by the end of the month, but the well over near the mess hall kept caving in for a long time. In fact, despite all efforts of Lt. Silverstein and Bates and Prim, the thing never did produce much water.

March was a bad month for the Squadron as far as casualties and loss of airplanes was concerned. We lost 16 men killed in action, six missing in action, and four planes were lost in combat. We were far ahead of any other Squadron in the Group in enemy shipping sunk and Jap planes shot down, but we also led in the number of casualties.

The camp area was completely set up by the end of March and we were now getting passes to some of the nearby towns. The barrios most frequently visited by the men were San Marcelino, Castillejos, Subic Bay, Olongapo, San Narcisso and San Filipe. Every night about 1800 a truck left for San Marcelino and Subic Bay. The truck would pick its passengers up at 2145 and bring them back to camp. The area itself proved very comfortable. There was ample room for each Squadron, the climate was very good and the surrounding hills gave us an attractive view. It was here that we had a much better chance to know the Filipinos. They did some work in our area such as constructing grass walls and caves for our tents, working in the mess, doing laundry or trading or selling fruit. Some of the men became acquainted with particular families and some interesting friendships were established.

Some of the things we can remember at San Marcelino: Joe Newman parading the area, wearing nothing but a helmet, a .45 and a Jap sword; the weird noises and raucous cries emanating nightly from the tent of Kusbaich and Norman, long after everyone else had gone to sleep; the phonograph from the same tent blaring forth with "The Fireman's Polka" at 0230 hours; the all-night poker games presided over by Canning and Loisel with the former's famous cry, "You lose!" becoming anathema to unfortunate losers; the night we had the Jap infiltration scare and we came piling across the road in shorts, shoes, and .45's to sleepily man the battle stations; the day the brush fire came uncomfortably close to our area (many a "wheel" was out there coughing in the smoke and beating out the flames); the hole that Rameses and Hardships, the two Squadron dogs, dug in the tent of the Lily Whiters, into which everyone fell the night of the famous Prayer Meeting, the "It's op to you, sor," of the Filipino girls, and last but not least, the adventure of 1st Sgt. Oskea and the incendiary latrine. Oskea had retired to the latrine one morning to smoke a cigar and read the paper. Being Saturday, the latrine orderly had poured an amount of 80-octane down the latrine to burn up the excess paper. Before he could light the gas he spied the inspectors making their rounds so he grabbed his broom and beat a hasty retreat. As the 1st Sgt. was enjoying his cigar and reading the sports page he casually lifted the neighboring cover to deposit some cigar ashes. There was a terrific explosion and latrine covers flew in every direction. Fortunately the Sergeant was not injured in this accident but the whole Squadron profited by his experience.

An advance echelon of 25 enlisted men under Capt. Erspamer was sent to Clark Field to prepare for our move there. It was to be a 65-mile move by truck to Clark, including a trip through Zig Zag Pass, site of a big battle and a rough enough road in its own right. The heavy rains were due to start at San Marcelino during early May and we wanted to move before they started.

On May 10th the Squadron officially moved from San Marcelino to Clark Field. The move was made by truck; however some of the equipment and personnel were flown up in our B-25s. The advance echelon had the area cleared and the main buildings set up so all the rest of the Squadron had to construct was their living quarters. Considerable ingenuity was exhibited in this construction and the shacks there were, on the whole, more elaborate than any we had elsewhere overseas.

An enlisted men's club was erected from two portable buildings and T/Sgt. Mohlke was elected president. The club was furnished very nicely with booths and tables occupying half the building while the other half provided a reading room and game room. Some condemned parachutes were dyed various colors and suspended from the rafters. This, added to the other efforts of the men to furnish and decorate the club, made it one of the nicest we had seen anywhere overseas.

With our arrival in the Phillipines and the consequent good laundry service, Capt. Carter's laundry contraption was abandoned at Tacloban. Here at Clark, just to keep things organized, we established some conveniences for a local citizen who had contracted to do the laundry for our Squadron; S/Sgt. Lanning was put in charge of the enterprise and any remaining laundry problems were quickly solved.

It was in May that we filled out our "Adjusted Service Rating Cards" and could begin thinking more or less seriously about going home. It was also about this time that we sent some of our over-40-year-old men home for discharge; we lost some of our old standbys when they left us.

Other memories of Clark Field: Paukovich and Sawyer allowing themselves to be put in for captaincies, and then sweating it out in reverse, both hoping desperately that the tracks wouldn't come through. When Sawyer's bounced, remember the hopeful expectant look on Pauk's face waiting to learn his fate, and then his downcast countenance when he learned that he was now a captain and Sawyer was going home while he remained overseas? Remember the nightly "monster demonstrations" at the shack of Loxell, Lovett and Buffington? The chaos that existed as the Lily Whiters built their shack . . . Loisel's unfortunate propensity for either stopping on Reheis' wounded foot or hitting him on the head, accidentally, of coruse, with two by fours; Andrews' still more unfortunate propensity for crash-landings; the stirring "love affairs" of certain members of the Squadron with Caroline, Christina, Victoria and "Blow Torch" Annie; the grounding of Rameses from any further flights; and many Manila escapades, to numerous to mention.

Then on July 11th, on a shipping strike to Formosa, the Squadron was dealt its hardest blow. Maj. Robert Canning, who succeeded Maj. Bazzel in May and was one of our most beloved C. O.s was shot down in flames at Hukuko point. We could scarcely realize the fact, so great was our sense of personal and communal loss. He was a great and respected leader.

Despite the fact that Clark was to be "permanent base" we were planning to move up. Our new home was to be Ie Shima, just west of Okinawa.

With Maj. Robert Todd as our new C. O., a detail was sent to Subic Bay to attend to loading Squadron material aboard our LST and on about the 10th of July we left Luzon bound for Ie Shima which we reached on July 25th. Our landing there, while not as grueling

That Dulag Christmas Dinner

as that on Leyte, was rather a muddy one. The air echelon remained back at Clark for a few days, but the ground echelon sweated out a very muddy casual camp and Squadron area, complete with red alerts. After three days, however, things got fairly well organized, the flight echelon joined up, and we began to fly missions.

The first was a strike on July 29th aimed at the heart of Japan, the Inland sea. Weather forced us to hit a secondary target which turned out to be a radio and radar station near the southernmost point of Kyushu. The 500th, incidentally, was the first Squadron of the Group to drop bombs on the Nip homeland.

And then V-J Day came, preceded by red alerts, gas alerts, paratrooper alerts and some of the roughest enemy raids that many of us had experienced. The war was over for us and we sat back and waited. We sweated out all sorts of rumors and false alarms. The new men were transferred out to other outfits and we waited—the next stop for us was Home.

Bottoms up at EM Club, Clark Field: Jacobson, Heath, Elwell, Ready, Wachtel, Luno, Doran, Ferry Mohlke, Murry.

179

The Administrative Building at Clark

Some of our men wrote the following accounts of the individual sections in the 500th. To those readers who were not with us in the Pacific they will present a first-hand account of life with the Rough Raiders.

We dedicate this section to the men of the 500th who have gone down, and to the memories and the traditions they have left us.

The scoreboard at Clark Field and Lt. "Salvo" Swallow, Squadron Navigator who went down with Major Canning.

The Staff—Eager Beavers "Pete" Peterson, Joe Gamino (standing), Al Stern, John Dinges (seated) Capt. Sam Andrews.

COMMANDING OFFICER

Being a Squadron Commander was no easy job in the Pacific war. It called for a great share of responsibility and no notable amount of glory. If things went well, the missions were successful, the crews got the credit; if crews were lost in action, the C.O., aside from the grief he naturally felt at the loss of dear friends, would have additional responsibility; if the Squadron area was comfortable, the troops felt that they had only their due; if the area and chow were poor the C. O. was liable to be blamed—so it went. Anything wrong with the organization could be laid at his feet or, more often, would be on his desk in the form of a letter.

Consider the situation. Our youngest commander was 23; our oldest was 26. It was upon the shoulders of young men such as these that the responsibility for the training, physical and mental welfare and combat record of 500 men was placed. As often as not these Commanders had no extensive training for such tasks in civilian life but they rose to the occasion and with the cooperation they inspired in their staffs, officers and enlisted men, welded us into the famous "Fighting Five Hundredth."

As a tribute to the Commanding Officer whom we feel best illustrates these attributes, we dedicate this portion of the 500th's story to Maj. Robert B. Canning, who was tragically lost in battle.

It is a privilege to pay tribute to Maj. Canning, a man truly admired by those who served with him. He commanded men with whom

he had flown and who had watched his quick rise from second lieutenant to major. He never lost his friendly manner but always inspired respect and admiration in all who knew him for his sense of fair play, his manliness in its finest sense of the term, and his all-around leadership.

As a flier, as well, he was far above average and led some of our best-executed missions. He was lost the day his majority came through. He did not even know of his new honor. Word of his promotion reached the Squadron after he had left for the Line and he could not be notified as he was already taxiing for the take off. He had already flown his share of "rough ones" but still carried on,

182

almost beyond the call of duty. Needless to say, his loss was very deeply felt by his Squadron—but even further than that and the loss to his family, do we feel that in Maj. Canning's death the Nation lost a real man. He was still very young but the marks of true manhood and leadership were already upon him.

Our first Commander was Maj. Charles M. Hagest who led us from activation until Nadzab. He was a stocky, good-natured individual and a fine flier, having flown since his youth and with the RCAF until just prior to his entry into the American Air Force.

He was succeeded on March 29th by Maj. Keith E. Dougherty, a flight leader since we left the States, who commanded the Squadron

Major Keith Dougherty

lieutenant colonel. He was a wonderful flier with an extensive flying background, both as a commercial pilot and in the RCAF, and was the second ranking man in the entire Group in combat missions (109), and combat hours (607:45), being exceeded only by his navigator, Lt. Neal Ryan, another 500th man. These

Major Charles Hagest

until he left for home from Biak. He was recommended for the DFC for his important part in rescuing Capt. Hochella's crew which had been shot down near Kavieng. He had over 64 missions when he left the Squadron.

Next was Maj. Max H. Mortensen; we all knew and admired him for he stayed with the Squadron from activation until San Marcelino, where he left us to become first Group Operations Officer, then Deputy Commander, and a

Lt. Col. Mortensen

183

Major Thomas Bazzel

two flew many of their missions together, and left a string of air victories behind them of which the 500th is justly proud.

As a commanding officer, Maj. Mortensen was excellent. He had native ability and experience. His men knew that whatever he asked of them, he could do and probably had done it himself. His fine record won him a reputation as one of the most able and respected airmen in the Theatre. We are proud indeed to know that so much of this record, which began with the Group's activation and ended with its de-activation, was achieved in the 500th.

Maj. Thomas A. Bazzel joined the Squadron as a captain at Biak after having served a tour of duty in the Carribean. He was a quiet, tall, capable, easy-mannered Southerner and things ran smoothly during his administration which covered the San Marcelino period. He left the Squadron to accept the post of Group Operations Officer, when we moved to Clark Field, and was replaced there by Maj. Canning, then a captain.

Major Robert F. Todd filled the sudden and large vacancy left by Maj. Canning's loss and at a difficult time for any C. O.—during the Squadron's move from Clark Field to Ie Shima. He had served ten months in the Aleutians in B-26s and as Group Air Inspector just prior to his arrival in the 500th. He immediately took hold of his duties in a quiet, efficient manner and the Squadron flew on its missions to the Japanese homeland under his capable administration which carried us through to VJ Day.

Major Todd

OPERATIONS OFFICERS

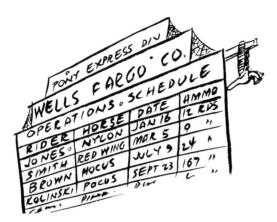

Operations' primary duty was the scheduling and briefing of combat crews to fly on all combat missions and local flights. There were numerous forms to be filled out and many individual records to be kept up to date. The

Weekly Status and Operations Report, the most important of all submitted by the Office, gave complete coverage of all combat experience by the Squadron with a detailed explanation of the happenings on each mission, such as results of strikes, losses, ammo and bombs expended, etc. A report on the status of our aircraft was submitted daily showing how many airplanes the Squadron had in flyable condition for the following day. Operations scheduled all flying personnel for rest leaves to Sydney or Manila when they began to show signs of fatigue and when such leaves were possible. S-3 also had the responsibility of seeing that each crew member's name was submitted for return to the States when he had completed his tour of combat duty.

Upon arrival at Port Moresby the Operations personnel consisted of Capt. Cavoli, Operations Officer; Lt. Cecil Jones, Asst. Operations Officer; Lt. Woldman, Asst. Operations

Captain Cavoli

Captain Speicher

Officer (Adm.) and a host of enlisted men headed by Sgt. Franks as head, Sgt. Epstein, Cpl. Schalla and approximately five more men who were soon to be transferred for lack of seating facilities, or for reassignment to other sections. A few months after the Squadron

Captain Ames

after ditching and this was declared his final mission. At the time of Capt. Mortensen's inaugural the Operations personnel was reduced to Sgts. Franks, Epstein, Schalla, and the newly acquired Sgt. Jones but to the surprise of everyone Operations functioned with its usual brilliancy. Capt. Mortensen continued as Operations Officer during the entire stay at Dobadura and for a period at our next base, Nadzab, from where he left the Squadron on DS to Port Moresby where he was to set up a system of training newly arrived pilots from the States.

In his absence he was succeeded by Capt. Speicher. During his tour of duty, Capt. Speicher will long be remembered for his breaking of the New Guinea mark for the 100-yard dash which he ran in 9.6 when his co-pilot accidently released the bombs of his plane before take off. "I'd of knocked a few more seconds off that figure if I could have gotten rid of that parachute on my back" panted the Captain from a respectable distance. After rattling off 61 missions, Capt. Speicher was grounded from

commenced combat flying Lt. Jones was killed when his plane crashed in the water during a practice bombing run on the Moresby wreck. Lt. Woldman, after six months of operational work was transferred to VBC.

During the reign of Capt. Cavoli some of the most important targets in the New Guinea area were attacked, including Wewak (when it was rough) and Rabaul. Of all the Operations Officers, Capt. Cavoli was perhaps the most accomplished administrator, and he undoubtedly had the finest tenor voice in Squadron history. He was leader of the local choir which besides himself included Capt. Fleury, Lt. Wallace (later pilot of the Squadron's most noted flight), and any one else who happened along. Although their renditions were greatly enjoying to themselves, unfortunately the rest of the Operations personnel did not always share their enthusiasm.

Capt. Cavoli was succeeded on the operational throne by the very capable Capt. Mortensen after the Squadron had moved over the hump to Dobadura. On his 36th mission, a strike on Kavieng, Capt. Cavoli got in the way of Jap ack-ack. He was rescued

Lieutenant Dick

186

combat flying and was transferred to other duties in the theater.

The next Operations Officer was Capt. Ames, an easy-going young man and well liked by the Operations personnel (by this time reduced to the old standbys, Franks and Epstein) as he respected the experience of these two operational experts. By the time Capt. Ames was nearing the end of his tour of combat he was relieved by the returned Capt. Mortensen. The latter continued in office until he became C. O. at the next base at Biak, NEI, and Lt. Dick became S-3. Before the move to Biak, Operations was augmented by Cpl. Marcet, a new arrival from the States whose

Captain Lewis

Captain Reheis

youth and vigor added a refreshing touch to the now wilting Operations enlisted personnel.

Lt. Dick was probably the most popular of all the Operations Officers. Not one to be dictated to, he ran Operations with a gentle but firm hand. While on a routine courier flight to Tacloban, Leyte, he volunteered to lead a mission against Jap supply ships coming into Ormoc Bay, at that time a main Jap bastion on Leyte. Lt. Dick picked out a destroyer as his target but was badly hit before releasing his bombs. Although his plane snap-rolled, Lt.

Dick still continued on his bombing run. After toggling his bombs, his ship was seen headed back for Tacloban but it never reached there. Despite numerous search missions for him nothing was found. His loss was deeply felt by the entire Squadron.

Capt. Symington was appointed the new Operations Officer. He might be best described as an able and progressive leader. Before leaving Biak the Operations personnel was blessed with a new typewriter, and acquisition by the Commanding Officer that was, at first, prized as if it were solid gold and for a time there

Captain Waring

187

was talk of assigning a crew chief for the typewriter. Soon after Capt. Symington's taking over, the Squadron moved to Tacloban. While on a shipping mission Capt. Symington was forced to ditch and was picked up at sea. As was customary, he was given a ten-day leave to Sydney.

Due to transportation difficulties the ten days blossomed into nearly five weeks and a replacement for Capt. Symington was assigned in the person of Capt. Reheis, an officer with considerable Army background. Under the efficient administration of Reheis, the 500th was greatly considered the best Squadron in the Group in formation flying and all other combat performances.

On his scheduled last combat mission, Capt. Reheis was hit in the foot but doggedly continued to fly the plane back to the home base. When asked how it happened he told his listeners: "I guess I forgot to jump."

Capt. Lewis was number eight. This Operations Officer came up the hard way, entering the Squadron as a co-pilot, he soon won the respect of all by his friendly manner and admiration for the way he soon became an accomplished first pilot. Although Capt. Lewis was in office but a short time it was long enough for every one that came in contact with him to label him "a swell guy."

Capt. Waring was next. Hastily put in office, he astonished all with the way he handled his new position and conducted himself as if he were born to the job. His judgment

of men was excellent and when he finally accomplished the impossible by getting Franks and Epstein, both after years of long and arduous service, a promotion, he even won the respect of these two skeptics. Capt. Waring was one of our all time greats in the buzzing department as he proved on a supply hop from Biak to Dulag. He was instructed to fly low over the Squadron area to acquaint the Squadron of his presence but his instructor seemingly failed to tell him how low to fly. In his eagerness to obey instructions Capt. Waring apparently was a little too low and for his pains he was fined $75.00. Capt. Waring was also the enterprising pilot who, in order to confirm a ship sinking, brought back part of it in his engine nacelle.

Upon finishing his tour of duty Capt. Waring was succeeded by Lt. Harper, a former employee of the 501st Squadron, who, after flying 71 missions with that organiaztion was returned to the States.

After spending approximately four months in the States he returned overseas and was assigned to the 500th Squadron where he was installed as Assistant Operations Officer under Capt. Waring and after a short time in this capacity, took over Operations as the "supreme wheel." At this time fate dealt Lt. Harper a cruel blow as Sgts. Franks and Epstein both were to be returned to the home land. In their places Sgt. Marcet became Operations head NCO with a staff consisting of Cpl. Jones and Sgts. Norrick, Kirby and Teats.

Standing: Lt. Harper, Franks, Epstein, Horrick.
Kneeling: Marcet, Jones, Kirby.

The Paddle Feet

EXECUTIVE OFFICERS

The executive officer is the medium through which the commander transmits his orders to the organization. He must translate the wishes of the commander into action and relay them to lower echelons. The executive officer is second in command of the unit; he must know his commander very well, his mental attitudes and the thinking processes by which he reaches his decisions or forms his judgments. He must be prepared to handle any problem at any time.

His responsibilities are many. Overnight he must help turn a wooded plain or hillside, swampland or kunai prairie into a home for his men. Upon arrival from the States our "Table of Basic Allowances" authorized one carpenter's chest consisting of a hammer, saw, square and a rule. We also had six shovels, a few axes and very few picks. These were the tools available to construct the camp.

Trained personnel were not to be had. Our Table of Organization lacked a Utilities Section. Cooks, clerks and airplane mechanics became carpenters, masons and plumbers overnight and our homes were built.

Sanitation is the biggest problem in the field and included such things as drainage of the area, mess facilities, properly placed latrines and an adequate water supply.

Capt. A. T. McCurdie was the first executive to encounter these problems. Fresh from the States and with a Utilities Section to depend upon, under his direction we managed to have one of the finest camps in our area. Capt. McCurdie served as executive until January 1945, and the officers who succeeded him in this position gained a great deal of experience by going through these early days in Moresby and other subsequent moves to new bases.

Capt. Curtis R. Erspamer moved from S-1 to the executive post when Capt. McCurdie was transferred to a higher echelon and capably handled the moves to San Marcelino, Clark Field and Ie Shima. At this last base,

Captain McCurdie

190

Capt. Erspamer was assigned to Group Headquarters and our Adjutant, Capt. Munro succeeded him. Capt. Munro's extra curricular claim to fame was his basketball and volley ball prowess. He was the athletic mainstay of the 500th.

Our executives have always been fortunate in having capable first sergeants with whom to work. As the executive is the liaison between the Commanding Officer and organi-

1st/Sgt. Burnett and Capt. Erspamer

M/Sgt. Oskea

ban. It was our loss when he was hospitalized and finally sent home as a result of a severe case of fungus infection contracted in New Guinea.

He was succeeded by T/Sgt. Robert Oskea of the Communications Section who carried out his new duties very well, but Oskea's real love was Communications and he returned to that section at San Marcelino. Sgt. Eddie Ison, previously of Tech Supply, then was chosen to occupy the "top kick's" desk and established a fine record in that position which he held until he left for the States and civvies from Ie Shima. He also improved Squadron morale by his excellent softball pitching, winning 50 out of 52 games he pitched for the outfit.

zation as a whole, the first sergeant is the liaison between the executive and the enlisted personnel, carrying out the orders of the executive, based on the decisions of the commander. He also acted as a liaison from the enlisted men to the command as it was his duty to keep his fingers on the pulse of the troops and do his best to provide for their needs as circumstances dictated.

A good first sergeant could do much to make or break the Squadron and we were fortunate indeed that ours were of the best. Our original first sergeant, Claude V. Burnett, was really a good man for the job and served in that position until the outfit reached Taclo-

1st/Sgt. Ison

191

ADJUTANT

The Adjutant is the Administrative Representative of the Commander. His duties are to correlate, consolidate, record and forward information to the proper places. He is also responsible for the mess, billeting officers and enlisted men, duty assignments, Squadron finances and transportation.

His duties are always tedious. They may seem unimportant from the administrative standpoint but there is no more important man in the Army. He assumes numerous responsibilities that do not come under the heading of his duties. He is more or less a "jack of all trades;" he must have a knowledge of legal affairs, personnel affairs and civil affairs. Along with this he must have patience and be a man of understanding to aid the men with their numerous personal problems.

Capt Erspamer served as S-1 until Tacloban, where he advanced to the Executive position and Capt. Munro became Adjutant. When he became Executive, Lt. McGarry, former Group personal equipment officer, became our S-1.

Captain Erspamer

It was through the machinery of the Orderly Room that the Adjutant carried out his many responsibilities. The Chief of the section was Eddy Lund. He would do the worrying for us on many matters that might otherwise go unheeded. He also saw that everything pertaining to us in the matter of promotions, recommendations, personal papers and unusual records were properly handed. Both the officers and enlisted men appreciated his efforts.

Any problem concerning allotments, flying pay, per diem, PTT or numerous other financial questions could always be solved out of the maze of records and the information in the files and the memory of the Finance Clerk "Danny" Horikowa.

Information on previous service in the 500th or another outfit could be obtained from S/Sgt. Lovett or Sgt. Buckley. They also made sure that our Adjusted Service Rating Scores were figured correctly and that we were listed on the all important Redeployment Roster.

S/Sgt. George Stanberry very capably handled his responsibility of submitting all Squadron statistical reports, a tedious job in itself, and maintaining the enlisted men's classification cards. He also had charge of the distribution of documents and correspondence between the Squadron and the Group Message centers.

Preparations of recommendations of 500 awards and citations were capably handled by S/Sgt. "Jake" Jacobson. He also worked on the preparation of the Squadron history and recording of events in the organization since activation.

The final and very important task of keeping the Squadron morning report and officer's classification records in order was well performed by Sgt. Freddie Heath.

Thus, it is readily apparent that the men who pushed the pencils and pounded the typewriters are really deserving of much credit and that they have done their part in building and maintaining the excellent record of the 500th.

Captain Munro

Lt. McGarry

Rear: Horikawa, Buckley, Jacobsen, Lambert, Willing, Dunbrack.
Front: Heath, Sgt/Maj. Lund, 1st/Sgt. Ison, Stanberry.

193

INTELLIGENCE

S-2. It was S-2's responsibility to provide combat crews with all possible necessary target information and maps, inform them of enemy capabilities, brief and interrogate crews, submit reports to higher headquarters and construct and maintain a briefing room. The Section usually consisted of two officers and four enlisted men; one of the latter was a sergeant in charge of Public Relations who produced a multitude of news items on men who joined the Squadron and their subsequent activities while in the organization.

As originally organized the S-2 Section was composed of 14 officers and men but by embarkation time it was whittled down to Capt. John C. Hanna, Intelligence Officer; 1st Lt. Clyde C. Carter, Assistant; 1st Lt. Elon H. Bomberger, Photo Interpreter; S/Sgt. Fred Guetgemann, Section Chief; Sgt. Bob Bynum, Administrative Chief; Cpl. Jim Dorran, Public Relations Clerk; and Cpl. Jay Albright, File Clerk. Being one of the smaller sections of the Squadron and because of the nature of their work, these men and their replacements were to have an

Major Hanna

insight into the combat operations of the Squadron that made it one of the most interesting jobs one could have.

In the States, S-2's duties included instructing on enemy equipment and tactics, target recognition, etc. Old timers will recall that at that time many of us expected to go to the ETO; the enemy wasn't the only one fooled on that deal.

The three-and-a-half day simulated combat at Aiken was as rough on the S-2 Section as anything they met in the Pacific; they handled 17 missions and had six hours sleep in the whole period. The return to Columbia was a relief, but then they started packing for the trip to the staging area at Walterboro, where the S-2 enlisted men set up their coke stand and had a section party on the proceeds.

Enroute to Stoneman, they were still selling refreshments, but this time at cost—and their wares were really welcome on the long ride across the continent. At Stoneman, their first real non-training work began—sealing and stamping the censored mail accumulated during the train ride.

At Moresby the crews started combat operations and so did S-2. Intelligence procedures were refined and streamlined to fit conditions.

The job to be done was clearly defined and it was evident that the task was not going to be an easy one. It was the start of the midnight sessions, the hurried chow, pre-dawn briefings, the excitement of returning crews with their stories at interrogation, and the grind of completing accurate reports and overlays upon which future missions would be based. Jim Dorran had a major task too, covering activities in his hundreds of public relations stories. In addition, he had the daily news and all war theatre situations to keep currently posted. Guetgemann and Albright toiled long hours putting up neat maps, drawing detailed over-

Captain Carter

lays and generally keeping the briefing room in excellent shape. The men in the photo division were busy in the lab or on the Line installing and repairing cameras. Grant Ross and "Fitz" Fitzpatrick worked closely with the section and Lt. Bomberger, who was eventually assigned to the Group Lab. Earl De-Castro and Bill Miller were also assigned duties in the Group Photo Lab.

It was at Moresby that Capt. Timms and Cpl. Tully, Aussie liaison personnel, were assigned to the Squadron working as part of the Intelligence Section. Their friendship will always be treasured by all who knew them and we were sorry to see them leave at Nadzab.

At Dobadura the Rabaul raids, complex in all respects, kept the Section busier than usual. Remember how we used to joke about

Captain Strauss

Capt. Hanna's temporary duty trips to Sydney for the purpose of processing the Squadron films? Joking aside, the films grew in length through many campaigns and are a valuable part of our Group's combat record.

Sgt. Bynum and Albright were on furlough in Australia and missed the move to Nadzab where the Section was set up in a new building. It was here that Capt. Hanna went to Group and Lt. Carter took over the 500th Section with Lt. Hutchinson as his assistant. Pfc. Anthony, an Army-trained draftsman, joined the Section and soon proved his worth. While Guetgemann and Dorran were furloughing in Australia, Capt. Carter was assigned to Group as Public Relations Officer; Lt. Strauss was transferred from the 501st as our Squadron S-2.

Shortly thereafter missions were staged

Captain Hutchinson

Lt. Bomberger

our clothes. The missions flown from there were more or less routine from the Intelligence standpoint.

During the settling down period at Tacloban, Bynum remained with the flight echelon at Biak. In the meantime after the section had been working in temporary tent set-ups at Dulag and Tanuan airfields, it settled at Tacloban and Guetgemann engineered an attractive S-2 tent-building. It was here that Lt. Strauss was promoted to Captain and assigned to Group and Lt. Hutchinson took charge of the section with a new assistant, Lt. John F. Dinges, a recent arrival overseas. Lt. Dinges had been a Squadron S-2 back at Greenville Army Air Base, an RTU from which many of our replacement crews came and was happy to find some old acquaintances in the 500th.

Tacloban was fairly peaceful for the section, except for the night that a jeep rolled into the Section's enlisted men's tent. It was here that Fred Guetgemann returned to the States on Temporary Duty; he was eventually re-

out of Hollandia and Wakde Island. Intelligence was represented by one officer and one enlisted man accompanied the staging crews and worked out of these advance areas. Lt. Hutchison and Sgt. Bynum, working on tiny Wakde, will long remember the all-night bombing they underwent there.

At Biak, that hot, rough coral island, the S-2 jeep was usually busy in the afternoon at the creek where we washed ourselves and

T/Sgt. Bynum and T/Sgt. Guetgemann

assigned there and Sgt. Bynum became Section Chief.

S-2's biggest difficulty at San Marcelino was the wind and dust which assailed us from nearly every direction, and papers and maps presented us with new problems. Paper weights and wind screens were valuable items indeed. Sgts. Ross and Fitzpatrick were presented with Air Medals by General Crabb for their fine work photographing enemy targets hit by our aircraft and Lt. Dinges was able to obtain

Lt. Dinges

196

about 20 sheets of plywood which were to be very useful at our next base, Clark Field.

Clark was said to be our permanent base and it was here that S-2 had one of its nicest buildings. The plywood afforded excellent space for maps, wall displays and a fine read-

Captaincy for "Hutch," a silver bar for Dinges, and a sergeancy for Albright.

On the move again to Ie Shima by LST, the Intelligence Section looked forward to its part in the final blows against Japan. Rotation was still around the corner. Bob Anthony fell

Rear: Epstein, Franks, Marcet, Dornan.
Front: Albright, Lt. Dinge, Bynum.

ing table. Lt. Hutchinson painted the walls green and our new benches a bright red. This color scheme was the object of some good natured joking for awhile and "Hutch" felt much better when the paint finally dried, but the final effect was really "solid." We even promoted ourselves a much-needed fan made from an old teletype motor and some sheet metal. Intelligence became quite a popular place, especially after *Impact* Magazine came out with a very complimentary issue featuring the deeds of the Air Apaches. Among the other good things that came S-2's way at Clark were a

sick and was evacuated to Guam. "Stop Press" Dorran reached the height of his overseas career as he calmly announced that the Japanese surrender was entirely official, and that we should "pack our bags" immediately.

At Ie Shima, the old Intelligence Section underwent a great change. Sgts. Dorran, Ross, Fitzpatrick and Albright left for the States in August. Bynum, now a T/Sgt. left in September, along with Capt. Hutchinson.All that were left were memories—of the old Section and the men who made it work so well.

ENGINEERING

It is the men of the Engineering Section who really "Keep 'Em Flying" and who too often receive insufficient recognition for the wonderful work they have done. It is in large measure through their back-breaking efforts that the Squadron has achieved its excellent wartime record.

Credit for the 500th's high standard of maintenance goes not only to the crew chiefs but also to the specialists; the electricians, instrument men, propmen, sheet-metal men, and to every man who worked on "The Line;" their efforts resulted in our record of one hundred per cent aircraft in commision the greater part of the time.

These men spent much time in training both in schools and on the Line before leaving the States and when they reached combat, they were well-prepared for the task ahead. Long hours in the heat and rains of the jungles

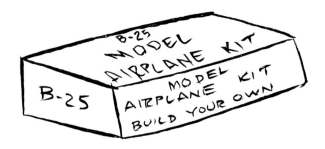

wore on them, but in spite of hardships they always had the ships ready for a mission. Their only satisfaction was knowing their job had been done and done well. They may feel justly proud that they had such an important part in keeping our air power flying against the enemy.

The Squadron came of age on a cold November day at Columbia with the arrival of the 500th first three airplanes. Sgt. Effa worked all that first night on his ship so that it would be the first to fly for the 500th. Things were beginning to happen. Work went well under the guidance of our able Line Chief, M/Sgt. Eichten, probably the most heard from man on the Line. Never a day went by that he couldn't be heard yelling at one of his flight chiefs—Njaa, Cate or "Spud" Murphy.

It was during the stay at Columbia that Sire showed so much interest in his work; every day he would go to the Depot Engineering Office to check his reports—of course the

Captain Hessel—Engineering Officer

Captain Cole

Line Chief "Eich"

fact that so many young ladies worked there had nothing to do with it. We also noticed Werner and Ison spending many hours chasing parts at the depot. They seldom got any parts, but they made some good contacts—and sometimes got a date for the following night.

It was near the end of the year, and about the time Reilly got a bit too close to the stove, that the boys in barracks 142 thought they were being picked on. It seems that after too many Saturday morning inspections they would be confined to the Base for another week. They didn't realize that it was irritating for the inspecting officer to cut his shoes on the broken beer bottles just walking from one end of the barracks to the other.

After the first of the year the Section was waiting to go overseas and the Squadron moved to Walterboro where it got its new airplanes and all was ready for the long trip over. Woodcox and Cullitan were both married on three-day passes about this time; Cheney went on an RON and returned a married man, but

M/Sgt. Gillis

M/Sgt. Efta

before too many more men took such a step the Group was on its way over.

With the planes safely landed at Reid River, Australia, all the men were happy except Andy Rezin whose plane had a single engine and was crash-landed by Lt. McLean at New Caledonia. All Andy had left was a pair of pants.

We were all glad to be together again at Moresby and it was there we learned about war. It was in June of '43 that our planes were over Lae that we first tasted combat when H. S. Smith's 048 was liberally holed and landed at Dobadura. From this time on Woodcox and his crew of sheet metal men were busy patching holes. It was also at Moresby that "Salvo Joe" Ulazewski won his name by salvoing a life raft and bomb bay tank on a hardstand.

After just a few missions the planes were taken to Australia to be modified into strafers

and it was at this time that the section lost five of its finest men in a tragic transport crash. They were: Sgts. Lee, Rapp, Bury, McKenna and Simpson.

Staging missions to Dobadura and Kerowina meant working day and night with a minimum amount of equipment to keep the planes flying in one of our roughest targets—Rabaul. It was on one of these missions that Lt. Wallace flew Puckett's Tondelayo on single engine in a 70-minute battle with Nip fighters.

Some of the highlights of the section's days at Nadzab are the recollections of the hours Brasco spent in painting the large horse's heads on the tails of our planes—or the day when the Squadron was released for Maintenance and Training and the call came through for ten ships to be ready in an hour

(continued on page 220)

Going Stateside: Murphy, Cates, Njaa, Eichten.

ARMAMENT

It is the responsibility of the Armament Section in a tactical outfit to maintain all armament with which the modern combat airplane is equipped. To fulfil this responsibility the aircraft armorer must be a highly technically trained soldier, possessing the knowledge of the complicated electrical and mechanical theory which makes up the bomb racks, gun sights, power turrets, and the gun and rocket firing systems. He must be able to dis-assemble, clean, repair and re-assemble all of the weapons in the shortest possible time and with the greatest degree of accuracy, for these weapons must function properly at any and all times. He must spend many early morning hours loading the bomb bays with all of the many types of bombs used on tactical missions. For this job, he must have a background of training on explosives and ammunition.

All of the duties required of the armorer must be done correctly the first time; for when the bombing run is started, the enemy is in the sights, and the firing button is pressed, it is his knowledge, toil and sweat that contributes so much towards a successful mission.

NOTES FROM A 500TH ARMORER'S DIARY
PORT MORESBY
September 1943

Those long days and nights of training in South Carolina have finally paid off. The 500th was overseas and pounding the Nip every day that the weather permitted.

An old life has been laid aside, and a new life begun. Gone are the "you all" girls of Columbia and Walterboro, gone is that ice cold beer at the P.X., gone are the neat, clean uniforms. Yeah, gone are the days when—oh, well—our hearts are still young if not quite so gay.

We rode on a train, we sailed on a ship, we flew in a plane. And when we set our barracks bags down and looked around we found ourselves in a dusty little valley seven miles from Port Moresby, New Guinea. It's called Jackson Drome and it's here that we are making the difficult transition from training to combat.

Transition is a pretty mild word to use in connection with the hectic activities of our first months of operation. Something more apt would be the war-born term "Snafu." Yea, verily, I say unto you, confusion reigneth.

Lt. Johnson

200

We found that the new situation called for three things: (1) the knowledge that the Air Force Training Command gave us; (2) native American "know how"; (3) sweat and profanity. Sometimes, it seems, that the final factor considerably overshadows the others. However, we've mixed them all together and the bombs got loaded, the guns got cleaned, and the turrets respond to the gunners' touch. And that is the work of the Armament Section. All the intricate paraphernalia of war that goes with a modern fighting plane . . . Keep it clean, keep it in tip-top shape, and see that it works when needed. Wewak and other north coast targets continue to receive their apportioned tonnage of bombs.

The Moresby wreck, whose battered and riddled hulk offered a practice target for our anti-shipping tactics.

February 1944 — DOBADURA

The pattern of our life overseas has gradually emerged as we have become familiar with every detail of our work and better acquainted with the men around us.

Last September our planes were converted to low-level strafer-bombers. For the Armament Section this means more guns to clean, more ammunition to load.

Our original section chief, Arah Doolittle of Los Angeles was killed in a regrettable transport crash in Australia last year. Our new boss is "that man with a screw driver" Allen O. Jones of Lafayette, Georgia. He is the cloven-hoofed individual whose habit it is to rout us out of bed in the middle of the night to crank up the bombs for the next day's mission. And like as not when we are through with that, back he comes to tell us that the target has been changed and a different type bomb is required. Up and away again in our rickety old weapons' carrier, drop the old bombs out, put the new bombs in. Gale Bradley of Mason City, Iowa, claims that he's dropped more bombs on the hardstand than any of our bombardiers dropped on the Japs.

Some of the familiar memory pictures of those days are:

Big John Davis of Westfield, New Jersey, bending over his little canvas bag of tools . . . Guns, gun-mounts, and ammo chutes spread all over the area. . . Dave Williams of Shreveport, La., overhauling his ship again . . . Hank Just of New York City and Al Heydt of Allentown, Pa., continuing their endless argument . . . Walter Rouse, Excelsior Springs, Mo., saying: "I look on gambling and drinking as cardinal sins. Pass the bottle and shoot a pound." . . . A cheery whistle and there goes Bob Chandler, Vernon Center, New York, quietly carrying out the endless tasks of an assistant section chief.

Lt. Macauley

June 1944 — NADZAB

The end of our first year overseas. For 365 days we've been changing worn-out gun barrels, fixing amplydine motors, adjusting bomb rack controls . . . One redeeming factor is that the speed and efficiency born of our twelve months' experience has lightened the burden somewhat.

Quotes from a bull session held under the wing of an airplane while waiting to go on a staging mission . . .

. . . "Six more months and we're eligible for rotation . . . Somebody left the damn belt stud out . . . This Aussie babe I had in Sydney could drink more beer than Tony Galento . . . I'd like to get home in time for the hunting season . . . Three broken mounts in two days . . . Yeah, Murphy was really putting out the chow . . . Couldn't find 'Pop' Welch anywhere."

* * * * *

During our stay at Nadzab a tragic accidental explosion had taken the lives of several armorers including old timers:

Kenneth Preston, Louisville, Ky. Soft-spoken, always ready with a pleasant smile or a helping hand.

John Summerson, Perry, Iowa. Good natured. "I want to get back to Vera and the farm."

Robert Earhard, Cincinnati, Ohio. Always puttering around with something—the amiable junk collector.

And Joe Mettam, San Diego, Calif. Killed in a crash of a furlough-bound plane.

December 1944 — BIAK ISLAND

Rain, coral dust, and a limited water supply. New developments which bring us new problems to be solved. R-2 frag racks, double suspension parademo bombs, new type turret, early morning loading only . . . The pace accelerates . . . Tokyo, here we come.

MEN AND WORDS

Don O'Shell, Belwood, Pa., singing "More Precious Than Diamonds, More Precious Than Gold."

"Annie and I were still pretty young then. Things will be different . . . " Pete Luciano, Jersey City, New Jersey.

"Ya damn betcha, I'll be out to your place for the pheasant season, first year . . ." Herman Ryerson, Highland Falls, New York.

"By God men are men out in West Texas." "Come to East Texas and you'll eat those words, podner." Allie Roberts, Dallas and Norm Williams, Tatum.

"Now back in Ohio . . ." Charles Dusenberry, Zanesville; Harold Wilson, Cambridge; John Romine, Columbus.

"Remember that night on Wakde when a square foot of foxhole was worth a year's pay?" William Stewart—Regular Army.

"Who wants to read the Yonkers' Home News?" Stanley Tauber, Yonkers, New York.

June 1945 — PHILIPPINE ISLANDS

Out of the jungle at last! Civilian services again—laundry, professional mess attendants, places to go during off duty hours, three-day passes to Manila.

And North American has come through with a new armament set up and pneumatic charging system which eases our work considerably.

Capt. Jack (where's my jeep?) O'Brien, Chicago, Ill., our original armament officer, has been transferred out and replaced by Lt. Willard Johnson, Courtland, Virginia, assisted by Lt. Bill Macauley, Hutchinson, Kansas.
Seen and heard around the line:

"Where do you get that magnet stuff? I'm head of the brass and links section." Nathan Gregory, West Hartford, Conn.

Calvin Pechham, Oakland, Calif., in abbreviated shorts, bubbling over with plans for his 45-day temporary duty in the States.

"It's all good but I'll take Canadian Club." Bert Yinger, Pittsburgh, Pa.

Jack Warren, Covington, Ky., with his oil can and rag.

T. M. "Slim" Williams, Colorado Springs, Colo., hammering on a steel watch band.

Bill Price, Lawrence, Kansas efficiently overhauling an energizer.

"I don't need a tool box. Just give me a screw driver and an oil brush." Harold Litteer, Rochester, New York.

John Sibson, Philly, Pa., ex-armorer, saying goodby after completing his missions as an air crewman.

Chester Buckner, Pasadena, Texas lugging hydraulic fluid around for the tail turrets.

September 1945 — IE SHIMA

Along came the Air Apaches and the atomic bomb and the Nips threw in the towel but quickly. Our bombs and our guns have done their part. So stow'em away boys, and it's home to the wife and family.

The Armament Section is gradually breaking up as the old timers go home and the not so old timers take over and await their turn for the trip to the promised land.

Parting remarks:

Kenneth Ostroot, Minet, North Dakota saying: "Anybody pick up any going-home rumors?"

M/Sgt. Jones

"I'd like to get discharged here and go home by way of China." Vick Goodwin, Dallas, Texas.

"Hey fellas, respect my age, willya?" William Jay, Cordell, Okla.

Rear: Buckner, O'Farrell, Brewster, Gregory, Wartena, Blumquist, King, Keenan, Ryerson, Buckley.
Middle: Jay, Tauber, N. A. Williams, Enoer, Romine, MacMahon, Wallace, Ostroot.
Front: Lt. Macauley, Lt. Johnson, Braun, Crago, Goodwin, Ross.

203

ORDNANCE

Ordnance's mission in the Squadron was to supply and maintain the ammunition and armament necessary for the tactical operation of the organization. For this purpose the section was composed of ammunition and armament specialists. It was the responsibility of the armament men to repair all weapons that could not be repaired while still installed in the airplanes and also to furnish whatever technical advice necessary to their effective operations.

The ammunition men were trained in the handling and storage of all types of ammunition. They were skilled in fusing the bombs properly and delivering them to the planes prior to take off. Upon the proper fusing of the bombs depends, to a large degree, the effectiveness of the bombing and the safety of the planes and crews.

The Ordnance Section, furthermore, must study and stay abreast of all the technical developments in weapons. This was particularly true of the introduction of aircraft rockets. Had it not been for the previous studies of our Ordnance specialists we might have encountered great difficulty in the effective employment of this new weapon. As it was, T/Sgt. Moore, our section chief, was able to instruct

the combat crews in the proper use of the rocket.

The Ordnance Section became a part of the Rough Raiders at Columbia on November 11th, 1942. At the time it was headed by Lt. DeWeil who directed the section until replaced by Lt. Gilardi at Nadzab. Lt. Gilardi remained with the section to June 20th, 1945, when he was replaced by Lt. Mueller at Clark Field.

Under the able guidance of Section Chief T/Sgt. Fred Moore the section established a fine record of efficiency. It is in this respect, by maintaining the guns and supplying the ammunition with which the 500th blazed her way to fame, that the men of the Ordnance Section are justly proud of the part they played on the road to victory.

As the months rolled into years, some of the men of the section came to make pretty definite impressions on their fellows, among them especially, S/Sgt. Leonard (Pop) Welch, one of the older men and a man who took great pride in his specialty—machine guns—and kept the best guns in the Group. "Pop" was also a bit of a gadgeteer; he made a clever set of burners for the mess kit washline and a handy washing machine from rocket and P-61 parts.

Lt. Gilardi

Standing: Spray, Stone, Talley, Kennedy, Moore, Foxworth, Dubose, Rollin, Minnicozzi.
Kneeling: Corrotto, Strassheim, Linville, Beecher, Bardino, Welch, Sekula, Horne.

Sgt. Everett (Tojo) Kennedy was also a bit older than the majority of the fellows and his judgments were well regarded. "Tojo" was in charge of the Squadron's Automotive Section and did much to keep the jeeps and trucks rolling—in all a hard worker and a good man to have around.

S/Sgt. Sydney Strassheim served as section clerk and was also very valuable in obtaining needed material. T/Sgt. Joe Sankowski worked as Section Chief from Tacloban to Clark Field while Fred Moore was Stateside studying rockets; one thing remembered about Joe was the enthusiasm with which he welcomed those beer issues . . . Sgt. Charles Sekula took the blue ribbon among the section's chow hounds, but he was always one of the hardest workers . . . Sgt. Rollin was a quiet, good natured fellow, but Sgt. Charlie Horne says he will never forget the night he was loading bombs with Rollin and one fell on Charlie's head; Horne says he'll settle to call it an accident . . . Cpl. John Tally was a born Rough Raider, either on horseback or driving a truck in the Pacific area; he is an Alabaman who migrated to Texas. John was

Preparing eggs for Tojo: O'Farrell, Warren (on hose), Sekula (on ground), Beecher (in truck).

a crack shot and had a mighty cool nature about him as demonstrated in his capable handling of an armed frag bomb at San Marcelino . . . Sgt. David Beecher became section chief at Ie Shima; he was a real veteran of the Philippines although "Buck" Bardino might question as to whose side he fought on. Seems someone hit "Buck" with a chair one time. And then there was the night Beecher and Lt. Gilardi were scared by the buzzing sound in a 100-lb. bomb crate—and found a cricket inside!

Pfc. James Mullins was one of the best-liked fellows in the section; he suffered a leg injury and was the first man from the section to return to the States—the boys really missed him . . . Cpl. Irwin (Rip) Spray joined the Section at Nadzab; he worked in armament and ammunition and finally as section clerk, performing all of his duties well . . . Cpl. William Boehme was our fastest man when frag bombs popped; even a trailer failed to stop him and it was thus he won his name "The

Lt. Mueller

Flying Dutchman." . . . Cpl. Alfred Stone joined the section in the Philippines; he just loved to load bombs! Cpl. Merle Cross came in at San Marcelino and was a great pipe smoker . . . Cpl. William Gerarden was a combat man who joined the section after being wounded in action over Luzon . . . Cpl. Herman Linville was a fast bomb handler and also one of the Squadron's watch repairmen.

Four men in the Section proved themselves heroes at Hollandia when they were awarded Soldier's Medals for their part in rescuing men from a plane which burned after a bomb fell from it while the plane was on a hardstand. The men are Sgt. Leo Bardino, Cpl. Charles Foxworth, Cpl. Irwin Spray and Pfc. James Mullins.

MEDICS

"First echelon maintainance of the troops," might well describe the function and duties of the Squadron Medics. This included: sick call; first aid; recommendation for hospitalization in serious cases; preventive medicine, including sanitation in all its phases; immunization; and malaria control. The Flight Surgeon himself had the added duty of maintaining the physical and mental well-being of combat crew personnel, grounding and ungrounding them as circumstances dictated and sending personnel home for combat fatigue. The Medics also served as alert emergency crews in case of crashes on or near the Strips, often resulting in extremely dangerous and heroic work on their part.

So quiet were the Medics about their achievements overseas, that an investigation

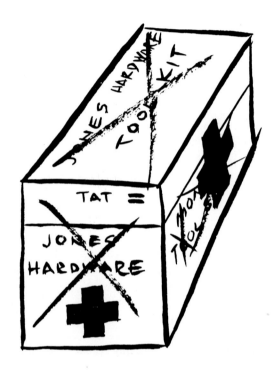

Captain Fleury

of their records is guaranteed to amaze one. It is commonly and erroneously believed that when the Squadron came overseas, Capt. Fleury told Sgt. LaRose to have the men, namely: Chytalo, Horme, Borton, Kay, Cobb, and "G. I." Maxwell, pack a foot locker full of aspirin and another full of codiene. This is obviously untrue, as any fool knows that a cure for anything from "Creeping Crud" to a nose bleed is two aspirin and one codiene.

We rode the Medics about their cures for our various ailments, but no one who has ever had anything seriously wrong with him will deny that he got the best possible treatment from them while he was in the Squadron, and if he went to the hospital "Doc" Fleury and one of the men would be among his most frequent visitors.

To get back to the record mentioned earlier, it will probably surprise later additions

Medics at Nadzab: Chytalo, Kay, Cobb, Williamson, Burton (in front).

to the Squadron to learn that while the Squadron was at Moresby, Maxwell, Cobb, Borton and LaRose were awarded Soldier's Medals for the job they did in saving the lives of Aussie paratroopers who were hit by a B-24 while they were waiting to take off for the famous Markham Valley drop. The B-24 hit the Aussies when it crashed and burned on take off, and the Medics were in constant danger from unexploded bombs in the burning ship. And that is not the only time that our men did a job we can all be proud of. Besides the time the Kamikaze plane hit the SS *Morrison Waite* in Tacloban Harbor, there was the night that the L-5 hit a transport in flight; the transport crashed and hit two B-24's and another transport killing 40 men. The Medics were on line duty that night, and did a great job.

The Medics aren't given to hanger flying like the air crews, and there is a tendency for the rest of the men in the Squadron to give them credit only for what is easily seen. For example, when they built a dispensary like the ones we had at Port Moresby or Biak, everyone commented on the fine job, but it is nice for the men in the Squadron to know that there is another side to the story, like the night they gave a 498th man first aid within 50 yards of a burning plane and a bomb went off.

There have been changes in the Flight Surgeon's Section, just as in any other. At Nadzab, Horne transferred to Armament and Williamson came in. LaRose, a fine man and well-liked worker, joined the combat crews and was killed at Biak, and there were also a few other changes. There was always someone in the dispensary, however, to murmur a few sympathetic words to the sick and press two aspirins and one codiene tablet into his palm— and their little white pills for the G. I.'s were especially handy when needed.

Near the end of our stay at Clark Field the Medics obtained a large trailer whose interior they remodeled into a gleaming white dispensary that would have provided excellent sick call facilities wherever we might go. VJ day, however, apparently put and end to its usefulness.

In speaking of the Medics we might add that, should any of your recollections of your days as a Rough Raider grow dim, they could always be refreshed by the fine pictorial record both in color and black and white kept by Capt. Fleury, one of the Squadron's most ardent photographers.

And it would hardly be proper to mention the Medics without including a very popular phase of their activities, namely the issuance of combat liquor and fruit juice chaser after each combat mission. The picture of "G. I." Maxwell astride a bench doling out his "Old Methusalem" is one that will live long in our memories.

The New Trailer Dispensary: Kay, Williamson, Capt. Fleury, Magnon.

COMMUNICATIONS

The 500th Communications Section could easily be termed the nerve center of the Squadron. It not only operated telephone switchboards and teletype-writers but was responsible for their installation and maintenance. Besides this the section maintained generators and telephone lines in the immediate area, providing the Squadron with power for lights, radios and for mess hall refrigeration.

Communications handled all cryptographic work for the benefit of all airborne radio personnel. Codes and radio facilities changed daily; all these changes had to be relayed to airborne personnel. We received this information by teletype and passed it on immediately to radiomen at briefings. We were also held accountable for training pilots and radio men in radio procedure, code and blinker practice.

We operated our own ground station to aid radio men in training flights. This station kept a log of encoded radio traffic which was submitted to high headquarters at the end of the month.

All of these duties were but part of our daily routine. Our main task lay in maintaining airborne equipment on the line. In this we are proud of our record. Since this outfit has been overseas very few aircraft were ever grounded because of faulty radio equipment.

Our maintenance men were divided into flights. These flights, along with the Line chief, made daily inspections of all airborne radio

equipment in our planes. This equipment was thoroughly checked for faulty operation. All inoperative equipment was replaced with spare servicicable equipment. Every morning these same men again frequented the Line to pre-flight all communications' equipment in planes scheduled for next day's take off.

The Communications Section, made up of several eager beavers just out of school soon found many bugs not in text books. These proved to add humor and comfort to the men who were to carry on for the 500th. Our good Lt. Levy, being a Bronxite and familiar only with the "A" subway train took to a jeep like a veteran to a Stateside blonde; his experience behind the wheel had Kovacs bailing out as he scattered a fence for a ten-yard repair job.

Some of our memories from Columbia training days on include: Larry (Henry) Ford keeping warm by burning the alert tent down two nights running . . . Eddie Martin, learning to climb a pole, had the fire department rescue him the first trip up, with Don Arbagast pleading with him to come down and forget the ladder. Aiken gave us our first test of long hours and just how it would be to stand off Banzai and paratrooper attacks. We had our phone lines in before anyone knew it and those who knew it took off for town, so no one knew it anyway. Our losses were one field switchboard and lots of sleep. We were at full

Captain Farias

Rear: Mannon, Capt. Farias, Kaplan, Oskea.
Center: Baker, Coleman, McCrea, Klugman.
Front: Blauvelt, Dobbs, Grigg, Seaton.

strength in Walterboro and almost knew something of what we were doing, and going to do overseas.

Six weeks later we were on our way to Port Moresby. Kovacs led a brigade of deck swabbers each morning while crossing the great Pacific. At Moresby we had our first introduction to the inevitable "C" rations and we thought it tasted better than steak.

Capt. Levy once tried to pitch a soft ball victory against the enlisted men. There were the long night pinnocle games between Capt. Levy, Sid Goldberg, Nick Carro, Kovacs and Martin.

The first air raids found Volz latrine-bound after the first shot, and Burke's laughter nearly got him a section eight. Bumpass, captured by the paratroopers (so he said), returned three days later speaking the native language of the Fuzzy Wuzzies. We were glad to see Kovacs made section chief.

Mannon acquired the name "Scoop" at Dobo after announcing rotation was in order. Our first replacement, Klugman, showed up at Nadzab (our next home) and we all thought that we would soon be on our way home. Capt. Levy left the Squadron and Lt. Farias was his replacement. Coleman, Gritz, and

Athletic Director Baker

Kovacs got their first furloughs to dear old Sydney. Brigg came into the section about this time and "Long John" Koonce with Vic Ascenzi made those long hikes into the hills in search of souvenirs which they seldom found. Coombs and Ascenzi were on the same shift on the switchboard and teletype. Martin and Coombs made 500th Communications known in baseball.

How about those delicious snacks at the lunch wagon on the line, with everyone taking his turn making the coffee and sandwiches? Remember when the Communications tent collapsed, and when a bomb exploded down the Line?

Biak found us digging bigger and better fox holes and turned Martin to prayer. Kaplan who was slightly inebriated, fell into a fox hole and Baker, who was sober, jumped into the garbage pit by mistake. "Cassanova" Coleman dated Ruth Terry, the first Stateside white woman we saw in months. Then there was

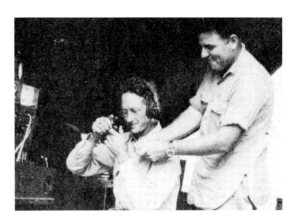

Time out for a smoke: Coombs and Seaton.

"Shorty" Bryant who was always condemning the "Temperance Union" and Kovacs who shaved off his mustache.

Dulag gave Larry Ford an extra five points when he won the Purple Heart, the hard way, our first day on shore. How wonderful the fruit cocktail tasted—those cans we managed to lift before leaving ship, remember? Also there were the lectures on beer and other intoxicating beverages which Kovacs gave us. Then there was the time "Professor" Behymer strolled into the section and started to fly a kite during a red alert.

Kovacs took over a platoon to guard the airstrip and Oskea was in charge of the first detail ashore. Communications set up a front

(continued on page 220)

SUPPLY

Captain Holtzman

Lt. Finklestein

S/Sgt. Parks

Supply, overseas, is often just about a week behind its needs—or to put it in other words, what you need today is expected to come in sometime next week. Seriously, supply had a hard job overseas. They were caught between the two fires of what the Squadron needed and what they could not draw, which often amounted to about the same thing.

Actually, Supply did a good job of caring for the Squadron, although a lot of it was off the record and due only to the winning ways and personality of the various men who filled the jobs of Supply Officer and Supply Sergeant. Some of the things they procured may have been intended for some other less deserving Squadron, but their efforts were always appreciated.

Once or twice a month came a day when no one groused at the Supply sergeant; that was beer issue day. For twenty-four hours Supply was then the center of a circle of affection, but only too soon came the old cry: "If you don't have it, why the hell don't you, and when the hell will you have some in?"

The official data on Supply is that it was founded at Columbia way back in November, 1942 with Lt. Holtzman, S/Sgt. Roth, Cpl. Parks, and Pfc. Eckstein. Those were the days that the men dreamed about in later days. Every man's needs could be satisfied in that shop, militarily speaking. At Walterboro, S. C., the set-up was again very good, but the Squadron moved on again, this time to Aiken, and then to fool the Japs, we were doubled back on our tracks to Walterboro, where we really went to work packing for the trip overseas, supposedly to the ETO.

Down at Moresby the set-up

wasn't bad. There was quantity at least, even though the local tailor shop did do a land office business in alterations. As we moved from place to place in our travels through New Guinea and the Philippines, the personnel of this section changed somewhat. Toward the end of our stay at Moresby, Lt. Holtzman was replaced by Lt. Garren, who was in turn replaced by Lt. Mawrence at Nadzab. Parks eventually took over as section chief, and when he left Clark Field to return to the U. S., O'Hara and Lanning took over and did the same excellent job of it that the others had before them. Lt. Norman Finkelstein served as Supply Officer for a time at Clark and Ie Shima while Lt. Mawrence was occupied with Group duties in Manila.

MESS HALL

Army chow is a difficult thing to write about. Much has been written before (especially in letters home) and so much more said, that whatever we may add here risks being superfluous. Nevertheless we dare not attempt an evaluation of our lives overseas without some mention of this vital section of the Squadron.

First of all, the Mess accomplished its mission: Mansueto's men fed the troops. Very often it was a thankless job but the less savory meals only made us appreciate the better ones more. A proper evaluation of what we ate overseas might wait until five or ten years after discharge when we try to count our ulcers —but seriously speaking, it wasn't so bad. After all, so much of the food came from cans that even the worst cooks couldn't harm it much—but when our cooks had some better than usual food to work with they did a good

Peanut Butter sandwiches and Attabrine Pills: Mansuetto, Buffalino, Quiak.

job. Remember the good chow at Clark Field? Some really attractive pastries made a welcome appearance ever so often and brightened our meals considerably.

Some of the things we would just as soon forget are the: seemingly countless meals we ate in which meat was ground, chopped, or shredded; salty bacon and powdered eggs; dehydrated potatoes; hot coffee three times a day in the tropics; and a few other little things we won't mention here.

Some of the things we missed most (besides chinaware): fresh fruit, fresh vegetables, fresh milk, napkins. "What's napkins?"

The old mess kits can't go unmentioned: We will probably all recall some embarrassing incident when we first "checked out" on the things and how the "chow hounds" loved to

clatter them as they led the troops to chow. As awkward as our eating irons were, they still were a big improvement over the old Army type in which the upper part of the meat can was shallow and undivided . . . and couldn't those canteen cups conduct heat from the blistering hot coffee?

The one big question or gripe that could always be found in an Army chow line was the alleged excellence of Navy chow—but we reckon there were enough reasons for this and we always remember that when it was rough and we were sufficiently hungry whatever the Army fed us tasted good enough, especially during a strenuous move from one base to another.

Rear: Niblack, Ready, Gonzales.
Front: Mansuetto, Quirk, Motroni.

PARACHUTE

The important job of the 500th Parachute Department was the supply and maintenance of air crew safety equipment which helped assure the safe return of our airmen.

Originating back at Columbia as a part of the Engineering section, it later took its place as a independent department with many other important duties such as maintaining and issuing flying equipment, flak suits, fire extinguishers, fire axes, sun glasses, flying helmets, watches, etc.

Under the able leadership of Sgt. Carnot Valiton, better known as "Ripcord," the Parachute Department soon become known for its efficiency. It was even said in those days that "Ripcord" was willing to jump with any 'chute he repacked. His assistant in the early days of the department was Sgt. John "Butch" O'Hara who later transferred to Squadron Supply.

When Sgt. Valiton left the Squadron at Nadzab because of illness, the work of the Parachute Department was taken over by Sgt. Arthur E. Rodekuhr and Cpl. Edward G. Elwell who carried on the high standards set by "Ripcord."

At Biak the Parachute Department took

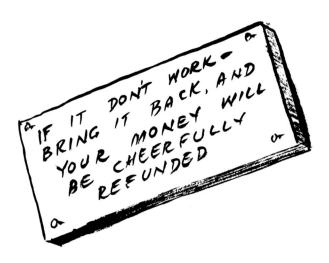

over the additional duties of a Personal Equipment Section and attained its independence. It now had the added job of equipping our air crew members with flying clothing, B-4 bags, glasses, watches, etc., and became the sole responsibility of the new Personal Equipment Officer, Lt. Lawrence N. Pence, Jr., and soon after that of Lt. Robert Silverstein.

Lt. Silverstein soon became known, in fact he became so well known in the Squadron that it was not unusual to hear someone shout out during the day or night: "Hey, Silver, do you have a watch?" or "Lt., do you have any sun glasses?" or "Hey, Silver, how many points do you have?" With the introduction of Personal Equipment it soon became necessary to add a new member to the Parachute Department, Cpl. John Plage, Jr., who with the assistance of Cpl. James C. King, carried on in the usual 500th tradition and manner. Sgt. Rodekuhr and Cpl. Elwell, both having enough discharge points, left for the States from Ie Shima.

King, Lt. Silverstein, Plage.

MAIL

Aside from actual combat time, the humble mail room may well have been the source of more personal, individual drama than any other thing overseas.

Mail call had a universal interest, but to each of us it meant something very personal: news of births, deaths, marriages and engagements and all the other bits that meant home. As important as the re-

clerk and worked in that capacity until he left for home from Clark Field. He was replaced by Cpl. Frank Dietz, a former Communications m a n who went home on points from Ie Shima and left the section in the hands of Cpl. Joseph King, former armorer, an extremely pleasant, courteous and able "mailman."

Cpl. King

ceipt of the mail was, the lack of it could be equally important—as anyone who has sweated out letters will know. Those letters took us all back across the miles to our homes and for the moment the war was erased from our minds.

The postal section consisted of one man, but his importance is fairly obvious. Sgt. Thomas McDaniel was our original

Mail call at Nadzab: Sgt. McDaniel.

UTILITIES

Sgt. Prim

T/Sgt. Pallister

and Friend

Two men who contributed much to our comfort overseas were the Squadron Carpenter and our Plumber.

T/Sgt. Marvin J. Pallister was assigned to us back in the States, but most of his work was done overseas. He was a contractor in civilian life and so fell to his duties in the Army quite naturally. They consisted largely in erecting administration buildings, mess halls and shower rooms—and then, not long after he completed them, of tearing them down and packing them in preparation for our next move when he could start the whole cycle over again. As proof of his industry, by December of 1944 he was credited with eighteen latrines, six administration buildings, nine mess halls and six shower rooms. His work was always done promptly and well and did much to add to our comfort and efficiency in combat.

Sgt. Marion L. Prim was called the "Jungle Plumber."

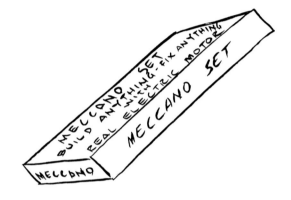

Such a commonplace thing in the States as water can be quite a problem overseas. His work consisted of laying in lines to the Squadron from a main line, if one existed, or fitting showers, etc. We needn't say much more, for we all know how welcome a daily shower was wherever we were overseas.

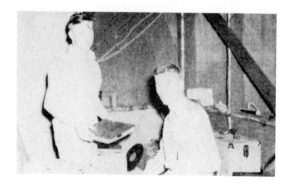

Stufflebeam and Lanning

Carpenters at Ie Shima: Achard, Seery, Schoettner, Grover.

214

Local Talent

A FEW 1000 WORDS"

The "Old Boy" rubbed his cherubic cheeks, took a long drink from his canteen cup, tilted his chair back against the wall and said: "You shoulda been here when it was rough!" The "Old Boy," who was 21 years old, had been in the Squadron for a month now, and was, therefore, eminently qualified for this title. The

"New Boy" who had been in the Squadron for only one week, but who was already shockingly familiar and disrespectful toward the ancients of the 500th, smiled sardonically, yawned and said: "Give us a few thousand words on how hot you are." The needle slipped back into the well-worn groove, and the endless bull session was on, once more.

It becomes necessary, at this point, to give forth with a definition of terminology. An "Old Boy," as you may already suspect, has nothing to do with chronological age. The term relates solely and strictly to time in the Squadron, and is, therefore, purely relative. Thus we have a confusing multiplicity of designations. A "New Boy," fresh from the States, his eyes wide in awe and admiration of some grizzled veteran of six months—a real "Old Boy"—has

his tin god rudely shattered as an older and more grizzled veteran of seven months contemptuously refers to his erstwhile hero as "that rookie!" The only recourse left open is blanket respect of everyone, or, of course, blanket disrespect, an alternative to be deplored by any right-thinking combat man. After all, "us 'Old Boys' wuz here when it wuz ruff!"

So we come to another term. When was it "rough?" We may use the following rule of thumb in this case:

It was rough

(a) Any period in the history of the Squadron dating from the day you reported for duty until the day your audience reported, after which it became practically Stateside.

"The chow bad now?" (This is to be uttered with pained incredulity.)

(a) "Listen, boy, you shoulda seen the chow down at X———," (the station just before the one at which the complainer reported.) "Why, we ate nuthin' but peanut butter and atabrine for three munts. Vienna sausages was a luxury."

A discussion about any place where the orator happened to be when no one else in the Squadron was around.

(a) "You think Manila is beat up now? Lissen, when I first came down here on rest leave, they was still fightin' in the streets."

And so forth.

There were also, of course, the "rough" combat missions. "Yulin Bay—flak? Samah? Lissen—lemme tellya about Wasile Bay, or Cabcaben. Why the flak was so thick you could drop your wheels and taxi on it. There I was, see, flat on my back—" The tales are endless, and modesty, of course, forbids . . .

As a character in that admirable book, *Shore Leave*, says: "It was nothing, really. Any man with unlimited courage and a genius for flying could have done the same thing."

Unfortunately, ever since one Ralph J. Norman, the pride of Lake Crystal, Minn., coined the phrase, any attempt by an "Old Boy" to set some "New Boy" right is met by the disparaging: "Give us a few thousand words——'

"Yessir, that's the trouble. No respect for the old men in the Squadron. You guys never had it *rough*. Lissen, lemme tellya about Dulag. There was this mud, see——"

ATHLETICS

Whenever sacktime permits, you'll usually find a few of the boys out throwing a ball around. This, in most cases, is the extent of athletic endeavor, for the Air Corps man is not the most energetic of individuals. Every once in a while, though, you get some eager beaver who stirs the boys from their slothful life and starts "Organizing Teams." The 500th has been bountifully blessed with these entrepreneurs, without whom many ballads of athletic heroism might have been forever unsung.

With Whit Baker, former Cornell "flash" as athletic director, a softball loop was set at Moresby shortly after our arrival there. In addition to intra-Squadron games among the sections, the Rough Raiders turned out a Squadron team which proved to be the scourge of the southwest Pacific. With Eddie Ison pitching, and Frank Buckley managing, they piled up eighty-eight victories against three defeats. The team was composed of Ison, Baker, McLean, Burton, Brasko, Martin, Eichten, Coombs, Sire, Werner, Durmeyer, Marcet, Stevenson, Fritzshall and Kay.

Ison who once pitched for a semi-pro team back in Memphis, was virtually unbeatable with his speed and control. The umpires usually admonished the batters "to swing at every pitch—I can't see them so they will all be strikes."

Unfortunately, at this time, the 500th was the victim of rank discrimination. Eddie Ison was evidently just a little too hot for the other Squadrons, and the poor dears prevailed upon the wheels at Group, who forthwith banned Eddie from pitching any further. Despite the handicap we still won our ball games.

At Nadzab, the Squadron team further endeared itself to the wheels of the Group by crushing would-be champions of other units. We garnered the Group championship by outclassing the 892nd Chemical Company, 17 to 0, behind the one hit pitching of Ison. The betting was high and heavy so the 500th rooters pocketed numerous pounds.

The Squadron played little softball during the next months, but a fair baseball club played at San Marcelino and Clark Field, winding up with a .500 average.

There was a lot of activity at San Marcelino centered on that dust bowl they called a volley ball court back of the officers' area. Anyone standing up by the orderly room could hear cries of "little men aren't worth a - - -"; "you lose"; "we'll let you know" (when we hit the net); or "I hate to play on a losing team."

Without a doubt the most voluble player on the court was "Horse" Reheis. Whatever he lacked in playing ability, he made up for by the use of his loud, clear baritone. Even after he was wounded over Formosa, he lent his refereeing talents and voice to the games. Among those routed out of the sack were: Bob Canning, Lew Rosenthal, "Whitey" Post, "Herky" Horowitz, C. John Loisel, Jay Lackey, Byrd Goodson and "Goofy" Gooban. The officers also had a softball team at Marcelino which was not too successful but which did provide a good deal of exercise.

Jack Parish became the athletic director at Clark Field. The officers' volley ball team distinguished itself there by running roughshod over the rest of the Group teams. Led by Bob Canning, the team consisted of Lew Rosenthal, Bill Price, Byrd Goodson, Bruce Munroe, Harry Meyers and "Stew" Malquist. A basketball court was set up and although no regular teams were organized, a lot of games were played between the officers and the enlisted men.

Ie Shima was pretty quiet as far as sports were concerned but everyone kept his hand in. All in all, through its history, the Squadron had been quite successful with its teams and the intra-Squadron games served their purpose in getting the boys' mind off the war we were fighting and in keeping them in good condition.

SHACKS

In the matter of shacks the men of the Rough Raiders seem to be possessed of the lore of the ancients. Through their knowledge of Alchemy they are able to take a bottle of Aussie liquor and after making certain motions with it and pronouncing certain words, change it into the material necessary for building a tent floor. Some gifted individuals have been

able to procure the material for a complete house this way.

Of course, in the hands of amateurs the use of this method often had dire results. Once at Port Moresby Capts. Erspamer and Fleury were forced to play hide-and-go-seek in a field with some Aussies in order to appease the spirits who take offense when the incantation prior to the change is not made properly.

Capt. Andrews and Lt. Grush returned one night on Ie Shima from trying to do business with these spirits with the story that they had been frightened away from a lumber pile and had left Grush's shirt behind in the confusion. Everyone realized that they had become con-

fused in making the spell, and instead of changing liquor to wood and tin, they had conjured up a captain in the Engineers. Of course, they didn't know how to send this Engineer back to the dark realms from whence he came, and for several days the life of these two gentlemen was made unhappy by him, until someone who knew how to deal with spirits, said the proper words to get rid of him. For several days all conjuring activities in the Squadron were suspended.

Besides the Alchemy, wide use was made of whatever materials were naturally found in the various areas. At Port Moresby many shacks were partially constructed of Kunai grass, and the same was true at Nadzab. At Biak, our amateur architects were given free rein and some unusual but comfortable shacks graced the heights of King's Row as a result. Some had porches on two or three different levels with private showers attached. At our later bases, the design was more restrained on the whole, except for the "monstrosity" as we kindly called the two-story structure that housed eleven men, including Hutchinson, Dinges, MacCauley, Silverstein, Gilmore, Besch, Decker and Montgomery, and which graced our area at Clark Field.

At San Marcelino which we passed over in our haste to describe the charming chateau mentioned above, we lived mostly in plain tents without floors. A few ambitious individuals, who placed no faith in the warnings from above that we were to move shortly, had the Filipinos build nipa grass walls around the out-stretched tent flaps. Needless to say, they got their money's worth from them when the rainy season rolled around to find us still there.

On Ie Shima the men went all out to build floors and porches, which turner out to be a wise investment of liquor and time when the first typhoon hit.

The fact that we are still alive, though at this writing, slightly wet and mildewed we owe to this warm climate, which is also responsible for jungle rot and a few near-fatal cases of athlete's foot. If the weather had been cold we might have frozen to death, which on a few occasions hadn't appeared as an exactly horrible death.

PRAYER MEETING

Every once in a while, on some soggy afternoon when all of the sacks were occupied with sagging bodies reclining in sodden stagnation, an idea would appear, germinate and begin to spread. Soon the word was being broadcast, heads would poke through tent flaps, and the project was on—Prayer Meeting tonight.

Now there may not be, as leading intellects would have us believe, any atheists in the fox holes, but the Prayer Meetings conducted in the 500th were no indication of this. In these gatherings, religion was not the main theme. To put it bluntly, the main idea at a Prayer Meeting was to get good and drunk—and have a lot of fun doing it.

The reason for Prayer Meetings were varied and many. A promotion, a new baby, the passing of the hundred combat point mark, the receipt of a "Dear John" letter, someone going home the next morning, a sudden acquisition of beer or liquor, or perhaps the mere fact that it had been a long time since the last one.

The boys would root around through their gear, and precious bottles, long-hidden, would be unearthed, anything from Stateside stuff to Flip rotgut, from Aussie Plonk to hospital brandy.

Now there are two types of Prayer Meetings. Toward the end, when most of the "old boys" had gone home and the Squadron had mostly "new boys", the men would get drunk all over the area, and about three o'clock in the morning, you'd have to fish them out of the mud puddles. This alien type of blowout was viewed with scorn and disgust by those "old boys" still remaining. The first, the only, the original Prayer Meetings were conducted solely in one dwelling. Everyone would congregate, bringing along a chair, a canteen cup, any liquor he might have, and most important of all, a lusty and willing singing voice.

For it was around the songs that most Prayer Meetings revolved. Much can be said about our Squadron songs, very little of it printable. They were, to put it mildly, somewhat obscene, replete with many picturesque Anglo-Saxon words. They were not subtle songs, one never had to ponder over some possible hidden meaning. But they were enthusiastically sung, and the pleasure they provided was more then enough justification for their existence, despite any fears that they might corrupt our minds. You could do a great deal of introspective delving to find the psychological reason for these songs. Let's put it simply and call them a release. There isn't much to do in the Pacific, and chastity is enforced by geography. This was our chance to be wicked and there was no one to be shocked.

Some of the songs we sang were: The—Big Wheel; Hardships, You B - - - - - - s; O'Reilly's Daughter; 'Twas a Cold Winter's Evening; The Fighting 500th; I Wanted Wings, Till I Got the G - d d - - - d Things; Blood on Your Tunic; Roll Your Leg Over; Cats on the Rooftops; I Used to Work in Chicago; That Was a Very Fine Song; Gathering of the Clan, and numerous other masterpieces.

Among the more famous, or notorious, if you will, Prayer Meetings, was the revival of the Civil War at Moresby, which resulted in a Mason-Dixon line painted on the bar, to divide the space between Yanks and Rebs. .

Perhaps the greatest of the Prayer Meetings, and the last of the good ones, was the one held at San Marcelino in the tent of the Lily Whiters, led by "Ox" Kusebauch, Ralph Norman, Jack Roe, Jim Geyer (the last two lost in action in the same plane over Formosa), and a few other men, equally famous for their Prayer Meeting voices. There were 48 men wedged in one pyramidal tent that night, all singing loudly, all drinking happily. No one remembers what occassioned the shindig but all agree it has never been equalled. It was climaxed by the amazing capacity and still more amazing energy and recuperative powers of the aforementioned Norman. No one who attended that Meeting will ever forget it.

V-J Day on Ie Shima was marked by a few appropriate gatherings and the songs rang out once more, probably never to be heard in public again.

219

to hit a convoy just reported. A quick survey revealed that all the ships were being worked on or were torn down for inspection. The situation looked critical but each man saw what had to be done and within the hour ten ships were back in commission, gassed loaded with bombs, preflighted and on their way. The entire convoy was either sunk or damaged—an indication of the spirit and coordination of those men who together accomplished the almost impossible. But of course Nadzab had its good points too—such as those ten o'clock sessions around the lunch wagon for discussions of military strategy, etc. Capt. Hussel, who headed the section from the beginning to VJ Day, was sure to take a prominent role in these sessions.

As far as engineering was concerned, the Biak period was largely spent preparing for the Philippine campaign. The planes brought from the States had been babied along for a thousand hours flying time and were turned over to the depot and replaced with new ships. Combat missions were few, but work on the Line was heavy preparing the planes for the move north.

The Philippines campaign presented some of Engineering's toughest problems. There were no replacements for the ships lost and during the China Sea blockade operations had to be carried on with a minimum of planes. Keeping all aircraft available every day was a job the Squadron may well be very proud of. The dust at San Marcelino was wearing on men as well as airplanes. During one week eight engines were changed and not required over ten hours. By starting at dawn a ship would be ready to fly that same afternoon. Although no records were broken for the time involved for an engine change made under perfect weather and working conditions, the work done during this period was outstanding.

The move to Clark was a welcome relief to the section as it brought more favorable working conditions and the passes to Manila served to relieve the monotony. New planes arrived and preparations for the move to Ie Shima were begun. Here it was that the "point system" reared its lovely head and the section lost one of its most able and best-liked men, M/Sgt. Eichten; M/Sgt. Effa replaced him and carried on with excellent results. Tech Supply was not the same after 44-year-old Joe DiNino left for home. But in spite of losing so many good men the section carried on.

A fine compliment was paid the Squadron at Clark when VBC Tech. Inspectors told M/Sgt. Tate that his ship was in the best condition of any B-25 they had ever inspected.

The move to Ie Shima was much like the others. The Squadron was just settling down after the move when the Great News arrived—which brings us to the end of our story.

COMMUNICATIONS SECTION
(continued from page 209)

line defense with the assistance of the Infantry. It was at Tacloban that Al McCrea joined the section. He was our third replacement. The "Flip" house boys will always be remembered especially by Oskea and Kovacs who invested one hundred hard earned pesos to supposedly finance one boy's way through school. As yet no word has been heard from him. The day Nick Carro was trapped inside a B-25 with a fire in its bomb bay will long be remembered.

Bob Oskea became our first sergeant shortly after moving to San Marcelino. His longing for those code books soon found him back at his desk. Bleuvelt and Dobbs, the fourth and fifth replacements, were welcomed into the section at this time. Who will forget the cigar Oskea dropped in an adjacent gas-filled hole in the latrine one morning? Not Bob! Madeo was assigned to the section and immediately dispatched on an advanced echelon. Seaton and Carro always boosted those wonderful Stateside women, particularly, at this time. We started getting three-day passes to Manila. Ford, Champ, Bump, Mannon, Seaton and Bryant made frequent trips to Castilljos. Then Farias was made Captain.

Clark Field has us think of Coleman again and his stories of the wild ride through Zig Zag Pass while the Nips shot at him. The good food, which all the boys enjoyed so much. Volz and Oskea bought transportation tickets to Manila while Koonce objected to Oskea's "international affair." Remember the two pesos a glass for ice cream? Several of the boys won't forget that.

The trip to Ie Shima was objected to by Koonce who is against moving in an LST. The card sharks, Champ and Baker, were taken over by a couple of beginners, Bleuvelt and Mannon. Remember how we felt in the fox holes the night after Japan accepted the peace terms . . . while we wore gas masks? Madeo finally strung up the ground station antenna and Behymer, the new Squadron electrician, restrung it the next day.

It was always the policy of this section to run 500th Communications much in the same way as a business. Every man had a job to do and as long as he did that job the section functioned smoothly. We are proud of our past record and the men who made it.

THE war is over now. The bulletin board is empty of combat schedules. The bombs no longer huddle sinisterly under the yawning bomb bays in the early mornings before the missions. The ammunition is out of the guns. Combat as a subject has been relegated to the nostalgic talks over the liquor glasses in the now lifeless "prayer meetings." The tales of Kavieng or Yulin Bay no longer have the same immediate sharp applicability as they did when strikes to Fusan or Tarumizu hovered on future schedules.

Perhaps, then, we can look in somewhat calmer retrospect, over a period in our lives, easily distinct from all others in our experience. Distinct and distinguishing, for combat men are marked indelibly, not always similarly, but always definitely. It may be in a studied arrogance, or in amused tolerance of the ground men. It may be in a marked disregard for the mores and morals of conventional *hoi polloi*. Or it may be in the nervous twitch, the involuntary shudder, the recurrent nightmares of those who have been too close to Death for too long a time.

For the essence, the cause, the premier motif of combat is Death. Whether we inflicted it on the enemy or had it visited upon us, Death was always there, riding with us. It is the ultimate purpose in conflict, the driving force of the combat man, and too long association with its influence has had its effects.

We do not, and did not, consciously think of these things. We did not approach or fly our missions with any preconceived philosophy of life and death and their effects on our characters. The possibility, the danger was always there, and we feared it, some more than others. Our reactions varied to the extremes. To some, each mission was an ordeal, to be sweated out from the moment their names were seen on the schedule in the late afternoon, until the pilot shouted, "Switches off," and we climbed wearily from our cramped quarters on the plane. To others, each combat mission was a job, an assignment, to be carried out as efficiently and expertly as possible, from the methodical copying down of plane numbers, headings, rescue facilities, all of the seemingly endless data so necessary on a combat mission, to the careful wearying hours of formation flying, ending in the final triumphant peel-off as we passed over our home field.

And to some, combat flying was like nothing else in the world. It was a thrill, a supreme exciting experience, a veritable orgy of man-made power and destruction.

The chief factor in this excitement, the main reason for the thrill, for those who experienced it, was this: The Air Apaches are a minimum level outfit. The differences between medium or high-altitude bombing and strafing and skip-bombing, are enormous.

Combat at 10,000 feet is abstract and impersonal. You fly your straight and level couse, unconscious of speed or distance. The point is reached, the bombs are dropped, and two miles below you, a puff of smoke or flame rolls up. Was it your bombs or those of your wingman? No matter. It was the target, and the target was hit, and slowly and methodically the great planes wheel around and plod home, still speedless, still aloft from the earth. And the automatic pilot is credited with another mission.

But down there, on the deck, things are different. Hopping over hills and around trees, buildings flashing by, the pale blur of upturned faces, there you have, for the first time, the realization of the actual and terrifying speed of the airplane. The B-25 is not the fastest plane in the world, nor is it the most maneuverable. But it has one distinction. It is, by far, the noisiest, and that characteristic makes up in impression for the other two. The engines don't purr or hum. They roar, they shake, they scream in rage. You hurdle through the air in a rising crescendo of noise, the angry barking of the machine guns, added to the explosions of the bombs of preceding planes. Acrid smoke from the nose guns fills and heats the cockpit, as you yank and pull and kick the controls to dodge through the rising columns of smoke, dust and flame. It's a personal war down here. You can watch your tracers run their deadly tracks up and into a machine gun pit, that suddenly ceases firing at you. You pick your own target and go after it, and you'll know if you got it, right then and there. The war is suddenly immediate and close and you're very much a part of it.

This, then, was combat as we knew it, and now it's all over. Are we now so different? Has it changed us irreparably? Shall we be forever apart in mind and heart from those who have not experienced what we have?

It seems doubtful. Oh, there will still be those who will walk down the humming city street, oblivious to the peace, their hands articulate in swooping patterns, their heads in the sky. "Kee-rist! What a run you could make on this town!" Lessee, you'd come in over those hills, say in three ship passes, start your strafing when you hit the canal, come right down the main street between the buildings and string your parafrags right over that R.R. yard, then rack 'er over to the right, hop over those hills and be away before they know it."

But that will pass, our hands will lose their wings, and our eyes will come down to earth. A church steeple will be a church steeple and not a possible flak tower, a ship something to take a ride on and not a possible target, and the green fields will no longer be a possible grave. We'll be home.

And we will have with us a sense of accomplishment, both personal and communal. We will have finished our job, and finished it well. We fought the greatest war in history, and we won it, each of us, individually, and all of us, together.

And with that feeling of pride and satisfaction, we can stop—stop, and relax, and rest. A chapter in our lives is over, as we finish the chapter in this book. We'll never forget it.

51st BOMB SQUADRON
BLACK PANTHERS

FOREWORD

Every department and activity of the Army Air Forces functions so that pilots, the leaders of air crews, may take their pay loads into the air and heap destruction upon our craven enemies. It might lead one to the assumption that the pilot is the most important element of aerial warfare, but this is not true. The combat team and the infinity of technically-trained men who keep this team on the field is likened to the intricate mechanism of a clock; each integral part is dependent upon and of no consequence without every other part. It is not the generals of our armies who have won this or any other war; these men, although they have played their role magnificently, are dependent upon their subordinates who are, in turn, dependent upon Joe Smith, American, a man of intense industry and astounding ingenuity. It is apparent that the average member of the civilian public pictures the Air Force as nothing more than a pilot holding his plane steady through innumerable black puffs of flak, a gunner shooting down an enemy fighter, or a bombardier calling "bombs away." They cannot see behind the glamour, which has originated in their minds, the sweat, the nights without sleep, and the anxiety for the air men by the crew chiefs, armorers, ordnance men, cooks, drivers, men with clerical jobs, and the others which make up the bulk of any bombardment squadron. It is to each indispensable individual whether, in the over-all scheme his job be great or small, that the following story is dedicated.

224

Captain Nevenschwander

Captain Nusbaum

COMMANDING

OFFICERS

Major Fain

Major Geise

Major Jones

THE

Captain Fridge

Captain Manders

OPER

Captain Fisher

DRONES

Captain Musket

Captain Fox

S/Sgt. Brown

THE

ATIONS

WORKERS

Sgt. Franko

Captain Green

INTELLIGENCE

1st Lt. Strauss

1st Lt. Baker

T/Sgt. Devecchio   Sgt. Blackwell

S/Sgt. Blaylock

ORDERLY ROOM

S/Sgt. Light

Sgt. Major Robinson

Captain Holtzman Exec.

T/Sgt. Gebhart

Sgt. Watson

Capt. Atteridge Adjutant

S/Sgt. Keller

1st/Sgt. Kelly

M/Sgt. "Pappy" Doerr—Killed in action

Captain Timmerman—Engineering Officer

T/Sgt. Albright

M/Sgt. Passodelis

T/Sgt. Blackwell

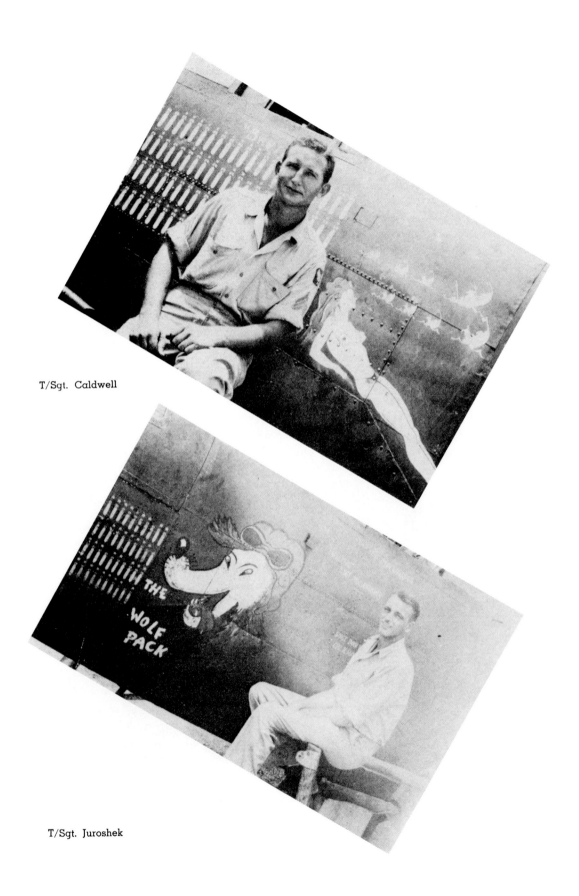

T/Sgt. Caldwell

T/Sgt. Juroshek

T/Sgt. Greenquist

Lt. Bayer

COMMUNICATIONS

Captain Meyers

T/Sgt. Abbey

Cpl. Kovak

Lt. Galloway

Capt. Geer

M/Sgt. Norton

ARMAMENT

ORDNANCE

Lt. Staply   S/Sgt. Schweitzer

MESS
MASTERS

What did you see, Soldier? What did you see at war?
I saw such glory and horror as I've never seen before.
I saw men's hearts burned naked in red crucibles of pain.
I saw such godlike courage as I'll never see again.

What did you hear, Soldier? What did you hear at war?
I heard the prayers on lips of men who had never prayed before.
I heard men tell their very souls, confessing each dark stain
I heard men speak the sacred things they will never speak again.

What did you eat, Soldier? What did you eat at war?
I ate the sour bread of fear, the acrid salt of gore.
My lips were burned with wine of hate, the scalding drink of Cain.
My tongue has known a bitter taste I would not taste again.

What did you think, Soldier? What did you think at war?
I thought, how strange we have not learned from wars that raged before,
Except new ways of killing, new multiples of pain.
Is all the blood that men have shed but blood shed all in vain?

What did you learn, Soldier? What did you learn at war?
I learned that we must learn sometime what was not learned before,
That victories won on battlefields are victories won in vain
Unless in peace we kill the germs that breed new wars again.

What did you pray, Soldier? What did you pray at war?
I prayed that we might do the thing we have not done before;
That we might mobilize for peace . . . nor mobilize in vain
Lest Christ and man be forced to climb stark Calvary again.

Our saga is not unusual, although there are few squadrons which can boast a more impressive record, but it is a story of sweat and tears, fidelity, patience, and courage. During the early period of the war, we were out-numbered in men and equipment; it should not be difficult to understand, therefore, the pride in achievement which is irrevocably ours. As the war progressed, more men and machines seeped into this theater and those who had fought so valiantly were either replaced or promoted; those who returned to the United States trained new young men who eventually carried this war to its successful consummation. Those who remained and were promoted worked assiduously to maintain the degree of efficiency of which we have always been so proud. It is our desire that the reader should realize that, irregardless of assigned tasks, the men of the 501st never waivered in their determination to achieve the inevitable victory.

When at some future time those who have lost loved ones read this story, feel that we too have mourned the death of these same friends. If consolation is possible, let it come from a letter by Abraham Lincoln to a woman who gave five sons during the Civil War: it expresses our concern for your more eloquently than we ever could.

Executive Mansion
Washington, Nov 21. 1864

To Mrs Bixby, Boston, Mass,

Dear Madam,

I have been shown in the files of the War Department a statement of the Adjutant General of Massachusetts that you are the mother of five sons who have died gloriously on the field of battle. I feel how weak and fruitless must be any word of mine which should attempt to beguile you from the grief of a loss so overwhelming. But I cannot refrain from tendering you the consolation that may be found in the thanks of the republic they died to save. I pray that our Heavenly Father may assuage the anguish of your bereavement, and leave you only the cherished memory of the loved and lost, and the solemn pride that must be yours to have laid so costly a sacrifice upon the altar of freedom.

Yours very sincerely and respectfully,

A. Lincoln

Whenever a group of men, of people rather, assemble and live together for a period of time, memories are stored in the heart and mind of each individual from the experiences which ensued. In the story, your story, which follows, we would like you to reminisce with us about the humor, the ebullience and depression, and the pathos which made this odyssey personal . . . ours alone. I think if we reflect upon the episodes which seem funniest to us now, it will be found that, at the time, they were not funny at all . . . for example, the times at Dulag when Jap raiders came over when we were on our way to chow and everyone fell flat on his face in that mud which had the consistency of molasses and the job it was to unscramble the mess kits; these scenes had the flavour of a Buster Keaton comedy and, now that they're over, are deliciously drole. To some men, the life that we lived overseas was satisfactory and pleasurable; to others it was merely an experience which had to be born; and to many others it was very nearly intolerable. But to all, irregardless of how distasteful it may have been, there are friendly memories and desirable acquaintances which should be renewed from time to time.

Our story begins in the USA—to be precise, in Columbia, South Carolina. The city of Columbia would seem heaven to us now here in the Pacific, but at the time, to the person educated or brought up in a large and cosmopolitan area, it appeared to have nothing save one excellent hotel, the Wade Hampton, and several others of mediocre quality. In comparison to other Army Air Bases, the food served at the field was inferior and a restaurant of distinction was an unknown quantity. The varieties of recreation were limited; those places which appeared interesting at first became trite and one was bored quickly. In addition to these undesirable qualities, neither officer nor enlisted man could safely walk down the main street of town. The local gestapo had cloak and dagger men lurking about ready to pounce upon any unsuspecting recruit who, confused by so many people milling about, inadvertantly failed to salute his superior officer; it was immaterial whether he were private soldier or full colonel; if he had committed the unpardonable, it was unquestionably the guillotine or, if there were extenuating circumstances, merely life imprisonment. Perhaps the facts have been somewhat enlarged, but that was the general impression left upon a not too pliant and impressionable personality. However, those were the days when "things were rough."

To get on with our story, this was the place where the original cadre was formed with Maj. Fain as C.O. The training program progressed in very much the same manner as any such program and, after many arduous hours in the air . . . and months on the ground . . . our merry throng departed. The ground echelon entrained at the local station with bag (not the feminine version) and baggage which included, as usual, numerous bottles of whiskey, gin, and any other fluid which boasted a high octane rating. As one casual observer remarked: "Gawd, but it's gonna be drunk out tonight!", his comment was not far from the absolute truth. Dirty, tired, and definitely seedy in appearance, we trudged into Camp Stoneman. Private Buckanan was especially seedy because a baggage car, in which he spent most of the trip, doesn't seem to be the place to maintain a well-groomed appearance. His communion with the mail sacks was the result of having handed a letter out of the window and even the greenest second lieutenant knows that that sort of thing is definitely "verboten." It seemed a shame and rather absurd that he was compelled to remain in this stable by guards bearing sub machine guns and was allowed not even the "necessite de toilette" in the usual manner; however, as Sherman so aptly put it: "War is Hell."

We remained at Stoneman a week, more or less, having received no more freedom than five-hour-passes into Pittsburg, California, and boarded the ferry for San Francisco and embarkation. Virtually everyone was burning up the wires with the final adieu to his family or friends; such a conversation at this moment is a morale-builder the equal of which I have never found and it seemed to transform our boys into bouyant and carefree lads.

The USS President Johnson a World War I transport, hadn't been claimed by Neptune merely because he didn't want it . . . and that was readily understandable. This vessel, even at its launching during the Boer War, was not fit to carry human cargo and its qualifications for this use had decreased measurably. In the bottom hold, one expected to see tre-

PANTHERS' PRIMITIVE PETS

Capt. Gallagher—To the rescue

mendous black Nubian slaves, chained to their benches, pulling heavy oars. There were two reasons for this. First, we couldn't imagine to what use the abysmal depths could be put and second, it was difficult to tell what means of locomotion was in use. It was with foreboding and extreme consternation that we followed our guide down innumerable steps toward our quarters. To make a distasteful story brief, we were to live where Nubian blacks should have been and there was but one consolation—we didn't have to row.

Eggs, eggs, eggs. Now eggs are all right in moderation and they certainly have a place in the well-balanced diet, but to eat them for breakfast, lunch and dinner for thirty days is a bit more than the average man can go. Nevertheless, these were the circumstances and everyone was surprised that his stomach hadn't rebelled and at the end of the voyage if one more hard-boiled egg had been served, not only stomaches, but the men as well, would have revolted. However, those were the days when "things were rough."

It was a tired bunch of boys that climbed off the boat in the harbor at Brisbane. The long march to Camp Doomben was gruelling, and many of the boys were picked up by the ambulances where they dropped. The troops spent only a few days here, but this period was filled to overflowing with peculiar happenings. Nearly everyone climbed the fence and hitched-hiked to town, but there are al-

ways those who become the victims of circumstance and they were charged AWOL. The consequences were not dire, but they seemed too harsh because the boys only wanted something to eat . . . they were actually hungry. Never have I tasted anything quite so good as the first plate of hot pork and beans with good Aussie beer to wash them down.

Brisbane is a city of approximately 150,-000 people and, during our stay there, it was swelled to bursting with Americans; the city is not beautiful, but it has a certain charm through the friendliness of the people and clean cafes where good substantial meals were to be had by men who were very nearly starved. Before we left the camp, the C.O. threw a big party with plenty of beer and whiskey and, since the situation was already at rock bottom, it improved infinitely and a good time was had by all.

We bid farewell to the land of kangaroos, for the present, and again boarded the *USS President Johnson* for the perilous journey to Port Moresby; since "general quarters" was sounded frequently and Corvettes dropped "ash cans" continuously, all men were engulfed in a blanket of pessimism. It was not

Original Camp Site

P.M., NEW GUINEA

244

Guard Inspection

the general concensus of opinion that we would reach our destination.

At this point it might be well to go back to Columbia, to Walterboro rather, and pick up the flight echelon. During the period when ground personnel were battling the elements on the high seas, the fly-boys were still training. Equipped with new aircraft, we moved to Walterboro, were processed, flew to a westcoast embarkation field, changed carburetors, and made the usual southern route flight to Australia and on to Moresby. I have made this section of our travels brief because it was uneventful and routine. This is the point at which the first chapter of our odyssey is concluded . . . this is the point at which Stateside living and thinking ended and combat began. We take you now to Port Moresby and "combat."

Our first impression of Port Moresby and our final analysis were completely dissimilar due to the fact that unloading was accomplished at night in a driving rain. Capt. Gallagher saved the day by issuing "C" rations and quartering the men in an old mess hall which had been previously used by the 3rd Attack. On the downbeat, the mud resembled mush and, attempting to release one foot, glue; the night was spent miserably, but the morning found the weather CAVU and definitely conducive

to good hard work. We were stationed at 14-mile strip, so-called because of its distance from the town, an area vacated shortly before by the 3rd and 13th Bomb Groups. By nightfall, the area was cleared of bushes and large rocks and although not comfortable yet, it was adequate.

The Fuzzy Wuzzies must be mentioned at this point because they made themselves indespensible as general workers, "wash-wash" boys, and because of their unwavering loyalty to us. It's incidental to the story, but they admired us so much that many of them cut their hair either "butch" style or in the latest Hollywood fashion. In two weeks' time, the Squadron was well settled and we found the varieties of recreation abundant in this new world. For example: There were the fat-cat rides to 30-mile strip for pineapples and bananas, the river which offered excellent swimming, the deer hunts . . . the meat supplemented our diet deliciously, and we had fun domesticating and training Wallobies for pets. Two of the boys were out in the jungle hunting and came upon a thirty-foot python. If they had not been armed, the snake would probably have mesmerized them, but stout fellows that they were, the lads killed the monster and returned to the area carrying their burden and each thinking himself Frank Buck.

Guard Duty

With General Ramey as guest of honor, the enlisted men formally opened the most outstanding club in southern New Guinea. Girls from the Australian Women's Army Service (Nurses' Aids) were invited for this and many parties afterwards. None of them resembled Lana Turner, but they served their purpose amiably and well. Three months after arrival, the officers' club opened officially and, according to the "old boys" who were here when "things were rough," it was the finest that the brass has ever had at any station to which this group has moved. Our Australian Liaison Officer, who set up the rescue for airmen and occasionally briefed the crews, added a certain touch which seemed to say: "Boys, you're not alone over here; there are other countries fighting this war too," and at times it was very comforting. The spirit of the Squadron was wonderful to watch; every man from C.O. to cook was out to watch take off and sweat out the return; it is just such pride and mutual interest in our fellows that has made this one of the outstanding squadrons of the war.

Among the officers there were several changes toward the end of our stay at this station. The Engineering Officer, Lt. Hopkins, was transferred to a service group and, to fill the vacancy, Capt. Timmerman moved in. Capt. Fridge, who later went to VBC and was promoted to the rank of Lt. Col. was ordered to Group as Operations Officer. Lt. Epstein became Assistant Adjutant and the inimitable Capt. Andrew went to the Dutch Air Force as Liaison Officer. Although we were fed-up, literally, with Aussie chow, fresh milk was served and we've cried for it ever since. There were numerous leaves to Sydney while our planes were modified to strafers and to those who have been to Sydney, nothing more need be said.

Concerning combat, although many dangerous missions were flown, we lost but one airplane. Lt. Aubrey Morre and his crew were shot down over Rabaul and, since we were hitting everything from battleships to sugardogs, it's surprising that our losses weren't heavier. We experienced few air raids and flew many. The terrain was difficult, over the Owen-Stanley range, but we managed several raids,

staging out of Dobadura, on Rabaul. These lasted for two months, in addition to supply-dropping missions over Southern New Guinea, and on these we met our first Jap interception. The count may be somewhat inaccurate, but we chalked up twelve and three probables. For our attacks on the Imperial Japanese Air Forces and bases, "Toyko Rose" announced that the 345th Bomb Group, the "Dobadura Butchers" would be completely wiped out within a month. Foolish, wasn't she?

In December of 1943 we moved to Dobadura to a temporary area which had previously been occupied by the 22nd Bomb Group. We had to build nothing since all of their buildings had been left intact and moving into such an area was quite pleasant and simple. The enlisted men had brought several cases of gin from the PX and there was no little agitation when the entire supply disappeared. The drawbacks to Dobo consisted mainly of the lack of sleep brought about by the numerous Jap air raids and, since enemy troops were close at hand, the long hours of guard duty. Fortunately, we lost nary a man due to either of these discomforts.

Life is generally dull and boring overseas and any diversion is welcome. Before we arrived the Australians had promised the natives a party, the splendor of which was beyond their imaginations, if they would resist the Japs and remain loyal to the white man. Thus about the midpoint of our stay at Dobo, a party was given for all the natives within a hundred mile radius; food aplenty was imported for the black boys who, for the occasion, had attired themselves in the very latest in New Guinea war costumes. As the accompanying pictures show, the garb is primitive

but interesting. It was also interesting to observe how drastically different their standard of living is from ours, and although their life expectancy is only one-half of that of the Occidental, how sturdy and energetic they are considering the ill-balance of their diet. Although they would be considered a bit dull in the better circles, these natives are really a most amazing people. The Australians have introduced the game of soccer football to them; their rapid understanding and agility are surprising and, if it were not for the native attire and dark skin, one could easily imagine that the match was being played between Oxford and Cambridge. Many are the times that we stood and marveled at the effortless performance and skill of these primitive boys who, in so far as I know, seldom saw a white man prior to the war. Travel enhances the understanding between peoples—it was certainly true of Americans, Australians and Filipinos. Our customs may vary, but our moral principles and aims run parallel.

During our stay there, three of our ships went down due to enemy action but, owing to the efficient rescue system, several of the crew

Capt. Still—Flight Surgeon

248

members returned not much worse for the experience. It's strange how pilots and crews can see their friends go down and yet say to themselves: "It's unfortunate, but it won't happen to me." Every man, if he thinks about it at all, seems to feel that it won't happen to him.

In all probability Capts. Kilroy, Bailey and Manders and their crews thought so on the mornings of their respective flights. Capt. Kilroy and his crew took off one morning on what they thought to be just another mission, but it turned out to be something entirely different. They were briefed, went out to the ship, took off, hit Wewak and were hit over the target. Returning home, Capt. Kilroy found that

Mess Hall

he couldn't hold altitude and informed his crew that he was about to crash land. Looking about, he spotted a likely spot. After the usual preliminaries, he set it down in a field of deep grass just west of Modango. When they didn't return, search missions were arranged and patrols flown covering the area of his possible return route. Concealing themselves from the Japs, they attracted the attention of our searching party and, now that their position was

known, went back into hiding. On Christmas day, an Aussie patrol having been summoned for the rescue, dinner and mail were dropped to the men and it was undoubtedly the most welcome meal which any of them had ever tasted. None of the crew had been injured in the crash. After a couple of days, they were picked up and returned to the Squadron in comparatively good shape.

Captain Bailey and his company were not so fortunate. Again the mission was over Wewak and again the ships were hit; on the return trip, having sufficient altitude, the pilot instructed his crew to bail out—and when such an order is given, very few men stop to question or weigh the relative merits of the command—they hit the silk. Just afterward, the Captain sighted a stretch of river and it seemed to be a fielder's choice whether to follow his men or ride it down. However, he decided on the latter and ditched successfully. He, like Kilroy, was just west of Modango, was sighted by our patrol, and was picked up and returned by the Aussies; but unlike Kilroy, the other members of the crew were never recovered or heard of again. It's always difficult for the men who remain to lose their buddies, but the show must go on—"c'est la guerre."

The last of our unfortunate losses at this station occurred to a pilot who was well liked by everyone. Capt. Manders was always happy, the life of every party, and it didn't seem in the cards that he should go, but one becomes a fatalist quickly in war and apparently his time had come. There was no Air-Sea rescue in those days and if you ditched near enemy troop concentrations, there was little

Capt. Nusbaum—Our New C.O.

Capt. Jacobson—Our Operations Officer

first replacements for whom a training program was immediately arranged. In addition to the new flying personnel, ground replacements in small numbers joined the Squadron, and, needless to say, they were welcome. Maj. Fain, our C.O. at that time, and many of the "old men" started their journey home; everyone was glad to see them go because they had worked assiduously and were largely responsible for the progress of our part in the war effort thus far.

For those men who have never been stationed at Nadzab, let me say that, although our area was more than adequate, it is a festering sore on the face of the earth and definitely should not be the destination of any post-war traveler. There are seasons of the year, short in duration, during which it's unbearable; but for the most part, it is hot, intolerably hot, and humid . . . a humidity which leaves one's skin oily and sticky . . . and makes one feel that he is constantly in need of a bath. As has been true in most places where lumber was available, we lived in wooden shacks, the floors of which were raised about two feet above the ground to exclude some of the vermin, and pyramidal tents served as roofs. During our stay there, screening wasn't necessary because mosquitoes were not to be seen or felt and malaria and dengue fever were almost a non-entity.

Our recreational facilities were probably as good or better there than at any station to which this group has gone. There were soft-

left but prayer and that, to my knowledge, hasn't saved most crews in this position. The strike was on shipping in Hansa Bay and Capt. Manders was hit as he started his run on a large freighter; the ack-ack was heavy and fairly accurate . . . as it always is in a bay . . . and rather than be taken alive by the Japs, he dove his ship into the boat and sank same. For this superb action, he and his crew received the Distinguished Service Cross and Purple Heart; decorations hardly compensate for the price they paid.

This period of activity ended on a much happier note when the orders arrived sending several men back to the U.S. for a well-earned rest—something like a reprieve from the governor—and the morale of those who remained was buoyed by a glimmer of hope. So much for Dobadura.

We arrived at Nadzab in February with seventeen crews and soon after received our

Capt. Epstein

Martinez

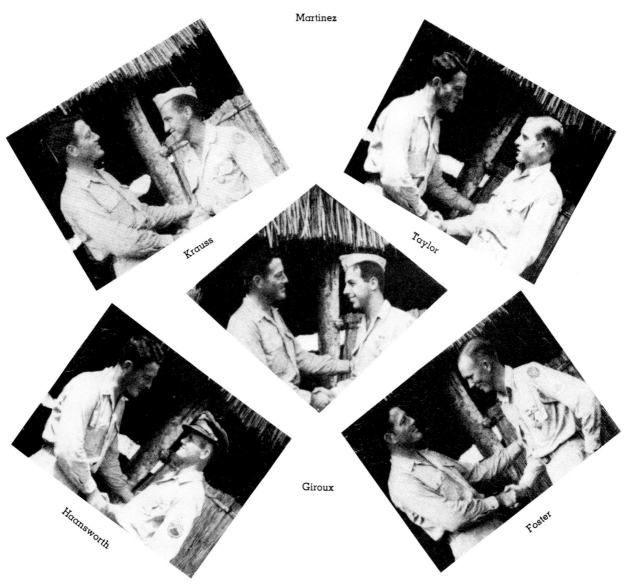

Krauss

Taylor

Giroux

Haansworth

Foster

ball tournaments for both enlisted men and officers . . . and we held our own very well. Our theatre was excellent and this was a form of recreation to which all men looked forward, and the Aussies put on boxing matches for us. Nadzab bears no resemblance, even in the wildest imagination, to New York but, all in all, our stay there was relatively pleasant.

A forward area combat unit never eats well, but we became so tired of bully beef and other items on the Aussie menu that the situation became critical and the brass fretted about the impending mutiny; putting aside such levity, the meals w e r e deplorable and the change, when it came, was appreciated like nothing else I have even seen. To alleviate boredom and jangled nerves and to put combat into the innermost recesses of our psyche, parties on a magnificent scale were thrown in the mess hall and liquor and relaxation were in abundance; in addition, each tent was issued a supply of gin. Drunk or sober Nadzab wasn't a good place to be, but it was better drunk. To give you some idea of just how bad off you really were there, the main man had a nervous breakdown and went home on a section eight . . . and was glad and proud of it.

We had our moments of excitement too. One day a B-24 returned from a mission and couldn't lower his wheels; it was nip and tuck for a while, but finally we saw some chutes blossoming out and it was interesting because

none of us had even seen a man bail out. There was another instance when T/Sgt. Decopelis walked into a prop. It was a gruesome sight and one which no one forgot for some time to come.

From Nadzab we said goodbye to our Australian Liaison Officers. They had done a fine job for us and we were genuinely sorry to leave them. During the same month the Group celebrated its first annual milestone wedded to VBC and a mutually beneficial union it had been. The Group offered a couple of quarts of liquor to the man suggesting the best name and submitting the best poster for an insignia. I don't recall just who won the prize, but the Group officially adopted the name "Air Apaches." Leaves to Sydney opened up and 1/Sgt. Kelly left on a well earned rest. Leaves to Sydney were given only to flying personnel hereafter for rest from combat but, rather than resting, most men returned weaker than when they left.

One fellow to whom I spoke had some very interesting views on this fair city—let me relate them to you and bring some familiar names to mind at the same time. He had an apartment at Bondi Beach which was three or four miles from the center of town; in order to find the largest selection of pulchritude, he arrived at Mansion's or any of the bars on Kings' Cross at about five o'clock. Before he had

Capt. Nevenschwander

252

der of the evening was spent, but he ended by saying that these girls were very much the same as American girls in appearance, but the Aussie lassies know why they were put on earth. What do you suppose he meant?

The system of penalties overseas varies somewhat from that in the States; in some cases the judgment was more severe while in others it was very mild. For instance: Corp. Harry Yeager, always a joker, was sent to Australia on furlough; apparently he overslept because he turned up thirty days late and everyone assumed that the proverbial book would be thrown at him; but, to our surprise . . . and his I imagine, a fine of $12.00 was imposed; rather drole, n'est ce pas?

downed his first scotch and soda, one of the innumerable leaches cornered him and stated, quite frankly, that he wanted to take his girl out and he needed a few coins. When asked why he nedeed money, since it was well known that Aussie couples usually go "dutch", he replied that he wished to be a gentleman and buy her a cup of tea later. Having cast this worm aside like an old shoe, my friend spotted the likely object of his choice. Kings' Cross is the area where most of the single working girls live. Having quickly acquired her assent, they retired to the best restaurant in the city— the best was none too good for our boy. He failed to mention in what manner the remain-

Sgt. Blackwell and The News

"The Character"—Cpl. Yeager

Headquarters

"Poop From The Groop"

Many awards and promotions came through and many men changed jobs; our boys received three D.F.C.'s, 25 Air Medals and Clusters; and Lt. Michael Murphy received the Purple Heart for wounds received over Wewak. Capt. Neuenschwander was appointed C.O. and one week later was sent to Group. Capt. Nusbam was then made C.O. and Capt. Coffman was Operation Officer. Capt. Gallagher was appointed Executive Officer, but not for long because he went to the hospital for a serious eye injury sustained in a jeep accident. Lt. Mather was made Armament Officer and Lt. Strauss, our Intelligent Officer, was transferred to the 498th Squadron. Bruce Marston was made assistant Group Operations Officer and Capt. Malliet went to VBC as Armament Officer. So much for that. About the middle of the last month at Nadzab, the men were in a turmoil because the Group was alerted for the move to Biak. At this time, Biak was not definitely ours and the though of becoming an infantryman as well as an airman was a trifle alarming. However, the move was made several weeks later with complete safety—for the time being!

The move to Biak was much different from any that we had made before or since because none of the heavy equipment was taken and everything we had was moved by air. Every jeep, weapon carrier, and truck shuttled back and forth between the line and the area for a

couple of days loading the C-47s which, in turn, shuttled back and forth between Nadzab and Biak.

We have all heard of and wished for fat-cat jobs and sinecures and the following is an anecdote about a man who fell into just such a position. After the group had moved ahead to the new station, Lt. Staply, having been so ordered, had every bit of the heavy equipment trucked down to Lae. This required only one or two days and, for him, it wasn't really hard work at that. From then until the group moved from Biak to Dulag, some two and a half to three months, he stayed at the officers' club at Lae, ate the excellent food which they served, drank the "Black and White" scotch which was abundant, and had a pleasant association with the Red Cross girls who arrived soon after the squadron left Nadzab. He lived this life of Riley until the boat came down from Biak to pick him up and the

Lt. Erspamer

equipment. Oh, well, these were the days when "things were rough."

Our area was adjacent to Mokmer strip and this was fortunate because we didn't have to travel too far to the planes. There was nothing resembling an area when we arrived, but by hook or crook we managed to find tractors and trucks to haul in coral and level and roll it into shape. We had the natives working the whole day burying dead Japs and the officers

APACHE

PLAY

HOUSE

and enlisted men rolling and carrying bombs away in order that the coral could be moved in. We lined up the tents and tied them down; the living conditions weren't good, but eventually some of the boys built wooden floors and rigged up parachutes as ceilings and a little more comfort was enjoyed. After the cool green shades of Nadzab, the bright glare off the coral was hard on the eyes and pilots had trouble for a while with depth perception. There seems to be a tendency to level off high on a bright strip and most of us did just that the first few landings.

We had several promotions and a good addition in the person of Lt. Ike Baker, assistant Intelligence Officer; Capt. Erspamer became Executive Officer, Lt. "Lucky" Holtzman was appointed Adjutant; a memorandum was sent to Group by our C.O. and I think it's worth mentioning here because it proved that he had the interest of the men at heart. It runs as follows:

"The general effectiveness of the Squadron during August as reflected by the esprit de corps, morale, general health, living conditions in the Squadron Camp Area, and combat operations, has been very good.

Morale of our officers and men has been very good, due largely to the following factors: New flying personnel replacements are eager and anxious to 'get going' on their jobs; very favorable progress of the Allied Armies in all theatres of operations; the apparent inability of the Japanese to make an effective stand against our aerial attacks; and a decided improvement in our squadron mess.

New officer promotion regulations have made it difficult to fill T.O.'s and put rank in the right places. The overall effect of this remains to be seen. Some initiative and enthusiasm may be destroyed, but it is hoped some let up may occur in the future. A more lenient policy would enable the outstanding men to attain the rank they deserve before war weariness sets in.

A definite policy for return of combat men to the States for rehabilitation would be welcomed. Reversals of policy have made it difficult to plan in advance. Morale is definitely affected, and the men do a much better job if there is a goal to reach. Adequate replacements seem to be available at present and the future looks bright.

Health of our men has been very good. The initial fears of typhus, malaria, and other tropical diseases have not materialized, due to prompt, thorough, and effective preventative measures taken by our medical authorities. The initial problem of an adequate water supply for drinking, cooking, and personal cleanliness has been met in a very satisfactory manner.

All in all, this organization has shown once again that it is sound in every department and that whatever problems may arise, our officers and men can cope with them efficiently and ingeniously and carry through to a successful conclusion."

John B. Nusbaum
Captain, Air Corps.
Commanding

10 September 1944

Shortly after this was written, Capt. Nusbaum went on leave and Lt. Davis assumed command. Capt. Underwood was transferred to Group and Capt. Lewis and Lt. Monaghan returned to the States. These last two men were of the original cadre and rotation was certainly due them. Lt. Jacobson became assistant Operations Officer under Lt. Coffman.

There was one mission which was flown that was particularly interesting to all concerned. The strike was on Ternate, the Halmaheras, the former seat of the Dutch Government in this group. We came in low and bombed the Sultan's Palace and, we cursed ourselves later, blew up part of the harem. A sad bunch of boys returned that afternoon. There were many exciting incidents which occurred on the island and one of them was very sad. Sgts. "Pappy" Doerr, Green Overcash, and Wagner were killed one night in one of the numerous Jap air raids; we mourned these boys particularly because they were indispensable and so well liked. In this same raid, many of our boys were injured and it seemed small compensation to give them, and those who were killed, the Purple Heart.

This same night, just off our area in the bay, a P-61 shot down a Jap Bomber and we

257

thought this to be the prettiest fireworks which we had ever seen. Shortly afterwards, we received B-25-Js in small numbers and the men immediately set to work on the modifications. Capt. Timmerman and Sgt. Holsonback installed a new innovation in ship No. 437, the first wing camera used by bombers in the southwest Pacific. It took frontal photos and gave us a true picture of any target before and after the attack. We lost only two planes during our many months on Biak. Lt. Nird-

Lt. Ed Kasten

linger and his crew were killed on a combat mission; the crew members were Lt. Scalzone, Lt. Hedenquist, T/Sgt. Welch, S/Sgt. Romaine and Sgt. Ratnoff.

Lt. Edward Kasten and his crew were on a weatherrecco mission and were intercepted by several Jap fighters. T/Sgt. Hazelrig bagged two Zeros, but the plane was shot up pretty badly and they were forced to crash land on the beach near the strip. The terrain was bad and none came out alive; for the two Zeros, Sgt. Hazelrig received the D.F.C. posthumously. After three years of separation, 1/Sgt. Kelly met his brother and a happy reunion it was. After leaving, his brother found himself in the unfortunate position of riding in a plane which was to crash land, successfully I might add, in the jungle of New Guinea. Everyone came out without a scratch and apparently the trek out was very interesting.

There were always couriers going to Nadzab for food and all kinds of supplies and everyone wanted to get on them. Our chow was better at Biak than at any station at which we had been stationed before or since; we had fresh fruit and vegetables and eggs and

the coke and ice cream shack functioned with amazing regularity; we received our first issue of Stateside beer and only God knows how good it tasted. Have you ever been to a night football game and heard the announcer ask the audience to light matches? At night, the Japs who were imprisoned in caves in the hills, lighted their cooking fires and it immediately reminded everyone of the night games in the States. During our stay here, Spanish classes were held for anyone wishing to attend; some fellows thought that it would be useful in the Philippines but, as it turned out, Spanish was of no use. The Filipinos don't speak the language.

Several of our boys attended the Birthday Party for the Queen of the Netherlands and said that they enjoyed themselves immensely. We had a fine theatre, the "Apache Playhouse," and fine shows which included many USO shows, movies, and the Bob Hope Show. Theatrical shows became our most pleasant pastime. A unique organization was started by a group of our enlisted men and from what I can gather, it promises to be a gala affair. The "Black Panther Bombers" of which 1/Sgt. Kelly is president and S/Sgt. Valentine treasurer, are going to meet for a three-day reunion at the Hotel Pennsylvania in New York City; to defray expenses, they had already collected from its members $1500.00 and there is more to come. Since there are only twenty-five members, there should be no suffering from want.

One Squadron landed the first B-26, or any other kind of bomber, on the Philippines; the crew of this plane consisted of Capt. Brigham, Capt. Jones, Lt. Robin, Lt. Moore, Lt. Ohnelius, T/Sgt. Casty, T/Sgt. Greenquist, and T/Sgt. Pitzner. When the plane had come to the end of its landing roll, Connie Greenquist jumped out and had the distinction of being the first Air Corpsman on the Islands; the plane, after completing official business, returned to Biak. The ground echelons moved to Dulag.

With the opening of October our ground echelon was alerted for a move and immediately departments began to check equipment and supplies that might not be needed until further operations. On the 10th of October orders were given that we were to be loaded on a boat by the 12th of the month. Upon receipt of orders, crews were formed for packing and boxing of supplies and the disassembling of

THE

AREA

THE

QUICK

And The

DEAD

buildings. The Ringling Brothers Circus preparing to leave town never packed with such speed and efficiency as that of this Squadron. At 1620 hours October 12th the last man clambered on board the troop transport, the SS Charles Loomis.

Other organizations aboard were the 500th Bomb Squadron, 892nd Chemical Company and a few men from the 498th and 499th Bomb Squadron. Soon after the coming of darkness the ship got under way for Lae, New Guinea. Everyone was much pleased over his quarters

Capt. Smith—Well Liked

as each enlisted man had a troop transport bed and plenty of room for comfort and the officers occupied rooms containing six to twelve beds. It was a very comfortable set-up and all enjoyed the ice cold water from the drinking fountains.

The troops' food was prepared in a large galley and the table space was excellent. Regular cafeteria trays were used and the meals were far above the expectation of any man on board the ship. We reached Lae on the 16th of October and much to our surprise discovered we were to be transferred to a cargo ship, the SS Morrison R. Waite, as the SS Charles Loomis had insufficient cargo space for our large equipment that was to come aboard. The cargo was then shifted

to the SS Morrison R. Waite and on the 19th of October, four days later, we pulled out of Lae harbor to catch our convoy which was due to sail from Hollandia, Dutch New Guinea. Living conditions were much different on the SS Morrison R. Waite. Tents and all types of shelters were erected on the deck to weather the troops from the storms. The "Waite" reminded one of an overgrown family barge in some of Mark Twain's books on the Mississippi River. A mess shack was erected near number two hold and troops could be seen winding their way around and between vehicles of all types to reach the serving line. Mess kits were again used by everyone. There was only one drinking fountain aboard and it contained cold water which was much welcome; but due to the shortage of fresh water aboard the ship there were several hours a day that this water fountain was turned off.

On the 20th of October we steamed into Hollandia Harbor and on the morning of the 23rd, we were well out to sea in a 32-ship convoy. On October 29th we dropped anchor in Leyte Bay, Philippine Islands. Early that evening we were greeted by a typical tropic typhoon and although pretty nervous, we weathered the storm in good condition. On the evening of October 31st we watched the Japs pull a "Hallowe'en Prank." Two planes came from out of nowhere to strafe our shore installations and bomb a fuel dump. This was only a mild prelude to that which awaited us at this new station.

Our stay on Leyte was brief, but certainly not uneventful. When we came into the harbor at Dulag, Lt. Galloway went ashore with the advance detail to San Pablo Airdrome No. 2 at Buraugen, but VBC deemed it unsuitable and we changed our site. What happened to our ships in the harbor is the most gruesome experience which the 501st had ever suffered. Both our transports, the SS Thomas Nelson and the SS Morrison Waite were hit by suicide bombers and the consequences were ghastly.

Capt. Shetron was up front in the hold with the enlisted men on the Nelson when she was hit and he and 25 of our boys were killed and 40 more wounded seriously; on the Waite, 15 were killed in a similar manner and about the same number wounded. While the Merchant Marine sat idly by, a few of the

WHITE WING OLDIE BUT GOODIE

WEARY BUT WILLING

men worked like men possessed to remove the wounded from the burning hold. Sgt. Allday seemed to have the constitution of a bull; he did the work of three men and, in addition, piled the pieces of the dead bodies into one corner so that they might later be identified and receive a proper burial. There were many heroes that day who were never rewarded! The main body finally went ashore to the area, three miles south of Dulag, which offered little except a really excellent beach toward an eventually satisfactory camp. The mud here was so deep that it mired down the "Ducks" which had come ashore with supplies and, brother, that's mud! After the area was completed, the boys had plenty of free time and recreation and this wonderful beach and here we had our first laundresses; heretofore, we had either washed our own clothes or, at best, a washing machine was set up to accommodate the entire Squadron. This was adequate but not good. Services were held on Thanksgiving Day for those who had been killed upon

our arrival at Dulag and, although it inspired deep pathos, the services were beautiful and fitting. This was really our first baptism of fire; everyone was "trigger happy" and, after learning the events which followed, it is easily understandable.

One night a Jap transport, which closely resembles a C-47, entered the downwind leg and landed; an Infantry guard opened the door of the plane and was immediately shot. Men poured out of the ship and rushed toward one of the Infantry camps, intent upon wiping it out, but the damage to nerves was done. Later in the week, paratroops landed and surrounded VBC. Machine guns were put into every window and riflemen filled every foxhole to ward off the impending attack, but this attack never came; reinforcements eventually arrived and the situation was again in hand, but most of the men were becoming slightly neurotic.

Our own boys couldn't walk about in the evening for fear of being shot by the guards,

263

Under Construction

who shot at anything which moved. We had "red alerts" constantly and the evening that the paratroops came over, the anti-aircraft batteries, because the planes were so low, shot holes in the tents. One of our carriers not far from Leyte had been hit and the planes which were airborne at the time circled our strip for some time. The traffic was so heavy that 200 assorted airplanes crash landed on the strip or the beach and the wrecking crews worked night and day clearing them away. The next day a C-46, which had just taken off, was hit by a low flying L-5 and the 22 passengers aboard the transport were killed in the ensuing fire. That night, a string of frags from a Jap bomber completely demolished a row of aircraft. In addition, several evenings on the way to chow, our little yellow brothers strafed and bombed the area. Although no damage was sustained, hours were required to unscramble the mess kits and scrape the mud off our bodies. After all this. nerves were at the breaking point; understandable, what?

While we lived through this holocaust, the flight echelon was living a fat-cat life at Biak which was no longer under attack; our food was intolerable while they still existed on those nasty old fresh vegetables and fresh meat. Ah, well, things were tough all over. The flight echelon had modified all the planes and trained the new crews and shortly after Christmas, they and our wounded men arrived.

The move to Tacloban was short and with very little inconvenience. Upon arriving, we observed a sea of mud and our first thought was "Oh, God, deliver us," but the area was easily and quickly drained and a semblance of order ensued. Living conditions are never satisfactory overseas but various places impress one as either above or below the mean and Tacloban was slightly above. They showed movies three times weekly; there were the news talks every evening by Lt. Baker; we had ice cream and coke almost daily; a sandy beach was available; occasionally there was sunshine; and life in general carried a bright hue. Lt. Gross flew a courier to Lingayen and, upon returning, held our interest . . . which is something of a feat . . . for hours with many interesting tales.

There were new crews to be trained, several promotions, a few men sent back to the States, the departments used squad tents because it was only a temporary base, we shared the mess hall with the 500th, T/Sgt. Casty, a radio operator, flew 104 missions before they caught up with him and now, he's back in the States enjoying the fruits of civilization. Some weeks before, the ground echelon had pulled out for San Marcelino. With the planes loaded to bursting, we took off for the Philippines.

Upon arriving, we found ourselves in an extremely precarious position which was frought with sinister aspect. Clark Field, which lay over the mountains, was not fully in our possession at the time and the Infantry was pushing the Japs toward our camp. We had been told to get out if we valued our necks, but we weren't informed where to go so we set

up defenses and remained. During the days between sleepless nights, the enlisted men and officers moved their areas as close together as possible, set up machine guns at strategic points, and appointed a rotating guard which watched with inexorable vigilance. Apparently our fears were groundless, for neither were we attacked nor did we ever see a Jap . . . alive, that is.

There seemed to be a certain divergence of opinion concerning the relative merits of our present area and climate. The nights were cool and definitely conducive to sleep, the days were balmy and clear, and we hadn't far to go to the airplanes . . . these are all true; on the other hand, there was an acute lack of fresh water; this was particularly tiresome because the heavy winds kept the area inundated in dust, and thirst and a desire to bathe were always with us. In addition, we were forced to live on the ground and, due to the fact that it was only a temporary base, even

the departments were housed in squad tents. The food was intolerable and boredom reigned supreme. It even became so intense that the fellows were starting to make passes at the laundry girls. However, near the close of the first month, the area was arranged, the danger of attack had passed, and life became relatively pleasant.

Entertainment at this station was at a new high; the volleyball and baseball teams were well represented on each and every night of league play. Everyone had a big old time in the town. Manila whiskey flowed in the gutters . . . just where it belonged; the theatre was excellent and, in addition to "This Is The Army", the shows were of unusually good quality; occasionally the Seabee Band played a concert, the ETO walk chalk talks by Ike Baker, which attracted the notice and attendance of men from other groups, were excellent. Most enjoyable and sought after of all were the four-day passes to the Group house in Manila. We had two houses, one for the enlisted men and one for the officers, the excellence of

which was not to be surpassed anywhere in the city.

SHANGRI-LA

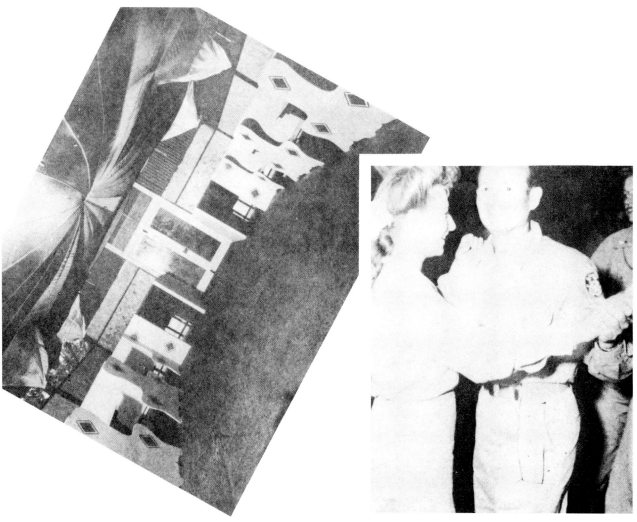

267

Capt. Marcus—Flight Surgeon

Probably the attacks for which our Group is best known are those which were carried forth from San Marcelino for the China Sea blockade. Our Squadron lost more that its share of planes, but we did more than our share of destruction. Capt. Timmerman and Lt. Bayer did more than was required and kept 94 per cent of the planes available at all times; the crew chiefs worked like dogs night and day and proved their indespensability. About a month before we left Marcelino, Capt. Holtzman and the advanced detail were at Clark Field constructing the building which would house the orderly room, operations, the mess hall, etc. When the Group moved sometime later in May, there was little to do save erect tents in which to live, and move in our furniture. Because of the short distance between the two stations and the efficiency of Holtzman and Co., this was the easiest move we had ever made.

Although we ran several missions to the China Sea and many to Formosa—over which the casualties were heavy—our Clark Field period was devoted primarily to checking out new first pilots and practice bombing on the old hull just off shore at Marcelino. We made a stab at "Glip" bombing on the range at Fort Stotsenburg, frequently ferried the war-wearies to Biak via Peleliu—the garden spot of the Pacific—and flew pathfinder missions to Okinawa for several fighter groups.

Without minimizing the importance of our attacks, it seemed to the men that this was more a period of preparation for Okinawa, which it turned out to be. Maj. Jones, a graduate of the Point, had been our C.O. at Marcelino and had been so fine that it was difficult to imagine any new man filling his shoes adequately; Maj. Giese took the reins and, although he lacked his predecessor's military background, filled the position with proficiency and poise. Capt. Foy was the new Operations Officer, filling the very capable shoes of Capt. Muskey, and a harder-working officer I've never seen; his job was particularly difficult since the lack of first pilots was acute and new men had to be trained and checked out; in short, he did a beautiful job! There were several promotions among the officers: Lts. Steel, Chealander, Stone and Wilkinson received their

Upon arriving at the Group house with clean clothes and mosquito bar, the first indication that one's stay here was to be pleasant was the savory smell of edible food . . . in our straits, meals fit for a king. The first thought that came to mind was "Get on the telephone, you chump, and sound out the hospital for dates for the next four nights." This every man did and, strangely enough, the hospital could always furnish, not necessarily queens, but attractive and charming nurses for every occasion. Sun baths with a book and a highball in hand had special appeal to the escapists. In the afternoon, the trips into the shopping district relieved us of some combat fatigue and a great deal of money; exorbitance is a euphemism for the price system in Manila. With a jeep and command car at our disposal any time of the day or night, just being apart from the Army camp and routine and just everything in general made these leaves purposeful and successful.

269

firsts; Flight Officers Mathews, Casky and Opdyke received commissions; and Capt. Foy, then a first, was given his new rank.

When we reached Clark from Marcelino at seven o'clock in the evening, the usual evening clouds had gathered and the impending rain forced us to work like mad to raise the tents before the deluge. New men moved into any tent in which there was space and a modicum of hospitality. By the time the rain began to fall, everyone was under protection. The following morning the sun shone brightly and organized construction was underway; by nightfall, the area had assumed new proportions but, since everyone knew this to be only a temporary area, few wooden floors were laid. Our mess hall was already built when we arrived, but it took a few days to make the improvements which eventually ensued.

In the officer's side, knives, forks, spoons, plates, and cups in addition to the Filippino waiters, helped to make existence more supportable and the colloquial expression "you've never had it better" was really a truth. The meals served were, during the first weeks, not too tasty but toward the end of our stay, steaks, chops, and fried chicken were the order of the day. Happiness and contentment reigned supreme. Our area rested directly in the middle of a barrio and, consequently we

had numerous laundresses, house boys, and a barber shop at which a shave could be had at a price which was left entirely to your conscience. Yes, upon reflection, I can see that life was relatively superior at Clark. Our little barrio offered in smaller doses what many of the larger towns, Angeles and San Fernando had, except the "swing bands" of questionable quality. San Fernando was the town at which the march of Bataan ended and each and every Filipino told us that he had thrown banana skins filled with rice and bananas to the suffering soldiers; every time we asked them why they charged so much for everything which they sold, they replied: "We been under Jap heel for three year . . . we poor . . . we starved" and if one pressed the issue they would say "I go now" and the conversation was closed.

We had our leaves to Manila which, as time slid by, became more and more enjoyable. There was 100 per cent co-operation when the enlisted men started to build their club; the spirit was tops among our 400 enlisted men and the club "Shangri-la," the equal of which I've never seen, was quickly and beautifully erected. "Mother Mason's" snack bar was the busiest place and had there been any charge, he would have made a fortune. T/Sgt. Albright was elected president of the club and handled his new position with firmness and tolerance. It was, all in all, a very happy place. Here the beginning of the first big redeployment started and we sent numerous high point men back to the States; we hated to see them go but were extremely happy for them.

On the Line, the crew chiefs took on one extra job, that of painting Indian head insignia on the tail and stripes on the wings of each airplane. There were instances coming off the target when one element leader would lose his Squadron and join the Group out of position; he could quickly change his position by finding the squadron with striped wings and much of the confusion was eliminated. About a week before we flew to Ie Shima the fellows on the boat echelon moved out of our area at Clark and were taken by truck to Subic Bay, the port of embarkation. That night was spent in rain without the aid of too much cover; port control would not let the men on the boat while it was being loaded and there weren't tents enough for all present. The following morning, they went aboard and remained in port for the remainder of the day and night, pulling out the next morning, traveling north and keeping west of Formosa. Lying between the LST and our destination, a typhoon of unusual intensity was raging and consequently, our path was erratic and delayed us three days crossing back and forth to the east and to the west, the convoy changing its arrangement constantly.

On the sixth day they docked in the little harbor at Ie Shima but it wasn't for another day and a half before unloading was effected. Trucks were not permitted to take the men

Jap Burial Vault

directly from the boat and each individual was instructed to carry all his baggage to the top of the hill and wait transportation there. It was a matter of some agitation and concern since the distance was about one-half mile. It was a weary bunch of boys who arrived bedraggled at camp, puffing and prespiring profusely and moaning and groaning that there is no justice.

The flight echelon flew to this fair island . . . on which I am now writing this story . . . without mishap and landed at seven in the evening. While we erected the tents, the wind commenced to blow heavily and rain fell. The earth was soft and throughout the night stakes would pull loose and the center poles would swing merrily in the breeze, making life complicated and definitely uncomfortable. We were briefed the night on which we arrived and took off for our first mission to the Inland Sea of Japan at six the next morning after an unholy night.

Our losses wer considerable for the number of missions flown and the quality of the targets hit. Capt. Burg was shot down over Kyushyu; his plane was hit just before the bombs were dropped and his plane, not out of control, remained steady long enough to unload. Apparently both men at the controls were wounded because the ship was observed to level out just above the water and a successful ditching would have been accomplished had it not been for the excessive speed, which was estimated at 200 mph. There were no survivors and the reports read: "Mission accomplished and successful," but it lacked details such as the pathos which existed in the hearts of friends of the crew. Lt. Vincent and his crew were shot down while making a run on a destroyer in a harbor on the island of Tau Shima. Neither he nor his crew had a prayer; the hit was direct and the plane went nose first into the water.

Lt. Philips followed him in the pattern and sank the destroyer and had half his tail shot away; however, he was more fortunate and nursed the plane home. On the same mission Lt. Wilkinson was hit over another target and started back on one engine. The crew sweated for about an hour before the gas ran low and ditching was inevitable. The landing was excellent and with the exception of wrenched legs and shattered nerves, everyone got out safely and paddled around in the water for some six hours before a "Jukebox" dropped the Higgins Boat. The boys remained afloat until noon the following day when a sub appeared and fired several shells at them thinking that they were a decoy for a Jap sub. Finally, after frantic waving and signaling, the sub recognized them as friendly survivors and came alongside. The following day the sub contacted a Cat and, with no little discomfort to the injured men, took them aboard and returned them to the station hospital at Ie Shima. When the men returned to the area, they were immediately put on orders to go home.

The living conditions at this station have been vastly superior to anything the Squadron has seen previously. The Negro truck drivers were immediately contacted and lumber of every conceivable size and shape, including plywood, was in over-abundance. The shacks were palatial and life was ever so comfortable. "C" rations and "10 in 1" were plentiful and over little gas stoves delicious meals were cooked. Except for an occasional typhoon, the weather at Ie Shima was beautiful and numerous sun tans walked about the area. Although cans of spaghetti, baked beans and plum pudding are tasty supplements to a diet, they aren't' fresh meat, fresh vegetables, fresh eggs, fresh butter, or fresh milk and these small items, common to every civilian table, were never seen on our table. If a man had been afloat on a life raft for twenty days with only crackers or nothing at all to eat, bully beef or canned stew might look good but, receiving nothing else day after day, it almost turned our stomachs.

When the war ended and high point men became eligible for return to the states and discharge, the responsibility for all jobs previously held by ground personnel fell on the shoulders of combat men who knew nothing more than how to fly or shoot a gun and we soon found out just how indispensable these other boys were. It wasn't until they were gone that we realized how valuable they were to us. American ingenuity is famous and it wasn't lacking here; men who had never cooked before became bakers and we had pies, cakes, and cookies; the looks of pleasure on the faces of the boys said thanks better than any of us could have with words and everybody was happy. It seemed funny that the crew chiefs should be the engineers with whom we'd flown so many missions and know that the fellows who were cooking our food were radio men and on flying pay; necessity seems to be the madre of ingenuity.

Today most of our airplanes have been given away as fat-cats or transferred to other groups who will remain in the army of occupation. All of the old ground men are probably starting their furloughs, the Group will fold up tomorrow or the next day, the old combat men will go home, the new will transfer to other groups and life for us will again assume reasonable proportions but indelible images of experience are stamped into our memories and no one will be quite the same person that he might have been. We haven't fought the dirty war of the foot soldier, but we've carried the war to the enemy, cut off his supply lines, bombed his cities, factories and air fields and made the war infinitely easier for those men who fought with other branches of the service. If one scans the pages of history, he is impressed with the fact that, so far, man's ingenuity has surpassed his intelligence. For the future, we can hope, through education and that ability which makes us different from animals, that instead of inventing new tools of destruction he will think . . . think of some way to make their use unnecessary.

IN GOD WE TRUST

345th Bomb Group

HEADQUARTERS
ALBUM

Headquarters
Album

Group Headquarters was composed of officers and men from the squadrons and an original cadre of 75 men. It contained the C.O.'s staff, S-1, S-2, S-3, S-4, communications, utilities, the photo lab, the dentist, and other administrative departments.

Adams, Haskell A., 314 Rodgers Street, Marianna, Arkansas
Adkins, Henry G., Jr., Keysville, Georgia
Akerley, Howard P., 295 Prospect Street, Manchester, New Hampshire
Alex, Peter E., 16 Mechanic Street, Fair Haven, Virginia
Allport, Edward H., 924 Iowa Avenue, Iowa City, Iowa
Ambrose, John P., 307 Montgomery Street, Jersey City, New Jersey
Andrau, E. W. K., P.O. Box 2408, Houston, Texas
Attebury, Marshal E., 604 E. Commercial Street, Weiser, Idaho
Bacon, Raleigh D., Jr., 2550 E. 5th Avenue, Knoxville, Tennessee
Baldwin, Charles R., 6848 Greton Street, Forest Hills, New York
Baldwin, Harry A., Jr., 110 S. Pioneer Street, Lyons, Kansas
Banks, James P., High Springs, Florida
Bardweil, Allen R., 122 Pine Street, Florence, Massachusetts
Bartlett, Kenneth C., 48 Lehigh Street, Caledonia, New York
Bazzel, Thomas R., Box 166, Clanton, Alabama
Beck, Robert F., 310 Naylor, Taft, California
Benedum, Max G., 485 Ripley Avenue, Akron, Ohio
Bennett, Harry L., 715 Moore Avenue, Bryn Mawr, Pennsylvania
Beran, Robert J., Snyder, Texas
Berger, Julius M., 3657 Broadway, New York, New York
Bishop, Donald B., Quincy, Pennsylvania
Bitel, Joseph A., N. Farms, Wallingford, Connecticut
Blair, Cebet C., 418 Taylor Boulevard, Louisville, Kentucky
Blazer, David H., Stanford, New York
Bloomenthal, Sanford R., 400 Mt. View Avenue, Mt. Holly, New Jersey
Boing, William F., Jr., Box 404, Carthage, North Carolina
Bomberger, Elon H., 516 W. Amador Street, Las Cruces, New Mexico
Boulahanis, Peter G., 3718 N. Greenshaw Street, Chicago, Illinois
Boulay, Richard M., 126 Fairmont Avenue, Worchester, Massachusetts
Bowen, Calvin M., 1608 Anthony Street, Columbia, Maine
Bradley, William T., 1504 Murray Avenue, Pittsburgh, Pennsylvania
Brady, Thomas M., 40 Oxford Road, Rockville, New York
Breen, Donald C., 98 South Street, Hingham, Massachusetts
Brewer, Jay N., Box 50 N., Wilkesboro, North Carolina
Brigham, Howard H., 33 Stratford Terrace, Springfield, Massachusetts
Brister, Raymond J., General Delivery, Smiley, Texas
Brock, Albert J., 5555 Palm Street, St. Louis, Missouri
Brodnax, Grover C., Jr., Box 344 A, Andrews, South Carolina
Brown, Martin A., Route 1, Box 112, Salley, South Carolina
Buchinsky, Theodore E., 148 Franklin Avenue, Hasbrouck Heights, New Jersey
Buckley, Wesley D., 520 Clinton Avenue, Newark, New Jersey
Bullard, Bynum B., Miller, Arkansas
Burks, Woodrow W., Box 134, Jasper, Texas
Burson, Jones, 29 N. 54th Street, Birmingham, Alabama
Byars, Rodney L., Box 1333, Blanco, Texas
Cady, Robert T., 96 Park Avenue, Passaic, New Jersey
Call, Silliam C., (Address Unavailable)
Calvin, Crim O., 1647 E. Broad Avenue South, Spokane, Washington
Canter, Reuben H., 503 Nicholas Street, Vincennes, Indiana
Carbajal, Manuel B., 749 E. 29th Street, Los Angeles, California
Card, George W., 1707 Tracy Street, Endicott, New York
Carso, Michael A., II, 2717 Audubon Street, New Orleans, Louisiana
Carter, Clyde C., 60 Maple Avenue, Windsor, Connecticut
Catron, George B., RFD 2, Flora, Indiana
Cavette, Roy T., 244 Rexford Drive, Beverly Hills, California
Cavoli, William J., 133 Myrtle Street, Vineland, New Jersey
Cefale, Albert, 32 Michigan Avenue, Lynn, Massachusetts
Celvin, John L., 1522 Western Avenue, Topeka, Kansas
Character, Hyman, 15 Market Street, Salem, New Jersey
Chistenson, Lawrence E., 831 A. West Walker, Milwaukee, Wisconsin
Christi, Daneil L., 135-41-234 Place, Laurelton, Queens, New York
Clavenlin, Frank L., Box 512, Green Cone Springs, Florida
Cleverdon, Alton A., (Address Unavailable)
Coleman, Clarence L., RFD 2, Piedmont, Kansas
Coltharp, Chester A., Jr., 45 Holden Street, Newport, Arkansas
Conner, Ian B., Perth, Australia
Conners, William F., 3200 Forbes Street, Apartment 2, Pittsburgh, Pennsylvania
Conroy, Ralph J., 1227 Bell Avenue, N. Broddock, Pennsylvania
Cook, Charles J., 617 W. Mairn Street, Lansdale, Pennsylvania
Coone, Y. Anthony, 2 Warren Street, Rockport, Massachusetts
Cosgrove, Edward P., 3006 Decatur Avenue, New York City, New York
Crabb, Jerred V., 5023 N. Troy, Chicago, Illinois
Craig, Johnson, Saluda, South Carolina
Culpepper, Jason A., Jr., Box 13, Little River, Texas
Curry, John W., 619 S. 27th Street, Philadelphia, Pennsylvania
Darwin, William N., 15 E. Norris Road, Norris, Tennessee
Davis, George C., 136 Elyton, Apartment H., Birmingham, Alabama
Deis, Martin B., 13505 La Salle, Detroit, Michigan
Del Vecchio, Leonard J., 77 Francis Avenue, Hartford, Connecticut
De Rusha, Raymond G., 18 Lincoln Street, Newton Highland, Massachusetts
Devore, James H., RR 2, Horsecave, Kentucky
Devroy, Eugene A., 230 N. Madison, Green Bay, Wisconsin
Dilling, Chester I., 623 E. Front Street, Port Angeles, Washington
Dimmick, Robert L., Route 3, Parkersburg, West Virginia
Domenenus, Frank A., 200-13 201st Street, Bayside, New York
Doolittle, Glenn A., 937 Waverley Avenue, San Antonio, Texas
Downen, Wm. R., Trisbrins, Ohio
Du Bose, George D., 929 S. W. 1st Avenue, Portland, Oregon
Echelmeyer, Wm. M., 1414 Hamilton Avenue, St. Louis, Missouri
Ellen, Cicero J., Jr., Apt. 2-B Gameron Court Apts., Rawleigh, North Carolina
Elliot, Jack T., 207 S. Maple Avenue, Martinsville, West Virginia
Ellis, Wm. L., Jr., 3242 Park Avenue, Memphis, Tennessee
Eppstein, Maurice J., 2235 Rose Street, Berkeley, California
Erspamer, Curtis R., 512 Stephenson Street, Norway, Michigan
Espinosa, George A., 282 Lucy Street, Salt Lake City, Utah
Eubanks, Albert D., Mer Rouge, Louisiana
Evans, William E., 912 Jefferson Avenue, Clairton, Pennsylvania
Fare, Joseph, 2356 Lorillard Place, Bronx, New York
Faircloth, Clifford W., 203 N. Orange Avenue, Dunn, North Carolina
Farias, Alfred J., 8712 Hoover Avenue, Richmond Heights, Maine
Farrell, Martin J., 1268th Street, Des Moines, Iowa
Fersyth, Robert H., 33 Hubbard Park, Red Bank, New Jersey

Finn, Albert M., 7217 Princeton Avenue, St. Louis, Missouri
Finney, Brandon W., 1620 N. Fuller Avenue, Hollywood, California
Fleury, George J., 1523 22nd Street N. W., Washington, D. C.
Freilich, Irving C., 900 Riverside Drive, New York City, New York
Fridge, Benjamin W., 706 Pine Street, Boulder, Colorado
Fucha, Marie J., 1232 40th Street, Brooklyn, New York
Gasnik, Frank, 905 Austin Avenue, Flint, Michigan
Gastgeh, Kenneth C., Route 1, Washington Pike, Kerwan Hts., Bridgeville, Pa.
Gay, Charles F., 706 East Main Street, Costesville, Pennsylvania
Geer, Merrill H., 61 Hartley Street, Portland, Maine
Gelman, Joseph, 204 E. 96th Street, Brooklyn, New York
Genuth, Nathan, 2903 Victoria Avenue, Los Angeles, California
Gibberman, Stanley A., 5012 7th Street N. W., Washington, D. C.
Goldberg, Louis, 253 Belmont Avenue, Newark, New Jersey
Gonzales, Manuel B., 723 Live Oak, Miami, Arizona
Graham, Henry Z., 2614 Chester Avenue, Bakersfield, California
Graham, Malcolm J., 2204 N. W. 4th Avenue, Mineral Wells, Texas
Gregory, James E., 816 Walker Avenue, Greensboro, North Carolina
Grigsby, Chester E., (Address Unavailable)
Grumet, Sanford, 971 E. 129th Street, Cleveland, Ohio
Gurowitz, Gustane, 504 Grand Street, New York City, New York
Gwinn, John W., 720 Highland Avenue, Princeton, West Virginia
Hagan, Crandall H., (Address Unavailable)
Hall, John R., 925 12th Street, Ogden, Utah
Hanlon, James J., (Address Unavailable)
Hanna, John C., 1004 E. Jefferson Avenue, Detroit, Michigan
Hardy, Vernon L., 42 Mayo Street, Nelfast, Maine
Harkins, Vernon J., 3922 N. 19th Street, Tacoma, Washington
Harley, John L., 1106 Maple Street, Columbia, South Carolina
Hassey, Sterling O., 1814 E. Menwood Boulevard, Milwaukee, Wisconsin
Hatcher, Ollie E., 1942 S. Lafayette, Denver, Colorado
Hatfield, Aster J., Printer, West Virginia
Hawkins, James W., 603 Avenue B. S. E., Childress, Texas
Helt, Harry L., 1715 Telephone Road, Houston, Texas
Heyes, Gordon H., Route 1, Monongalhia, Pennsylvania
Hill, Claude J., 930 N. 28th Street, Milwaukee, Wisconsin
Hoffman, William M., 949 Glue Hill Avenue, Dorchester, Massachusetts
Holtzman, Martin M., 5520 Pershing Avenue, St. Louis, Missouri
Houck, Wendell G., 98 Montans Street, W. Ashville, North Carolina
Hubert, Peter, Elmhurst, Illinois
Hudson, Henry F., 529 Deleware Street, Denver, Colorado
Huff, Robert G., Route 2, Newcomerstown, Ohio
Huffman, George W., Route 1, Box 84, Belzoni, Mississippi
Hugaboom, Delbert H., 28 Carroll Street, Binghampton, New York
Hurdle, Albert N., La Harpe, Illinois
Hutcherson, James E., 514 Arnold Avenue, Box 432, Greenville, Mississippi
Jackson, Ernest P., Jr., Box 83, Tanonia, Georgia
Jackson, Kenneth L., 2210 10th Street, Oakland, California
Jones, Clifford F., 156 Marsh Avenue, Trion, Georgia
Jones, John D., Route 4, Jackson, Mississippi
Jones, John J., Route 1, Charlotte, Tennessee
Jones, Wingate B., Canton, North Carolina
Johnson, Harold C., 2553½ Corralitas Drive, Los Angeles, California
Johnson, Rodney, 323 7th Street S. E., Puyallup, Washington
Kahn, David S., 793 Man Street, Lynnfield Center, Massachusetts
Kase, James M., 2338 Perkiomen Avenue, Mt. Penn, Pennsylvania
Katz, Simon D., 3561 Bogart Avenue, Cincinnati, Ohio
Keller, George R., 754 W. 42nd Street, Miami Beach, Florida
Kerestes, Steve, Jr., 349 44th Street, Pittsburgh, Pennsylvania
Klein, Benjamin F., Jr., 14925 Shaker Boulevard, Shaker Heights, Ohio
Korthals, Francis J., 9363 Richter, Detroit, Michigan
Kozlowski, Edward A., 78 Genung Street, Middletown, New York
Kregas, Antonio G., 244 Marlboro Street, Keene, New Hampshire
Lacey, Theodore W., 8708 Germantown Avenue, Chestnut Hill, Pennsylvania
Lahikaninen, Alde H., 87 Coleman Street, Gardner, Massachusetts
Lambert, Bruna, Route 1, Cragford, Alabama
Langstaff, Maurice M., Allenville, Michigan
Laughlin, Palmer G., 524 W. Herash Street, Salisbury, North Carolina
Law, Lawrence E., 1918 S. 6th East, Salt Lake City, Utah
Lee, Clark S., 911 E. 6th Street, Santa Ana, California
Leffman, Pal H., 5461 Everett, Chicago, Illinois
Leirsch, Paul J., 455 E. 135th Street, Bronx, New York
Leper, Merida W., Box 2712, Odessa, Texas
Levine, Leonard J., 1345 Shakespeare Avenue, Bronx, New York
Lewis, Roer K., 1641 S. 11th Street, Lawrenceville, Illinois
Lilek, Albert P., 7611 S. Hermitage, Chicago 20, Illinois
Long, Connelius W., 706 Gallatin Road, Nashville, Tennessee
Lucente, Vincent A., 112-08-3-th Avenue, Larona, New York
McCarthy, John J., 343 D. Street, S. Boston, Massachusetts
McClure, Jack C., Jr., 852 E. 13th Street, Brooklyn, New York
McGarry, Andrew T., 2300 66th Avenue, Oakland 3, California
McGuire, Samuel T., Route 3, Coshacton, Ohio
McIntyre, Robert J., Falfurrias, Texas
McKay, Harvey J., St. Paul, Oregon
McKenzie, Patrick N., Mission, South Dakota
McLaughlin, Daniel D., 3028 34th Street, Astoria, Queens, New York
McRoberts, Reed A., 9306 Caroline Avenue, Silver Spring, Maryland
Macrepoulad, Constantinos, 309 W. 28th Street, New York City, New York
Marsh, Robert F., 1907 N. Leavitt Street, Chicago, Illinois
Marston, Bruce T., 560 E. California Street, Pasadena, California
Martini, Robert J., 115 30th Street, San Francisco, California
Marwedel, Charles A., Jr., 68 Rosewood Drive, San Francisco, California
Mather, Virgil W., 507 N. 30th, Waco, Texas
Metzel, Charles O., 280 Rnner Street, Cincinnati, Ohio
Meinert, Henry, Jr., 60-10 Putman Avenue, Brooklyn, New York
Meridith, Joseph W., (Address Unavailable)
Mhore, Edgar E., 1325 E. 20th Street, Independence, Missouri
Michalowiski, John, 2864 Constitution Road, Fairview, New York
Midlan, Thomas L., 20 S. Jackson Avenue, Eagle Grove, Iowa
Mintz, Morton, 1323 Park Place, Brooklyn, New York
Mooney, Joseph P., 235 Centennial Avenue, Roosevelt, New York
Moore, Patrick J., 706 S. Judson Street, Ft. Scott, Kansas

Morgan, Merle H., Box 1376, Mullens, West Virginia
Mortensen, Max H., 906 S. Locust, Champaigne, Illinois
Murphy, Mack W., O-Meare Court, Charlestown, Massachusetts
Murphy, Paul M., Pine Meadow, Connecticut
Nace, Harrison E., 616 Washington Street, Red Hill, Pennsylvania
Nelson, Frederick E., 706 Brown Street, Healdsburg, California
Nerbert, Milair M., 10 Hill Street, Cortland, New York
Neuendorf, Harold A., 37 Neptune Avenue, New Dorp, Staten Island, New York
Nelenschwander, Darwin G., 3168 S. 20th E., Salt Lake City, Utah
Nichols, Aldridge R., 1126 E. Prairie Street, Decatur, Illinois
Nick, John E., 1130 S. 48th Street, Milwaukee, Wisconsin
Noble, James H., 549 Washington Avenue, Portland, Maine
Oliver, Hugh, Route 2, Mexia, Texas
O'Brien, Daniel J., 155 Atlantic Street, Warren, Ohio
O'Connell, Francis A., 34 Peace Street, Clifton Springs, New York
O'Dall, Bruce, 1224 Shirley Street, Columbia, South Carolina
O'Connor, John F., The Square, Denmare, Ireland
O'Neill, Arthur F., Alda, Nebraska
Orem, William M., Bay Street, Lakeland, Florida
Ouellette, August R., 20 Kick Street, Lowell, Massachusetts
Owenx, John E., Charleston, Maryland
Parr, Hugh V., 23 Elm Street, Granville, New York
Pauli, John T., 174th Floral Park, New Jersey
Pendreck, John J., 517 Ontarie Street, Port Huer, Michigan
Perkins, Warren E., 65 Linden Avenue, Bloomfield, New Jersey
Perkins, Whitney T., 16 Corning Street, Beverly, Massachusetts
Perrin, Thomas C., 1106 Brooks Street, Greenwood, South Carolina
Petre, Alex P., 2092 Northwestern Avenue, Racine, Wisconsin
Pitman, Wilton, Route 1, Box 103, Pachuta, Mississippi
Pitts, Lydon D., Sandborn, Iowa
Powell, Allden M., Price, Utah
Pretti, Raymond J., 1627 Humbolt Street, Denver, Colorado
Priest, Wiley T., 2455 Newton Street, Denver 11, Colorado
Puleston, Charles S., 1225 Molendon Avenue N. E., Atlanta, Georgia
Rainville, Jean A., 13½ Washington Avenue, Holyoke, Massachusetts
Rainwater, William F., 120 Third Street, Cheraw, South Carolina
Ramey, Alvin D., Route 14, Box 552, Portland, Oregon
Reedington, Delbert T., 1658 Clarkson Street, Denver, Colorado
Reilly, Hugh M., 435 West 125th Street, New York, New York
Reissig, Irving, 748 Trinity Avenue, Bronx, New York
Reynolds, Robert G., 122 Hamilton Street, Ogdensburg, New York
Rice, Robert T., 5570 Cates Street, St. Louis, Missouri
Richards, Arthur, Monongah, West Virginia
Richardson, William B., Route 1, Del Kalb, Texas
Ridout, Leon E., Route 2, Box 91, Weaverhuser, Wisconsin
Robers, Lewis G., 2813 Murphy Street, Ft. Worth, Texas
Roberts, August E., 1616 Lycamon Street, Cincinnati, Ohio
Roberts, Ben I., 919 Sheldon Avenue, Norfolk, Virginia
Roberts, Bryant R., 108 Washington Street, Leaksville, North Carolina
Robertson, Everett E., 4637 San Jacinto, Dallas, Texas
Rockefeller, George R., 1250 Market, Sunbury, Pennsylvania
Roper, Thomas J., 621 Sycamore Street, Santa Paula, California
Rosenbaum, Bert S., Fairplay, Kentucky
Rosiecki, Mathew E., 17161 Syracuse, Detroit, Michigan
Rowe, Eliot M., 21 South Street, Friendship, New York
Rox, Warren H., 58 Lake Street, Bloomfield, New Jersey
Sages, Royce M., Glenn Avenue, Mt. Vernon, New York
Sanders, Edgar S., Route 1, Wauchula, Florida
Santillo, Americo, 104½ Washington Street, Auburn, New York
Sasina, Harold V., 166 William Street, Perth Amboy, New Jersey

Schroeder, Louis E., Arcade, New York
Schulte, John W., 813 Gearing Avenue, Pittsburgh, Pennsylvania
Searles, Robert W., 7742 Latona Street, Seattle, Washington
Seidel, Henry H., 2435 N. 4th Street, Harrisburg, Pennsylvania
Seilbert, Clyde D., 2802 Jackson Street, Amarillo, Texas
Selimenson, Warren E., 2446 25th Avenue, S. Minneapolis, Minnesota
Semikoff, Nick J., 53 South Arizona Avenue, Los Angeles, California
Shaklee, Harold O., (Address Unavailable)
Shoup, Charles E., Route 1, Scenery Hill, Pennsylvania
Siet, Morton J., 145 S. Central Avenue, Chicago, Illinois
Smith, George E., 99 Lafayette Street, Bridgeport, Connecticut
Smith, George L., Box 105, Decherd, Tennessee
Smith, John A., 711 Mabette Street, Kissimmee, Florida
Smith, Robert N., Box 102, Pstoka, Illinois
South, Wm. E., Route 2, Robinson, Illinois
Springer, Jack W., 2062 Davidson Avenue, New York, New York
Stanten, Jury D., Box 101, Alamo, California
Stapkey, Paul E., Box G., Schroen Lake, New York
Stearns, Lewis F., 1109 W. Green Street, Champaign, Illinois
Stevens, Stewart O., 1209 Old Orchard Road, Vincennes, Indiana
Story, Thomas P., Route 1, Waysate, Minnesota
Stowarz, Valentine W., Wallington, New Jersey
Strals, Leonard M., (Address Unavailable)
Strauss, Carl A., 3428 St. John's Place, Cincinnati, Ohio
Strauss, Philip, 1534 Selwyn Avenue, New York City, New York
Strausser, Robert B., 361 Arayon Drive, Denmore, New York
Susan, Herbert S., 303 W. 80th Street, New York City, New York
Swannack, George E., V-2 Apt., Colonial Village, Columbia, South Carolina
Sweigard, Roy R., Box 203, Route 3, Marshal, North Carolina
Swinney, John G., 2920 Devine Street, Columbia, South Carolina
Szikszay, Zelton, 1585 Second Avenue, New York, New York
Taggett, George U., 350 N. W. 11th Street, Miami, Florida
Tarwater, William R., 803 N. 10th Street, Duncan, Oklahoma
Taylor, Vember D., Box 46, Clarkton, Maine
Thornton, Aren G., 1601 N. Broad Street, Rome, Georgia
Threlfall, John C., 427 Fowler Avenue, Pelham, New York
Treganza, Paul B., Benton, Wisconsin
True, Clinton R., RFD 3, Vaughn Road, Montgomery, Alabama
Tubbs, Eugen H., 574 Huron Street, Pontiac, Michigan
Tyson, Clayton L., 425 S. Center Street, Bremen, Indiana
Valanderen, Russell B., 2459 McKinley Street, Sioux City, Iowa
Vanderveer, Lindsley D., 67 Bridge Street, Somerville, New Jersey
Vanne, Eugene, 9002 7th Street, Richmond Hill, New York
Velanski, John, Route 1, North Hampton, Pennsylvania
Velkman, Albert E., (Address Unavailable)
Waterman, Joseph R., 38 E. 4th Street, Oswego, New York
Weiner, Abraham, 87 Broad, Midway, Massachusetts
Wernimon, Frank A., Evergreen Avenue, Oceanside, New York
White, Francis W., 1201 Edwards Street, St. Helena, California
White, Harold F., 3404 Lyndale Avenue, Baltimore, Maryland
Whitworth, Rans A., 424 Boulevard S. E., Atlanta, Georgia
Williamson, Kenneth J., 506 Norris Street, Norriston, Pennsylvania
Winters, Robert K., 208 West Stranage Street, Champaign, Illinois
Witherell, William R., Jr., 17 N. Clover Drive, Great Neck, New York
Womack, Homer E., Route 3, Winnsboro, Louisiana
Woodward, James C., Holly Springs, Massachusetts
Wrigg, Herman, 220 Auusta Avenue E., Willman, Minnesota
Wyckoff, Eldon J., Darlington, South Carolina
Zacek, Joseph F., 33 George Street, Westfield, Massachusetts
Zipprich, John B., 623 Forest Avenue, Wilmett, Illinois

498TH SQUADRON

Ables, Norman E., Route 242, Criahes, California
Acree, Richard J., RR 5, Brazil, Indiana
Adams, James M., 2840 Peachtree Road N. E., Atlanta, Georgia
Adams, William E., Route 1, Roland, Arkansas
Adams, Stuart E., 5890 Gardena Avenue, Long Beach, California
Adelman, Monroe G., 125 W. Trement Avenue, New York City, New York
Agatielli, Ottavo T., 34 Cherry Street, New York City, New York
Aikin, Steard C., c-o U.S. Engineers, New Orleans, Louisiana
Albertson, Bernhard T., Battle Creek, Iowa
Alito, Joseph F., 1004 Rutgers Street, Utica, New York
Allain, David E., 193 Phillips Avenue, New Bedford, Massachusetts
Allen, Douglas M., Jr., 2969 Annwood, Cincinnati, Ohio
Allen, Richard, Jr., Box 95, Sentinel, Oklahoma
Aloia, Patsy H., 384 Houston Street, Washington, Pennsylvania
Ambrose, John C., 522 16th Avenue, Minneapolis, Minnesota
Anderson, Barney B., Potect, Texas
Anderson, Frank E., Route 1, North Street, Greenwich, Connecticut
Anderson, Robert E., (Address Unavailable)
Anderson, Vernon L., Red Granite, Wisconsin
Anderson, Wayland R., 32 Monterey Road, Pontiac, Michigan
Andrews, David E., 103 Clayton Avenue, Laurel, Delaware
Andrews, Robert J., RFD 2, Belmont, New York
Angeletti, Telio T., Stump Creek, Pennsylvania
Apai, Gustave R., 110 Kenwood Street, Elyria, Ohio
Apelt, August L., 2737 Penn Avenue, Beaumont, Texas
Arklander, Arthur W., 3218 E. Atherton Road, Flint, Michigan
Armigo, Joe F., 1 Pueblo Drive, Santa Fe, New Mexico
Arnett, Fred E., Box 1229, Midland, Texas
Arnold, George C., Route 1, Macon, Georgia
Arruda, James R., 124 Eagle Street, Tall River, Massachusetts
Augustine, Edward T., 287 Sixth Street, Brooklyn, New York
Austin, Kenneth L., Rio, Wisconsin
Bagula, Oliver J., Route 2, Box 425, San Diego, California
Baker, Haskell C., Jr., Box 9B, Hope Hall, Alabama
Baker, John G., 25 E. 9th Street, Duluth, Minnesota
Baker, John M., 92 E. Dakota Avenue, Detroit, Michigan
Ballain, Dale R., (Address Unavailable)
Ballirano, Gaetano, 65 Woodhall Street, Brooklyn, New York

Baran, Anton C., Route 1, Taylor, Texas
Baranko, Frank R., 334 Alpha Street, Perth-Amboy, New Jersey
Barkau, John F., 7441 Vine Street, Carthage, Ohio
Barnasky, George I., 35 New Street, Tuckahoe, New York
Barnard, Milton J., 4010 Avenue T., Galveston, Texas
Barnes, Cecil L., 219 N. Clara Street, Deland, Florida
Barnes, Levi A., 805 Market Street, Emporia, Kansas
Barnett, Robert E., RR 7, Butler, Pennsylvania
Barney, Francia E., 60 Border Street, Whitinsville, Massachusetts
Barnhart, Paul A., 2131½ McClain Avenue, Butler, Pennsylvania
Barter, William H., 200 Dicsane Street, Avalon, California
Bauer, August F., Jr., 28 Cross Street, West Orange, New Jersey
Beard, Edward J., 166 Bouck Street, Tonawanda, New York
Beard, Milton V., Vale, Oregon
Beardsley, Harrison T., 210 W. Harrison Avenue, Wheaton, Illinois
Beasley, Smillid B., Box 231, Graham, Texas
Beattie, James J., 9 Staple Avenue W. W., Hartford, Connecticut
Beauseleil, Eugene, 11 Bloomfield Street, Lynn, Massachusetts
Beavers, Rex B., Renick, West Virginia
Becker, Charles H., 350 N. Point Road, Baltimore, Maryland
Beebe, Lynn L., 245 N. Millwood, Wichita, Kansas
Beedle, Richard, 1115 Maple Street, S. Pasadena, California
Beiga, Albert J., 85-48-98 Street E., Elmhurst, Long Island, New York
Belew, Yoeger H., General Delivery, Ethridge, Tennessee
Bell, John G., 111 Liberty Street, Booton, New York
Bellise, Louis T., 2542 99th Street, Corona, New York
Benson, Harold D., 122 Birch Street, Manchester, Connecticut
Berends, Kenneth E., Middleville, Michigan
Berg, Ward S., Kendall, Wisconsin
Berman, Martin J., 173 89th Street, Jamaica, New York
Besecker, Walter E., 520 Welworth Avenue, Delaven, Wisconsin
Best, Melvin L., 2606 23rd Street, Lubbock, Texas
Best, Robert D., 272 N. Harris Street, Sandersville, Georgia
Bianconi, Owen M., 2604 Sunset Place, Nashville, Tennessee
Bissell, Alfred E., 1106 Hopeton Road, Wilmington, Delaware
Biunno, Vincent J., 323 N. 11th Street, Newark, New Jersey
Black, John R., 5428 Laconia Avenue, Cincinnati, Ohio
Blackstone, Carl R., Lincoln Way W. Ext., Massillion, Ohio

Bladell, Ralph R., 206 W. 6th Street, Monroe, Michigan
Blaeske, John F., 19 Myrtle Street, Bloomfield, New York
Blake, Robert G., 1304 Blaisdell Street, Rockford, Illinois
Blanchard, Frank E., 208 Callenger, Peoria, Illinois
Blase, Albert C., 5201 McBryde Avenue, Richmond, California
Blevins, Clinton E., Decatur, Nebraska
Blevins, Virgil L., 2706 Cayuga Street, Granite, Illinois
Bobbett, Dale L., RR 2, Fairfield, Illinois
Bodell, Lloyd E., 1414 Longacre Road, Detroit, Michigan
Boden, Alvin O., Adams, Nebraska
Boehnemann, Lee T., Greer, South Carolina
Bokenyi, Julius F., Jr., 9423 Heath Avenue, Cleveland, Ohio
Bolick, Paul, Brookford, North Carolina
Boorman, Eric V., Jr., 326 N. University Avenue, Provo, Utah
Boroshafsky, Allan A., 730 Oakland Place, New York City, New York
Boroski, Mitchek, Kimball, West Virginia
Bosley, George M., St. Ignatius, Montana
Botti, John J., 540 Park Avenue, New York City, New York
Boutwell, Doyle F., McLautin, Mississippi
Bowen, Edwin L., Greer, South Carolina
Boyer, Bernard F., 13 Elm Street, Williamstown, Massachusetts
Brainard, Webster, Chautauqua, Illinois
Brand, Robert W., 475 14th Avenue, San Francisco, California
Brandser, Ralph R., 3201 Bowdein, Des Moines, Iowa
Brandt, Raymond H., 319 N. Prospect Avenue, Park Ridge, Illinois
Brashers, Hassel, Oscaloosa, Iowa
Brass, Charles E., Jr., 1151 Scott Street, Baltimore, Maryland
Branstad, William T., Leland, Iowa
Breen, Francis R., 5776 Whitter, Detroit, Michigan
Brennan, Charles, 117 3rd Street, Elizabeth, New Jersey
Bridges, Harold L., 1607 W. 47th Street, Los Angeles, California
Bridges, Kenneth L., (Address Unavailable)
Brimer, Edgar O., 24 Milton Avenue S. E., Atlanta, Georgia
Brinkerhoff, Robert S., 514 Richmond Terrace, Staten Island, New York
Britton, David H., Route 1, Sumter, South Carolina
Brooks, John C., Peters, Florida
Brooksby, Victor C., Fredonia, Arizona
Bronson, John P., 629 Washington Street, Monroe, Michigan
Brown, Donald F., 206 N. Pear, Havana, Illinois
Brown, Harold, 1024 N. Townsley, Los Angeles, California
Brown, James W., RFD 1, Box 715, Wilkinsburg, Pennsylvania
Brown, Lawrence R., 602 Jefferson Street, Cairo, Delaware
Brown, Leo, 1505 Charlotte Street, New York City, New York
Brown, William M., Route 1, Crosell, Oregon
Browne, Edward H., 257 Hosea Avenue, Cincinnati, Ohio
Bruce, Arthur A., 1125 E. Freemont, Bronx, New York
Brvnik, Julius F., 711 S. Prince Street, Lancaster, Pennsylvania
Buchwald, Anthony, 3068 N. Davlin Street, Chicago, Illinois
Buckman, Wesley H., 15 N. Front Street, Harrisburg, Pennsylvania
Bueno, Jerome, 276 New Lots Avenue, Brooklyn, New York
Bukky, Edward R., 14112 Thames Avenue, Cleveland, Ohio
Burns, Richard F., 203 Westford Street, Lowell, Massachusetts
Burns, Robert E., 207 S. Broad Mt. Avenue, Frockville, Pennsylvania
Burns, William A., 365 Hershberger Road, Johnstown, Pennsylvania
Busha, Thomas S., 612 5th Avenue N., Great Falls, Montana
Bushong, Olpha G., 19 Winding Way, San Francisco, California
Butier, Ralph, 20 Bates Avenue, Greenville, South Carolina
Byrd, William E., 212 Washington Street, Salisbury, Maryland
Cahill, James D., Radiun Springs Road, Albany, Georgia
Calabrd, Thomas C., 60 Carroll Avenue, Valley Stuam, Long Island, New York
Camene, Leander P., 118 W. 90th Street, New York City, New York
Campbell, Lonnie R., Jr., 1347 Beverly, Houston, Texas
Campbell, Marvin L., Athens, Texas
Cann, Robert E., 413 W. Mahl, Edinburg, Texas
Capiniski, Alexander J., 606 E. 4th Street, Swedesburg, Pennsylvania
Capobianco, Nicholas J., 121 George, Brooklyn, New York
Caputo, Fred, 626 W. Leacock, Pittsburgh, Pennsylvania
Carey, Henry S., Jr., 59 Summit Avenue, New London, Connecticut
Carr, Albert I., 1116 Hemphill Street, Ft. Worth, Texas
Carr, William L., Jr., 183 Nicols Street, Everett 49, Massachusetts
Carter, Curtis L., Route 2, Box 14, South Boston, Virginia
Caruso, Paul, 251 Stanhope Street, Brooklyn, New York
Card, August D., 353 E. Cady, Northville, Michigan
Carfello, Roco, 59 Wallace Street, Newark, New Jersey
Carlson, Harry I., 98 N. Main, Concord, New Hampshire
Carlton, Leroy N., 401 S. 10th Street, Yakima, Washington
Carmichael, Morris C., 832 Holden Street, Ft. Worth, Texas
Carrington, Carrol D., Box 21, Saltillo, Texas
Carroll, John R., 52 Gahl Terrace, Reading, Ohio
Carroll, Joseph W., Jr., 2835 Kingston Street, Dallas, Texas
Carter, James B., 2400½ Cyprus Street, Columbia, South Carolina
Casselman, Lloyd W., McIntosh, Minnesota
Cassiani, John B., 1107 Idlewood E., Carnegie, Pennsylvania
Catlin, James B., Box 87, Baldknob, Arkansas
Cavin, Edgar R., 1520 N. 47th St., E. St. Louis, Illinois
Cavorti, Joseph W., 46 Huber, Yonkers, New York
Chadrow, David B., 3236 N. Carlile, Philadelphia, Pennsylvania
Chalifoux, Wallace W., 3357 W. Flournox Street, Chicago, Illinois
Chambers, Benjamin F., Box 383, Willcox, Arizona
Chanier, Joseph H., 1325 Rathbone Street, Grand Rapids, Michigan
Chard, Charles A., 2023 E. Biddle Street, Baltimore, Maryland
Charles, Frank I., 43 Penrose Street, Rochester, New York
Chase, Leo J., 4736 Moran, Detroit, Michigan
Cheek, Alvin R., Route 1, Box 254, Scappose, Oregon
Chiappe, Anthony N., 2176 Walton Avenue, New York City, New York
Chittendon, Quentin D., RFD 2, Gilford, Connecticut
Chorney, Michael J., 1214 Lilly Avenue, Akron, Ohio
Cicci, Edward F., Box 292, Bentleyville, Pennsylvania
Clark, Albert D., Leavenworth, Texas
Clark, James L., 148-28 87th Avenue, Jamaica, Long Island, New York
Clarke, Elias D., 448 E. Orr Street, Anderson, South Carolina

Clary, John Q., Mountain Grove, Missouri
Cleary, Lloyd G., 2696 Montgomery, Detroit, Michigan
Clemens, G. E., 3207 Elmora Avenue, Baltimore, Maryland
Cludston, William H., 3631 Fourth Street, Detroit, Michigan
Cochran, Robert J., 32 N. Mill, New Castle, Pennsylvania
Coen, John J., Jr., 6824 Jackson, Guttenberg, New Jersey
Cohen, Bertram L., 652 Morton Street, Mattapan, Massachusetts
Cohen, Herbert J., 86 Tudor Street, Chelsa, Massachusetts
Cohen, Irving I., 1945 S. 4th Street, Philadelphia, Pennsylvania
Cohen, William W., 5 Minerva Place, New York City, New York
Colburn, Jerry C., Aberdeen, Idaho
Cole, Alfred J., 141 Ackley Avenue, Johnson City, New York
Collier, Marian G., Route 1, Surgoinsville, Tennessee
Collier, William M., 511 Lathrot Avenue, Boonton, New Jersey
Collins, Ralph, 701 W. 17th Street, Connersville, Indiana
Coloff, Mike, 261 Collver Street, Long Mont, Colorado
Colquitt, James A., 126 Charles Street, Macon, Georgia
Combs, Arnold N., RR 3, Bloomfield, Indiana
Comstock, Joseph W., (Address Unavailable)
Conner, Kenneth F., AAron, Kentucky
Connery, Robert I., 1136 Scamore Street, Steubenville, Ohio
Cooper, Benajmin, Wendover Apt., Pittsburgh, Pennsylvania
Cooper, John T., 517 N. Church Street, Visalia, California
Cope, Haldene A., 622 6th Street, Sulphur, Oklahoma
Coppotelli, Lawrence A., 522 E. Call Street, Algona, Iowa
Corley, Joseph A., 227 W. Fishers, Philadelphia, Pennsylvania
Cornwell, Robert P., 904 N. Maple Street, Royal, Michigan
Correll, William C., 211 Wilson Street, Albermerla, North Carolina
Cota, LeRoy, 216½ Morrison, Dubois, Pennsylvania
Cote, Paul M., 369 Main, Auburn, Maine
Cottam, Clifford C., 4252 Vinton Avenue, Culver City, California
Cotton, Homer O., 8946 San Juan, South Gate, California
Council, William D., Jr., Pine Hall, Alabama
Cousino, Leo R., Route 4, Gouverneur, New York
Craig, Mark O., 677 Fair, Salem, Ohio
Crain, John R., Route 1, Lucerne, Indiana
Cranford, Elmo L., 1027 Franklin Street, Winston-Salem, North Carolina
Cribaro, Sam M., 3380 W. 29th Avenue, Denver, Colorado
Crose, James H., 1412 4th Avenue, Council Bluff, Iowa
Cross, John E., (Address Unavailable)
Cross, R. A., c-o States Oil Corp., Eastland, Texas
Cross, Robert A., 1330½ Douglas Road, Los Angeles, California
Crum, Bardell A., Charmco, West Virginia
Curtis, Leonard M., Webster, Iowa
Cutinelle, Robert W., Etra Road, Hightstown, New Jersey
DaPrato, Charles P., 312 W. Locus Street, Canton, Illinois
Darnell, Lester E., 9 Nen Street, Swaton, Vermont
Davern, John W., 40-40 Crescent Street, Long Island City, New York
Davis, Franklin D., 237 Pine Street, Reno, Nevada
Davis, Grady L., Route 1, Samson, Alabama
Davis, Gwllyn W., Route 1, Box 511, Pittsburgh, California
Davis, Harry E., 1716 Ann, Portsmouth, Virginia
Davis, Lawrence, 968 Florence Avenue, Duwmuir, California
Davis, Neal B., RR 3, Shonandoah, Iowa
Davis, Paul D., Parlin, New Jersey
Davis, William D., Jr., Route 1, Emory, Texas
Davidson, George B., 1215 N. Plumer, Tuscon, Arizona
Davidson, John F., 931 S. Hobard, Los Angeles, California
Dawson, Kenneth L., 217 W. Kee Street, Weatherford, Oklahoma
Dean, Jesse L., 111 Kent Place, Dayton, Ohio
Dean, Kenneth C., Route 1, Foster, Oklahoma
Deeb, Michael, 63 Herbert, Geneva, New York
Delagado, Andrew A., 846 Maple Avenue S., San Francisco, California
Dell, Robert, (Address Unavailable)
Delaney, Richard E., 430 Ash Street, Osaje, Iowa
Demetre, George S., Route 1, Rexford, New York
Demijan, Adam V., 286 Burritt Street, New Britan, Connecticut
Demos, Peter P., Jr., Breakers Rese, Moultrieville, South Carolina
Denney, Paul W., YMCA 1st Emporia Street, Wichita, Kansas
Depascale, Carmine A., 4117 E. Douglas, Wichita, Kansas
DePietro, Richard A., 369 Forbes E., Hartford, Connecticut
Devers, Philip T., Jr., 33 Short Street, Edwardsville, Pennsylvania
Devinney, Tobert H., Arkport, New York
Dewar, Steward A., 729 Dickason Street, Flint, Michigan
Dewey, James L., Route 2, Williamsport, Ohio
Dibbern, Edward J., 2033 E. Eager Street, Baltimore, Maryland
Dickert, George R., 705 E. 22nd, Anniston, Alabama
Diedrich, Orville H., 1435 Idlewood Road, Glendale, California
Dietrich, Howard E., 2217 42nd St. N. W., Washington, D. C.
Dillard, Frank L., 315 Hawkins Avenue, Sanford, North Carolina
Dilling, Delbert D., Box 47, Woodburn, Indiana
Disalvo, Frank F., 594 Wethersfield Avenue, Hartford, Connecticut
Doggett, Glen N., 120 Birch Street, Ottumwa, Iowa
Donald, Hugh H., 20 Sylvester, Lynbrook, New York
Doty, Walter R., 351 Hill Drive, Glendale, California
Dougherty, Frazer L., Millwood, Virginia
Dowdell, John H., 625 Alder Street, Scranton, Pennsylvania
Dow, Bob J., 343 E. Bodger, El Monte, California
Downey, William R., Route 3, Oneida, New York
Drabicki, Raymond A., 22 Roving Street, Sharksborough, Pennsylvania
Dreibelbies, Rowland G., 221 Jarclan Street, Allentown, Pennsylvania
Drake, William H., (Address Unavailable)
Drinkard, Paul B., 1 Coytonrace, Wheeling, West Virginia
Dubane, Harry F., 1157 W. 21st Street, Erie, Pennsylvania
DuCharme, Arthur A., 3837 35th Avenue S., Minneapolis, Minnesota
Dudas, John B., Box 129, Stump Road, Ottumwa, Iowa
Duff, Eugene F., 7614 Union Avenue, Chicago, Illinois
Dunnigan, Hiram E., (Address Unavailable)
Durbahn, Albert M., Buhl, Minnesota
Dziewit, Francis S., 8 Catherine Street, Amsterdam, New York
Earsom, Robert M., 407 E. Colton Avenue, Redlands, California

Easter, John B., Nitta Yuma, Mississippi
Eastman, Oran S., Box 575, Richeyville, Pennsylvania
Ebersole, Harvey N., 522 Clark Street, Hollidaysburg, Pennsylvania
Edelstein, Harold, 7904 Michigan Avenue, Chicago, Illinois
Edwards, Bryant, Bloomfield, Missouri
Edwards, James D., 1308 E. 39th Street, Savannah, Georgia
Egerman, Robert G., 912 8th Avenue, St. Cloud, Minnesota
Eider, James J., 5163 Venus Street, New Orleans, Louisiana
Eiko, Charles, Wharton, New Jersey
Eisiman, Theodore N., General Delivery, Metter, Georgia
Elam, Victor O., Route 5, Box 14, Elgin, Texas
Ellard, John E., 309 S. Knox, Houston, Texas
Eminizer, Albert E., (Address Uavailable)
Enright, David F., 5088 Vermont Avenue, St. Louis, Missouri
Erickson, Lloyd M., Hettinger, North Dakota
Espevik, Leife E., (Address Unavailable)
Evans, Gordon G., 22 Highland Avenue, North Hampton, Massachusetts
Everett, Jesse J., Route 2, Moselle, Mississippi
Fabale, John L., 242 Burritt Street, New Britain, Connecticut
Fabian, Norman, 5 Boulevard Knolls, Poughkeepsie, New York
Fair, Fredrick, 301 El Cerrito Avenue, Piedmont, California
Farabaugh, George S., Road 1, Carrolltown, Pennsylvania
Farmer, William P., 483 Milton Street, Manchester, New Hampshire
Favata, Charles C., 804 N. Simmons Street, Montebello, California
Fay, Frederick J., 58 Gordon Avenue, Providence, Rhode Island
Feder, Harry R., 275 Madrone Avenue, Larkspur, California
Ferris, Robert C., Upper Broadway Grand View, Hudson, New York
Feucht, Richard R., Reynoldsburg, Ohio
Fezatte, Richard E., 1818 Arizona, Flint, Michigan
Fick, Charles W., Box 546, San Bernardino, California
Figuero, Raymond J., Jr., 117 Bergen Street, Brooklyn, New York
Fisher, Clarence J., Bellville, Texas
Fitch, Billie E., Box 182, Julio, Texas
Flaminio, Peppino' J., 514 Walnut Street, Springdale, Pennsylvania
Flanigan, William E., 332 Kyle Street, Youngstown, Ohio
Flentz, John B., 2004 S. Albany Avenue, Chicago, Illinois
Flinton, Jack G., 2407 Campbell Street, Greensboro, North Carolina
Flom, Leroy C., Frost, Minnesota
Flynn, George T., Evan Avenue, Tiverton-Newport, Rhode Island
Flynn, Jack J., 344 Irving Place, Elmira, New York
Foley, Bernard L., 322 McDowell Road, Lexington, Kansas
Folkerth, Robert L., RFD 6, Sidney, Ohio
Forenza, Russell R., West New York, New Jersey
Fortman, John, 152 Frontenac Avenue, Buffalo, New York
Fowler, George E., 84 Winter Street, Newport, New Hampshire
Fox, Eli H., 201 Live Oak Street, McComb, Mississippi
Fox, Mark R., 6127 Frontonac, Philadelphia, Pennsylvania
Frawley, Edward H., 118 Lincoln Street, Pittsfield, Massachusetts
Frazier, George L., Rollins, Montana
Free, Coy B., Route 4, Canton, Georgia
Freedman, Jerold A., 8684 20th Avenue, Brooklyn, New York
French, Alexander S., 16350 Libbly Road, Maple Heights, Ohio
Frey, Otto F., 29 Linden Street, Yonkers, New York
Friese, Donald O., 5017 Fletcher Street, Chicago, Illinois
Fulkerson, Floyd H., Jr., North Little Rock, Arkansas
Gagen, Robert E., 642 39th Street, Des Moines, Iowa
Gale, John H., Tuckerton Ocean, New Jersey
Gallagher, John F., 946 N. Genesee, Los Angeles, California
Galletti, Elliot R., 65 Lowell Street W., Springfield, Massachusetts
Garland, Herbert B., 229 Goodfellow Avenue, St. Louis, Missouri
Garner, Wade B., (Address Unavailable)
Garrison, Walter B., Jr., (Address Unavailable)
Gasper, Robert E., 1229 Twin Pine, Canton, Ohio
Gatwood, Robert D., 3241 W. Michigan Avenue, Kalamazoo, Michigan
Gearhart, Orval L., Jr., 721 S. Ottawa Avenue, Dixon, Illinois
Geer, David A., 819 Woodland Drive, Columbia, South Carolina
Gelfand, Jack E., 522 Alabama Avenue, Brooklyn, New York
Gerber, Frank A., Jr., 10 Ewington Avenue, Trenton, New Jersey
Gerharter, Erwin P., Route 4, St. Joseph, Missouri
Gerlando, James V., 349 68th Street, Brooklyn, New York
Gervais, Norman D., (Address Unavailable)
Gexetski, Tony, 709 Grant Street, Piertage, Pennsylvania
Giab, Steven, 41 Carolina Avenue, Yonkers, New York
Giacobbe, Louis, 56 Madison Street, Revere, Massachusetts
Giacolette, John, Dalzell, Illinois
Giffin, Earl L., 1321 Greenwood Avenue, Wilmette, Illinois
Gilbert, John C., 6th Street, Barnegat City, New Jersey
Girdler, Edgar E., Route 3, Box 231, Somerset, Kentucky
Gilstrap, Tommy O., (Address Unavailable)
Givens, George A., Jr., 323 Fisk Street, Pittsburg, Pennsylvania
Glachman, Harvey, 1450 Jesup Avenue, Bronx, New York
Gladych, Frederic A., 7267 Cadillas Avenue, Van Dyke, Michigan
Godorecci, Alfred F., 2127 Mt. Street, Philadelphia, Pennsylvania
Golden, Frank, RFD 1, Rayland, Ohio
Golden, Norman E., 81 Burritt Avenue, Stratford, Connecticut
Goldman, Nathan, General Delivery, c-o Horowitz, Chamberino, New Hampshire
Goldstone, Richard H., 2118 Quentin Road, Brooklyn, New York
Gott, Willard C., RR 2, Bluntville, Tennessee
Goulet, Robert W., 28 Elmwood Avenue, Buffalo, New York
Gowan, Truett C., 104 Forrest Avenue, Montgomery, Alabama
Grabbe, Philip J., 938 W. 12th Street, Dallas, Texas
Graber, James W., Mound Ridge, Kansas
Graves, George R., 344 S. Fremont Street, Los Angeles, California
Green, Milton, 566 Beach Street, Revere, Massachusetts
Green, Milton J., 69½ Hillside Avenue, Bradford, Pennsylvania
Green, Robert L., 419 19th Street, Virginia Beach, Virginia
Gregory, Harold J., (Address Unavailable)
Grier, Baudin R., 2118 Biddle Street, Wilmington, Delaware
Gross, William D., 355 Northway Street, Northcumberland, Pennsylvania
Gruer, Albert W., Jr., 719 E. Big Bend Road, Webster Groves, Missouri
Guay, Joseph G. L., 7 LaFayette Sereet, Biddeford, Maine
Gucciardo, Frank, 99 Lake Street, Newburgh, New York

Hagedorn, William, 281 E. Walnut Street, Wadsworth, Ohio
Hagerup, Robert O., 6836 Olcott Avenue, Chicago, Illinois
Haggard, Pope J., RR 3, Ahelbyville, Kentucky
Hah, Walter R., (Address Unavailable)
Haijoakiewica, Victor, 127 Connant Street, Gardner, Massachusetts
Halferty, John T., 731 Griffin Street, Watertown, New York
Hall, Albert C., Jr., Rosehill, North Carolina
Hall, Lee V., 360 N. Main, Randolph, Massachusetts
Hall, Russell H., Jr., Madison Avenue, North Vernon, Indiana
Haller, Kenneth E., Bycoda, Washington
Hallum, Allen L., 610 Lee Avenue, Hereford, Texas
Halver, Ralph S., Wing, North Dakota
Halvorson, Gilbert G., General Delivery, Medford, Oklahoma
Hamilton, Ward E., 59 Judson Street, Canton, New York
Hanley, John D., 1515 Addison Street, Berkeley, California
Hansen, George K., 1168 MacArthur Boulevard, Oakland, California
Hanson, Albert T., 15 Talmadge Street, New Haven, Connecticut
Hanson, Earle R., 422 Laurel Avenue, St. Paul, Minnesota
Hanson, George W., 115 E. Main Street, Havana, Illinois
Harrel, Tonnyson C., Chattanooga, Tennessee
Harris, Perry R., 211 Cherry Street, Cookerville, Tennessee
Harris, Robert E., 4 Silver Avenue, Auburn, New York
Harrison, Edward L., Spartanburg, South Carolina
Hasselbauer, Ferdinand E., 723 Augusta Street, San Antonio, Texas
Haugen, Ray H., RFD 2, Taylor, North Dakota
Havrelock, Frederic J., Jr., 223 Deacon Street, Bridgeport, Connecticut
Hawkes, Robert W., South Road, Orange, Massachusetts
Hawks, Alfred J., Route 5, Box 1042, Modesto, California
Healey, John J., 57 Magoun Street, Cambridge, Massachusetts
Heath, Clarence R., Jr., 705 18th N. W., Washington, D. C.
Heimann, Wilfred S., 620 N. Broadway, Stanley, Wisconsin
Heinbockel, Florian H., Norwood, Minnesota
Henderson, Lawrence W., 1331 Hendricks, Dallas, Texas
Hendrichs, Wayne, 2104 N. W. 27th, Oklahoma City, Oklahoma
Henson, Thomas H., 2420 Atherton, Berkeley, California
Henwood, John B., 311 5th Street, Ridgefield Park, New Jersey
Herbst, Emmett L., 513 North A Street, Farmington, Missouri
Herbst, Lawrence R., RFD 1, Farmington, Missouri
Hetherington, Ralph W., 520 Weld Street, Benton Harbor, Michigan
Heuser, Francis J., 2415 More Street, Chicago, Illinois
Hicks, Billie G., 1507 Poag Road, Edwardsville, Illinois
Higgins, John W., 3125 Potomac Avenue, St. Louis, Missouri
Hight, William S., 7029 Van Dyke Street, Philadelphia, Pennsylvania
Hilbert, Harry C., 12 Rockland Street, Nashua, New Hampshire
Hill, Claude E., Battle Creek, Michigan
Hinkle, Julian, RR 4, LaFayette, Louisiana
Hitt, Earl J., 1505 Keeler, Bartelsville, Oklahoma
Hix, William T., Jr., 1518 Lee Street, Charleston, West Virginia
Hochadel, Richard A., Route 2, Albion, Pennsylvania
Hochgesang, Robert N., (Address Unavailable)
Hodener, John J., Jr., 3837 Broadway, Sacramento, California
Hodges, James A., 3032 Arrowhead Avenue, San Bernardino, California
Hoey, Thomas J., 8 Koury Court, West Haven, Connecticut
Hoffman, Robert E., 1710 Edmund Terrace, Maplewood, New Jersey
Holly, Harry C., RR 2, Factoryville, Pennsylvania
Holmes, Melville W., 814 Sackett Avenue, Cuyahoga Falls, Ohio
Holz, Frank, Orchard Street E., Patchogue, Long Island, New York
Hosiba, Edward A., 280 Shaw Street, New Bedford, Massachusetts
Hosmer, Elbridge E., 210 Cresswell, Ridley Park, Pennsylvania
House, Ray A., 1632 19th Avenue, Moline, Illinois
Hover, Arthur G., Box 305, Arkansas City, Arkansas
Howard, Lester S., Route 2, Merry Oaks, North Carolina
Hozza, Frederic J., 438 Myrtle Avenue, Irvington, New Jersey
Hudson, William P., Garlin, Kentucky
Huffman, Robert W., 823 W. 3rd Street, Davenport, Iowa
Huftless, Frank A., 2918 S. 23rd, Omaha, Nebraska
Huking, Leonard J., 535 Lowell Avenue, Palo Alto, California
Hull, Robert E., RFD 1, Port Jervis, New York
Hume, Billie E., 1531 E. 24th Street, Minneapolis, Minnesota
Humphreys, Lenley, 713 N. Olie Street, Oklahoma City, Oklahoma
Hupp, Leon C., Route 3, Wayne, Nebraska
Hurley, John R., 1515 Northwestern Avenue, West Lafayette, Indiana
Hurst, James A., Jr., Route 1, Apopka, Florida
Hurt, John T., Lancaster, Missouri
Hustad, Maynard H., Room 228 Fess Hotel, Madison, Wisconsin
Hyde, Ralph J., Box 54, Haleyville, Alabama
Hzizdak, George J., 3124 Elm Street, Weirton, West Virginia
Inderbitzin, Fredrick D., 215 S. Goodman Street, Rochester, New York
Ireland, Theodore B., 12778 Promenade, Detroit, Michigan
Iscm, Ben L., 2241 S. 2nd Street, Abilene, Texas
Jack, John H., Jr., 3120 Bessemer Road, Birmingham, Alabama
Jackson, Robert E., 240 Oxford Road, Upper Darby, Pennsylvania
Jacobs, Herbert R., 6121 N. Claremont Avenue, Chicago, Illinois
Jarman, Roy K., 439 N. Cherry, Galesburg, Illinois
Jenkins, Philip J., 19 Baldwin Street, Cambridge, Massachusetts
Jensen, Floyd R., 183 E. Hazel Street, Gridley, California
Jenson, Alfred C., Bear River City, Utah
Jenson, Doule R., Tendoy, Idaho
Jentzsch, Gerald J., 327 17th Avenue, Moline, Illinois
Janovec, Delmar L., Box 7, Nebraska, Nebraska
Johnson, Albin V., Route 2, Box 7-A, North Branch, Minnesota
Johnson, Howard W., 68 S. Main Street, North Field, Vermont
Johnson, Leonard E., 163 N. 9th Street, Newark, New Jersey
Johnson, Melvin E., Route 1, Hope, Arkansas
Johnson, William H., Cumberland, Maryland
Jones, Charles Q., Route 2, Bloomington, Indiana
Jones, John W., 64 Nulp Street, Wilkes-Barre, Pennsylvania
Jones, Mitchell J., 2121 E. 12th Street, Oklahoma City, Oklahoma
Jones, Robert E., 118 W. Pine Street, Santa Ana, California
Jordan, Kenneth H., 7675 N. Rogers, Chicago, Illinois
Joy, James W., 559 Second Street, Albany, New York
Judd, Robert W., 305 N. Locust, Jefferson, Iowa

Jurgelewicz, Chester B., 2633 Hirsch, Chicago, Illinois
Keith, Frank C., P. O., Eaton, Georgia
Keller, Earl W., 910 Park Street, McKeesport, Pennsylvania
Kelley, Virgil R., Box 68, Cottonwood, California
Kelly, John, 3316 Mantoose Avenue, LoCrescento, California
Kelly, John W., Valatie, New York
Kemp, Harold J., 6816 Bellevice Avenue, Guttenburg, New Jersey
Kendirck, Warren, Route 9, White Bear, St. Paul, Minnesota
Kenyon, Carlton W., 509 Pine Street, Yankton, South Dakota
Keown, James E., 528 Hall Street, Owensborough, Kentucky
Kesler, William P., 965 Carter Road, Roanoke, Virginia
Kienholz, Joseph H., 932 Mount Curve, Altadena, California
Kierst, Kenneth W., 2013 Key Boulevard, Arlington, Virginia
Kilgore, Marton P., 1317 Salt Air Avenue W., Los Angeles, California
Kimball, Raymond, RFD 1, White River, South Dakota
Kimble, Richard M., Daring, Missouri
King, Arthur J., 2 Hamilton Avenue, Crawford, New Jersey
King, Matthew B., 510 E. Monroe Street, Austin, Texas
Kingsbury, Walter E., 643 W. Main Street, New Britain, Connecticut
Kirkland, Elmer J., 4805 Guernsey Street, Bellaire, Ohio
Kirkpatrick, Lyle B., General Delivery, Celina, Kansas
Kizzire, William L., 518 S. 5th Street, Laramie, Wyoming
Kline, James W., 215 15th Street, Douglas, Arizona
Knauf, Robert J., 64 Norwood Avenue, Albany, New York
Knepper, Ralph L., Skidmore, Missouri
Knight, Charles R., 1515 S. 15th Street, Lincoln, Nebraska
Krebs, Miller M., Jr., Country Club Village (271 Azales Circle), Spring Hill, Ala.
Krempasky, George T., 229 Hickory Street, Peckville, Pennsylvania
Krikorian, Mihran, 150 Randall Street, San Francisco, California
Kristy, Harry, 340 N. Vendome Street, Los Angeles, California
Kuechler, Robert, 6325 Alabama Avenue, St. Louis, Missouri
Kushner, Herbert, 496 Greenwood Avenue, Trenton, New Jersey
Kuzmick, Matthew J., 2923 N. Oak Park Avenue, Chicago, Illinois
Kyger, Donald A., 605 W. Washington Street, Bloomington, Illinois
Kyle, Thomas J., 73 Elm Street, Marlboro, Massachusetts
LaBrizzi, Frank H., 131-68 Maple Avenue, Flushing, Long Island, New York
LaBaunty, Dolthers A., Coldwater, Michigan
Ladner, Purvis J., Route 1, Box 840, Pass Christian, Mississippi
LaFond, Wilfred M., 94 Arnold Street, Woonsoket, Rhode Island
Lagemann, Roy E., Godfrey, Illinois
Lamb, Roland F., Jr., (Address Unavailable)
L'amoreaux, Raymond C., 225 N. "G" Street, Tulare, California
Landfair, James B., Tillar, Arkansas
Landsness, Donald O., Jesup, Iowa
Lane, James L., 142 Hillcrest Road, Mt. Vernon, New York
Lane, Berry V., Sharon, Tennessee
Lane, Richard S., 232 Claremont Road, Ridgewood, New Jersey
Langer, George, 1326 St. Johns Place, Brooklyn, New York
Lankheit, Edward H., 36 St. Josephs Lane, Covington, Kentucky
Lassiter, Sherrod B., Floraia, Alabama
Lateer, Ralph M., 410 Empire Street, Montpellier, Ohio
Lauer, William F., (Address Unavailable)
Law, George M., 18 Helen Avenue, Niles, Ohio
Lawrence, Frank H., Jr., 2615 N. Charles Street, Baltimore, Maryland
Leach, Frank, 10 Atherton Street, Ft. Devens Ayer, Massachusetts
Leffier, Donald E., 6 Steward Street, Trafford, Pennsylvania
Lentine, Charles J., 3594 E. 139th Street, Cleveland, Ohio
Leon, Joaquin, 3111 S. San Pedro, Los Angeles, California
Leone, Philips F., 1410 Hobart Avenue, Bronx, New York
LeTourneau, Raymond J., 2 Farrar Avenue, Worcester, Massachusetts
LeVasseur, Napoleon L., 304 11th Street, White Bear Lake, Minnesota
Leveridge, James B., Decide, Kentucky
Leverock, John H., Richmond Hill, Queens, New York
Liles, William G., 606 W. Wilson Street, Farmville, North Carolina
Linberg, Robert S., 1364 Crescent Road, Canton, Ohio
Lipman, Warren A., 2541 Aqueduct Avenue, New York City, New York
Liposky, Walter, 34 Stearms Street, Malden, Massachusetts
Lipschutz, Nathan, 7522 20th Avenue, Brooklyn, New York
Little, Cyril M., 1016 Vermont Street, Quincy, Illinois
Littleton, Lewis J., General Delivery, Gillette, Wyoming
Loeb, Jerbert R., 1509 S. Livonia, Los Angeles, California
Logan, Howard P., 216 Rock Street, Pomroy, Ohio
Lohwater, Robert K., 4223 Lake Avenue, Rochester, New York
Lopez, Joe S., Box 336, Alpine, Texas
Luhta, Adolph J., 234 Billette Street, Plainesville, Ohio
Lurix, Joseph W., 81 Franklin Street, Bridgeport, Connecticut
Maassen, Elden L., Dakota City, Iowa
MacBeth, Robert E., 829 Baldwin Avenue, El Monte, California
Macone, Francis V., Box 18, Beaufort, South Carolina
Magee, Milford M., 2420 California Avenue, Topeka, Kansas
Mahany, Julain A., 2632 Dixie Highway, Covington, Kentucky
Malcolm, Melvin C., 75 Baumer Street, Johnstown, Pennsylvania
Malone, Frank P., 30 Canson Street, N. Tonauanda, New York
Malone, Frank R., 322 S. High Street, Lancaster, Ohio
Mangano, Salvatore P., 1837 Van Vran Ken Avenue, Schenectady, New York
Manners, James P., 704 Boyd Street, Kelso, Washington
Marchand, Leo P., Pulasky Boulevard, Bellingham, Massachusetts
Marcusson, Edmond A., 32 Courter Avenue, Maplewood, New Jersey
Markowski, Frank W., 2814 S. Kenneth Avenue, Chicago, Illinois
Markwalder, Derrald L., RFD 1, Box 372, Cuyahoga Falls, Ohio
Marlin, Celetis A., 2504 1/2 Indiana Street, Kansas City, Missouri
Marlowe, Coleman B., Route 1, Collands, Virginia
Martin, Charles P., 1462 Wirt Street, Omaha, Nebraska
Martin, Robert J., 3636 N. Whipple Street, Chicago, Illinois
Martin, Roy D., Route 1, Rentz, Georgia
Mason Caldin J., 812 Atate Street, Ft. Wayne, Indiana
Mason, Francis J., 419 Sunset Drive, Murfreesboro, Tennessee
Mason, Frank E., 705 Sunshine Drive, San Antonio, Texas
Masterson, Peter J., 2969 Briggs Avenue, Bronx, New York
Matthews, Billy, 19 Grace Street, Montgomery, Alabama
Mattson, Clair E., Bremerton, Washington
Mayerson, Robert, 945 E. 26, Brooklyn, New York

Meadors, Irby H., 522 2nd Avenue, Albany, Georgia
Medina, Louis L., 484 Tenorio, Santa Fe, New Mexico
Medway, Marvin, 5405 Berks Street, Philadelphia, Pennsylvania
Melieste, William, 280 N. Chester Avenue, Pasadena, California
Mesthos, George A., 10 Pine Street, Mt. Holly, New Jersey
Middleton, Curtiss O., 4314 Gibson Street, Houston, Texas
Miller, James A., General Delivery, Box 90, Jasper, Texas
Miller, John (Address Unavailable)
Miller, Keith E., Box 65, Mesick, Michigan
Miller, Merlin D., 276 E. 14th Street, Chicago Heights, Illinois
Miller, Raymond A., 611 S. Avenue B., Washington, Iowa
Miller, Thomas G., 1735 Roscoe Street, Chicago, Illinois
Miller, William E., 611 Walton Street, Ft. Atkinson, Wisconsin
Millett, George E., 71 Larch Avenue, Dumont, New Jersey
Millikin, Clifford J., Farmingham, Massachusetts
Millstein, Stanley, 138-49 77th Avenue, Flushing, Long Island, New York
Milstein, Alexander S., 6220 Leland Way, Hollywood, California
Mitchell, Harold J., Lexington, Kentucky
Mitchell, Louis D., Route 1, Negley, Texas
Monahan, Thomas F., Burlington, Massachusetts
Monroe, Irving B., RFD 2, St. Louis, Michigan
Monteith, Leon, Bartrain & Cook Avenue, Darley Township, Pennsylvania
Montgomery, Owens L., Box 1111, Colorado City, Texas
Montney, Russell L., RFD 1, Clio, Michigan
Montville, Harold C., 43 Summit Street, Woonsocket, Rhode Island
Moon, Jack F., Mertzon, Texas
Mooney, Robert E., Woodville, Texas
Moore, Clifford A., 1409 Vinewood Street, Detroit, Michigan
Moore, Roland H., 4 Courtland Avenue, Charleston, South Carolina
More, Joseph C., 888 Dowling Street, Kendallville, Indiana
Morgan, William O., Route 6, Box 516, Dallas, Texas
Morrett, Denzil J., Route 1, Dallas, Pennsylvania
Morris, Thomas R., Estancia, New Mexico
Morris, Wilmer W., 810 Allen Way, Visalia, California
Mulner, Martin H., Jr., 39 Exchange Street, Uttica, New York
Murphy, Joseph H., Route 1, Filton, Georgia
Murray, Donald G., 427 Fairfield Woods Road, Bridgeport, Connecticut
Murray, William A., 216 Depew Avenue, Mayfield, Pennsylvania
Murray, William S., 42-60 Ketcham Street, Elmhurst, New York
Murtach, James J., 1431 Bedford Avenue, Brooklyn, New York
Musgrave, James R., 18804 Iron Woodore, Cleveland, Ohio
Muster, Henry J., East Bernstadt, Kentucky
Mutchler, Miles G., 51 Business Street, Hyde Park, Massachusetts
Muth, John S., 117 Skelly Street, Johnstown, Pennsylvania
Muto, Dominic E., 49 Herber Street, Farmingham, Massachusetts
Myers, Charles E., Jr., 120 Prospect Avenue, Phillipsburg, New Jersey
McAdam, John W., 2400 D. Street, Sacramento, California
McArn, John J., Box 74, Rowland North Carolina
McArthur, Lachlan, (Address Unavailable)
McClannahan, Charles L., Box 95, Clemscot, Oklahoma
McCall, Garvis D., 620 Spring Street, Hendersonville, North Carolina
McCann, John M., 4952 Baynton Street, Philadelphia, Pennsylvania
McCarthy, Donald J., 1803 Bayard Avenue, St. Paul, Minnesota
Mc Closkey, Edwin J., 154 Franklin Street, Cambridge, Massachusetts
McCullough, George L., 148 Fairbanks Avenue, Morehead, Kentucky
McDonald, Orlando M., 4836 N. California Avenue, Chicago, Illinois
McDowell, Claud E., Inman, South Carolina
McEwen, Donald D., 3147 W. Washington Boulevard, Chicago, Illinois
McFarland, Roy C., Route 2, Box 132, Snyder, Oklahoma
McFerrin, Harold, Jr., 1405 9th Avenue, Great Falls, Montana
McIntyre, Paul A., 1004 Washington, Wellington, Kansas
McKaskle, Clarence W., 1505 Linden, Memphis, Tennessee
McKenna, John J., Route 2, Poland Road, Youngstown, Ohio
McKeller, Jack A., Atlanta, Michigan
McKibbon, John B., 1185 Green Street, Gainesville, Georgia
McKinney, Issac H., RFD 4, High Point, North Carolina
McLaughlin, James E., Dixon, Montana
Nagy, Charles A., 13081 Clifton Boulevard, Cleveland, Ohio
Nalley, John B., Route 2, Springfield, Kentucky
Nass, Raymond E., 517 E. Bergen Street, Springfield, Illinois
Neal, Harold H., 110-49 107th Street, Ozone Park, Long Island, New York
Neal, Robert G., 121 Minnesota Avenue, Buffalo, New York
Neal, Thomas F., RR 1, Bradley, Oklahoma
Nebinger, Robert F., 1114 W. North Street, Bethlehem, Pennsylvania
Neblett, Walter H., RR 1, Clarksville, Tennessee
Neimeyer, Edwin A., General Delivery, Magargel, Texas
Nekhay, Peter, 1603 Warren Street, Roselle, New Jersey
Nelson, Gynn H., Amery, Wisconsin
Nelson, Donald E., Box 161-A, Moline, Illinois
Nettles, Stephan, 1821 Green Street, Columbia, South Carolina
Neuendorf, Theodore G., 748 Fuller Street, St. Paul, Minnesota
Newman, Carl H., 561 21st Street, Richmond, California
Ng Richard Y., 228 W. Anderson, Stockton, California
Nicora, Mike, Jr., 456 Franklin Street, Salem, Ohio
Nightwine, Fred D., (Address Unavailable)
Nordin, Robert M., 10 Perkins Street, Lynn, Massachusetts
Norman, Rex M., Beatrice, West Virginia
Norman, John S., 2037 N. W. 19th Street, Oklahoma City, Oklahoma
Nutting, Elmer W., 1104 Cedar Street, El Paso, Texas
O'Brien, James J., 1109 Kirkpatrick Avenue, N. Fradford, Pennsylvania
Ochsner, Walter H., Box 506, Sutton, Nebraska
O'Connor, William F., 312 17th Avenue, Tuscaloosa, Alabama
O'Dell, Lloyd E., (Address Unavailable)
O'Donnell, John C., (Address Unavailable)
Oliver, Bradley B., 5238 Ellsworth, Pittsburgh, Pennsylvania
Olson, Howard A., 1020 S. Catalina, Los Angeles, California
O'Neill, Joseph A., (Address Unavailable)
Ong, Robert F., Ripley, West Virginia
O'Rear, Theodore, 1315 16th Street, Wichita Falls, Texas
Orloff, John S., 28 Mohawk Avenue, Waterford, New York
Osterhout, Jesse C., Halsterd, Pennsylvania
Ottaviani, William F., 49 Railroad Street, Glen Lyon, Pennsylvania

Owens, William J., 1 Ainsley Street, Dorchester, Massachusetts
Ozimek, Louis J., 14901 Edgewood Avenue, Cleveland, Ohio
Pack, Doyle D., 1450 Lemoyne Street, Los Angeles, California
Paden, Neil R., 11 W. Central, Miami, Oklahoma
Padgett, John D., 1700 S. 12th Street, Waco, Texas
Palansky, John J., 4782 N. Ellston Avenue, Chicago, Illinois
Palmer, Paul H., 1604 N. W. 36th Street, Oklahoma City, Oklahoma
Panciocco, Paul J., (Address Unavailable)
Pantello, Charles C., Hoagland Avenue, Ft. Wayne, Indiana
Paquette, Wilfred J., (Address Unavailable)
Parin, Aldin A., 335 N. Stileo Street, Linden, New Jersey
Parrott, William J., Box 219, Camino, California
Parsons, Edwin A., Jr., 34 Hart Avenue, Nuckham, West Virginia
Patton, Weldon F., 26 27th Avenue, St. Cloud, Minnesota
Patty, Ernest N., Jr., 4411 55th N. E., Seattle, Washington
Paxton, Thomas T., Route 1, Central City, Kentucky
Pearson, Silas W., Box 521, Louisville, Mississippi
Pedelty, Rodger D., 323 N. Adams, Mason City, Iowa
Pederson, Jens N., 450 E. 80th Street, Chicago, Illinois
Pennington, Wallace C., 253 Dexter Avenue, Mobile, Alabama
Perocchi, Alfred A., 55 Portland Street, Laurence, Massachusetts
Peters, Richard J., 1118 Washington Avenue, New York City, New York
Petersen, Harvey J., 3340 Federal Boulevard, Denver, Colorado
Peterson, Theodore J., 1608 Belvedere Avenue, Berkeley, California
Phillips, James O., Box 248, Mineola, Texas
Pickard, Earl, (Address Unavailable)
Pitek, Mike, Farmington, West Virginia
Pittman, Halloway B., 134 Thack Avenue, Auburn, Alabama
Plumb, Charles W., Box 208 RIS, Santa Fe Road, Chanute, Kansas
Ponder, Harold H., Route 1, Clarkesville, Texas
Poole, Ephriem R., 1025 Barber Street, Columbia, Pennsylvania
Portnoy, Saul, 625 E. 96th Street, Brooklyn, New York
Pospisil, Edwin S., 1550 11th Avenue, Sacramento, California
Powers, Edwin A., 40 U. S. Customs, Coburn Gore, Maine
Procaccio, Ernest A., 4408 Parrish Street, Philadelphia, Pennsylvania
Propes, John C., 2103 Mable Street, Shreveport, Louisiana
Purser, Edwin F., Hoguiam, Washington
Purtee, John W., RFD 1, Edwardsville, Kansas
Pushetoneque, Charles, Iama, Iowa
Putman, Robert E., 3541 Greenmouth Avenue, Baltimore, Maryland
Quarterman, Peter C., 315 W. Central Avenue, Valdosta, Georgia
Quesenberry, James P., Box 386, Las Cruces, New Mexico
Quinn, Guy H., 6 Melrose Street, Brattleboro, Vermont
Quinn, Herman P., 1025 N. 11th Street, Albuquerque, New Mexico
Quigley, Daniel J., Jr., Poplar Street, McKees Rock, Pennsylvania
Rader, Irvin B., Box 102, Roulette, Pennsylvania
Radke, Lucus M., 3825 W. 60th Street, Seattle, Washington
Rainey, Fred R., Jr., 2580 W. Lloyd Street, Pensacola, Florida
Ranek, Walter K., 2650 E. 33rd, Salt Lake City, Utah
Raney, Charles P., 1719 Que Street, Sacramento, California
Ranger, Richard L., 9 Farragut Road, Squamscott, Massachusetts
Raper, Troy L., 1500 Pine Street, Little Rock, Arkansas
Ratliff, Isaac L., Jr., 3117 S. Cincinnati, Tulsa, Oklahoma
Ratterree, James G., 611 W. Mt. Street, Kings Mountain, North Carolina
Rau, Charles H., (Address Unavailable)
Rauzon, John A., (Address Unavailable)
Rayfield, Harold W., 608 W. Hill Avenue, Valdosta, Georgia
Redwine, Carrol R., 209 W. 2nd, Morristown, Tennessee
Reed, Henry M., Jr., 1232 Jenks Avenue, Panama City, Florida
Regan, Andrew C., 826 Locust Street, Pittsburgh, Pennsylvania
Reiser, John, 1809 Mascher Street, Philadelphia, Pennsylvania
Renaud, Bernard W., 27 Ashley, Pittsfield, Massachusetts
Reseck, Albert T., 653 Kern Avenue, Los Angeles, California
Rettich, Charles L., 1719 Morton Street, Ann Arbor, Michigan
Reynolds, Charles G., Lombardy Heights, Bridgeport, Ohio
Reyns, Henry J., Rock Tavern, New York
Rhode, Jonathan C., Tabor, Iowa
Rhodes, Orville J., 4214 Cleveland, Spokane, Washington
Richard, Raymond J., 2733 Lincoln Avenue, Chicago, Illinois
Riggle, Robert E., Oregon, Mississippi
Rishel, Lee M., 4323 Century, Inglewood, California
Ristau, Robert E., 3586 6th Avenue, San Diego, California
Robinette, Ralph R., Box 230, Conroe, Texas
Robinson, James D., 3930 30th, San Diego, California
Robinson, William A., 92-31 53rd, Elmhurst, Long Island, New York
Rocca, James D., 221 Culver Avenue, Jersey City, New Jersey
Rocheleu, Michael J., 707 Houstonic, Pittsfield, Massachusetts
Roddy, Everett R., Route 1, Mountainview, Oklahoma
Rodriguez, Frank, 859 42nd Street, Brooklyn, New York
Rogers, E. H., 609 Oak Street, San Angelo, Texas
Rodgers, James F., 1526 Ft. Ashby, San Antonio, Texas
Roketzke, Edward W., 111 E. 7th Street, New York, New York
Rone, Hugh P., Methodist Orphans Home, Tahlequah, Oklahoma
Rooney, James A., 945 Federal, Philadelphia, Pennsylvania
Roser, Clarence E., 209 Elm Street, Leavenworth, Kansas
Rosevear, Charles F., 109 Frey Street, Union, New York
Ross, Cader E., Bradford, Arkansas
Rosseau, William J., 4 Clifton Street, New Haven, Connecticut
Rotko, Eugene, 128 Ft. Washington Avenue, New York, New York
Rounds, Lloyd J., 13 Allen Avenue, Pittsburgh, Pennsylvania
Rubal, Arturo C., Klondyke, Arizona
Rubottom, Ernest L., 1919 N. 6th Street, Clay Center, Kansas
Ruhland, Clayton H., 1221 Cross Street, Baltimore, Maryland
Rumery, John W., Route 1, East Lake Road, Harbor Creek, Pennsylvania
Rumplik, Robert H., Carleston Avenue E., Islip, New York
Runnels, Ralph N., Route 1, Broaddus, Texas
Russell, Daniel J., 238 86th, Brooklyn, New York
Russell, William H., 4107 Lakeshore, Oakland, California
Rustad, George H., 3618½ Washington, Los Angeles, California
Rustin, Thomas N., Jr., 108 E. Moor Street, Valdosta, Georgia
Ryals, George R., Goodnoe Hills, Washington
Ryals, Nolan C., 601 Vine Street, Orville, Ohio

Ryder, George M., 73 Center Street, Middleboro, Massachusetts
Sagendorf, Arthur J., 114 Boorasm Street, Jersey City, New Jersey
Sahoenberg, Norman, 3804 N. Fremont, Chicago, Illinois
Sainato, William J., 763 Union Street, Brooklyn, New York
Sandler, Harold M., 3016 S. W. 1st Avenue, Miami, Florida
Sargent, Richard T., 1325 Inglewood, Cleveland, Ohio
Saunders, Howard, Troy, North Carolina
Sauceda, John, 1105 S. 40th, Kansas City, Kansas
Sawyer, Paul, Monument Street, Wenyan, Massachusetts
Seaman, Glen F., 1873 Boy Street, Lanning, Illinois
Segal, Leon, 4751 Mervine Street, Philadelphia, Pennsylvania
Sellards, William D., 2419 1st Avenue, Juntington, West Virginia
Scanlon, Thomas A., Raymond Boulevard, Jackson, Mississippi
Schexnayder, Raymond H., Route 1, Jeanerette, Louisiana
Schack, William R., Jr., 452 Oakwood Street S. E., Washington, D. C.
Schaefer, Richard C., 138 Church, Ballston Sp., New York
Schallern, Riner B., Jr., 1161 S. W. 19th, Miami, Florida
Schaub, Ira O., Western Boulevard, Raleigh, North Carolina
Schmidt, Orville R., Route 1, West Bend, Wisconsin
Schoenbert, Norman, (Address Unavailable)
Scholl, John D., 705 Elton, Bronx, New York
Scholz, Frank M., Route 1, Box 395, Jacksonville, Florida
Schreiber, Leslie L., (Address Unavailable)
Schreiner, Phillip, Torrington, Wyoming
Schricker, Robert E., 6441 N. Artesian, Chicago, Illinois
Schuster, Arnold L., S. Fallsburg, New York
Scott, George E., 113 E. 14th Street, Idaho Falls, Idaho
Scow, Fredrick T., Shelby, Nebraska
Seguin, Donald R., RR 1, Eleva, Wisconsin
Selestak, Stephen, Box 144, Okalona, Mississippi
Shakar, Sammy M., 2781 Holly Street, Dearborn, Michigan
Shalala, Francis L., 2094 W. 85th Street, Cleveland, Ohio
Shapiro, Aaron A., 49 Brownell Street, Worchester, Massachusetts
Shaw, Paul M., 907 S. Washington, Roswell, New Mexico
Shea, William D., 332 Owens Street, Portsmouth, Virginia
Shelton, Ross G., c-o Florence M., 1200 10th Street, Modesta, California
Sherman, Ronald J., 2621 Highland Avenue, Rochester, New York
Sherr, Robert, 2402 Orleans Street, Baltimore, Maryland
Shoms, Roy E., Pampa, Texas
Shotwell, John L., 1979 Myrtle Avenue, Long Beach, California
Showers, Roy E., Jr., (Address Unavailable)
Shubley, Harry E., Jr., 83 Hall Street, Waltam, Massachusetts
Sievers, Gerald V., Route 2, Fremont, Nebraska
Simmons, Robert G., 2704 N. Avenue, Baltimore, Maryland
Simsonson, Orville A., Andover, South Dakota
Simpson, Ralph L., 1324 1st Street, Coffeeville, Kansas
Sindeldecker, Lloyd R., Box 27, Mackey Avenue, Martin-Ferry, Ohio
Skelskie, Stanley I., 147 Columbia Road, Dorchester, Massachusetts
Slater, James C., 2029 Melrose Street, Chicago, Illinois
Slauson, Benjamin A., Box 60, Lowhill, Connecticut
Slutzky, Samuel J., 905 2nd Street, Peekskill, New York
Smaus, Richard F., (Address Unavailable)
Smith, Frank D., 89 Harding Street, Lynbrook, Long Island, New York
Smith, Frederick E., 426 Beach Street, Kearny, New Jersey
Smith, George L., RFD 5, Bowling Green, Kentucky
Smith, George R., Raymonds, South Dakota
Smith, Herman A., Box 1, Caddo Mills, Texas
Smith, Kenneth W., 224 2nd Avenue, Long Branch, New Jersey
Smith, Leon E., Jr., 18 Sququoit Street, Whitesboro, New York
Smith, Leo V., 1223 B'hoffair, Utica, New York
Smith, Merritt L., Jr., 1032 Mauch-Chunn, Bethlehem, Pennsylvania
Smith, Millard A., 601 Horley Avenue, Bucyrlis, Ohio
Smith, Robert S., General Delivery, Hallsville, Texas
Smith, William M., Jr., 8 Wheatland Avenue, Dorchester, Massachusetts
Smith, Woodrow W., Overton, Nebraska
Snyder, Robert T., 102 Vista Place, Mt. Vernon, New York
Solomon, Benjamin, 54 Seward Avenue, Port Jervis, New York
Solomon, Joseph A., 76 King Street, Burlington, Vermont
Son, William B., 43, Greenley, Colorado
Sova, Lawrence A., Box 232, Sauk Rapids, Minnesota
Spence, Robert H., York, Pennsylvania
Sperling, Harold H., Box 132, Trumball, Connecticut
Springer, Loyal H., 347 S. 6th, Indiana, Pennsylvania
Stambaugh, Quentin R., RFD 1, Spring Grove, Pennsylvania
Stapleton, Howell H., Box 735, Raymondville, Texas
Stawarz, Valentine E., 29 Hayward, Wallington, New Jersey
Steele, Paul E., 2 Wendell Terrace, Worchester, Massachusetts
Stefanowski, Edward J., 1724 Banks Avenue, Superior, Wisconsin
Stevens, Edward J., 3226 Lincoln E., St. Louis, Illinois
Stickler, Stanley C., (Address Unavailable)
St. Julian, George L., 2615 Beaumont, Port Arthur, Texas
Stockman, Allan J., RR 2, Crooksville, Ohio
Stott, John J., 13 Home Place, Danbury, Connecticut
Stout, Donald E., 324½ S. Miram, New Ulm, Minnesota
Street, Charles E., 1608 Howard Avenue, Burlingame, California
Strommen, Richard S., 605 Short Street, Fort Atkinson, Wisconsin
Strever, Raymond G., 518 N. View, Aurora, Illinois
Stroz, Henry E., 386 Lafayette, Newark, New Jersey
Strickland, William I., 959 Kern Avenue, Richmond, California
Studer, Lyle E., 515 Blackman, Jackson, Michigan
Subel, Henry J., 2005 S. 8th, Milwaukee, Wisconsin
Sullivan, Calvin A., Box 431, Fredricksburg, Virginia
Sullivan, George M., 422 Market Street, Johnson City, Tennessee
Sullivan, James W., 190 Spring Street, Winchendon, Massachusetts
Sullivan, Odis A., 517 B. Street, Meridian, Mississippi
Swan, Maurice J., Route 1, Box 150, Aptos, California
Swartley, Robert B., 133 W. Tobias Street, Flint, Michigan
Sweeney, Charles J., 50 Beech Street, Framingham, Massachusetts
Sweet, Russell H., 28 Canal Street, Machanville, New York
Szalanski, Harry J., 314 Railroad Street E., Vanderbrift, Pennsylvania
Szmytkowski, Stanley J., 1671 Grove Street, Ridgewood, New York
Tait, Fred E., Jr., 1517 S. 78th Street W., W. Allis, Wisconsin

Talbot, Michael P., 315 Fenimore, Momaroneck, New York
Taylor, Douglas C., 30 South Street, Westfield, Massachusetts
Taylor, Edward H., Box 114, Alma, Georgia
Taylor, Roger M., 84 Myrtle Avenue, Cedar Grove, New Jersey
Tate, Verley, Route 4, Jonesboro, Tennessee
Teague, William R., 2309 6th Terrace, Birmingham, Alabama
Teal, Lloyd L., 906 Ellis Street, Dallas, Oregon
Templin, Jack D., (Address Unavailable)
Thayer, Gale M., 801st Avenue, Brookings, South Dakota
Thomas, Ben H., Jr., Route 3, Newport, Tennessee
Thomas, Donald I., Box 185, Houlton, Oregon
Thomas, Karl N., Arlington, Minnesota
Thomas, Peter C., 526 Walker, Stockton, California
Thomas, Victor M., 1209 Crotin, Newcastle, Pennsylvania
Thompson, Harry A., 16 Harvey, Dorchester Terrace Navy Yard, South Dakota
Thompson, Norman P., General Delivery, Ontonagon, Michigan
Thompson, William J., 416 Bay Avenue, Buckroe Beach, Virginia
Tilton, Thomas K., 514 Johnston, Trenton, New Jersey
Tinsley, William C., Easley, South Carolina
Topal, Jack M., 1200 Orinoco, Alexandria, Virginia
Townsley, Harold R., 128 N. 4th Avenue, Coatesville, Pennsylvania
Treadwell, Walter L., 2325 10th Avenue, Oakland, California
Treece, Henry R., Boza, Alabama
Trohimivich, Stanley J., Route 1, Elma, Washington
Truitt, Jake A., Jr., Box 822, Gladewater, Texas
Tuchler, Robert J., 120 Grant, Creeskill, New Jersey
Tuel, William O., Gilmer, Texas
Tuftie, Robert W., RFD 2, Ottawa, Illinois
Turk, Roy S., O. V. G. Hospital, Wheeling, West Virginia
Turgeon, James B., 166 Brown Street, Pittsfield, Massachusetts
Underwood, Harvard L., Palace Theatre, Brady, Texas
Urdahl, Nordeen S., Route 4, Thief R. Falls, Minnesota
Usnick, Raymond R., 9301 Kentucky, Kentucky City, Missouri
Valentine, Edward M., (Address Unavailable)
Van Etten, Francis J., (Address Unavailable)
Vann, George N., 1606 Scales Street, Raleigh, North Carolina
Varvello, Edward J., 4273 22nd Street, San Francisco, California
Vavases, Joseph J., Water Street, Coal Center, Pennsylvania
Villa, Frank E., 452 Garretson Avenue, Rodeo, California
Vincenti, Amdeo J., (Address Unavailable)
Vollmer, Raymond W., 1123 Mason Street, Springfield, Ohio
Vosevich, Milan, St. Louis, Missouri
Waldo, John H., (Address Unavailable)
Walker, John J., 1849 N. 72nd Street, Wauwatosa, Wisconsin
Wanzer, Charles R., 2111 Briarwood Road, Charlotte, North Carolina
Wradle, Elbert J., 1742 Menloway Street, Klamath Falls, Oregon
Wargel, William A., 520 S. E. Riverside Drive, Evansville, Indiana
Warrington, George L., Rehoboth, Delaware
Ward, Wilbur D., Rural Route 3, Fostoria, Ohio
Ward, William W., 1425 E. Marquette Road, Chicago, Illinois

Weaver, James W., 309 E. 19th Street, Indianapolis, Indiana
Weber, Hubert E., (Address Unavailable)
Weich, Bertram, 287 Leslie Street, Newark, New Jersey
Weikel, Clyde C., 502 Thomas Avenue, Williamsport, Pennsylvania
Welch, Joseph D., 20 Mercier Avenue, Boston, Massachusetts
Wessels, Howard J., 324 6th Street, West New York, New Jersey
Westfall, Wade, 3830 N. E. 21st Avenue, Portland, Oregon
Whitlock, James C., General Delivery, Washington College, Tennessee
Wickman, Warren J., 1087 Pier Avenue, Hermosa Beach, California
Wienstrom, James C., 3924 Woodland Avenue, Western Springs, Illinois
Wiesenberg, A. P., 134 E. 2nd Street, New York City, New York
Wilder, Deloss D., Box 642, Coast Road, Santa Cruz, California
Wilhelm, Louis J., 74 Park Dale Terrace, Rochester, New York
Wilkinson, John H., 2442 McGee Avenue, Berkeley, California
Williams, Jack J., Ben Wheeler, Texas
Williams, Joseph E., Box 241, Odenton, Maryland
Wills, Thomas C., 726 37th Avenue, San Francisco, California
Wilserson, Charles R., 623 W. Hayes, El Reno, Oklahoma
Wilson, Charles M., Spiceland, Indiana
Wilson, Robert G., 1153 E. Fox Street, South Bend, Indiana
Wilson, Roy J., 2035 Ivar Avenue, Hollywood, California
Wilson, William C., 100 Lynwood Avenue, Wilkes-Barre, Pennsylvania
Wingard, Darrell C., 5906 13th Street N. W., Washington, D. C.
Winiecki, Louis J., 44 Erie Street, Lancaster, New York
Wolf, Charles A., Dyersville, Iowa
Womble, George L., RR 1, Box 6, Enid, Oklahoma
Wondree, Robert E., Star Route, Salem, Virginia
Woodard, Neill S., 2705 E. 4 Place, Tulsa, Oklahoma
Wooden, Merl G., General Delivery, Guymon, Oklahoma
Workman, Dennis, Lansing, West Virginia
Worthington, Hersel, General Delivery, Eagan, Tennessee
Wozlek, Stanley S., 2900 W. 12th Avenue, Gary, Indiana
Wright, Edward A., Frost, Minnesota
Wright, Hans N., 2345 W. 33rd Avenue, Denver, Colorado
Wright, Robert B., 2516 Buchanan Street, Nashville, Texas
Wright, Theodore R., 3844 Wellington Road, Los Angeles, California
Wyatt, George S., Big Green Street, Vincennes, Indiana
Wyler, Daniel E., (Address Unavailable)
Wynne, Pruitt W., Route 1, Westminster, South Carolina
York, Avery J., 17 Spring Road, Yonkers, New York
Yorke, Wilbert R., 72 Church Street, Belfast, Maine
Young, Hommer G., 2238 Wrightboro Road, Augusta, Georgia
Young, James O., 30 Salem Street, Niwot, Colorado
Zackovsky, Brownie, 7937 White River Drive, Indianapolis, Indiana
Zellers, Guy G., 21395 S. Penn Street, Denver Colorado
Zimibovitz, Stanley J., 8580 White Street, Detroit, Michigan
Zimmerman, Eldor E., 1206 Mathews, Merril, Wisconsin
Zucaru, Harold, 10 Portrio Street, Little Falls, New York
Zukoski, Paul O., Robison Springs, Elmore, Alabama
Zollinger, John K., 1427 Pythian Avenue, Springfield, Massachusetts

499TH SQUADRON

Adair, Walter E., 13 Cottage Avenue, Chicago Heights, Cook, Illinois
Adams, Ewell B., (Address Unavailable)
Adamsky, Benjamin, (Address Unavailable)
Adrion, Charles L., (Address Unavailable)
Akers, L. B., Vicksburg, Mississippi
Alger, Harry N., 1202 Idaho Street, Deerlodge, Montana
Allen, Edward J., 2232 Andrews Avenue, Bronx, New York
Allen, Richard R., 30 Lincoln Avenue, Norristown, Pennsylvania
Alleman, Martin L., Water Street, Abbottstown, Pennsylvania
Allenson, Clifford A., 79 Olive Street, Pawtucket, Rhode Island
Amos, Bevil T., Biloxi, Mississippi
Anderson, Alan S., 111 E. 36th Street, Minneapolis, Minnesota
Anderson, Earl J., 1818 Mary Street, Pittsburgh, Pennsylvania
Andrezjewski, Andrew, Pittsburgh, Pennsylvania
Andrews, Kenneth T., 84 Walker Street, Saylesville, Rhode Island
Andrews, Thomas B., RR 1, Mt. Gilhead, North Carolina
Anuta, Russell E., (Address Unavailable)
Anthony, Palmer L., 45 Beardon Arkansas
Apetz, John H., Rochester, New York
Arkes, Nathan, 2637 W. Patomic Street, Chicago, Illinois
Armbruster, Glenn L., 42 Marion Street, Cumberland, Maryland
Arnest, William W., 214 W. Walnut Street, Kokoma, Indiana
Atkelski, Bernard, 816 West 17th Street, Lorain, Ohio
Attanassie, Peter J., 131 Pyerson Street, Brooklyn, New York
Augustine, Edward T., 387 6th Street, Brooklyn, New York
Austin, James C., Vidolin, Georgia
Avedisian, George, 219 East Street, Pawtuckett, Rhode Island
Awenius, James G., 850 Jersey Street, Denver, Colorado
Axelrod, Edward I., 5617 Pemberton Street, Philadelphia, Pennsylvania
Axmark, Roger E., RFD 1, Star Prairie, Wisconsin
Babin, Lee O., Duplessis, Louisiana
Baccelli, Ferdinand, Madford, Massachusetts
Bader, Walter E., 3705 Monerey Road, Baltimore, Maryland
Baeta, John R., 3536 20th Avenue, Sacramento, California
Bailey, Donald W., (Address Unavailable)
Bailey, Louis M., (Address Unavailable)
Bailey, Robert B., Box 32, Wolf Summit, West Virginia
Bailey, Robert L., (Address Unavailable)
Baird, Julian B., 1028 Elmwood Avenue, Ft. Worth, Texas
Baker, Pax D., 3987 Kalomath Street, Denver, Colorado
Baker, Raymond A., 605 Wood Street, Philadelphia, Pennsylvania
Baker, Richard, 2451 Scottwood Avenue, Toledo, Ohio
Balochke, George J., (Address Unavailable)
Balla, Ernest A., 32 Ullmen Street, Buffalo, New York
Ballnich, Frank C., (Address Unavailable)
Bankston, Buell A., 302 Archer Street, Houston, Texas
Bannister, Lawrence R., 1007 Aviant Avenue, Clinton, Oklahoma
Banz, Charles L., 5719 Kavon Avenue, Baltimore, Maryland

Barber, Russell J., 85 Forest Road, West Haven, Connecticut
Barnes, Walter S., Santa Fe, New Mexico
Bartlow, Jack B., 8624 Woodbridge, Cincinnati, Ohio
Barton, Daniel, General Delivery, Granger, Texas
Bartzokes, Christopher, 52 Nedgewood Street, Philadelphia, Pennsylvania
Barry, John V., 12 Estes Street, Lynn, Massachusetts
Bauer, Robert W., Mancos, Colorado
Beadles, John D., RFD 1, West Burlington, Iowa
Beard, Ray E., 236 N. 32nd Street, Kansas City, Kansas
Beisty, Thomas F., (Address Unavailable)
Belanger, Maurice, Lock Street, Nashua, New Hampshire
Benjamin, Lawrence, 3929 Haines Road, W. St. Petersburg, Florida
Bennett, Frederick E., (Address Unavailable)
Bennett, Henry B., 1755 15th Avenue, Birmingham, Alabama
Bennett, William W., RR 2, Childress, Texas
Bennett, William H., (Address Unavailable)
Bergh, Fred A., Box 361, Delray Beach, Florida
Bies, Stanley J., (Address Unavailable)
Bingham, Paul, Cornich, Utah
Bivins, Alston F., 1219 Dodd Street, Shelby, North Carolina
Blair, Raymond D., RR 2, Independence, Oregon
Blatherwick, Charles A., Box 206 Atco, New Jersey
Blumstein, Robert, 1738 University Avenue, Bronx, New York
Bobay, Francis A., (Address Unavailable)
Boghesean, Edward L., 4865 Ravenswood, Chicago, Illinois
Boight, (Unavailable), (Address Unavailable)
Bolinger, Freddie H., RFD 1, Galesburg, Kansas
Bollinger, Joseph C., 2334 S. D. Street, Elwood, Indiana
Bolte, George M., 514 Jersey Avenue, Jersey City, New Jersey
Bone, Walter R., (Address Unavailable)
Books, Donald L., (Address Unavailable)
Book, Robert S., (Address Unavailable)
Borders, James J., RFD 1, Commarce, Georgia
Borton, Daonald R., RR 2, Hastings, Michigan
Boudreau, Normand, 9 Pleasant Street, Nashua, New Hampshire
Boule, Arthur I., 18 Davis Drive, Bristol, Connecticut
Bowerstock, Raymond B., RR 1, West Salem, Ohio
Bowker, Otto L., (Address Unavailable)
Boyd, John B., 1502 N. Wanamassa, Ashbury Park, New Jersey
Boyd, Walter R., 204 Ducan Avenue, Jersey City, New Jersey
Boyna, Andrew T., (Address Unavailable)
Boyns, Herbert C., (Address Unavailable)
Braconi, Americo J., (Address Unavailable)
Bradley, William F., 8434 Howard Drive, Houston, Texas
Bradshaw, Morris H., Petersburg, Texas
Brandon, (Address Unavailable)
Bray, Roy R., 8821 2nd Boulevard, Detroit, Michigan
Brennan, Thomas J., 230 Doyle Avenue, Providence, Rhode Island

Brevitz, Harry F., (Address Unavailable)
Bright, Victoria, 110 Balsan Street, Rome, New York
Broadhurst, Jack L., Ideal Brick Company, Fayetteville, North Carolina
Brock, Willard, Rax, West Virginia
Broman, Carl D., 13th Avenue, Lakewood, Colorado
Bronson, Theodore C., 517 Hill Street, Prescott, Arizona
Brown, Archie F., 1815 West View Drive, Indianapolis, Indiana
Brown, Barney A., Richland, Missouri
Brown, Gaylord L., Star Route 2, Rhinelander, Wisconsin
Brown, John D., 244 Westfield Road, Eggertsville, New York
Brown, John J., (Address Unavailable)
Brown, J. A., RFD 2, Ashville, New York
Browngardt, Arthur, Sag Harbor, Long Island, New York
Browning, Archie W., (Address Unavailable)
Brundidge, Roy B., 4309 Speedway Drive, Austin, Texas
Brunnemer, Robert W., 1311 Spring Street, Jeffersonville, Indiana
Brydges, Harold R., 1257 Beaconsfield, Grosse Point, Michigan
Bryan, James T., 110 Nowland Avenue, Hillsboro, Texas
Bryan, Wilson S., Box 26, Tracy, Missouri
Bryant, Clifford B., 1110 N. Broadway, Leavenworth, Kansas
Bryzenyski, Daniel, 4217 Martin, Detroit, Michigan
Buck, George H., S. Willington, Connecticut
Buck, Howard M., S. Willington, Connecticut
Buckingham, Harry W., 701 Grany Street, Corinth, Mississippi
Buckwald, Anthony, 3068 North Daulin Court, Chicago, Illinois
Buczkowski, Louis T., Hazard Avenue, Thompsonville, Connecticut
Budde, Henry H., 5914 Pailade Avenue, West New York, New York
Buedhler, Wilbur C., (Address Unavailable)
Bullitt, George R., 7907 Winston Road, Chestnut Hill, Philadelphia, Pennsylvania
Burbank, William F., (Address Unavailable)
Burbank, William B., RFD 4, Waterloo, Iowa
Burger, Claude W., 1058 Texas Street, Mobile, Alabama
Burke, Elwyn R., (Address Unavailable)
Burke, Frank J., Dennis, Massachusetts
Burks, J. R., (Address Unavailable)
Burnese, Frank, (Address Unavailable)
Burney, Theodore M., 3807 Tenth Street, Tampa, Florida
Burns, Chester F., (Address Unavailable)
Burns, Edwin J., RR 2, Rimington, Indiana
Burns, James F., (Address Unavailable)
Burns, Odie H., Halayville, Alabama
Burris, John S., 2532 Dryden Road, Houston, Texas
Bursath, Douglas, 35th Street, Sacramento, California
Bussler, Jack V., 838½ Arch Street, Williamsport, Pennsylvania
Butiscaris, John, 1823 Van Dyke Avenue, Detroit ,Michigan
Butler, Dean W., 7044 Irving Avenue, Minneapolis, Minnesota
Butts, William G., 4484 Ciaque Road, Olmste, Ohio
Buxton, James M., (Address Unavailable)
Cabell, William W., Tuchahoe Apartments, Richmond, Virginia
Cade, George E., 417 Lyceum Avenue, Roxborough, Pennsylvania
Cagle, George W., Bartlett, Texas
Calengor, Donald S., 2333½ 1st Avenue, Hibbing, Minnesota
Campbell, Robert E., 1508 Avenue, Terre Haute, Indiana
Campbell, William J., 521½ Starr Avenue, Toledo, Ohio
Camelleri, James, 303 14th Street, Detroit, Michigan
Camper, Hubert A., 725 Anderson Street, Beixtol, Tennessee
Campo, Joseph, 711 Avenue N. W., Childress, Texas
Cantwell, Martin, 2910 6th Avenue, Troy, New York
Caouette, Rene, 51 Mill Street, Brunswick, Maine
Capachietti, Umberto F., 51 Kimble Street, Lawrence, Kansas
Carlton, Everett E., (Address Unavailable)
Carrico, Leo C., Quinton Drive, Route 1, Meridan, Mississippi
Carroll, Joseph A., (Address Unavailable)
Carrilo, John W., Louisville, Kentucky
Carson, Catuin S., 2217 S. Broad Street, Philadelphia, Pennsylvania
Carter, William G., (Address Unavailable)
Casler, Harold, 71 Glen Avenue, Amsterdam, New York
Center, Elbert R., (Address Unavailable)
Cesolini, Bruno, 775 Merrimack, Lowell, Massachusetts
Cessna, Carl L., 307 Wills Street, Cumberland, Maryland
Chalon, Joseph F., 412 West Bell, Houston, Texas
Chance, Daniel A., 4115 Sullivan Street, Beaumont, Texas
Charlesworth, Donald E., Waterman, Illinois
Checinski, Walter J., (Address Unavailable)
Chesanck, Andrew T., 897 Asylum Avenue, Hartford, Connecticut
Chiado, Joseph J., Route 1, Box 249, Albuquerque, New Mexico
Childers, Ralph H., 523 N. 3rd Avenue, Upland, California
Cianflocco, Daniel J., (Address Unavailable)
Ciaramella, Joseph, 319 Moore Avenue, Pittsburgh, Pennsylvania
Clark, Daniel, (Address Unavailable)
Clark, Edward L., (Address Unavailable)
Clark, William F., 60 Dickinson Street, Lisbon, New Hampshire
Clarks, Vincent, 149 Ridge Street, Glen Falls, New York
Clarkens, Henry, 8651 Ferris Avenue, Morton Grove, Illinois
Clay, Jack C., 500 N. E. 11th Street, Oklahoma City, Oklahoma
Clevenger, Lyle J., 436 Sedgwick Place, Richmond, Virginia
Cloud, Curtis L., 43 E. Easton Street, Tulsa, Oklahoma
Coates, Roy B., 4941 N. Troy Street, Chicago, Illinois
Cobb, Byron E., 5613 Loraine Avenue, Detroit, Michigan
Cohen, Joseph, 1580 Theriot Avenue, New York, New York
Colihan, Eugene, 75 S. 3rd Street, Ashland, Pennsylvania
Collinan, Richard M., 83 Gardner Avenue, Buffalo, New York
Collins, John F., 643 River Street, Scranton, Pennsylvania
Collins, Lawrence, (Address Unavailable)
Colton, Michies, 612 5th Avenue, Brooklyn, New York
Conant, Carl C., 4045 Brooklyn Street, Seattle, Washington
Conn, Donald Y., (Address Unavailable)
Connor, John B., 158 Foster Street, New Haven, Connecticut
Converse, Stanley M., (Address Unavailable)
Cookman, Calvin L., 14 Anacostia Road, S. E. Washington, D. C.
Cooley, Edward J., 136 Bowles Street, Springfield, Massachusetts
Cooney, Kenneth B., (Address Unavailable)

Cooper, George L., 702 Elm Street, Peabody, Kansas
Corcoran, Francis J., 2615 Glendale Avenue, Chicago, Illinois
Corley, Ernest G., 417 Memorial Drive, Decatur, Illinois
Cocoran, Robert E., 2500 Green Road, Cleveland, Ohio
Corrick, Merle D., 1124 Yosimite Avenue, Fresno, California
Cosaluzze, Rocco C., 13404 3rd Street, Brooklyn, New York
Cosentino, Joseph N., (Address Unavailable)
Coskrey, James O., RR 2, Troy, Alabama
Costa, Michael J., 1710 Sinate Street, Columbia, South Carolina
Cozzolino, Leo J., 312 22nd Place, Clinton, Iowa
Cramer, Basil G., 30 West High Street, East Hampton, Connecticut
Crane, John P., 2212 Giddings Street, Chicago, Illinois
Crocker, L. B., RR 2, Milan, Tennessee
Crockett, William J., (Address Unavailable)
Croft, Arthur F., 18 Tremont Street, Maynard, Massachusetts
Croop, Aaron B., 905 11th N. E., Massillian, Ohio
Crosland, William J., 2121 S. N., Ft. Smith, Arkansas
Cruz, Anthony A., 1620 San Francisco, Trinity, Texas
Cummings, William R., 3510 Park Avenue, Weehawken, New Jersey
Cunningham, Charles J., 6560 Roosevelt Avenue, Charleston, West Virginia
Curci, Joseph, 61 Stewart, Norwalk, Connecticut
Curtis, Lucious E., (Address Unavailable)
Cwiklinski, Robert E., 968 Filmore Avenue, Buffalo, New York
Czapski, Edmund, 8304 Badger, Detroit, Michigan
Dahlgren, Jack R., (Address Unavailable)
Daigle, Oscar L., 49 Pleasant Street, Ft. Kent, Missouri
Daleo, Benny J., (Address Unavailable)
D'Alessio, Pasquale C., 980 Grant Street, Denver, Colorado
Damour, Louis T., Henniker, New Hampshire
Dancer, Royee C., General Delivery, Greegtown, Texas
Deniel, Octave J., 10157 S. Morgan, Chicago, Illinois
Dapra, Gelid, (Address Unavailable)
Dauchess, Edward G., Philadelphia, Pennsylvania
Davis, Howard E., 2217 61st Street, Kenosha, Wisconsin
Davis, James A., (38 E. Babbitt Street, Dayton, Ohio
Davis, Lawrence B., 3001 Fawnee Avenue, Birmingham, Alabama
Deafenbaugh, Edward E., (Address Unavailable)
DeArmond, Henry W., 316 N. 18th Street, Independence, Kansas
De Canio, Anthony, 39 S. Penn Avenue, Atlantic City, New Jersey
Decker, Wendell D., 624 W. Wiley, Bluffton, Indiana
DeFrank, Pete, 222 Brennan Street, Houston, Texas
Den, Linger Carl, 2732 Whittier, Dayton, Ohio
DePrater, Robert A., (Address Unavailable)
DePra, Gelio, 6630 Lafayette, Detroit, Michigan
Deproteo, (Address Unavailable)
DeRight, Stanley R., 1513 Main Street, Kalamazoo, Michigan
DeSalvo, Joseph, 60 E. Park Avenue, White Plains, New York
De Santis, William A., 29 Chapel Street, Trenton, New Jersey
Desenberg, Franklin B., (Address Unavailable)
De Zonia, Lawrence E., 3029 E. Ocean Boulevard, Long Beach, California
Diberardine, Anthony F., (Address Unavailable)
Dietz, Frederick F., 44 Pineville Road, Central Islip, New York
DiGiovanni, Salvadore A., 502 Campbell, Kansas City, Missouri
Dillehunt, Richard M., 420 A. Street, Needles, California
Dobson, Arthur S., Box 45, Southview Ridge, Glendale, Connecticut
Donaldson, George P., (Address Unavailable)
Donohue, William H., (Address Unavailable)
Douglas, Denver C., 8627 Roulo Place, Detroit, Michigan
Doull, William, 54 Union Street, Belleville, New Jersey
Dovica, Nicholas G., 1452 S. Ringgold Street, Philadelphia, Pennsylvania
Dreper, Robert W., 340 N. Griffith Park Drive, Burbank, California
Driscoll, Robert E., 1602 West Boulevard, Rapid City, South Dakota
Dubuc, Raymond A., 265 Colony Street, Meriden, Connecticut
Dubois, Rosaire A., 122 Edgewood Avenue, Methuen, Massachusetts
Dugan, Frank M., RR 1, McConnelsville, Ohio
Dumas, Charles J., 1521 Spruce Street, Philadelphia, Pennsylvania
Dunn, Harold C., 45 State Street, Weatherfield, Connecticut
Dusen, Berry Robert C., 1005 Prentice Street, Ashland, Wisconsin
Dusterhoff, Waldo J., Route 1, Spokane, Washington
Duval, Clarence E., 651 Ashwood Avenue, Toledo, Ohio
Earhart, Robert E., RR 2, Chileothe, Ohio
Eastman, Eugene W., (Address Unavailable)
Eckard, Samuel R., Route 1, Box 23, Conover, North Carolina
Edwards, Carl B., 1374 Cohasseh Place, Lakewood, Ohio
Edwards, Robert J., (Address Unavailable)
Edwards, Thomas B., (Address Unavailable)
Egan, Edward F., 615 Church Street, Bound Book, New Jersey
Eichenberg, Royal, (Address Unavailable)
Eilmann, Fredericke, (Address Unavailable)
Ellis, William T., 3252 Parke Avenue, Memphis, Tennessee
Emley, Harold E., RR 5, Huntington, Indiana
Engle, Richard C., RFD 1, Cedar Lake, Indiana
Englehart, Frank, (Address Unavailable)
Englehart, Von Hobel, (Address Unavailable)
English, Nath L., Atlanta, Georgia
Ensor, Luther B., RR 1, Mt. Sterling, Kentucky
Epple, Edward J., (Address Unavailable)
Erb, Walter S., (Address Unavailable)
Erickson, Harold E., Andubon, Iowa
Erum, Russell N., 3234 42nd Avenue, S. Minneapolis, Minnesota
Ervin, Clair R., RR 3, Butler, Pennsylvania
Eseudero, Edward F., 117 N. Rutland Avenue, Watertown, New York
Estep, Don F., RR 1, Box 72, Ft. Smith, Arkansas
Estes, Roy W., 8132 Glinbrook Drive, Houston, Texas
Evans, William, 299 Hoyt Street, Brooklyn, New York
Ewing, Harold O., Turton, South Dakota
Fait, Albert, 400 Jackson Street, Manchester, New Hampshire
Falvey, Floyd R., 222 S. West Street, Waukegan, Illinois
Faris, Joseph A., (Address Unavailable)
Farkas, Elamer G., (Address Unavailable)
Farmer, Raymond V., (Address Unavailable)
Farmer, William P., 483 Milton Street, Manchester, New Hampshire

499TH SQUADRON

Farrell, Gabriel, Jr., Perkins Institution, Watertown, Massachusetts
Fazi, Frederick P., 207 LeRoy Street, Saulte St. Marie., Michigan
Feder, Herman J., 726 N. Benn, Allentown, Pennsylvania
Ferguson, Lyle, (Address Unavailable)
Ferguson, Max B., RR 2, Oskaloosa, Iowa
Fiebig, Clarence J., (Address Unavailable)
Fike, Earl J., RFD 3, Myersdale, Pennsylvania
Fisher, Andrew J., 1917 Stafford Avenue, Scranton, Pennsylvania
Fitzpatrick, Thomas J., 1539 Cambria Street, Los Angeles, California
Fitzpatrick, William F., (Address Unavailable)
Flanigan, Eugene, 1213 E. Calvert Street, South Bend, Indiana
Fleisher, Fredrick, 549 Euclid Avenue, Brooklyn, New York
Fleming, Fred B., 67 Berwick Street, Belmont, Massachusetts
Fleniken, Leo I., 2028 Winteria, Baton Rouge, Lousiana
Flight, John W., (Address Unavailable)
Fones, Theodore H., 15223 Centre Avenue, Harvey, Illinois
Ford, Davis, 6141 Sarchwood, Philadelphia, Pennsylvania
Forster, William S., 2607 S. Bancroft Street, Philadelphia, Pennsylvania
Foster, Stanley B., Route 2, Plainfield, Wisconsin
Fox, Floyd N., RR 3, Shelby, Michigan
Foxbenner, Ralph L., (Address Unavailable)
Frauenfelder, Carrett H., RR 1, Riley, Kansas
Frazier, Benajmin L., (Address Unavailable)
Frazier, Sherman J., 3730 Riverside Drive, Huntington, West Virginia
Frazier, Thomas L., Aprian, Georgia
Fried, Lawrence J., Route 2, Clara City, Minnesota
Fuller, Wallace H., (Address Unavailable)
Fulton, Kenneth E., Hillside Avenue, West Newton, Massachusetts
Gallagher, William F., 184 Roosevelt Street, Providence, Rhode Island
Galinkin, Claire, 119 Lyons Avenue, Newark, New Jersey
Gallagher, Edward F., 362 Lafayette Avenue, Brooklyn, New York
Gallows, Michael, (Address Unavailable)
Gamble, Shuler S., Stigler, Oklahoma
Gamblin, Willie R., 312 E. 16th Street, Amarillo, Texas
Gambon, John F., (Address Unavailable)
Garber, Harry, 1216 Empier Avenue, Camden, New Jersey
Gardner, Delmar R., 193 Houston Avenue, Muskegon, Michigan
Garris, Jack T., 1822 Country Club, Prado, Florida
Garza, Alexandro, 730 6th Street, Brownsville, Texas
Gath, Philip, 28 Wyoming Street, Warsaw, New York
Gearhart, William W., 750½ Kohn Street, Norristown, Pennsylvania
Geis, Raymond J., (Address Unavailable)
Gemmill, Richard H., 423 Perry Street, Prescott, Arizona
George, Jack L., 317 Main Street, South Park, Pennsylvania
Gerstner, Leo J., (Address Unavailable)
Giancario, Orlando J., (Address Unavailable)
Gilbert, Clarence H., (Address Unavailable)
Gilkinson, Robert D., Winona, Kansas
Gillim, Charles W., 432 Walnut Street, Owensburg, Kentucky
Ginnelly, Thomas J., 12828 Woodrow Wilson, Detroit, Michigan
Glass, Heath T., 4169th Avenue, N. E. St. Petersburg, Florida
Glenn, LaVance A., Box 144, Coolidge, Arizona
Goebel, Victor J., RR 2, Hermlish, Texas
Goehry, Erhart A., Route 1, Gothenburg, Nebraska
Goforth, Pat E., 424 E. 12th Street, Ada, Oklahoma
Goldman, Jacob H., 1305 Nedro Avenue, Philadelphia, Pennsylvania
Gomes, Clement F., 137-20 97th Avenue, Jamaica, New York
Goodwin, William T., 1017 E. Silber Street, Tucson, Arizona
Gordon, George A., Route 2, Box 450, Wheeling, West Virginia
Gould, Henry H., 922 Vance Street, Toledo, Ohio
Graham, William A., 327 Jefferson, Bloomsburg, Pennsylvania
Graham, William W., 30 N. Main Street, Bel Air, Maryland
Granosky, Anthony J., (Address Unavailable)
Grassel, Albert J., 214 E. 15th Street, New York, New York
Grauenfelder, (Address Unavailable)
Green, George W., Box 1152, Del Rio, Texas
Green, Harvey N., Parder, Idaho
Green, Robert E., Risco, Missouri
Greenwood, James W., (Address Unavailable)
Greenwood, Steve F., Snomac, Oklahoma
Gribble, Robert M., 1 West Green Street, Shiremans Town, Pennsylvania
Gribbon, Harold J., (Address Unavailable)
Grice, John C., Mulberry, Indiana
Griffin, James E., Dorchester, Massachusetts
Gross, A. J., Star Route, Knott, Texas
Gryzbek, Henry, (Address Unavailable)
Guido, Gye A., (Address Unavailable)
Gustafsom, Howard M., 1110 Summit Street, Red Oak, Iowa
Guthrie, John H., 520 Magnolia Avenue, Shebymite, Kentucky
Gwiazda, Adam A., 3046 N. 8th Street, Milwaukee, Wisconsin
Gwyn, Donald, 408 Woodland Drive, Denny Terrace, Columbia, South Carolina
Haber, Fred C., 28 Maple Street, South Hadley Falls, Massachusetts
Haire, Charles C., 25 E. 77th Street, New York, New York
Halcom, James H., 1229 54th Street, Oakland, California
Hall, Hugh D., Route 5, Box 193, Ft. Worth, Texas
Haller, William C., 3927 S. Clerose Circle, Cincinnati, Ohio
Hamlin, Paul A., 39 Frazier Street, Brockport, New York
Hanna, James, 222 77th Street, Chicago, Illinois
Hannan, Patrick J., 25 Church Terrace, Belleville, New Jersey
Hannon, John T., Jr., (Address Unavailable)
Hanson, Gorden B., Binderob Apartments, Minden, Nebraska
Harben, George W., 6507 S. Normandie Avenue, Los Angeles, California
Hardke, William F., Hazen, Arkansas
Harding, George W., 1419 Parke Lane, Spokane, Washington
Hardtke, Gerard N., 624 W. Main Street, Sumner, Washington
Hargis, Calvin G., 513 Meyton Street, Texarkana, Texas
Harmon, George W., 261 Ridgewood Circle, Lackawanna, New York
Harner, Kenneth E., (Address Unavailable)
Harner, Max R., 914 Homestead Avenue, Springfield, Ohio
Harper, Victor D., (Address Unavailable)
Harrigan, Francis S., 2530 Wyckuffe Road, Baltimore, Maryland
Harris, James B., (Address Unavailable)

Harris, Frank R., Joneoye Falls, New York
Harvey, Lawrence H., Conewant Valley, New York
Hathazi, George, 42 Alden Avenue, Roebling, New Jersey
Hattield, Donald J., RR 2, Manchester, Iowa
Haugen, Orville A., Route 3, Flandreau, South Dakota
Haugh, Francis, 14 Lee Street, Putman, Connecticut
Hawkins, Harry E., Jr., 2615 S. Harvey, Oklahoma City, Oklahoma
Hawyer, Owen A., Stafford, Kansas
Hays, Carroll W., 819 N. Gayese Street, New Orleans, Louisiana
Hazard, Clifton E., Washington Courthouse, Ohio
Hedges, Homer J., 306 N. 3rd, Clinton, Indiana
Heinbold, Richard D., 220 Hudson Avenue, Newark, Ohio
Heldman, George L., 740 Clinton Springs, Cincinnati, Ohio
Helms, James E., 1025 Stewart Avenue, Roanoke, Virginia
Hemness, Clayton J., 1350 S. Lybarger Street, Olympia, Washington
Hennen, Lee W., Morris, Minnesota
Henson, Robert J., Willis, Oklahoma
Herman, Frank I., 3404 Beach Avenue, Baltimore, Maryland
Hermanson, Earle S., Waterville, Iowa
Higgins, Louis E., 1361 N. Union, Decatur, Illinois
Hill, Fred R, Ashton, Idaho
Hillman, Myron R., 1604 Minneapolis Avenue, Gladstone, Michigan
Hilton, William, 17318 Curtis, Detroit, Michigan
Hines, Thomes E., (Address Unavailable)
Hinz, Raymond W., (Address Unavailable)
Hitchcock, Edwin H., Schenectady, New York
Hoffman, Edwin H., 4190 Utah Street, San Diego, California
Hofmeister, Anthony R., (Address Unavailable)
Hogan, Leroy J., (Address Unavailable)
Hollingsworth, James J., 3536 103rd Avenue, Corano, Long Island, New York
Holmes, Gail R., 1915 N. Nicholas Street, Arlington, Virginia
Hooks, Donald L., (Address Unavailable)
Hoopes, Jack G., Maryville, Ohio
Hopson, James F., 15 Faville Avenue, Dodgeville, New York
Hopson, Merritt M., Alpine, Texas
Horton, Rowland W., Jr., (Address Unavailable)
Hotz, Robert E., (Address Unavailable)
Howard, David E., 403 Wall Street, Jeffersonville, Indiana
Hoyak, Vincent J., (Address Unavailable)
Hubbard, Clinton G., (Address Unavailable)
Huddelson, John D., 603 3rd Street, North Morga, Alabama
Hudgins, Harry Q., Enfield, North Carolina
Hughes, Teman O., RR 1, Plainview, Texas
Hull, Arthur R., (Address Unavailable)
Hulsey, Robert E., Fulcom Road, De Soto, Missouri
Hunt, George F., 1248 Wash Street, Bronx, New York
Hyder, Norman W., 902 Miller, Buhl, Idaho
Irby, Sover A., (Address Unavailable)
Irish, George, 327 N. Bridge Street, Grand Lodge, Michigan
Ingle, Robert L., (Address Unavailable)
Inglis, Albert (Address Unavailable)
Jackson, Ray O., (Address Unavailable)
James, William H., 508 Portland Avenue, Belleville, Illinois
Jenkins, Kenneth D., 540 Main Street, Palmery, Ohio
Jenkins, Walter P., 759 S. Orange, Sarasota, Florida
Jenne, Robert H., 817 Jackson E., Sullivan, Illlinois
Jepson, Henry A., RR 2, Overton, Texas
Jetton, Eugene A., 822 W. 8th Street, Woodland, Kansas
Johns, Charles J., Box 423, Republic, Pennsylvania
Jordan, Conrad B., 195 Jefferson Street, Tenefly, New York
Jones, John L., (Address Unavailable)
Jones, Macleod, 116 E. School Street, Stillwater, Minnesota
Johnston, Arthur L., (Address Unavailable)
Johnson, Charles H., RR 1, Elkhart, Indiana
Johnson, Corydon M., 17 Macmi Street, Plattsburg, New York
Johnson, Harold L., Fargo, North Dakota
Johnson, Joe, Dodey, Kentucky
Johnson, Kenneth C., Box 483, Oak Hill, West Virginia
Johnson, Lloyd M., 63 Bay Shore, Marinette, Wisconsin
Johnson, Richard, Fountain City, Tennessee
Johnson, Robert L., 46 Main Street, Bonne Terre, Missouri
Johnson, William C., 793 Ohio Street, St. Paul, Minnesota
Joseph, John, (Address Unavailable)
Joyner, Alton F., 1318½ 7th Avenue North, St. Petersburg, Pennsylvania
Kahn, Joseph, 5728 Pine Street, Philadelphia, Pennsylvania
Kaminski, Stanley J., 15356 Broadway, Maple Heights, Ohio
Kaminsky, Wallace B., 1052 Clay Avenue, New York City, New York
Kantor, Alvin R., 3400 Lake Shore Drive, Chicago, Illinois
Karnegie, Martin S., 957 Cranston Street, Cranston, Rhode Island
Karnis, Edward J., 2304 S. Woodstock, Philadelphia, Pennsylvania
Katz, Morton, 1336 W. Buena Vista, Detroit, Michigan
Kaufman, Harold, 779 Riverside Drive, New York City, New York
Kauffman, Edgar, 400 5th Avenue, Pittsburgh, Pennsylvania
Kawka, Walter J., Chicago, Illinois
Kay, John W., 1408 Frame Street, Charleston, West Virginia
Keegan, Joseph, 2401 Prospect Avenue, Scranton, Pennsylvania
Keller, Billy, 310 Dwyer, San Antonio, Texas
Kelly, Charles S., 306 N. Broad Street, Grove City, Pennsylvania
Kelly, Thomas F., 806 N. Beechwood Street, Philadelphia, Pennsylvania
Kelly, Thomas R., 9 Belleview Avenue, Winthrop, Massachusetts
Kellison, Walter R., 1204 E. Street, Sparks, Nevada
Kenney, Robert H., 646 C. Street, Lemoore, California
Kennedy, William F., Route 1, Box 15, Peacock, Texas
Kepler, Maurice E., (Address Unavailable)
Kersh, Blake F., Jr., 310 S. Main Street, Shamrock, Texas
Kessinger, Otis H., 2601 N. W. Parkway, Louisville, Kentucky
Kilpatrick, Wofford G., 141 Pearl Street, Atlanta, Georgia
King, Edgar D., (Address Unavailable)
Kingsley, Robert L., (Address Unavailable)
Kinney, Robert F., 1948 Rodney Drive, Los Angeles, California
Kiskadden, Lawrence W., Seattle, Washington
Klander, Stewart W., 11325 E. 39th Street, Kansas City, Missouri

Kleb, Jack A., (Address Unavailable)
Klein, George D., 48 Broadway, Passiac, New Jersey
Klemp, Earl L., 310 Ridge Road, Highland Park, Illinois
Kluender, Stewart, (Address Unavailable)
Knappick, Floyd, Route 7, Box 404, San Antonio, Texas
Knerr, John W., 112 E. Carpenter, Hutchinson, Kansas
Knighton, Perley A., (Address Unavailable)
Knopp, Virgil B., 22 N,. New Stanton, Virginia
Knox, Charles S., 350 Pleasant Drive, Cedar Rapids, Iowa
Koch, Joseph O., 243 N. Fountain Street, Cape Girardeau, Missouri
Koller, Frank J., 813 14th Street, McKees Rock, Pennsylvania
Korch, Alexander, Upper Main & Lee Street, S. Ambor, New Jersey
Kornblau, David, 113th Street, Forest Hills, New York
Kovack, Frank A., 3451 Bosworth Avenue, Cleveland, Ohio
Koza, John, 140-20 117th Street, Richmond Hill, Long Island, New York
Kranz, Alfred R., 2 Golfwood Street, Nassan, New York
Kreshock, Mathew B., 220 2nd Street, Wilburton, Pennsylvania
Krug, Lewis W., Heilwood, Pennsylvania
Kull, William E., (Address Unavailable)
Kunkel, Delce W., Adama, Wisconsin
Kurowski, Walter C., 5234 S. May Street, Chicago, Illinois
Kusior, Thaddeus, 64 Newton Street, Lawrence, Massachusetts
Ladolecetta, John J., 206 32nd Street, Brooklyn, New York
La Forest, Frank R., Jr., (Address Unavailable)
Lamer, Lee P., Box 4112, Oklahoma City, Oklahoma
Lanchak, Stephen, 228 Chaterine Street, Philadelphia, Pennsylvania
Lasson, William F., 3502 Southport Avenue, Chicago, Illinois
Lawson, William D., Gastonia, North Carolina
Lebeck, Howard G., 93 E. Schley Boulevard, Bremerton, Washington
LeBlanc, Jean P., 50 Knox Street, Lewiston, Maine
Lechner, Allen W., 8349 Portland Avenue, Wauwatosa, Wisconsin
Lee, Richard T., Penllyn Pike, Blue Belle, Pennsylvania
Lee, Robert R., 2603 Lillian Street, Shreveport, Louisiana
LeFevere Bowe C., (Address Unavailable)
Lehane, Joseph P., 197 Weid Street, Roxbury, Massachusetts
Leite, Manuel G., 21 Union Street, Brooklyn, New York
Lem, David G., 114 Jefferson Avenue, Oshkosh, Wisconsin
LeMay, Robert J., 435 Mast Road, Manchester, New York
Lemery, Conrad A., 286 Park Place, Woonsocket, Rhode Island
Leonard, John H., Cornersville, Tennessee
Leonard, Maurice A., Alpha, Minnesota
Lester, Lawrence B., Box 86, Moore, Texas
Levy, Julian E., 437 Morris Park Avenue, New York City, New York
Liebowitz, David, 150 Brighton 10th Street, Brooklyn, New York
Lipp, John, Timberlake, South Dakota
Lippard, Luther A., 951 Maple Avenue, Salisbury, North Carolina
Litchman, Gabriel G., (Address Unavailable)
Livingston, Joe T., RFD 1, Onenta, Alabama
Loete, Donald K., Box 229, Spanaway, Washington
Loomis, Howard R., RFD 4, Fulton, New York
Lorens, Nicholas B., (Address Unavailable)
Loskill, Stuart R., (Address Unavailable)
Loscnoy, Louis, Jr., (Address Unavailable)
Lotsgezell, James A., Decatur, Illinois
Lousche, Joseph, Jr., Box 254, Harwick, Pennsylvania
Loveras, Paul J., (Address Unavailable)
Loverin, Oren N., Lemon Grove, California
Lucas, Paul D., 1003 Bazore, Streator, Illinois
Luenebrick, Charles H., RR 1, Bruceville, Indiana
Luhta, Adolph J., (Address Unavailable)
Luka, Steve C., 266 Harding Avenue, Clifton, New Jersey
Luttrell, Paul T., RR 3, Cumberland, Maryland
Lyons, Andrew J., 11 Sabin Avenue, Montpelier, Vermont
MacDonald, Harry L., French Street, Banger, Maine
Madigan, James E., 206 Stevenson Street, Gayre, Pennsylvania
Madson, Richard, Britt, Iowa
Magart, Harold E., Route 2, Cutler, Indiana
Magee, Thomas E., Route 2, Mart, Texas
Mahaffey, James M., 430 S. Lahoma, Norman, Oklahoma
Maloney, Charles F., 355 Grant Street, Phillipsburg, New Jersey
Maloney, John F., 110 Lewis Street, Bridgeport, Connecticut
Malone, Walter A., Miles City, Montana
Mandell, Sam, 166 Howard Avenue, Brooklyn, New York
Mangum, Thomas H., 204 E. Trinity Avenue, Durham, North Carolina
Manich, William S., 1423 25th Street, Sacramento, California
March, John A., 3100 Duncan Street, Columbia, South Carolina
Marcinkevich, George, 1415 Dickson Avenue, Scranton, Pennsylvania
Marks, Leon, 1832 N. 54th Street, Philadelphia, Pennsylvania
Marks, Richard F., 1425 4th Avenue, Cedar Rapids, Iowa
Marlatt, Dwight G., 619 N. Denver, Hastings, Nebraska
Marsili, Anthony, (Address Unavailable)
Marsten, Douglas F., (Address Unavailable)
Martin, Archie J., Box 343, Fowler, Colorado
Martin, Charles E., 5613 Lexington Avenue, Hollywood, California
Martin, James R., 357 Richton Avenue, Highland, Michigan
Martin, Ralph E., Haydenville, Ohio
Massengill, James E., (Address Unavailable)
Mathers, Chester J., (Address Unavailable)
Matthews, Walter S., (Address Unavailable)
Mattieson, George L., (Address Unavailable)
Mattson, Matt M., Box 314, Ruinklo, Minnesota
Maurer, Thomas J., (Address Unavailable)
Mavraides, William, 651 Varnum Avenue, Lowell, Massachusetts
Mavromates, Harry T., 107 N. Dewey Street, Philadelphia, Pennsylvania
May, Ralph E., Laconia, Indiana
May, Thomas F., 53 Hillside Street, Boston, Massachusetts
Meade, James J., Jr., 40 Seawall Street, Lynn, Massachusetts
Metcalf, Ralph, (Address Unavailable)
Melander, Lawrence H., 5137 Nakomis Avenue, South Memphis, Minnesota
Menefee, Jack V., 230 8th Street, Palisades Park, New Jersey
Miholovich, Albert G., (Address Unavailable)
Mikell, Louie A., RR 1, Savannah, Georgia

Miller, Benjamin J., Route 1, Box 164, Ontonagon, Michigan
Miller, Elsie L., 1022 11th Avenue, Hickory, North Carolina
Miller, James J., 321 N. Frances, Lansing, Michigan
Miller, Walter G., (Address Unavailable)
Miller, Wilbur F., 6539 Berdan Street, Philadelphia, Pennsylvania
Minarick, Roy H., 2111 S. Drake Avenue, Chicago, Illinois
Minghella, Thomas F., 109 Franklin Street, Stoneham, Massachusetts
Mitchell, Frederick, (Address Unavailable)
Mitchael, Samuel, 656 Mayville Avenue, Pittsburgh, Pennsylvania
Mittermaier, Gerhart, (Address Unavailable)
Mixon, James B., Barnville, South Carolina
Mock, Jack C., Route 3, Kirkland, Texas
Moeller, Gavian C., Somers, Iowa
Moir, Robert M., 2511 Tratman Avenue, Bronx, New York
Molhern, Thomas F., 448 Third Street, Albany, New York
Montgomery, Ralph A., 507 Franklin, Frederickstown, Maryland
Moore, Charles A., (Address Unavailable)
Moore, Howard B., Route 4, Salem, Indiana
Moore, Herman A., (Address Unavailable)
Moore, Richard E., 721 Ford Avenue, Odgensburg, New York
Morgan, Eugene C., 804 Orr Street, Miles City, Montana
Morris, Edward L., 611 Tyler Street, Waco, Texas
Morten, Lester W., 518 Meander, Abilene, Texas
Mortland, James C., Scotland, Indiana
Mosser, Irving M., First Street, Penquannock, New Jersey
Mote, William R., Route 2, Woodland, Alabama
Mottern, George A., Bluff City, Tennessee
Mousty, Claude F., 12799 Corbett Avenue, Detroit, Michigan
Mrazek, Charles R., 1301 S. Wesley Avenue, Burwyn, Illinois
Muhonen, Einar C., 27 Bacon Street, Westminister, Massachusetts
Mulherin, Edward L., (Address Unavailable)
Murati, Edward, 16 Hubbel Avenue, Buffalo, New York
Murray, Charles J., 195 Mission Street, St. Mary's, Kentucky
Murray, Elbert E., 126 Central Square, Pittsburgh, Pennsylvania
Muse, Clyde F., 11730 Riad Street, Detroit, Michigan
Mushok, John M., 638 Redman Street, Dunmore, Pennsylvania
McCabe, George B., (Address Unavailable)
McCall, Garvis D., (Address Unavailable)
McClure, Kenneth D., 862 Kenwick, Bexley, Ohio
McCune, Francis D., Glenville, Nebraska
McDaniel, Fred H., Jr., Columbia, Mississippi
McDonald, Harry W., 54 Vanderbilt Avenue, Manhasset, Long Island, New York
McDonald, Jack W., (Address Unavailable)
McDoniel, James H., RFD 3, Box 83, Batesville, Arkansas
McDowell, Harold H., RFD 1, Saunemin, Illinois
McEwen, Elbert W., 1111 Ordway Place, Nashville, Tennessee
McFarland, Donald E., RR 2, Delhi, New York
McFarland, Joe E., (Address Unavailable)
McGrath, William J., 1854 S. 13th Street, St. Louis, Missouri
McGrinn, Francis E., 22 Patterson Street, Port Jeruis, New Jersey
McIntire, Paul A., Jr., 1004 S. Washington Street, Wellington, Kansas
McKenney, Edwin J., 2 Garland Road, White River Junction, Vermont
McKinnon, Lawrence E., RR 4, Yakima, Washington
McKown, Edwin L., 2nd Western Avenue, Booth Bay Bar Harbor, Maine
McManos, David P., 4115 Falls Road, Baltimore, Maryland
McMinn, Charles R., 1420 Lagonda, Ft. Worth, Texas
McNeeley, George, (Address Unavailable)
McRenolds, Walter H., South Pittsburg, Tennessee
McShane, Isaiah E., Florence Station, Omaha, Nebraska
McWilliams, James H., 627 N. Bishop Avenue, Dallas, Texas
Naas, Walter R., 1216 N. 7th Street, Miles, Michigan
Nasif, Edmund B., (Address Unavailable)
Nazimek, Frank J., 567 Van Houten Avenue, Clifton, New Jersey
Nedeao, Raymond F., (Address Unavailable)
Nelson, Frank L., Casper, Wyoming
Nelson, Harold L., (Address Unavailable)
Nelson, Maynard O., Peetz, Colorado
Nemeeck, Frank E., 614 S. Trip Avenue, Chicago, Illinois
Neslund, Lloyd, Route 1, Oak Park, Minnesota
Newbauer, Edward M., 240 Liverpool Avenue, Egg Harbor, New Jersey
Newman, William F., 113 Clark Street, Hillside, New Jersey
Niles, Aaron L., Howell, Michigan
Noe, William H., (Address Unavailable)
Noland, Willis H., 205 Court Street, Scott City, Kansas
Nordquist, Emil, (Address Unavailable)
Nunes, Edward L., 300 Eucalyptus Drive, San Francisco, California
Oaks, Oscar, Jr., (Address Unavailable)
O'Brien, Fredrick, (Address Unavailable)
O'Brien, James M., Star Route B., Box 50, Austin, Texas
O'Chalek, Stanley J., 2438 N. Pierce, Milwaukee, Wisconsin
Olesick, James S., 16209 Throckley Avenue, Cleveland, Ohio
Oliver, Rufus L., (Address Unavailable)
Olmstead, Andrew, (Address Unavailable)
O'Meara, John F., 162 West 96th Street, New York, New York
Opie, Milton J., 1444 Rosedale, Pontiac, Michigan
Orzechowski, Joseph O., 357 E. Howard Street, Winonw, Minnesota
Ostland, John W., (Address Unavailable)
Osbourne, Douglas, 804 Park Avenue, St. Paul, Minnesota
Otey, Frank E., Grandview, Missouri
Owens, Harry E., 821 E. 40th Street, Savannah, Georgia
Oxendine, Raymond I., (Address Unavailable)
Pack, Brownlow W., Jr., 1553 Wilmore Drive, Charlotte, North Carolina
Palmer, Harry K., 204 Rodney Avenue, Buffalo, New York
Paplin, John E., (Address Unavailable)
Parke, William N. 918 Hill Avenue, Wilkinsburg, Pennsylvania
Parker, Daniel W., Route 1, Maxhan, North Carolina
Parker, Frank M., Jr., 607 Orange Street, Monroe, Louisiana
Parkhurst, William J., 1351 S. W. 3rd Street, Huron, South Dakota
Parks, Jack H. 502 W. Johnson, Sullivan, Indiana
Parisi, Vincent J., (Address Unavailable)
Pate, Paul M., Paint Rock, Texas
Patten, Harry O., 10702 Springfield, Queens's Village, New York

Patterson, Richard, 524 Louise Avenue, Morgan Town, West Virginia
Paul, Wesley B., Bruning, Nebraska
Paulis, William, RR 1, Eatonville, Washington
Pavelich, Joseph B., 219 S. Ohio Street, Butte, Montana
Peacock, Leonard F., 802 Williamson Drive, Raleigh, North Carolina
Pepper, John H., 2700 La Cresta Drive, Bakersfield, California
Perkins, Morris R., RR 1, Sycamore, Kansas
Petty, Harold A., Ferron, Utah
Pleiffer, Albert J., Route 1, Box 153, Kenoch, Wisconsin
Pfeiffer, Dominic E., 4632 Schenley Road, Baltimore, Maryland
Phillips, Charles C., 801 W. Franklin Street, Monroe, North Carolina
Phillips, Leo E., Jr., 5301 Byers, Ft. Worth, Texas
Phillips, Martin, 520 Arcadia Avenue, Chattanooga, Tennessee
Podas, Arnold W., (Address Unavailable)
Polenz, Clarence A., (Address Unavailable)
Poole, Thomas M., 2611 Godman Avenue, Muncie, Indiana
Pope, James H., 507 Walton Avenue, Altona, Pennsylvania
Porter, George, RFD 1, Cushing, Nebraska
Post, Robert A., 3157 Westover Road, Topeka, Kansas
Powell, James S., Lapwai, Idaho
Prassos, Nichkolas, 3612 21st Street, Astoria, New York
Prentice, Robert A., 1223 Smithwood Drive, Los Angeles, California
Preth, Raymond J., (Address Unavailable)
Price, Charles K., 501 Stanbridge, Norristown, Pennsylvania
Pridgen, John L., 177 Horner Street, Henderson, North Carolina
Prostem, Hyman, 2980 W. 27th Street, Brooklyn, New York
Pritt, Arthur L., RR 6, Lexington, Illinois
Pudas, Arnold, Box 138, Hurly, Wisconsin
Pulieri, Frank, (Address Unavailable)
Pulver, Frank C., Beaverton, Oregon
Putoff, Leroy, 124 Rische Street, San Antonio, Texas
Qualls, Clyde L., Route 8, Lamesa, Texas
Quinius, Herman L., 144 North Grove, Wichita, Kansas
Raff, Felicio P., 54 Alvarado Avenue, Worchester, Massachusetts
Ragan, Robert G., 1442 Chippewa Avenue, Akron, Ohio
Rainford, Walter T., 127 Katherine Street, Joliet, Illinois
Rains, Paul H., (Address Unavailable)
Ramsey, Jack A., (Address Unavailable)
Randall, Donald R., General Delivery, Woodland Park, Colorado
Rapp, Dale A., Axtell, Nebraska
Rassmussen, Edward, 474 Lisbon Street, San Francisco, California
Rassmussen, Tilford W., Box 18, McCamey, Texas
Rastuccia, Philip F., (Address Unavailable)
Rau, Robert J., (Address Unavailable)
Reavis, Charles B., RR 3, Henderson, North Carolina
Redel, Ernest F., RR 5, Guthrie, Oklahoma
Reed, Byron J., (Address Unavailable)
Reed, Hal W., (Address Unavailable)
Reel, Edward L., 5900 S. Flower Street, Los Angeles, California
Regan, Thomas P., Harrison Avenue, Helena, Montana
Rehart, Soloman T., Box 534, Lakeview, Oregon
Rehder, Roy G., 2748 West 36th Street, Chicago, Illinois
Resnick, Stanley M., (Address Unavailable)
Rexroat, George A., 3011 West Avenue, Newport News, Virginia
Reynal, Edward W., Bay City, Texas
Rhode, Howard F., 6 Lincoln Place E., Rutherford, New Jersey
Rhodes, Harold L., 1223 Orange Street, N. Little Rock, Arkansas
Rice, Charles E., Jr., 202 S. Ft. Meade Road, Linthicum, Maryland
Richardson, Fred L., 508 N. 9th, Enid, Oklahoma
Richardson, Henry A., (Address Unavailable)
Riddle, Larry E., 322-23 Luhrs Building, Phoenix, Arizona
Rider, James O., 3912 S. Harvey, Oklahoma, Oklahoma
Ridgeway, Lonzo T., 1804 W. 9th Street, San Bernardino, California
Rieper, Arthur B., 715 W. 6th Street, Los Angeles, California
Rinehart, Robert F., Langley, Washington
Riske, James O., Paducah, Kentucky
Rizzo, Richard A., 240 Rivere Street, Rivere, Massachusetts
Robatcek, Frederick H., (Address Unavailable)
Roberts, Clinton C., 306 Belded Avenue, San Antonio, Texas
Roberts, Julius J., Box 322, Floral City, Florida
Rodeghier, Andrew A., Whitt, Illinois
Rodgers, Lamont E., RR 6, Mercer, Pennsylvania
Rodgers, Marion J., Box 1509, Midland, Texas
Roe, James F., Jr., 775 Fairview Road, Ashville, North Carolina
Rogers, Frederick C., 631 S. 3rd East, Salt Lake City, Utah
Romano, Patsy A., (Address Unavailable)
Rose, Conrad A., 1049 N. Laramie Avenue, Chicago, Illinois
Rosenblum, William L., 675 Alabama Avenue, Brooklyn, New York
Rosentein, David, (Address Unavailable)
Ross, Morton D., 4147 Ridge Avenue, Philadelphia, Pennsylvania
Roth, Martin N., (Address Unavailable)
Rotunda, Armond, (Address Unavailable)
Rowe, Doyle C., (Address Unavailable)
Rowland, Edwin M., 106 Adams Street, Greenport, New York
Roy Richard E., 121 Morris Avenue, Winchendor, Massachusetts
Rugo, John V., (Address Unavailable)
Rund, Murray, 1325 Grand Course, Bronx, New York
Rushworth, William E., 2223 Hampton Street, Swissvaled, Pennsylvania
Salmela, Bernard, 122 Caspian Avenue, Caspian, Michigan
Salmi, Earle M., (Address Unavailable)
Salter, James A., 813 Springdale N. E., Atlanta, Georgia
Salzman, Reinhold, 428 15th Street, Greely, Colorado
Samsa, Edward, RR 1, Glen Field, New York
Sanford, Phillip N., Jr., 25 Watervale Road, Medford, Massachusetts
Sauraz, Peter P., (Address Unavailable)
Sawick, John J., (Address Unavailable)
Schaeffer, Walter R., 1320 Lincoln Avenue, Prospect Park, Pennsylvania
Schaffer, Arthur M., 611 Logan Street, Brooklyn, New York
Schaffrath, Anthony A., (Address Unavailable)
Schell, Charles L., General Delivery, Beaden, Oklahoma
Schertzer, Edward A., 12 Merrill Street, Cambridge, Massachusetts
Schiff, Bernard J., 3425 Know Place, New York City, New York

Schleh, James W., 1510 Scott Street, Williamsport, Pennsylvania
Schlotterback, F. D., (Address Unavailable)
Schmidt, Walter G., 7th & W. Avenue, Lebannon, Oregon
Schnitzer, Robert J., 322 Washington Avenue, Oil City, Pennsylvania
Scholer, Francis J., (Address Unavailable)
Schoonmaker, Robert J., 7 Sixth Street, Gloversville, New York
Schultz, Charles J., (Address Unavailable)
Schultz, Ted E., White Salmon, Washington
Schwartz, Sol, 946 E. 181st Street, New York, New York
Scott, Donald E., (Address Unavailable)
Scott, Perry W., RR 2, Luiderr, Texas
Scott, Wilson, RR 2, Fenton, Michigan
Selby, William A., 632 Payne Avenue, Akron, Ohio
Sell, Raymond F., 4444 W. Wilson Avenue, Chicago 30, Illinois
Serex, Robert H., 126 Grand Avenue, Rochester, New York
Shaber, Bert, Wetumka, Oklahoma
Shaffer, Junior C., 609 S. 22nd Street, Terre Haute, Indiana
Shane, William R., 1601 Crowe-Canyon Road, Haxward, California
Shannon, Glen W., Clinton, Minnesota
Sharpe, Edwin F., (Address Unavailable)
Sharpe, William R., 4210 Ala Avenue, Nashville, Tennessee
Shaw, Robert L., RR 1, Ravenna, Michigan
Shawhan, Harold L., Lond Jack, Missouri
Sheaffer, Owen O., Arnold, Kansas
Shelton, James D., RR 1, Box 321, Biloxi, Mississippi
Sherman, Leonard, (Address Unavailable)
Shields, Joseph G., (Address Unavailable)
Shrebnik, Samuel B., 205 Kelsey Avenue, West Haven, Connecticut
Shultz, Walter C., 280 Prevost Street, Ft. Worth, Texas
Siira, Herbert P., (Address Unavailable)
Simco, Andrew E., Taylor, Pennsylvania
Simcoe, Paul G., 210 Grand Street, Trenton, Pennsylvania
Simmons, Walter T., Jr., (Address Unavailable)
Simmons, William E., 164 Long Hill Avenue, Shelton, Connecticut
Simpson, John W., 12 C. Street, Spokane, Washington
Simpson, Robert L., RR 10, Box 1085, Portland, Oregon
Simmons, Theodore W., 249-02 Jerico Turnpike, Bellerose, Long Island, New York
Simons, William J., RR 2, Fort Scott, Kansas
Sims, Mack L., Box 662, Hedley, Texas
Sing, James, 614 S. 7th Avenue, Phoenix, Arizona
Singer, Sherwood J., 89 N. Main Street, Bangor, Maine
Sinnett, Matt M., General Delivery, Gilmore City, Iowa
Sisson, Clifford L., RR 1, Castle Brood, Washington
Sitek, Joseph, 3277 E. Thompson, Philadelphia, Pennsylvania
Slaughter, James E., Jr., 3442 Ethel Street, Columbus, Georgia
Slick, Clyde J., Jr., (Address Unavailable)
Sliney, Edgar M., 1967 Great Highway, San Francisco, California
Slining, Robert L., 409 Cuttriss Place, Park Ridge, Illinois
Slutsky, Samuel, 905 2nd Street, Peekskill, New York
Smelley, Robert L., RR L, Box 104, Ft. Worth, Texas
Smith, Arnold A., (Address Unavailable)
Smith, Charles R., Grenada Boulevard, Greenwood, Mississippi
Smith, Clinton A., (Address Unavailable)
Smith, Hiram E., Jr., Purvis, Mississippi
Smith, Jack, RR 1, Roy, Washington
Smith, Marion B., 1436 7th Street, New Orleans, Louisiana
Smith, Morgan A., 329 N. Holliston Avenue, Pasadena, California
Smith, William T., 2017 Mason Street, Houston, Texas
Snyder, Jack W., 130 6th Street, N. E. Brewster, Ohio
Snyder, George K., 910 Rural Avenue, Williamsport, Pennsylvania
Sodergren, Richard C., Box 232, Wayland, Iowa
Sorrelle, Glentis W., (Address Unavailable)
Sotirakopolus, Christ S., 1651 N. Mobile Avenue, Chicago, Illinois
Spear, Robert W., 531 E. Coldspring Lane, Baltimore, Maryland
Springer, Harold F., Parkdale Avenue, Cleveland, Ohio
Stacy, George W., St. Helena, Kentucky
Stanfield, Foster A., 3721 Hubbard Street, Los Angeles, California
Stearns, Ralph A., Jr., (Address Unavailable)
Stecz, Joseph M., Sloatsburg, New York
Stein, Francis E., RR 1, Vincinnes, Indiana
Stephens, Charles E., 1127 N. W. 23rd Street, Oklahoma City, Oklahoma
Stephens, James W., Grand Coulee, Montana
Sterns, Robert A., Dunstable Road, Nashua, New Hampshire
Stetzelberger, W. F., 1055 Wilbert Road, Lakewood, Ohio
Stevens, Joseph W., 163 Beaulah Road, Norwood, Australia
Stevens, Ralph M., Ellettsville, Indiana
Stevenson, Edward B., (Address Unavailable)
Stewart, Robert D., 905 5th Street, Brookings, South Dakota
Stockman, Allen J., (Address Unavailable)
Stone, Marvin S., 141 El Street, New York, New York
St. Onge, Alphonse L., 246 Gratton Street, Chicopee Falls, Massachusetts
Storck, William E., 815 N. 8th Street, Quincy, Illinois
Stott, John J., 13 Home Place, Danbury, Connecticut
Stowe, Jesse L., 312 Birdsall Street, Houston, Texas
Stricklin, Donald L., 3906 N. Park Drive, East St. Louis, Illinois
Stubbs, William B., 405 N. Randolph Street, Rockinham, North Carolina
Sucevich, John J., (Address Unavailable)
Summers, Hubert G., 1760 Glendale Drive, Lakewood, Colorado
Surface, Robert P., 931 N. Bradley, Indianapolis, Indiana
Svec, Adolph F., Schuyler, Nebraska
Swann, Earl S., 6 Lei Drive, Pearson, Maryland
Sweet, Charles H., 106 North Street, Fayetteville, New York
Switer, Stanley J., Pinconning, Michigan
Sylvanowicz, Charles, Shillaber, Massachusetts
Tacy, Arthur F., 25 Huntington Street, Springfield, Massachusetts
Taft, Jack N., Munith, Michigan
Taranuk, Peter E., Whitney Street, Westport, Connecticut
Tatelman, Victor W., 1619 4th Street, Terre Haute, Indiana
Taylor, Francis M., (Address Unavailable)
Taylor, Glenn W., Lebo, Kansas
Taylor, Otto J., (Address Unavailable)
Taylor, Roger M., 84 Myrtle Avenue, Cedar Grove, New Jersey

Terranella, Angelo L., 67 Sidney Street, Lodi, New Jersey
Terrell, William N., Jr., 1322 College Avenue, Hartsville, South Carolina
Theriot, Lloyd J., 116 French Street, New Iberia, Louisiana
Thimpson, William W., (Address Unavailable)
Thompson, Alden W., 233 High Street, Morgantown, West Virginia
Thompson, Francis A., 6798 California Street, Long Beach, California
Thompson, John W., (Address Unavailable)
Thomas, Donald E., (Address Unavailable)
Thornquist, Everett E., Fort Bragg, California
Todd, Robert, Dolliver, Iowa
Toler, Ira N., (Address Unavailable)
Tomblestone, Leroy B.,1918 Gadsden Street, Columbia, South Carolina
Torsella, Joseph, 1109 1st Avenue, Berwick, Pennsylvania
Tubez, Francis A., 2811 S. Lowe Avenue, Chicago, Illinois
Tudor, Kenneth M., (Address Unavailable)
Turnham, Thomas R., Long Lake, Minnesota
Tuttle, Royce E., Potect, Texas
Tyree, Harry E., Eldorado, Illinois
Tytler, John E., Jr., (Address Unavailable)
Underwood, Arthur D., (Address Unavailable)
Utley, David A., 319 Peoria Avenue, Dixon, Illinois
Vandergrift, Arthur P., 11 S. Idlewild, Nashville, Tennessee
Vanderventer, Blaine F., 318 Elder Street, Council Bluffs, Iowa
Van Hebel, Engelhart, (Address Unavailable)
Vaughn, Charles W., Block 48, House 4-16, Renton, Washington
Viggiano, William A., 152 Lexington Avenue, Jersey City, New Jersey
Vick, Clifford L., RR 3, James Road, Memphis, Tennessee
Villarreale, Lorenzo, 914 S. Park Street, El Paso, Texas
Voitier, George R., 255 N. Court Street, Opelousas, Louisiana
VonFlowtow, Walter E., 803-B Washington Boulevard, Venice, California
Voyna, Andrew P., 7336 Schley Avenue, Swiss Val., Pennsylvania
Voight, Merton E., 1827 Northwestern Avenue, Hollywood, California
Wade, Robert L., RR 1, Silver Creek, Georgia
Wagner, Elsie, RR 1, Wallingford, Kentucky
Wahlund, William B., Old Arcata Road, Ureka, California
Wakefield, Robert T., 1125 Rebella Street, N. Braddock, Pennsylvania
Wald, William J., Lisbeth, New Jersey
Waldo, John H., Jr., 1310 15th Avenue, Greely, Colorado
Walker, Clement M., 14811 Marktwain Avenue, Detroit, Michigan
Walker, James H., 818 American Avenue, Apartment 4, Long Beach, California
Walker, Julius C., Hazard, Kentucky
Walker, Norman E., RR 1, Rockwood, Pennsylvania
Walker, W. H., (Address Unavailable)
Wallace, A. D., 2 Sayer Street, Midland Junction West, Australia
Wallace, Billy J., Box 616, Wardell, Missouri
Wallace, George H., (Address Unavailable)
Walling, Donald J., 237 E. Robie, St. Paul, Minnesota
Walters, Edison K., RR 3, Oxford, Pennsylvania
Ward, Paul, (Address Unavailable)
Ward, Richard A., 6540 S. W. 13th Street, Box 1777, Miami, Florida
Ward, William B., 833 Whaley Avenue, New Haven, Connecticut
Warren, Clyde A., RR 3, E. State Street, Bristol, Tennessee
Warren, David, 1477 Washington Street, San Francisco, California
Warvel, Harold E., Palestine, Ohio

Watson, Christopher, 3928 Wood Street, Wheeling, West Virginia
Watts, Peter P., (Address Unavailable)
Weaver, Arthur W., RR 1, Gilman, Iowa
Weaver, Jack, General Delivery, Killeem, Texas
Weiss, Stanley, 604 S. Broadway, Younkers, New York
Whipple, Chandler, 781 Doresta Road, San Marino, California
White, J. P., 810 N. Main, Cleburne, Texas
Whittington, Arthur W., 392 Tibet Road, Columbus, Ohio
Whitt, Kenneth, 410 Downey Street, Radford, Virginia
Whittemore, Raymond, 6643 Gayer Avenue, Philadelphia, Pennsylvania
Whittier, George I., 6 Fillmore Street, Beverly, Massachusetts
Wickhorst, Milton J., 2011 Benjamin Place, Whiting, Indiana
Wiener, William B., 141 E. Peanco Street, Canton, Mississippi
Wilder, Benjamin, Box 192, Fairhope, Alabama
Wiley, Newton E., Box 103, Watsonville, California
Wilkens, Fredrick M., 94-05 35th Street, Jackson Heights, New York
Williams, Daryl D., 115 E. Water Street, Chillecothe, Ohio
Williams, Donald S., 3 Knight Street, Worcester, Massachusetts
Williams, F. A., Box 323, Bossiar City, Louisiana
Williams, John P., 5327 2nd Avenue, St. Petersburg, Florida
Williams, Morris C., 3100 Jefferson Street, Wilmington, Delaware
Williams, Ross H., Jacksonboro Pike, Mountain City, Tennessee
Williams, Wylie E., 3701 Urban Avenue, Dallas, Texas
Wilson, John D., Box 103, Somerset, Kentucky
Wilson, Marion F., Box 234, Schererville, Indiana
Wingertsahn, William A., 8 Renwick Street, Pittsburgh, Pennsylvania
Winterscheidt, Lawrence, RR 1, Fairview, Kansas
Wirak, Richard T., (Address Unavailable)
Wistron, John H., (Address Unavailable)
Witt, Jack R., 16526 Birwood, Detroit, Michigan
Wolfe, William T., 9 Ridge Road, Farmingdale, Long Island, New York
Wonn, George R., 673 S. Lincoln, Denver, Colorado
Woolcott, Earnest J., Agassiz Street, Bethlehem, New Hampshire
Wood, Martin D., 45 Edgewater Drive, Greenwick, Connecticut
Wood, William M., Box 80, St. Louis, Oklahoma
Worthington, Everett, 436 Main Avenue, Apartment 4, Long Beach, California
Worthington, Hudson G., Route 5, Box 267, Tallahasse, Florida
Wright, Donald D., 463 63rd Street, Oakland, California
Wright, Jack, Hardwick, Georgia
Wubbolding, John F., 508 Linden Avenue, New Port, Kentucky
Wyatt, Joseph L., Phil Campbell, Alabama
Yacher, Stanley, (Address Unavailable)
Yackiw, Charles, RR 1, Macedon, New York
Yarborough, John R., Mullins, South Carolina
Young, Grady L., (Address Unavailable)
Young, Percy K., Covington, Kentucky
Younklin, Frank E., (Address Unavailable)
Yoss, Edward W., 117½ 4th Street, Baraboo, Wisconsin
Zalesny, Joseph, Windmill Hill, West Groten, Massachusetts
Zarfas, Harry, 1161 Partridge Street, University City, Missouri
Zeikus, Edward L., 166 Howard Avenue, Brooklyn, New York
Zemer, John F., 242 W. Tiffin Street, Forsoria, Ohio
Zinda, Norman J., 481 East 1st Street, Fondcolac, Wisconsin

500TH SQUADRON

Acampera, Pasquale, 470 West Main Street, Northboro, Massachusetts
Achard, Francis H., Jr., 836 Boulevard, Westfield, New Jersey
Akers, Donald J., Fifth Street, Carreullton, Kentucky
Albright, J. W., Roanoake, Alabama
Alduino, Frank T., 124 Bush Street, Brooklyn, New York
Alexander, Jack H., 1021 Ninth Street, Durham, North Carolina
Allen, Franklin F., Naples, Florida
Altenback, Edwin J., 797 Broadway, Lina, Ohio
Alton, Omar L., Route 1, Mt. Clare, West Virginia
Ames, William H., Box 598, Bayard, New Mexico
Anacker, Lyle E., 1416 Fairview Drive, Columbia, South Carolina
Andrews, Stanley, 165 W. 197th Street, New York, New York
Anderson, Gordon J., 604 W. Luemis Street, Ludington, Michigan
Anderson, Harold W., Orleans, California
Anderson, Leslie H., 1104 South Porter Street, Stuttgart, Arkansas
Anthony, Robert E., 5125 W. Bloomingdale Avenue, Chicago, Illinois
Anderson, Richard C., 26 Rye Avenue, Elingville, Staten Island, New York
Anderson, William R., (Address Unavailable)
Arbogast, Donald H., Condon, Oregon
Arnold, Frank L., Box 272 M., Mt. Holly, North Carolina
Ascenzi, Victor P., 3628 S. W. Hillside Drive, Portland, Oregon
Assmann, Florian L., Route 1, Box 24, Wishicot, Wisconsin
Atwood, John R., 1773 S. 3rd East Street, Salt Lake City, Utah
Austin, Louis H., c-o Prennen Motor Co., 19th Street, Bessemer, Alabama
Avery, Richard T., 735 Tucker Street, Birmingham, Michigan
Babin, Lee O., Box 96, Gonzales, Louisiana
Bacher, Walter J., 512 E. 12th Street, New York, New York
Back, John J., 850 Albany Street, Roxbury, Massachusetts
Bade, Frank J., Jr., Plymoth, Wisconsin
Bagley, Edward D., 735 Heaton Street, Hamilton, Ohio
Bagley, Joseph H., 226 Main Avenue S., Fayetteville, Tennessee
Bagshaw, Herbert N., 307 Linnmoore Street, Hartford, Connecticut
Bagwell, William D., 3938 W. 27th Street, Los Angeles, California
Baker, Douglas C., 1421 S. Pine Street, Port Angeles, Washington
Baker, Isaac E., Hunnewell, Kansas
Baker, James D., Lawrenceville, Pennsylvania
Baker, Malvern W., 913 Bridge, New Cumberland, Pennsylvania
Baker, Ray L., 1209 Wattee, Kingsport, Tennessee
Baker, William A., Jr., 2056 N. Alabama, Indianapolis, Indiana
Bailey, Eugene W., (Address Unavailable)
Bailey, William S., 2315 Walnut Terrace, Huntington Park, California
Bane, Bryon E., Route 1, Box 254, Cumberland, Maryland
Barclay, Joe T., 1590 Wilson Street, Beaumont, Texas
Bardino, Leo H., 313 E. John, Martinsburg, West Virginia
Barlow, Elmer L., 114 Main Street, Peoria, Illinois

Baron, Harvey, 1301 Lucile, Avenue, Los Angeles, California
Barnes, George R., Big Spring, West Virginia
Barnes, Jack L., 223 E. 6th Street, Hastings, Nebraska
Barney, Henry P., III, 127 Apple Avenue, Hampton, Virginia
Barrall, Earle F., 37 South Allen Street, West Naticoke, Pennsylvania
Bartlett, James F., 5129 Claremont, Houston 3, Texas
Basore, Thomas S., Schellsburg, Pennsylvania
Bates, Stafford C., Brookneal, Virginia
Beaudoin, Sylvan A., Havre, Montana
Bechtel, Joseph R., 972 2nd Street, Beauer, Pennsylvania
Becher, Theodore R., 1220 Fourth Avenue, East Street, Twin Falls, Idaho
Beck, John G., 3019 Lake Avenue, Cheverly, Maryland
Beecher, David L., Route 1, Baxley, Georgia
Beeman, Harold O., Box 32, Admona, California
Behymer, Donald E., 1108 S. 11½ Street, Terre Haute, Indiana
Bellamy, John A., Fordsville, Kentucky
Bennett, Calvert H., Dry Ridge, Kentucky
Bennett, Samuel W., Box 512, Amite, Louisiana
Bennett, William W., (Address Unavailable)
Bennoit, Gorge A., (Address Unavailable)
Bentz, Edwin F., 3076 N. 12th Street, Milwaukee, Wisconsin
Bert, Henry C., 244 Brown Avenue, Turtle Creek, Pennsylvania
Besch, Marvin E., Route 1, Mingo, Iowa
Beswick, Melville, 4806 N. Monticello Avenue, Chicago, Illinois
Bevan, Billie B., 500 Fullerton Parkway, Chicago, Illinois
Bevis, George, Green Creek, Cape May, New Jersey
Bidgood, Robert B., Elm Street, Dublin, Georgia
Bigari, Louis, Route 2, Iron River, Michigan
Bilyou, Ronald B., 90 Tubby Street, Kingston, New York
Bingham, Gerlad W., (Address Unavailable)
Binsted, Hobart G., Accomac, Virginia
Bissell, John L., Gravelle, Arkansas
Bissell, Wayne M., 2214 E. Fifth Street, Vancouver, Washington
Bizub, Stephen B., 108 Depot Street, Youngwood, Pennsylvania
Bjerklund, Robert H., 1113 High Street, Bellingham, Washington
Blake, Clifford H., 9 School Street, Hudson Falls, New York
Blake, William J., 124-16 84th Road, New Gardens, Long Island, New York
Blakemore, Charles O., 1006 W. Rene Street, Oklahoma City, Oklahoma
Blaine, James L., 528 East Astor Avenue, Calville, Washington
Blair, Donald L., 3254 Ulysses Street N. E., Minneapolis, Minnesota
Blodgett, Robert R., 308 North Cedar, Creston, Iowa
Blowpuist, John P., 1426 Balmeral Avenue, Chicago, Illinois
Blum, Arthur D., 1514 Mace Avenue, New York, New York
Blumer, Harry F., 602 W. 132nd Street, New York, New York
Bobker, Oscar, 270 Harrison Avenue, Jersey City, New York

Boehme, William R., Route 2, Box 161, Latrobe, Pennsylvania
Boehrnsen, Walter N., 5941 S. Winchester Avenue, Chicago, Illinois
Boelter, Haold H., 616 N. W. 17th Street, Portland, Oregon
Bolka, Edward S., 103 Pulaski Avenue, Wallington, New Jersey
Borton, Donald R., Hastings, Michigan
Bowman, Charles, 65 B. Pulaski Avenue, Ft. Leonard Wood, Missouri
Boyce, William T., 1214 W. 6th Street, Little Rock, Arkansas
Bradley, Gale M., 709 N. Washington, Mason City, Iowa
Brady, David C., Sparta, Tennessee
Bradwell, Lloyd E., Arkadelphia, Arkansas
Braid, Albert W., 1412 Mount Hope Avenue, Pottsville, Pennsylvania
Brasko, George, 2818 Snyder Avenue, Philadelphia, Pennsylvania
Braun, George H., 575 Hamilton Street, Poughkeepsie, New York
Braun, Joseph W., 135 Spring Street, New Haven, Connecticut
Braund, Delbert, Route 2, LaValle, Wisconsin
Brester, McCluer, 4309 Stanford Street, Dallas, Texas
Brick, Daniel L., 4816 Park Height Avenue, Baltimore, Maryland
Bridsell, David D., E. 403 Walton Avenue, Spokane, Washington
Brine, Amos F., 225 Stetson Street, Whitman, Massachusetts
Brinkerhoff, Robert S., 514 Richmond Terrace, Staten Island, New York
Britt, Robert H., Biscoe, North Carolina
Brock, Robert M., 242A Brown Avenue, Turtle Creek, Pennsylvania
Brown, Charles W., Fig, North Carolina
Brown, Lee M., 731 S. Wayne Street, Piqua, Ohio
Brown, Robert L., 717 Santa Clara, Mission Beach, California
Brown, Warren B., 10 Kendall, Portland, Maine
Bruce, Merwyn W., 520 1st Street N. W., Fort Dodge, Iowa
Brunnemer, Robert W., 1311 Spring Street, Jeffersonville, Indiana
Bryant, Stewart L., 3357 Wellington Street, Philadelphia, Pennsylvania
Bryant, Ward D., General Delivery, Auburn, Heights, Michigan
Buchanan, Robert E., Manlex Road, Auburn, Maine
Buchanan, Vernon C., 2437 Stuart, Indianapolis 1, Indiana
Buchkoski, Michael, Boltz, Pennsylvania
Buckely, John P., Jr., 5017 Hazel Avenue, Philadelphia, Pennsylvania
Buckner, Chester L., 201 Jackson Avenue, Pasadena, Texas
Buckley, Frank J., 6400 Adems Street, West New York, New Jersey
Bufalino, Henry F., 10 Shelton Road, Swampeatt, Massachusetts
Buffington, James O., 426 Ease Main, Peru, Indiana
Buffington, Lawrence W., 7701 Georgia Avenue, Washington, D. C.
Buffo, John A., 509 W. Marion Street, Joliet, Illinois
Buhse, Carl G., 1918 Goulburn Street, Detroit, Michigan
Bumpass, William E., 10058 8th Street, Durham, North Carolina
Burbank, Orie W., Ritterly, Maine
Burgess, James O., Munford, Tennessee
Burnett, Claude V., 220 11th Street, Council Grove, Kansas
Burns, Robert B., (Address Unavailable)
Burke, Jerome J., 251 Hendrix Street, Brooklyn, New York
Burke, John F., 15 Gunn Square, Springfield, Massachusetts
Burrows, Robert A., 2041 Leuis Drive, Lakewood, Ohio
Burton, Herbert E., 1724 W. 12th Street, Muncie, Indiana
Butcher, Lee W., 1719 Edwardsville Road, Madison, Illinois
Buza, Theodore A., 514 Storra Avenue, Dickson, Pennsylvania
Bynum, Robert P., Oneonta, Alabama
Cahpman, Marion M., (Address Unavailable)
Cain, Jerome A., Box 704, Wilber, Nebraska
Callicut, James W., Route 2, Myrtle, Mississippi
Campbell, James S., Box 807, Charlottesville, Virginia
Campo, Joseph, Childress, Texas
Canning, Robert B., 140 St. Albans Road, Berkeley, California
Cantenacci, Francis J., 6 Bethoven Street, Boston, Massachusetts
Capute, William A., 107-17 Liverpool Street, Jamaica, Long Island, New York
Cardonick, Stanley, (Address Unavailable)
Carl, Robert L., 1010 E. Calvert, South Bend, Indiana
Carro, Nicholas A., 2339 W. 1st Street, Brooklyn, New York
Caswell, Harold V., 103 Lake Avenue, Middleton, New York
Catanzarita, Francis J., 30 Spring Street, Port Henry, New York
Cates, Charles A., Milan, Georgia
Cate, Lilburn N., 621 N. East Street, Benton, Arkansas
Cather, Delmas V., 9400 West 107th Street S., Palos Park, Illinois
Cellerini, John B., 335 34th Street, McKeesport, Pennsylvania
Champion, Bruce D., Pleasant Hill, Louisiana
Chandler, Robert H., RFD I, Brenon Center, New York
Chapin, William, 2714½ Santa Cruz Way, Sacramento, California
Chapman, John W., Jr., 445 Riverside Drive, New York, New York
Chatingy, Desire W., Jr., 22 Atwood Street, Newburyport, Massachusetts
Cheney, Clyde R., Route I, Lafeyette, Ohio
Chilla, John W., 917 N. Keeler Avenue, Chicago, Illinois
Christensen, Monte E., 110 Commercial Street, Waterloo, Iowa
Chronic, Jack G., 64 Chatterton Parkway, White Plains, New York
Chura, Elmer B., 215 Berner Avenue, Hazelton, Pennsylvania
Chused, Harry S., 39 Freeman Avenue, Haverhill, Massachusetts
Chytalo, John E., Jr., 48 Lambert Street, Roslyn Heights, New York
Cielo, Arthur P., Upper Main, South Ambory, New Jersey
Clarke, Alfred E., 2709 Hartford Street, S. E. Washington, D. C.
Class, Dean W., 805 Walnut, Emporia, Kansas
Cobb, Harvey M., Box 65, Fulton, Mississippi
Coffman, William P., Ronceverte, West Virginia
Cohen, Julius, 5026 N. Kimball, Chicago, Illinois
Cohen, Stanley L., 923 E. 28th Street, Brooklyn, New York
Cole, Eugene E., Box 47, Route 2, Galena, Illinois
Coleman, Dee B., Route 2. Pampa, Texas
Comstock, Ray A., 39 Henderson Avenue, Kenmore, New York
Conner, Donald G., Speiter, West Virginia
Cook, Orrin V., Alexis, Illinois
Cook, William L., 2612 W. 48th Terrace, Kansas City, Kansas
Cooke, Edward J., Jr., 238 S. Tenth Street, Philadelphia, Pennsylvania
Cooley, Harold J., Ellen Street, Amityville, New York
Coombs, Edward W., 72 Van Reypen Street, Jersey City, New Jersey
Coopola, Theodore A., 211 Jackson Street, Hoboken, New Jersey
Corder, Harry D., 305 N. 17th Avenue, Apartment D., Columbus, Ohio
Cornish, Charles W., 170 Allston Street, Cambridge, Massachusetts
Corotto, Eugene J., RFD I, Box 266, Hollister, California

Cotler, Irving H., 2076 Bronx, Park E., New York, New York
Couture, Joseph R., Box 408, Mexico, Maine
Crago, Nicholas J., Box 84, Beulen, Wyoming
Craig, Russell C., 2526 Washington Avenue, St. Albans, West Virginia
Crain, John R., Lucerne, Indiana
Crayton, Herman E., 3902 Oak Grove Avenue, Greensboro, North Carolina
Cross, Merle J., 33-6 E. 36th Street, Indianapolis, Indiana
Crosslin, Paul L., 509 N. W. 16th Street, Oklahoma City, Oklahoma
Crow, William C., 114 W. Lafayette Street, Decatur, Alabama
Crowley, Andrew J., Jr., 605 S. Main Street, Athens, Pennsylvania
Cubeta, Mike P., 90 William Street, Middleton, Connecticut
Culber, John S., 6620 S. Barton Road, North Olmsted, Ohio
Cullitan, Raymond F., 2311 Giddings, Chicago, Illinois
Culver, George W., 100 Hale Place, Bellmont, New York
Cummings, Herman N., 3017 Oakford Avenue, Baltimore, Maryland
Cunningham, Thomas H., Box 80, North Fork, California
Curran, Felix J., Clifton Springs, New York
Cutkosky, Harold C., 845 Custer, Billings, Montana
Cypert, Maurice N., Hillsboro, Texas
Dahlman, Enoch J., 1141 Porell Street, Chicago, Illinois
Daker, Lynn W., Box 57, Manchester, Iowa
Davis, George I., 916 63rd Street, Brooklyn, New York
Davis, Gwllym W., Route 1, Box 511, Pittsburg, California
Davis, Howard J., Kinzau, Oregon
Davis, Jack G., 2604 Columbus, Muskogee, Oklahoma
Davis, James L., 408 S. 20th Street, Birmingham, Alabama
Davis, John A., 632 Fairfield Circle, West Field, New Jersey
Davidson, Everett N., 323 Valley Avenue, Clover, South Carolina
Decastro, Earl W., 498 Fremont Street, Taunton, Massachusetts
Decker, Richard O., 3718 Carter Avenue, St. Louis, Missouri
Del Buono, Angelo, 91 Queen Avenue, West Springfield, Massachusetts
Deweil, Harold, Jr., 1302 Washington Street, Hoboken, New Jersey
Dick, Frederick W., South Congers Avenue, Congers, New York
Dickson, Charles W., Box 32, Escalan, California
Dietz, Frank W., 1309 Jefferson Street, Latrobe, Pennsylvania
Dinges, John F., 7857 South Shore Drive, Chicago 49, Illinois
Dinino, Joseph, 43-A Floyd Street, Everett, Massachusetts
Dinneen, Rodney L., 388 Pearl Street, Fitchburg, Massachusetts
Dobbs, David M., 320 Live Oak Street, Daytona Beach, Florida
Dobrinich, Charles A., Livingston, Illinois
Doherty, Lott J., 663 W. Onondaga Street, Syracuse, New York
Dolezal, Robert H., Mill City, Oregon
Doman, Francis P., RFD I, Valencia, Pennsylvania
Doolittle, Arah L., 5011 10th Avenue, Los Angeles, California
Dornan, James W., 1023 Fairfield Avenue, Niagara Falls, New York
Doudna, David E., (Address Unavailable)
Dougherty, Keith E., Williamsburg, Iowa
Douglas, Arthur A., E. Franklin Street, Horsehead, New York
Dowburd, Joseph A., 3934 Poplar Street, Philadelphia, Pennsylvania
Doyle, William T., Chart Hill, New Jersey
Draper, Leo C., North Adams, Michigan
Dubose, Emmett R., Route 5, Tiften, Georgia
Dubose, James W., 121 Gilmer Avenue, Montgomery, Alabama
Dunbrack, Gordon O., 91 Stow Street, Waltham, Massachusetts
Dugan, Willia F., 166 Grinell Street, New Bedford, Massachusetts
Duggine, John R., 206 Ridgemede Road, Baltimore, Maryland
Dunham, John H., 701 Russet Street, Racine, Wisconsin
Dunn, James M., Box 17, Mount Calm, Texas
Dunnavant, Bernard R., Victoria, Virginia
Durmeyer, Lloyd S., 619 Nashville Avenue, New Orleans, Louisiana
Dusenberry, Charles K., 17 Main Street, Zanesfield, Ohio
Duval, Clarence E., 2504 Walnut Street, Toledo, Ohio
Dwyer, John J., (Address Unavailable)
Dzury, Stephen D., Wilkes-Barre, Pennsylvania
Earhart, Robert R., Route 3, Eaton, Ohio
Eaton, Burton E., 5 Hendricks Avenue, Woodsocket, Rhode Island
Eckstein, Hyman A., 224 E. Broadway, New York, New York
Edukaitis, John A., 1462 E. 66th Street, Cleveland, Ohio
Efta, Francis J., Wibaux, Montana
Eichten, Vernon L., Webasso, Minnesota
Eley, Dale O., Cadillac, Michigan
Elgie, Augustus, Jr., 138 Altamont Boulevard, Altamont, New York
Elliot, David G., 24 Proter Place, Towanda, Pennsylvania
Elwell, Edward G., 127 Vernon Avenue, Irvington, New Jersey
Elwood, Homer E., Williamsfield, Ohio
Ender, Gustav O., 930 Broadway Boulevard, Benton Harbor, Michigan
Englehart, Donald L., 11218 Hopkins Avenue, Cleveland, Ohio
Epps, Talmadge O., Eachus Boulevard, Garett Hill, Pennsylvania
Epstein, Richard, 401 W. Girard Avenue, Philadelphia, Pennsylvania
Erdman, Norman J., 508 S. 20th Street, Harrisburg, Pennsylvania
Estey, Harold L., 6551 N. Richmond Street, Chicago, Illinois
Evans, Herschel D., 1516 Peyton, Little Rock, Arkansas
Fagan, Robert W., (Address Unavailable)
Farrell, Gabriel, Jr., (Address Unavailable)
Fawthrop, Wesley M., 1134 Hancock Street, Brooklyn, New York
Ferry, Charles G., RR 3, Ligonier, Pennsylvania
Feuerstein, Robert C., 4966 Saint Elmo Drive, Los Angeles, California
Fieder, Frederick W., 40 E. Pierrepont Avenue, Rutherford, New York
Finklestein, Norman, 1006 A. Florida Avenue N. E., Washington, D. C.
Finnegan, Thomas, 99 Riverside Avenue, Westport, Connecticut
Fiore, Vincent R., 2502 Avenue D., Brooklyn, New York
Fitch, Billie E., (Address Unavailable)
Fitton, Jeremiah J., 135 W. 238th Street, Bronx, New York City, New York
Fitzpatrick, Edward J., 867 9th Avenue, New York, New York
Flanagan, Robert A., 217 Washington Street, Hartford, Connecticut
Fleming, Newell D., Route 2, Box 282, Natchitaches, Louisiana
Fletcher, Maz E., 2317 North 9th Street, Fort Smith, Arkansas
Ford, Lawrence J., 2727 South Daring Street, Philadelphia, Pennsylvania
Foss, John D., 12 Rockaway Street, Lynn, Massachusetts
Foster, James W., 4347 Ellis Avenue, Chicago 15, Illinois
Fouts, Oliver E., Wingate, Indiana
Fowler, Wilmer R., 2590 W. Fayette Street, Baltimore, Maryland

Foxworth, Charles E., Route 2, Foxworth, Mississippi
Francis, Lew E., 4230 Montana, El Paso, Texas
Franks, Robert G., RFD 1, Homer Road, Sanborn, New York
Frederick, Joseph W., 1208 W. Market Street, Lina, Ohio
Free, Willie F., (Address Unavailable)
Freeman, Thomas B., 742 Maywood Street, Spartanburgh, South Carolina
Fresty, Mike F., 501 Ohio Avenue, Midford, Pennsylvania
Frey, Authur C., 405 E. 87th Street, New York, New York
Frietas, Francis F., 86 Linden Street, Attleboro, Massachusetts
Fritzshall, Richard B., 1239 Hood Street, Chicago, Illinois
Frye, William L., Route 1, Montgomery, Alabama
Fuller, Frederic W., Jr., 270 Maple Street, Springfield, Massachusetts
Fuller, Leslie C., Jr., 1232 W. French P., San Antonio, Texas
Funk, Glendon R., RFD 1, Beardon Road, N. Homestead, Ohio
Furlong, Richard J., 142-05 Lakewood Avenue, Jamaica, Long Island, New York
Gadbois, Robert E., 11 McCaffrey Street, Uxbridge, Massachusetts
Gamino, Joseph G., 1003 Armstrong Street, Barthlesville, Oklahoma
Gambon, John F., 5224 S. Oak Street, Tacoma, Washington
Garren, Alfred E., 14402 Idarose Avenue, Cleveland, Ohio
Garrison, Orville L., Route 1, Poplar Bluff, Missouri
Garza, Manuel C., 734 Monroe Street, Brownsville, Texas
Gautreau, Joseph A., 7 Arlington Street, Cambridge, Massachusetts
Gawryla, Frank L., 53 Wallington Avenue, Wallington, New Jersey
Gerarden, William F., 1010 E. 25th Street, Minneapolis, Minnesota
Geer, Raymond E., 304 Fairmont Street, Amarillo, Texas
Gerchow, Joseph A., 742 Lounge Place, New Orleans, Louisiana
Geremonte, Joseph B., 321 Main Street, Stonehan, Massachusetts
Gerhardt, Robert G., 6 Linden Avenue, Hempstead, Louisiana
Gerstein, Max, 712 North Denny Street, Indianapolis, Indiana
Geyer, James J., 396 Union Avenue, Irvington, New Jersey
Gibb, Donald J., 312 Icth Avenue S. E., Minneapolis, Minnesota
Gilardi, Stephen N., 110 William Street, Larkspur, California
Gillies, Walter J., 345 Holly Park Circle, San Francisco, California
Gilmore, Charles E., 490 S. Pearl Street, Denver, Colorado
Gietz, Charles F., Jr., 133-19 188th Street, Ozone Park, New York, New York
Glaccum, Joseph E., 3254 N. Marshal Street, Philadelphia, Pennsylvania
Glass, Joseph W., 620 N. Walnut Street, Harrison, Arkansas
Gloege, Orville C., Route 1, Odessa, Minnesota
Godgerg, Sidney M., 419 Wolf Street, Philadelphia, Pennsylvania
Godsey, Norman E., (Address Unavailable)
Goehring, Donald T., 806 Hiland Avenue, Corapolis, Pennsylvania
Goldston, Lewis, Route 1, Harrinman, Tennessee
Golightyly, James L., Melbourne, Florida
Gonyeo, Staley, 37 Ouclid Street, Gardner, Massachusetts
Gonzalez, Lewis R., 2018 Howard Street, Corpus Christi, Texas
Gooch, Ernest A., 3808 Woodland Avenue, Duluth, Minnesota
Good, Floyd J., 4909 Woodland, Kansas City, Missouri
Goodban, William T., 407 N. Santa Ana Avenue, Modesto, California
Goodson, Byre W., 702 E. 12½ Street, Houston, Texas
Goodwin, Victor B., 1619 Penn Avenue, Dallas, Texas
Gorham, Marshall, 37 W. 72nd Street, New York, New York
Gould, Charles C., N. New Portland, Maine
Graham, John W., 6850 Camrose Drive, Hollywood, California
Grasso, Victor A., 16 Stone Street, Newark, New Jersey
Gray, George M., 56 Stewart Avenue, Arlington, New Jersey
Gray, James A., 24 Halcyon Street, Scottia, New York
Gray, Roger W., 109 Terrace Avenue, Hempsted, Long Island, New York
Greenstein, Richard M., 1550 Edmond Avenue, Foleroft, Pennsylvania
Greger, Arthur L., 1550 Edmond Avenue, Foleroft, Pennsylvania
Gregory, Nathan W., 78 S. Quaker Lane, West Hartford, Connecticut
Grigg, Thomas N., 1474 Milburn Avenue, Toledo, Ohio
Gritz, Carl I., Box 142, Pond Creek, Oklahoma
Grosse, Leander A., Crossplains, Wisconsin
Grover, Carlton F., Killery, Maine
Grush, Lincoln H., 10 Tower Road, Lexington, Massachusetts
Guetgemann, Fred J., Route 2, Kimmswick, Missouri
Gulling, Donald D., Goddington Road, Route 3, Ithaca, New York
Gullette, Frank E., 1608 Hemphill Street, Dallas, Texas
Gunnels, Talmadge P., No. 3 Hanover, Camgron, Texas
Guy, Robert L., Cherokee Road, RFD 9, Richmond, Virginia
Guyer, Merle W., 105 E. Keller Street, Mechanicsburg, Pennsylvania
Hadzor, Robert V., 512S. Winebiddle Street, Pittsburgh, Pennsylvania
Hagest, Charles M., Las Vegas, New Mexico
Hall, Lacy B., Jr., (Address Unavailable)
Hallack, Jack G., 1728 S. Orange Drive, Los Angeles, California
Hamlin, Paul A., Brockport, New York
Harbert, Jackson D., Box 55, Wallace, West Virginia
Hardison, Earl L., Deep Run, North Carolina
Hardy, George M., Jr., 40 N. 18th Street, East Orange, New Jersey
Hare, Harold E., 3 Philips Street, Boston, Massachusetts
Harned, Poeter W., Alberson, New York, New York
Harper, Milton N., 767 Gresham Avenue S. E., Atlanta, Georgia
Harrell, Wood T., 314 Highland Avenue, Suffolk, Virginia
Harrison, Harold E., 28631 Avondale Road, Inkster, Michigan
Hart, Francis B., 522 W. 61st Street, Los Angeles, California
Hartmann, Roy W., 3743 N. 8th Street, Milwaukee, Wisconsin
Hartung, Harley D., New Port, Nebraska
Harvey, Delman, 5 Norvel Avenue, Stoneham, Massachusetts
Harviell, Eugene L., 5058-A Maffitt Street, St. Louis, Missouri
Hass, Robert O., 220 Olympia Street, Pittsburgh, Pennsylvania
Heath, Freddie A., 527 Ingleside Drive, Baton Rouge, Louisiana
Hecox, Thane C., Jr., Route 2, Canal, Winchester, Ohio
Heffner, Robert B., 133 Washington Street, Fleetwood, Pennsylvania
Hejl, Raymond J., 215 Virginia Avenue, Macon, Georgia
Helmick, Victor H., 607 Ward Avenue, Gerard, Ohio
Henderson, Robert T., Edri, Pennsylvania
Hennigan, Paul F., 404 S. Main Street, Old Forge, Pennsylvania
Herick, Joseph, 531 N. Maryland, Glendale, California
Hertz, Joseph, 120 Hopkins Street, Brooklyn, New York
Hessel, Farnham L., 1257 Park Row, La Jolla, California
Heydt, Albert C., 516 N. Penn Street, Allentown, Pennsylvania

Hicko, Edward J., 2046 Lake Avenue, Whiting, Indiana
Hill, William B., 1215 S. 3rd, Arkansas City, Kansas
Hinchman, Ross D., 426 Pine Street, Michigan City, Indiana
Hiner, James M., 3075 Dix Road, Lincoln Park, Michigan
Hines, Alvert K., Enfield, North Carolina
Hinton, James B., 327 Concard, Dallas, Texas
Hobbs, Murphy, Dryden, Virginia
Hochella, Michael F., (Address Unavailable)
Hofbuer, Frederick C., 38 Stephan Street, Kingston, New York
Hoffman, Sylvester A., 916 Van Buran Street, Madison, Wisconsin
Hoffman, Wayne W., 1662 East Fourth Street, St. Paul, Minnesota
Hoin, James J., 334 47th Street, Brooklyn, New York
Hoizbauer, Anthony G., 251 Vine Street, Ashkost, Wisconsin
Holm, Albert, Jr., Box 1164, Cook, Minnesota
Holz, Robert, Jr., 3550 Epwort Avenue, Cincinnati, Ohio
Hooper, Edward E., RR 2, Box 211, Delta, Colorado
Horikawa, Daniel, 9 Worcester Street, Natick, Massachusetts
Horne, Charles W., 25 Kittridge Road, Portland, Maine
Horwitz, Irving, 463 High Street, Burlington, New Jersey
Houdeshell, Robert E., 409 Wilson Street, Piqua, Ohio
Hourigan, William E., 69 Holmes Avenue, Buffalo, New York
Howard, Charles W., Jr., Greenwich, Connecticut
Hubert, Peter, Tallahose, Florida
Hudak, William G., 9901 Sophia Avenue, Cleveland, Ohio
Heubner, Carl J., 1020 Prospect Avenue, Portage, Wisconsin
Hughes, Leroy S., Elon College, North Carolina
Hunter, Charles S., Route 1, Glasgo, West Virginia
Hurt, George J., Jr., 1214 Rugby Boulevard, Roznoke, Virginia
Hutchenson, Jack E., 420 W. Copper Street, Slippery Rock, Pennsylvania
Hutchinson, Philip A., Bolten Center, Connecticut
Imperato, Edward M., 5822 20th Avenue, Brooklyn, New York
Isler, Weldon, Route 1, Irvington, Alabama
Ison, Edgar S., 644 New York Street, Memphis, Tennessee
Israel, Millard W., Hurley, Missouri
Jacobson, Robert E., 335 Middle Avenue, Aurora, Illinois
James, William A., 707 East 7th Street, Metropolis, Illinois
Jay, William E., 3534 Mentone Avenue, Los Angeles, California
Jenkins, Robert D., Route 4, Madison, Wisconsin
Jensen, Robert W., 391 Hope Street, Glenbrook, Connecticut
Jessen, Robert, 1124 Copper Avenue, Lansing, Michigan
Johnson, Cecil C., Route 3, Shell Lake, Wisconsin
Johnson, Glenn E., 301 S. Spruce, Nokonis, Illinois
Johnson, Willard L., Corruland, Virginia
Jones, Allen O., Lafeyette, Georgia
Jones, Cecil O., Box 853, Albuquerque, New Mexico
Jones, Donald R., 2001 Sanford Avenue, Sanford, Florida
Jones, Lorin L., 604 E. 9th Street, Trinidad, Colorado
Jones, Ted A., (Address Unavailable)
Jones, Robert S., Lawrenceville, Virginia
Jordan, Earl W., Route 3, West Chester, Pennsylvania
Just, Henry A., 9810 204th Street, Hollis, New York
Kahn, Joseph, 5738 Pine Street, Philadelphia, Pennsylvania
Kalland, Elwood A., 1035 N. Tacoma Avenue, Tacoma, Washington
Kapitzke, William J., (Address Unavailable)
Kaplan, William, 419 S. 56th Street, Philadelphia, Pennsylvania
Kay, Eugene V., Spencer, Indiana
Keenan, John E., Route 1, Box 201, Brush Prairie, Washington
Keener, William T., Box 302, Queenboro Street, Shreveport, Louisiana
Kehoe, Charles W., 611 N. Kansas Avenue, Hastings, Nebraska
Kellr, Samuel, Jr., Hanova Height Road, Pottstown, Pennsylvania
Kemp, Elias B., Jr., Route 5, Tahaka, Texas
Kempsey, Edward, 500 Southern Boulevard, Bronx, New York
Kendall, Robert E., Westbrook Street, S. Portland, Maine
Kennedy, Everett A., Route 1, Winchester, Ohio
Kent, Paul E., 1131 Thompson Street, Glendale, California
Kenyon, Russell A., 194 5th Street, Fond Dulac, Wisconsin
Keown, James E., 1420 Leitch Road, Argunburg, Kentucky
Kerr, David L., 3211 Seward Street, Okama, Nebraska
Kerr, Robert B., 1203 West 5th Street, Waterloo, Iowa
King, Bryan D., 113 Mohawk, Corpus Christi, Texas
King, Elmo, Rivermine, Missouri
King, Francis H., 2211 Persian Boulevard, Clinton, Iowa
King, James O., Route 5, Winston-Salem, North Carolina
King, Joseph A., 21 Lafayette Place, Arlington, New Jersey
Kirby, William R., Jr., Main Street, Summer Hill, Pennsylvania
Kirshaman, Stanley E., 202 Hickory Street, Linden, Michigan
Kistner, Charles L., 909 Grand Avenue, Dayton, Ohio
Kline, Clyde W., Route 2, Pennel Road, Village Green, Media, Pennsylvania
Klugman, Ruben, 102 Semeca Street, Seattle, Washington
Kneeland, Robert W., Pottsville, Iowa
Koenig, David E., Route 1, New Bremen, Ohio
Koenen, Walter L., Hanson, Kentucky
Kohlmeyer, Thomas W., 441 Baldwin Road, Hays, Pennsylvania
Koonce, William E., Route 4, Florence, Alabama
Korczynski, Michael R., 280 E. 10th Street, New York, New York
Kovacs, Eugene J., 133 Wartman Avenue, Dayton, Ohio
Kozak, William J., 4539 N. 16th Street, Philadelphia, Pennsylvania
Kresnicks, Alfred R., Box 198, Route 1, S. Coventry, Connecticut
Krieger, Arthur H., 1455 Sheridan Avenue, Bronx, New York
Krist, John J., Jr., 111 Sears Street, Ithaca, New York
Kuhn, Lloyd M., Jr., 1056 Kennsington Avenue, Buffalo, New York
Kusebauch, Anton K., 323 Gibham Street, Pittsburgh, Pennsylvania
Kuter, George D., 407 E. 2nd Street, Fond DuLac, Wisconsin
Kyser, William T., Box 42, Route 1, Minter, Alabama
Labatt, Simon E., Urania, Louisiana
LaBoy, Raymond A., (Address Unavailable)
Lackey, J. T., 515 E. Valentine Street, Tyler, Texas
Laird, Thomas H., 205 E. 48th Street, Savannah, Georgia
Laliberte, Leo R., 71 Springs Street, Minille, Rhode Island
Lamb, Glen A., (Address Unavailable)
Lamb, Ralph M., 612 South East Street, Fenton, Michigan

Lambert, Clyde R., 612 South East Street, Fenton, Michigan
Lambert, Jack, 233 West 83rd, New York City, New York
Lambert, Leon W., 122 Mt. Hope Avenue, Dover, New Jersey
Lamphier, Merlin, Reasnor, Iowa
Landon, Sturt G., 303 Vestal Road, Vestal, New York
Lang, Walter S., Jr., Houston Chronicle, Houston, Texas
Lancaste, Loui M., 3004 Farmington Road, Hutchinson, Kansas
Landon, Jack N., 1652 W. Indiana Avenue, Elkhart, Indiana
Lanning, Lester W., Box 13, Murray City, Ohio
LaPyrne, Anthony T., 516 Helen Avenue, Detroit 7, Michigan
LaRose, Wyman R., 1515 W. Monroe Street, Chicago, Illinois
Latawiec, Frank G., Philadelphia, Pennsylvania
Lawlis, Merrit E., 2021 Laurel Street, Indianapolis, Indiana
Lawrence, Charles S., 4 Brown Street, Hartford, Connecticut
Lawrence, Clifford J., 3445 S. 11th Easy, Salt Lake City, Utah
Lawrence, Geahart T., Route 2, Elroy, Wisconsin
Lay, Allan W., 3601 Belleview, Kansas City, Missouri
Layman, John R., General Delivery, Jeffersonville, Indiana
Lee, Francis M., (Address Unavailable)
Lee, Malachy J., 370 Communipew Avenue, Jersey City, New Jersey
Leet, Harold E., Turtle Point, Pennsylvania
Leete, Edward A., 616 West Walnut Street, Titusville, Pennsylvania
Lenhart, Maris A., 318 N. 7th Street, Adel, Iowa
Lentz, Kenneth L., 3021 S. 44th Street, Milwaukee, Wisconsin
Leonard, Donald H., 84 Union Street, Brunswick, Maine
Leto, James P., 317 Lottowattaie Street, Leavenworth, Kansas
Leventon, Marvin, 5803 Third Place, Washington, D. C.
Levy, Irwin S., 236 E. 5th Street, New York, New York
Lewis, James P., 1504 Second Street, Macon, Georgia
Lewis, Richard J., 1724 Coolidge Street, Eau Claire, Wisconsin
Lewis, Robert E., 218 South Rowe, Pryor, Oklahoma
Lexell, Roger H., 10 Park Street, Jamestown, New York
Lightfoot, Clair C., 519 N. 7th Street, Payette, Idaho
Lind, Robert A., 530 N. 15th Street, Escanaba, Michigan
Linville, Herman, Route 1, Broseley, Missouri
Litteer, Harold H., 95 Mason Street, Rochester, New York
Loisel, Cyriaque J., 146-17 Kolmia Avenue, Flushing, New York
Lometti, Adeino D., 14-16 Bedford Street, New York, New York
Long, Cecil L., Wellersburg, Pennsylvania
Long, Jack L., 2003 Wilshire Street, Los Angeles, California
Long, Robert R., Sac City, Iowa
Lorenz, Harold, Box 63, Route 2, LaSalle, Colorado
Lovatt, Robert B., 5023 Cedar Avenue, Philadelphia, Pennsylvania
Lovett, Roger W., Manly, Iowa
Low, Robert, 1 Arden Street, New York City, New York
Lowrey, Eugene D., 80 Main Street, St. Johnsbury, Vermont
Lowry, Frederick, 3427 Summer Avenue, Memphis, Tennessee
Lugrine, John J., 1429 M. Lawrence Street, Philadelphia, Pennsylvania
Lund, Eddy S., 8747 14th Street N. W., Seattle, Washington
Mackiewicz, Joseph K., 6541 Newman Avenue, Cleveland, Ohio
Madeo, Edward, 1529 W. 10th Street, Brooklyn, New York
Madison, Jesse H., 15310 LaSalle Boulevard, Detroit, Michigan
Magnon, Henry N., 97 Bushnel Street, Hartford, Connecticut
Maggi, Bortolino P., 4 Home Street, Springfield, Massachusetts
Mahan, Charles H., 9th Hill Street, Clinton, Massachusetts
Maish, Morton C., Jr., Box 187, Onekama, Michigan
Malchow, Arnold M. C., 722 E. 180th Street, New York, New York
Malendoski, Joseph M., 15514 Ohio Street, Detroit, Michigan
Malquist, Stewart R., 40 West 81st Street, Chicago, Illinois
Manley, Robert F., 72 Greenvale Avenue, Wevmauth, Massachusetts
Mann, Edward E., RFD 1, Austin, Pennsylvania
Mannon, Ralph J., 2149 Carmelita Drive, St. Carlos, California
Manthey, Robert H., 590 Prospect Street, Muskegon, Michigan
Marks, Marshall T., 5900 Fifth Avenue North, St. Petersburgh, Florida
Marrett, Joseph C., 4079 E. 106th Street, Cleveland, Ohio
Marso, Bernard J., 710 E. Chevey Chase, Glendale, California
Martin, Edward, 10 Salem Street, Newburgy Port, Massachusetts
Martin, Frank, Jr., General Delivery, Aracta, California
Martin, Roy H., Jr., 1007 E. Norwegian Street, Pottsville, Pennsylvania
Masueto, Dominick A., 138 Parkevill Avenue, Brooklyn, New York
Matuzic, Frank J., 52 Pearl Street, Lackawanna, New York
Mauldin, Myron J., 4955 Clay, Denver 11, Colorado
Mawrence, Silvert, 2528 N. California Street, Chicago, Illinois
Maxwell, Marvin, Hamilton, Alabama
Mayer, Elmer C., Austin, Indiana
Mayo, Howard F., Rowden, Texas
Mazeolle, Albert J., Limestone, Maine
Meech, Dick K., 747 Chapin Street, Birmingham, Michigan
Mele, Anthony A., 20 Stevens Street, Stoneham, Massachusetts
Mele, Joseph, 429 Orchard Avenue, Ellwood City, Pennsylvania
Mendes, John, 2122 69th Street, Oakland, California
Mensch, Edward T., (Address Unavailable)
Merril, Robert D., Jr., (Address Unavailable)
Mettam, James B., Box 214, Solana Beach, California
Meyer, Harry E., Route 1, Flatonia, Texas
Middlebrook, Carl L., Jr., 3206 Trice Street, Waco, Texas
Migliacci, Anthony E., 225 Elmer Street, Trenton, New Jersey
Millard, Nelson H., 245 Lawndale Avenue, Aurora, Illinois
Miller, George E., 12 River Street, Forestport, New York
Miller, James M., 219 E. 4th Street, Little Rock, Arkansas
Miller, Oliver O., Route 1, Council Bluffs, Iowa
Miller, Robert M., 515 Laura Avenue, Wichita, Kansas
Miller, William P., 2014 N. Washington Street, Scranton, Pennsylvania
Minicozzi, Bartholmess, 115 South Street, Oyster Bay, New York
Mitchell, George, Route 3, Burley, Idaho
Mohlke, Richard E., 408-9 Avenue N. E., Rochester, Minnesota
Monoghan, Philip A., 307 Bowdoin Street, Winthrop, Massachusetts
Montgomery, Edward F., 305 Galahan Street, Muskogee, Oklahoma
Montgomery, George D., Jr., 2553 Jasmine Street, New Orleans, Louisiana
Montieth, Robert L., 1003 Church Street, Iowa City, Iowa
Moore, Fred, 1621 S. Grand Avenue, Los Angeles, California

Moore, James R., 2 Riverview Terrace Street, Morgantown, West Virginia
Moore, Rufus A., 5009 Cunningham Road, Merriam, Kansas
Morawetz, Elmer C., 3924 M. Galema, Milwaukee, Wisconsin
Morman, Edward F., 4826 N. Talman Avenue, Chicago, Illinois
Moseley, James C., Champaign, Illinois
Moss, Clarence A., West Main Street, Millville, New Jersey
Motroni, Edward P., 38 N. Bennett, Boston, Massachusetts
Mozzetti, John P., 633 S. Carpenter Street, Chicago, Illinois
Mudis, Kenneth C., 1035 E. Market Street, York, Pennsylvania
Mueller, Wolfgang H., 2076 Greenleaf Avenue, Chicago, Illinois
Muller, Benjamin T., 1805 Arizona Street, El Paso, Texas
Muller, Frank J., 16 N. Main Street, Flemington, New Jersey
Muniz, Stanley R., 1511 Summit Avenue, Union City, New Jersey
Munro, James B., Jr., 18 Maple Road, Long Meadow, Massachusetts
Murphy, James B., 1818 E. 29th Avenue, Denver, Colorado
Murphy, John A., 3621 West 14th Street, Columbus, Nebraska
Murphy, Joseph W., 478 Poplar Street, Woodburn, Oregon
Murphy, William, Market Square, Country Cork, Ireland
Murry, William E., Jr., 55 Parkside Drive, Berkeley 5, California
Myers, Roland W., 105 West 4th Street, Florence, Kansas
McCauley, Bill T., 8411 11th Street, Tampa, Florida
McCaskell, Calin N., (Address Unavailable)
McCaw, Robert M., 9726 S. Hoywe Avenue, Chicago, Illinois
McClaury, Shelton H., Wray, Colorado
McClean, William R., 2111 15th Street, Moline, Illinois
McCollum, Ray H., 1207 S. Garden Street, Columbia, Tennessee
McCord, Henry E., 4002 Crest Haven Road, Dallas, Texas
McCrea, Albert M., Ridley Park, Pennsylvania
McCurdie, Alexander T., Jr., 130 N. Ore Street, Hattiesburg, Mississippi
McDaniel, Herbert A., 5209 Marburn Avenue, Los Angeles, California
McDaniel, Thomas B., 1103 Emmet Street, Augusta, Georgia
McFarland, Dale W., 2511 Daisy Avenue, Long Beach, California
McFarling, Glenn E., 815 East Parkway South, Memphis, Tennessee
McGeown, John M., 27 Princeton Boulevard, N. Chelmsford, Massachusetts
McGhee, Rolla Q., Gateway City Street, Pryor, Oklahoma
McGinnis, Thomas, 4127 Dehman Street, Elmhurst, New York City, New York
McGuire, James, Route 1, Box 364, Grants Pass, Oregon
McKenna, Laurence A., 408½ N. 2nd Street, Clinton, Iowa
McKenzie, George T., 725 Key Street, Mobile, Alabama
McKibben, Harold A., Beaverton, Michigan
McKinney, Arthur D., Pineville, North Carolina
McLean, John P., 4235 Bateman Street, Seattle, Washington
McLain, Gordon V., 518 15th Avenue, Moline, Illinois
McLeod, John E., Box 263, Homerville, Georgia
McMahon, Edward R., 1738 Boren Avenue, Seattle, Washington
McManan, Walter W., Jr., 320 Hunsork Avenue, San Antonio, Texas
McManus, Vincent J., 38 Ridgeway Street, Springdale, Connecticut
McMullen, Frank M., 511 Alta Avenue, San Antonio, Texas
McPherson, Charles E., Germantown, Tennessee
McRae, Leonard R., 3687 Rodgers Avenue, Muskegon, Michigan
Nagy, John W., 35 S. 13 Avenue, Monville, New Jersey
Naigle, Alfred J., Bechtelsville, Pennsylvania
Nasif, Edmond B., (Address Unavailable)
Nedic, Seymour, 11 Watson Avenue, Newark, New Jersey
Neely, James E., Route 2, Murfreesboro, Tennessee
Nela, Robert B., 225 S. Main Street, Punxsutawney, Pennsylvania
Nelson, Myron E., RFD 1, Nicktown, Pennsylvania
Nelson, Walter J., 3407 Hudson Avenue, Union City, New Jersey
Newman, Joel S., 20 Royal Road, Belmont, Massachusetts
Newton, Bertram H., 356 Essex Street, Salem, Massachusetts
Niblack, Thomas J., 1628 9th Street, Lubbock, Texas
Nicolazzi, Joseph A., 6526 20th Avenue, Kenosha, Wisconsin
Njaa, Reuben S., Northwood, North Dakota
Nordby, William E., 145 Spencer Street, Nanugatuck, Connecticut
Norman, Ralph J., Jr., RR 2, Lake Crystal, Minnesota
Norrick, Warner G., 618 Sherman Street, Oakland City, Indiana
O'Brien, John M., 6453 University Avenue, Chicago, Illinois
O'Connell, Robert L., 22 Hall Street, Grand Rapids, Michigan
O'Farrell, Kelvin N., 1509 Shenandoah Street, Los Angeles, California
O'Hara, John T., 545 Perry Street, Buffalo, New York
Olinger, Robert L., Vernonia, Oregon
Olsen, John E., 534 Anderson Avenue, Grantwood, New Jersey
Olson, Frank T., Jr., Holgate, Ohio
Omeara, Philip R., 22 Pine Street, Nashua, New Hampshire
O'Neill, John P., (Address Unavailable)
Orbinati, Anthony J., 811½ Dominick Street, Rome, New York
Orlando, Henry W., 72 John Street, East Haven, Connecticut
Orsak, Edwin J., El Campo, Texas
Orr, John D., 103 Main Street, Kingwood, West Virginia
Oshell, Donald W., 896 N. 5th Street, Bellwood, Pennsylvania
Oskea, Robert N., 2024 Pacific Avenue, Alameda, California
O'Slep, Pierre, 256 Preston Street, Hartford, Connecticut
Ostroot, Kenneth J., 505 W. Central Avenue, Minot, North Dakota
Ott, Clarence R., 1853 Niagara Falls Boulevard, Tonawanda, New York
Ow, Lee A., Jr., 1825 S. 13th Street, Lincoln, Nebraska
Owens, Albert W., 910 Washington Street, Atlanta, Georgia
Oxendine, Raymond I., 217 Peabody Street N. E., Washington, D. C.
Paiva, Alfred D., 19 Adrian Street, Sumerville, Massachusetts
Pallister, Marvin J., 13807 Anglin, Detroit, Michigan
Palmer, John B., 354 Goodnor Street, Jacksonville, Florida
Pannell, Ray, Box 107, Sterling, Oklahoma
Paquette, Gerald E., 26 Stearns Terrace, Chicopee, Massachusetts
Parker, Eugene J., 726 E. Howard Avenue, Biloxi, Mississippi
Parks, Fred, 391 E. Maple Street, Wabash, Indiana
Parlo, Peter A., 358 Elm Street, Elmira, New York
Parrish, Jack N., Jefferson, Oregon
Parrish, Demon W., 197 Dailey Road, Pittsburgh, Pennsylvania
Paugh, Rodney F., Route 5, Box 185, Tallahassee, Florida
Paukovich, William G., Box 310, Rock Spring, Wyoming
Paul, Raymond G., RFD 7, Evansville, Indiana
Paulis, William, Jr., Route 1, Eatonville, Washington

Paulson, Richard E., 6425 N. Francisco Avenue, Chicago, Illinois
Pavkovich, Mickey D., Box 168, West Pittsburgh, Pennsylvania
Payton, Louis L., 4040 S. Cedar Street, Spokane, Washington
Pease, Richard L., Stephentown, New York
Peckham, Calvin C., 68 Sheridan Road, Oakland, California
Pecora, Samuel A., Box 87, Boston, Pennsylvania
Peddicord, Marvin F., Glen Dale, Maryland
Pedersen, Jens N., 450 E. 89th Street, Chicago, Illinois
Pence, Lawrence N., Jr., Box 32, Chatham, Virginia
Penn, Carloton C., Jr., 506 5th Street, Panama City, Florida
Peregoy, Jos. N., Jr., (Address Unavailable)
Peterson, Erick W., 12 Eastland Road, Jamaica Plain, Massachusetts
Peterson, Harlan H., Route 1, Stanton, Iowa
Peyton, Joseph H., (Address Unavailable)
Phillips, William, 122 Gave S. W., Atlanta, Georgia
Piatt, John F., Box 303, Route 1, Lancaster, California
Picard, Earl E., North Williston, Vermont
Pierce, Clarence E., South Britain, Connecticut
Pitman, Elmer W., 5906 Genoa Street, Oakland, California
Plage, John H., Jr., 118 Wright Street, Marietta, Georgia
Pluth, Bernard J., 4212 Wyoming Street, St. Louis, Missouri
Poe, Delosse, Hotel Padre, Bakersfield, California
Pohlman, Frank C., 1027 King Street, Toledo, Ohio
Pollock, Melvin L., Adams, Wisconsin
Post, Amos G., 229 Washington Avenue, Clarksburg, West Virginia
Power, Jack W., (Address Unavailable)
Powell, Melvin, Bridgewater, Virginia
Pratt, Jackson T., 550 N. 17th Street, San Jose, California
Preston, James A., 4115½ Edenhurst Avenue, Los Angeles, California
Preston, Kenneth E., 1824 W. Main Street, Louisville, Kentucky
Preston, William S., 918 18th Street, Monroe, Wisconsin
Price, William J., 1258 S. Columbia Street, Frankfort, Indiana
Price, William L., Lawrence, Kansas
Prim, Marion L., 267½ Clarendon Street, Huntington Park, California
Proffitt, Raymond F., 804 W. Pine, Centralia, Washington
Puckett, Allen R., Route 1, Dustin, Oklahoma
Pugatch, Abraham, 2 Barton Place, Port Chester, New York
Purvis, Meredith, Box 74, Otho, Iowa
Quigley, John E., 8022 S. St. Lawrence Avenue, Chicago, Illinois
Quinn, James N., 405 S. Cherry Street, Marshfield, Wisconsin
Quirk, Charles J., 502 S. 25th Street, Philadelphia, Pennsylvania
Randall, James S., 415 N. Palm Canyon Drive, Palm Springs, California
Rankin, Hobart R., 1345 Cedar Drive, Springfield, Ohio
Rapp, Ezra E., 650 May, RR 2, Idaho Falls, Idaho
Rasmussen, Dean H., 781 Fountain Ave, Fresno, California
Rasulo, Vincent J., 28-16 37th Street, Long Island City, New York
Reaves, LeRoy J., Box 188, Demming, New Mexico
Rawlings, Donald E., 2624 West Groop, Franklin Park, Illinois
Ray, Virgil M., 41 Dayton Drive, Dayton 6, Ohio
Ready, Robert C., 13 State Street, Biddleford, Maine
Reed, Vergil E., Box 21, Shaw, Mississippi
Reed, Purrine C., 1231 Mt. Vernon Avenue, San Bernardino, California
Reeves, Jack B., 565 E. Erie Street, Painesville, Ohio
Regan, Andrew C., (Address Unavailable)
Regin, John J., 1209 Beach Avenue, New York, New York
Reheis, Herman F., Box 25, Douglas, Kansas
Repass, William F., Route 1, New Market, Tennessee
Rezin, Andrew M., Franklin, Kansas
Rielly, Herbert F., 30 Benjamin Avenue, Middletown, New York
Ritcher, Bergie A., RR 1, Alma, Wisconsin
Robar, Calvin J., 823 West 22nd Street, Sioux Falls, South Dakota
Roberts, Allie M., Route 1, Waxahachie, Texas
Roberts, Charles E., 217 E. 16th Street, Columbia, Tennessee
Roberts, Ernest S., Arapahoe, Colorado
Roberts, George A., Caraban, Texas
Robertson, Elbert G., 1034 7th Street, Huntington, West Virginia
Robertson, Reed S., 1037 Linwood Avenue, Collingswood, New Jersey
Rodekuhr, Arthur E., Deercreek, Minnesota
Roe, John W., 209 44th Street, Pittsburgh, Pennsylvania
Rogers, William D., 521 Poplar Avenue, Las Animas, Colorado
Roh, Clarence J., Linwood, Nebraska
Rohler, Lloyd E., Dayton, Indiana
Rollin, Herman A., 8114 Ellsworth Street, Detroit, Michigan
Roma, Gino, 209 Robble Avenue, Endicott, New York
Romans, C. W., Route 2, Cumby, Texas
Ronk, Robert E., 9315 Oakville Avenue, Plymouth, Michigan
Rosenthal, Joseph D., 1800 Commonwealth Avenue, Boston, Massachusetts
Rosenthal, Lewis, 43 64th Street, West New York, New Jersey
Ross, Grant D., 15 Mytle Street, Everett, Massachusetts
Ross, Herman L., West Union, West Virginia
Rosskopf, Harry F., 127 East School Street, Owatonna, Minnesota
Roth, Milton, 1555 Boston Road, New York, New York
Rouse, Walter E., Persimmon Grove, Excelsior Spring, Missouri
Rubin, Max, 73 Erie Street, Dorchester, Massachusetts
Rule, Clyde R., Milton, West Virginia
Rund, Murray, 1325 Grand Concourse, Bronx, New York
Rundle, Ralph P., Kaw City, Oklahoma
Rush, Paul W., 1323 Beecher Street S. W., Atlanta, Georgia
Rushman, Edward M., 2073 4th Street, Wyandotte, Michigan
Russell, Claude C., Kingston, Washington
Russell, Edward M., Elnora, Indiana
Ryall, Thomas L., 28 Milgwood Street, Brooklyn, New York
Ryan, Nel H., 218 E. 8th Street, Watson Town, Pennsylvania
Ryerson, Herman J., 17 Eagle Road, Highland Falls, New York
Sabo, Walter W., 2709 West Shorb Street, Alhambra, California
Sankowski, Joseph J., 1882 Jackson Street, Dubuque, Iowa
Santamari, Michael J., 598 St. Anns Avenue, Bronx, New York
Sapanaro, Rocco D., 714 Smith Street, Dunmore, Pennsylvania
Sargent, Linus R., Chittenden, Vermont
Sass, George W., Jr., Route 3, Grand Island, Nebraska
Sauer, John, 911 W. Monroe Street, South Bend, Indiana

Sawyer, Vernon L., 401 Norview Avenue, Norfolk, Virginia
Schaffer, Richard G., 87 N. Grand Street, Cobleskill, New York
Schalla, Alvin R., 5706 N. Bernard Street, Chicago, Illinois
Schallern, Riner B., Jr., 209 S. Avenue, Tampa, Florida
Schiebendrein, Robert J., 5440 Drexel Avenue, Chicago, Illinois
Schierman, Robert A., (Address Unavailable)
Schlagel, Cecil E., Howard Lake, Minnesota
Schmidt, George R., Box 336, Gooding, Idaho
Schneider, William, 2929 N. 25th Street, Milwaukee, Wisconsin
Schoettner, John E., 312 West Lynwood Street, Phoenix, Arizona
Schroeder, Walter C., Decatur, Indiana
Schryver, Robert G., 964 Columbia Place S. E., Warren, Ohio
Schultz, Carl D., 244 16th Street, Silvis, Illinois
Schulz, Herbert F., 1407 Potter Avenue, Merrill, Wisconsin
Scott, William B., 2700 Rogers Avenue, Ft. Worth, Texas
Scudder, Robert K., 33 S. Wolcott Street, Salt Lake City, Utah
Seaton, William J., 945 President Street, Brooklyn, New York
Sebastian, Charles S., 2036 S. 5th Avenue, Maywood, Illinois
Seery, Thomas J., 1727 Holland Avenue, New York, New York
Seger, Russell J., 1800 Goodman Avenue, N. Collegeville, Cincinnati, Ohio
Seitz, John Otis, 1719 W. 5th Street, Texarkana, Texas
Seiverson, Forest G., 1620 Markman Way, Sacramento, California
Sekula, Charles, 1075 Fairfax, Flint, Michigan
Shaffer, Ellis R., Route 2, Mt. Gilard, Ohio
Shaffer, Morris H., 10 Fabyan Street, Dorchester, Massachusetts
Shaffer, Raymond J., 2217 N. Honore, Chicago, Illinois
Sharpe, Raymond E., (Address Unavailable)
Shelton, Charles E., Stab, Kentucky
Shinn, Jack R., Route 2, St. Elmo, Illinois
Shirreffs, John A., Chicaken Pot Road, Port Washington, New York
Shivel, Lee E., 107 E. Harding Boulevard, San Antonio, Texas
Shock, Jese M., 932 14th Street, Rock Island, Illinois
Shott, John, 224 Erd Avenue, Aliquippa, Pennsylvania
Shubert, Norman, 85 Intervale Street, Roxbury, Massachusetts
Sibson, John M., 232 East Queen Lane, Philadelphia, Pennsylvania
Siegrist, William H., 819 Evelyn Avenue, Louisville, Kentucky
Silliams, Daryl D., 115 E. Water Street, Chillicothe, Ohio
Silvestri, Anthony J., 125 Harvard Street, Wailstab, Massachusetts
Silverstein, Robert, 80 Jackson Avenue, Jersey City, New Jersey
Simansky, Calvin D., 458 Chateworth Drive, San Fernando, California
Simpson, Floyd M., Caddo, Oklahoma
Simpson, James F., (Address Unavailable)
Simpson, William P., 705½ North West 17th Street, Oklahoma City, Oklahoma
Sims, Robert L., Box 328, Kilgore, Texas
Sire, William J., 235 Atlantic, New Orleans, Louisiana
Sirokman, William G., 3423 W. 36 Avenue, Denver 11, Colorado
Sisson, Clifford L., RD 1, Rock Castle, Washington
Sizemore, McKinley, Hyden, Kentucky
Skeets, Alfred W., 71 Saxton Street, Lockport, New York
Slagele, Robert G., 4319 Maple Avenue, Dallas, Texas
Sloan, Eugene B., 73 Musgroge, Clinton, South Carolina
Smith, Carl W., Kingsport, Tennessee
Smith, Edward J., (Address Unavailable)
Smith, Finley C., Jr., Mankato, Kansas
Smith, Hugh, D., 723½ W., Oklahoma, Oklahoma
Smith, James C., Yardelle, Arkansas
Smith, Oma S., General Delivery, Waconia, Minnesota
Smith, Roy E., 1425 Allison Street N. W., Washington, D. C.
Snable, Caro C., 1306 Bradfield Street, Bay City, Michigan
Sneed, Roy A., Gail Route, Howard, Texas
Somsel, Cameron N., (Address Unavailable)
Speicher, Dale, 2822 Charles Street, Wellsburg, West Virginia
Spencer, John E., 212 Birdwell Parkway, Buffalo, New York
Spickler, Wilbur L., 213 Main Street, Middletown, Pennsylvania
Spray, Irvin C., Fort Laramie, Wyoming
Sprowles, George H., 2627 W. Alleghing Avenue, Philadelphia, Pennsylvania
Spurlock, Chas. S., Jr., Box 75, Hillster, Texas
Stacey, Charles W., 908 Grove Street, Elizabeth, New Jersey
Stager, Joseph W., 12 Sowden Street, Elizabeth, New Jersey
Stalnaker, Alfred D., Jr., 613 Lula Street, Parkersburg, West Virginia
Stanbery, George W., Box 175, Jefferson City, Tennessee
Stanton, Donald H., 48 Broad Street, Pennsgrove, New Jersey
Steart, Horton R., 2445 Roosevelt Drive, Alameda, California
Steffe, William F., 426 Reef Road, Fairfield, Connecticut
Steifle, Ben W., Bradley, South Carolina
Stenlake, Raymond F., 623 S. High Street, Bangor, Pennsylvania
Stenmann, Edward J., RFD 1, Breese, Illinois
Stepanow, Samuel, Jr., 332 W. Washington Street, Paulsboro, New Jersey
Stephens, Elmore C., (Address Unavailable)
Stepp, Ira M., 1108 Penn Avenue, Fort Worth, Texas
Stevens, Gordon A., 4303 Birchwood Avenue, Ashtabula, Ohio
Stevenson, William R., Jr., Box 951, Mexia, Texas
Stern, Alfred W., 431 Roscoe Street, Chicago 13, Illinois
Stewart, Albert R., 170-07 Foch Boulevard, Jamaica, New York
Stewart, William F., 35 N. 15th Street, San Jose, California
Stine, Homer A., Box 67, New Martinsville, West Virginia
Stoddard, Ernest R., 31 Franklin Street, Bristol, Connecticut
Stokes, William R., 801 W. Va. Avenue, Kokomo, Indiana
Stone, Charles L., 429 Pleasant Street, Winthrop Center, Massachusetts
Stookey, Donald L., 424 Main Street, Gresham, Oregon
Stork, Harvey W., 1001 N. Ross Street, Santa Ana, California
Strassheim, Sidney, 2222 New Bold Avenue, Bronx 61, New York
Stratton, Morris M., Toluca, Illinois
Strelecki, Stanley A., Fort Jefferson Station, Long Island, New York
Stufflebeam, Kenneth E., 715 11th Street, Augusta, Georgia
Suarez, Peter P., 2410 E. First Street, Philadelphia, Pennsylvania
Suey, Charles L., 12621 Wyoming, Detroit, Michigan
Summers, Claude C., Edenwold, Tennessee
Summerson, John F., Dawson, Iowa
Suriano, Carmine J., 4023 4th N. E., Seattle, Washington
Svec, Millard, 970 N. Dedvale Avenue, Chicago, Illinois

Swallop, Paul G., 3207 Parkview Avenue, Pittsburgh, Pennsylvania
Swallow, Clarence E., 1123 E. 8th Street, Pueblo, Colorado
Symington, Thomas A., Jr., 56 South First Street, Paris, Texas
Symonds, Joseph W., 727 Wayne Street, Fefiance, Ohio
Szucs, Mike S., 1108 9th Street, Muskegon Heights, Michigan
Tackaberry, Thomas F., 9788 Avoca Road, Avoca, Michigan
Talbert, Carl S., Box 411, Winsboro, Texas
Tate, Milton M., 415 1st Street, Idaho Falls, Idaho
Tauber, Stanly, 39 Prospects Street, Yonkers, New York
Taylor, Floyd E., 11 Arlington Avenue, Greenville, South Carolina
Taylor, Thomas H., Roscoe, Texas
Teats, Roberts S., 1620 19th Street N. W., Washington, D. C.
Tenenbaum, Edward, 2257 University Avenue, New York, New York
Territo, Joseph N., 186 Auburn Avenue, Buffalo, New York
Terry, Clark M., 3724 W. Ellgrove Street, Seattle, Washington
Thomas, Roland P., Elm Street, Salisbury, Massachusetts
Thompson, Howard D., Fulton, South Dakota
Thompson, Mark A., 6323 Potomac, St. Louis, Missouri
Threadgold, Francis S., Main Street, Lancaster, Massachusetts
Tilson, William W., 413 Oak Street, Iowa Falls, Iowa
Tittle, Burton L., (Address Unavailable)
Tilley, John O., Toney, Alabama
Tredway, Bruce, 4308 Cedar Street, Spokane, Washington
Truman, Robert V., 501 Scenic Drive, Monrovia, California
Tryon, Harold B., 101 Gilman Street, Marietta, Ohio
Tubb, Frank M., 117 Bell Avenue, Festus, Missouri
Turkington, George E., 1924 Waveland Avenue, Chicago, Illinois
Turner, John, (Address Unavailable)
Tuttle, Charles W., Forest Hill Avenue, Lynnfield, Massachusetts
Tygart, John A., 547 Toronto Street, Toledo, Ohio
Ulaszewski, Jos. A., 7012 Gertrude Avenue, Cleveland, Ohio
Uzdarwin, William J., Box 65, Windsor, Connecticut
Upshaw, Harold C., 515 W. Rugby, College Park, Georgia
Waggle, James A., 171 Olive Terrace, Porterville, California
Waggy, Robert H., 14 Stephenson Street, Charleston, West Virginia
Wagner, Donald E., 15 Ledge Terrace, Stamford, Connecticut
Waite, Edgar A., 2213 4th Avenue, Scottsbluff, Nebraska
Waldheim, Alfred F., Jr., Stanley Street, Hartford, Connecticut
Walker, Ray S., (Address Unavailable)
Walker, Robert O., Charlottesville, Virginia
Walker, Von N., 2216 S. Taylor Street, Amarillo, Texas
Walker, James K., 2221 Church Street, Greenville, Texas
Wallace, Ralph G., Fayettville, North Carolina
Wallace, William H., Trooper Road, Route 2, Norristown, Pennsylvania
Waring, Kenneth B., 1026 N. W. 11th Avenue, Miami, Florida
Warren, Donald W., Merkel, Texas
Warren, Harold, Perintown, Ohio
Wartena, Robert B., 950 Belle Plaine, Chicago, Illinois
Waters, Leland H., Jr., 7326 Hermitage Road, Richmond, Virginia
Watne, Earl W., 38 E. 4th Street, Hannaford, North Dakota
Watt, George S., 506 W. College Avenue, Tallahasse, Florida
Webb, Paul P., Grain Valley, Missouri
Weimer, Jonas R., Oliver, Pennsylvania
Welch, Leonard W., 2153 Junction Avenue, Detroit, Michigan
Welch, William H., 127 Josephine Avenue, Somerville, Massachusetts
Werner, Herman, Peshastin, Washington

Wexler, Fred H., 5417 Gainor Road, Philadelphia, Pennsylvania
Wezel, Arthur O., (Address Unavailable)
Whitfield, George B., Jr., 701 W. Angela Boulevard, South Bend, Indiana
Whitehead, George W., Box 593, Vero Beach, Florida
Whitsell, Robert H., Route 1, Box 11A, Turlock, California
Whittington, Arthur W., 392 Tibet Road, Columbus, Ohio
Wicker, Walter V., 1111 E. Green Street, High Point, North Carolina
Wideman, Perry C., Homer, Louisiana
Wiggins, Robert C., 1622 N. W. 14th Street, Oklahoma City, Oklahoma
Williams, Burnie L., Star Route 2, Lamesa, Texas
Williams, Dave M., Castor, Louisiana
Williams, Donald H., 538 N. Summer Avenue, Scranton, Pennsylvania
Williams, Jack A., (Address Unavailable)
Wiling, John A., 200 N. 7th Street, Northwood, Iowa
Williams, Nelson, Route 1, Boaz, Alabama
Williams, Norman A., Route 2, Atlantic, Iowa
Willis, Samuel C., Box 237, Loyall, Kentucky
Williams, Theron M., 2322 West Platte, Colorado Springs, Colorado
Willoughby, Lloyd E., 7023 31st Avenue, Kenosha, Wisconsin
Wilson, Clive F., Route 5, Clinton, Missouri
Wilson, Harold J., 237 Browns Street, Crooksville, Ohio
Wilson, Lee, 718 Simpson Street, Evanston, Illinois
Willson, Lewis R., 522½ S. 9th Avenue, Pocatello, Idaho
Willy, Craig G., Madison, South Dakota
Wise, Milton B., 6950 Canal Boulevard, New Orleans, Louisiana
Woldman, Samuel C., 31 Maywood Street, Boston, Massachusetts
Wood, Walter V., 282 Greenwood Avenue, Trenton, New Jersey
Woodcox, James F., Box 26, Ubly, Michigan
Worley, Henry M., 904 E. Jessamine Street, Ft. Worth, Texas
Worman, Robert E., 458 W. 15th Avenue, Spokane, Washington
Wright, Jesse L., Cane Hill, Arkansas
Wyckoff, Eldon J., 404 Choctaw Street, Liberty, Missouri
Vail, John H., 201 Klotter Street, Cincinnati, Ohio
Valiton, Carnot K., 125 East G. Street, Ontario, California
Van Ausdell, Robert C., 335 Oak Street, Salem, Oregon
Vanderbeck, Edward L., 34 Walthery, Bridgewood, New Jersey
Vanderberry, Rolfe C., 130 Kentucky Avenue, Norfolk, Virginia
Van Etten, Francis J., 29 Arnold Road, Poughkepsie, New York
Van Huben, Leslie H., 80 Vayo Street, Rochester, New York
Van Patten, Willard G., Tawas City, Michigan
Van Scoyk, Ralph J., 315 E. Corrington Avenue, Peoria, Illinois
Veliquette, Raymond A., 3833 Herbert Street, San Diego, California
Vojnovich, Sam, (Address Unavailable)
Volz, Jack A., 4010 W. 8th Street, Cincinnati, Ohio
Wachtel, George J., 214 Locust Street, Ambridge, Pennsylvania
Wade, Charles H., Route 2, Chickamauga, Georgia
Yecker, Donald H., 1807 Amberly Avenue, Cleveland, Ohio
Yinger, Bert P., 516 Chalfont, Pittsburgh, Pennsylvania
Young, Otis H., 620 E. 73rd Street, Chicago, Illinois
Yovino, Philip E., (Address Unavailable)
Zacker, Leo, 4300 S. Mozart Street, Chicago, Illinois
Zahora, Charles J., 50 E. Railroad Street, Coaldale, Pennsylvania
Zimmer, Carl E., 210 Pardella Lemay, St. Louis, Missouri
Zimmerman, William C., Willow Bank Street, Bellefonte, Pennsylvania
Zollweg, Walter V., 303 3rd Street, Box 24, Tawas City, Michigan
Zorn, Edward C., Route 1, Helper, Utah

501ST SQUADRON

AAneson, Ole M., (Address Unavailable)
Abbey, Merlin, 135 Damon, Jackson, Michigan
Abernathy, Clifford L., Route 2, Jamestown, Alabama
Adams, Marcel W., 31 Saratoga Street, Springfield, Massachusetts
Adams, John K., 124 W. Ottawa Street, Sycamore, Illinois
Adamson, Kervyn R., 411 W. Washington, Chicago, Illinois
Adrian, Arthur C., 23 Stanton Street, West Pittston, Pennsylvania
Ahrendt, Donald C., Dubuque, Iowa
Akers, William, 1410 Porter Street, Helena, Arkansas
Albers, Joseph H., 551 York Street, Cincinnati, Ohio
Albert, Nathan, 5636 Phillips Avenue, Pittsburgh, Pennsylvania
Albrecht, John F., Box 103, Nettleton, Arkansas
Albright, Lester W., (Address Unavailable)
Albright, Richard W., 153 E. King Street, Lancaster, Pennsylvania
Alcalde, Joseph M., 1727 Clarke Street, San Leandro, California
Alday, Felipe, Box 481, Calexico, California
Alexander, Roy A., 168-20 88th Avenue, Jamaica, Long Island, New York
Allen, Carl L., Ooltewah, Tennessee
Allen, Glenn C., Route 2, New Albany, New York
Amurso, Nicholas J., 142-19 Rockaway Boulevard, Ozone Park, New York
Anderson, Arthur O., Route 1, Dalton, Minnesota
Anderson, Guy H., 428 Margareite Street, Corona Del Mar, California
Anderson, John R., 212 6th Street, Burlington, North Carolina
Anderson, William N., 351 Mildred Avenue, Syracuse, New York
Appello, Aubust, 6735 Hudson Boulevard, N. Bergen, New Jersey
Armel, John E., 870 Birch Street, Memphis, Tennessee
Arnold, Gordon W., 112 Myrle, Longview, Texas
Arnold, Newton A., RFD 1, Coal City, Illinois
Arpin, Norman R., 126 Tinkham Street, New Bedford, Massachusetts
Aslin, Harold C., 4344 Bayley Street, Wichita, Kansas
Atkins, Benjamin S., Box 325 Perry, Georgia
Atkins, John W., McKenzie, Tennessee
Atteridge, Arehur C., 19 W. 5th Street, Watsonville, California
Audas, James, (Address Unavailable)
Auclair, Ephrem J., 104 Tallman Street, New Bedford, Massachusetts
Auerbach, Samuel, 2562 83rd Street, Jackson Heights, Long Island, New York
Augusta, George, Box 136, Cumberland, Kentucky
Avant, Lawrence B., 5 Wayne Street, Montgomery, Alabama
Babcock, John H., Jr., Johnsontown Road, Slatotsburg, New York
Bagg, Albert S., Jr., (Address Unavailable)
Bagwell, Harold D., 226 Burlington Avenue, Logansport, Indiana
Bailey, Edward E., Box 145, Helen, West Virginia

Baird, Frank N., 101 Linwood Avenue, Pawtuckett, Rhode Island
Baker, Charles A., (Address Unavailable)
Baker, Isaac E., Hunnewell, Kansas
Ball, Gordon A., 1048 Altadena Avenue, Royal Oak, Michigan
Ball, Gordon B., Lake Shore Boulevard, Cleveland, Ohio
Balonier, Harold M., 1920 Brookline Avenue, Dayton, Ohio
Bannon, Mike F., Edgewater, New Jersey
Barbato, Ralph H., 158 Parkway, Rochester, New York
Barnett, Edward H., 2451 S. Percy Street, Philadelphia, Pennsylvania
Baross, James P., East Boulevard, Greenlawn, New York
Baron, Isidore N., 2045 Union Street, Brooklyn, New York
Barron, John M., 718 S. Tripp Avenue, Chicago, Illinois
Barth, Richard A., 28 Cross Street, West Orange, New Jersey
Bartlett, Hobert R., 1704 Sylvania Avenue, Ft. Worth, Texas
Bates, Glenn O., Route 1, Jefferson, Pennsylvania
Bauer, Walter E., Stewardson, Illinois
Bauman, John D., Box 164, Clarkson, Nebraska
Bayer, Abba, (Address Unavailable)
Beard, Clarence L., 1304 E. 6th Street, Little Rock, Arkansas
Beck, Calvin C., 4222 Dumesnil Street, Louisville, Kentucky
Beck, William F., Route 1, Box 52 Seagrove, North Carolina
Becker, Robert P., 21 Richmond Street, Carbondale, Pennsylvania
Becker, Walter E., 118 Trevor Street, Covington, Kentucky
Becon, Robert L., 37 N. 3rd Street, Sayre, Oklahoma
Bedell, Frank G., 16 Monroe Street, South Norwalk, Connecticut
Bedell, Gordon L., Bellaire, Michigan
Behrhorst, Donald, Sylvan Grove, Kansas
Belchik, George R., 7023 Columbia Avenue, Hammond, Indiana
Belknap, John W., Route 3, Forsyth, Georgia
Bell, Melvin R., Route 6, Box 662, Oklahoma City, Oklahoma
Bell, Victor N., 411 Southwest Avenue, Greensburg, Pennsylvania
Bell, William W., 708 E. 12th Street, Oklahoma City, Oklahoma
Bellew, Robert R., 6623 Avenue C., Houston, Texas
Belmont, Gordon W., 831 Church Street, Ripon, Wisconsin
Bemis, Fred D., 727 Dan Gaspar Avenue, Stnta Fe, New Mexico
Bench, William J., Route 1, Leonard, Texas
Berger, Martin S., Middletown, Missouri
Bernstein, Jack L., 2282 Ocean Avenue, Brooklyn, New York
Berry, Norman V., 341½ 31st Street, Ashland, Kentucky
Betz, Henry E., 3629 35th Avenue, Oakland, California
Bever, Robert E., Powell, Wyoming
Bianconi, Owen M., (Address Unavailable)

Bibeault, George L., 29 Huckins Street, Roxbury, Massachusetts
Billig, Harold L., Sealy, Texas
Bina, Edward L., 1328 3rd Street, Antigo, Wisconsin
Birchak, Steve J., RFD 2, Box 189, Laterobe, Pennsylvania
Bissesi, Sam T., 246 Locust Street, Akron, Ohio
Bizel, Frederick G., (Address Unavailable)
Blackerby, Adrian G., Route 3, Box 456, Bessemer, Alabama
Blackmon, Jeffery, Elberton, Georgia
Blackwell, George M., 1507 Avenue U., Lubbock, Texas
Blackwell, Henry C., Box 5, Adamsville, Alabama
Blair, George W., Tilford, South Dakota
Blaylock, Norton, 3550 Ellis Avenue, Chicago, Illinois
Blessing, Joseph C., 325 S. Maple Avenue, Ridgewood, New Jersey
Blount, Ralph E., 101 E. 20th Street, Big Spring, Texas
Boczan, Stephen M., 399 High Street, Perth Amboy, New Jersey
Boden, John V., 345 Albert Street, Turtle Creek, Pennsylvania
Boening, Alger L., 33171 Utica Road, Fraser, Michigan
Bogacz, Walter, 108-110 E. Vienn, Anna, Illinois
Boland, William T., Arcadia, Wisconsin
Bonadies, Eugene J., 29 Anthony Street, New Haven, Connecticut
Bonner, Leemon F., Chattanooga Road, Dalton, Georgia
Bonson, Harold, (Address Unavailable)
Born, Frank K., 6521 S. Morgan Street, Chicago, Illinois
Bosen, Frederick C., 717 Kent Street, Rome, New York
Boshko, John P., 54 Armstrong Avenue, South River, New Jersey
Bosworth, Elbert H., 126 Ferris Avenue, Chardon, Ohio
Boswell, Arnold B., Route 2, DeLeon, Texas
Botner, Wilson T., 18 Estill Street, Berea, Kentucky
Bowen, Charles B., Booker, Texas
Boyles, Guy C., Route 2, Barnwell, South Carolina
Bracebridge, Kenneth C., 40 Barclay Street, Canajoharie, New York
Bradebill, James R., 116 N. Oklahoma Street, Shawnee, Oklahoma
Bradley, Walter, RFD 3, Lancaster, Wisconsin
Brandt, Louis, 945 Leggett Avenue, Bronx, New York
Braid, Bernard, 2200 W. Jefferson, Philadelphia, Pennsylvania
Brecken, Wayne C., Comstock, Nebraska
Brewster, James R., Route 1, Asher, Oklahoma
Britton, Donald J., 1602 N. Mariposa Avenue, Hollywood, California
Brock, Robert A., Route 2, Mt. Healthy, Ohio
Brocker, Vernon O., 1425 42nd Street, Sacramento, California
Brown, Benson K., E. 208 Everett, Spokane, Washington
Brown, James, 1723 N. Atlanta Street, Tulsa, Oklahoma
Brown, James L., 2194 Fannin Street, Vernon, Texas
Brown, James W., 714 10th Street, Shelbyville, Kentucky
Brown, Kenneth R., 1376 Grant Street, Lincoln Park, Michigan
Brownell, Victor F., 280 W. Delauan Avenue, Buffalo, New York
Brownlee, John H., Route 1, Aledo, Illinois
Bruecker, John V., 213 Sherman, Peoria, Illinois
Brunkow, Merlyn C., 710 S. Garden Street, Lake City, Minnesota
Braun, Robert N., 1353 W. Rogers Avenue, Appleton, Wisconsin
Buchanan, Ronald S., 4930 Main Street, Crete, Illinois
Buffa, Sebastian, 11711 Elmdale, Detroit, Michigan
Bufkin, Earnest L., Stringer, Mississippi
Buitron, Ignacio G., 917 E. Alice Street, Kingsville, Texas
Bull, Billy A., Box 2, Agua Dulce, Texas
Burg, Richard L., 1089 Tonawanda Street, Buffalo, New York
Burall, John E., Mt. Savage, Maryland
Burnett, Robert L., RR 3, Batavia, Iowa
Burns, Chester F., 32 N. Market Street, Nanticoke, Pennsylvania
Burns, Paul A., 105½ Parsons Avenue, Endicott, New York
Burow, Milton A., Pecos, Texas
Bursic, Matthew J., 1113 Sylvan Avenue, Homestead, Pennsylvania
Burzynski, Herman F., 47 Deshler Street, Buffalo, New York
Butz, Harold C., 548 N. Mary Street, Lancaster, Pennsylvania
Byfield, Phillips, Jr., 350 Cabot Street, Newtonville, Massachusetts
Byrd, Joseph H., Route 2, Hurricane, West Virginia
Cade, Alfred E., Ingram, Texas
Caldwell, James T., 316 W. Willow Street, Durant, Oklahoma
Caldwell, Thomas E., 1404 Maple Street, Columbia, South Carolina
Callahan, John R., 1608½ S. Geddes Street, Syracuse, New York
Calloway, Robert D., Route 3, Florence, Alabama
Calo, Frank R., 132 W. First Street, Mt. Vernon, New York
Campbell, Leroy M., Oberlin, Kansas
Campbell, Leroy M., 2226 Larimer Street, Denver, Colorado
Campbell, Richard J., 113 Arthur Street, Ridgefield Park, New Jersey
Capp, Charles D., Route 1, Palmyra, Pennsylvania
Cardany, Stanley R., 2 Middletown Avenue, Wethersfield, Connecticut
Carlee, John L., (Address Unavailable)
Carrano, Nicholas P., 827 Martin Street, Elizabeth, New Jersey
Carretta, Alexander F., 506 Springdale Avenue, Long Branch, New Jersey
Caskey, Clair E., RFD 3, Council Bluffs, Iowa
Cate, Elton G., East Calais, Vermont
Caterina, Vincent A., 1133 Michigan Avenue, Niagara Falls, New York
Cather, William H., 2421 Avenue G., Birmingham, Alabama
Cavins, Robert K., 310 S. Michigan Avenue, Chicago, Illinois
Cera, Albert, 593 N. Wyoming Street, Hazelton, Pennsylvania
Chambers, Alpha L., Dequincy, Louisiana
Chance, James W., 401 B. Gilles Street, Alameda, California
Chapman, Richard B., Gray, Maine
Charron, Howard H., 1845 S. Carona Street, Denver, Colorado
Chealander, Jerry L., 604 W. Avenue, Los Angeles, California
Christensen, John E., Newport, Nebraska
Christenson, James, (Address Unavailable)
Clancy, Paul J., 21A Spring Park Avenue, Boston, Massachusetts
Clark, Donald L., RFD 1, Fenton, Michigan
Clark, Thomas P., Jr., Indian Agency, Sells, Arizona
Clark, William H., 542 Lewis Street, Hammond, Indiana
Clark, William O., 3176 N. 40th Street, Lincoln, Nebraska
Clayton, Fred A., Fairmont, South Carolina
Cleveland, Norman, 429 W. Main Street, Lebanon, Tennessee
Close, James, 402 4th Street, Brooklyn, New York

Closson, Chalmer C., 1213 Airgrake Avenue, Turtle Creek, Pennsylvania
Cloyd, Donald L., Cozad, Nebraska
Coffman, Charles E., Allen, Kansas
Cohn, Martin M., 8100 Bay Parkway, Brooklyn, New York
Cohron, Henry E., Katy, Texas
Collis, Arthur C., Route 1, Herkimer, New York
Concelmo, Dominick, 73 Chamberlain Street, New Haven, Connecticut
Conley, Joseph F., 3407 Greenview Avenue, Chicago, Illinois
Cook, Harry G., 324 N. Star, El Dorado, Kansas
Cook, Joe, (Address Unavailable)
Cook, John W., Jr., 75 Fairmont Avenue, Glenbrook, Connecticut
Cook, William O., Ross Building, Hugo, Oklahoma
Coons, Noland S., 512 Margaret Avenue, Los Angeles, California
Corbett, Roland N., Utica, Minnesota
Corbin, Clarence N., (Address Unavailable)
Corder, Owen B., 139 River Side, Little Rock, Arkansas
Cortesio, Sandy A., Mystic, Iowa
Coscia, Patrick J., 118 Columbus Place, Roselle Park, New Jersey
Coryell, Harry E., 515 N. Sheffield Avenue, Indianapolis, Indiana
Costellio, John J., 73 Norfolk Street, Worcester, Massachusetts
Costner, Robert K., 1954 Pattie Avenue, Wichita, Kansas
Coursey, Harwede, 1239 E. Myrtle Street, Lakeland, Florida
Cousens, Charles H., 23 Wepple Avenue, Brockton, Massachusetts
Cottingham, Morrison, (Address Unavailable)
Cowell, Glen W., Box 295, Harlem, Montana
Coyel, Joseph M., 112 E. Patterson Street, St. Clair, Pennsylvania
Craig, George, Box 375, Route 5, Tucson, Arizona
Craig, Jack, 1113 E. 37th Street, Savannah, Georgia
Crawford, Herbert D., 517 Rose Street, Clifton Forge, Virginia
Creager, John R., Route 1, Fairfield, Pennsylvania
Cronin, Kenneth R., 1300 31st Street, Sheffield, Alabama
Crusenberry, Harry, Box 211, Saltville, Virginia
Crutchfield, John, (Address Unavailable)
Crutchfield, William, Box 201, Monroeville, Alabama
Cullina, John F., Main Street, Millbury, Massachusetts
Culpepper, Reginald, Route 3, Hickory, North Carolina
Czechorowski, John, 1417 Fort Avenue, Niagara Falls, New York
Daihl, Jason D., RFD 1, Newburg, Pennsylvania
Dale, Stanley L., Route 3, Dawsonville, Georgia
Davis, Edwin, Jr., 1320 Washington, Fort Worth, Texas
Davis, Emery, 230 S. Broadway, Baltimore, Maryland
Davis, John F., 132-17 Maple Avenue, Flushing, Long Island, New York
Davis, John L., Route A, Americus, Georgia
Davis, Raymond L., Quinton, Oklahoma
Davis, Warren E., 6237 S. University Street, Chicago, Illinois
Davis, Fred P., Jr., 520 E. Illinois Street, Evansville, Indiana
Davis, William F., RR 1, c-o E. M. Bishop, Traveler Rest, South Carolina
Deady, Frederick W., 10608 Almira Avenue, Cleveland, Ohio
Dean, Guy I., Alden, Michigan
Dean, Howard D., Sparrowbursh, New York
Decobellis, Fred J., 19 S. W. 2nd SEtreet, Chisholm, Minnesota
Deetz, Milton E., 3103 Triumbull Avenue, Detroit, Michigan
DeJong, Doyle G., Box 11, Lyneen, Washington
DeKay, Harold G., 216 Lincoln Avenue, Chicago, Illinois
Delk, John R., 1902 Pecan Street, Texarkana, Arkansas
DelVecchio, Leonard, 77 Francis Avenue, Hartford, Connecticut
DelVecchio, Carlo C., 174 Hachensack Street, Woodridge, New Jersey
Demoskio, Steve C., 2864 Sanborn Street, Pittsburgh, Pennsylvania
Denny, Herbert B., 811 Jackson Street, San Antonio, Texas
DePiano, Neal J., (Address Unavailable)
De Turck, Ellwood R., Esterly, Pennsylvania
Devore, George W., (Address Unavailable)
Dew, Dudley Z., 383 High Street, Benton Harbor, Michigan
Diedrichs, Herman J., 146 S. Main Street, Dodgeville, New York
Diedrich, Robert M., 2906 E. 3rd Street, Dayton, Ohio
Diemer, Russel B., 464 Pen Street, Spring City, Pennsylvania
Ditetrich, George H., 2747 N. 11th Street, Milwaukee, Wisconsin
Dixon, Ira J., Route 1, Cashion, Oklahoma
Doerr, John W., RFD 2, Vergennes, Illinois
Doerner, Joseph S., 166 Clinton Place, Newark, New Jersey
Donovan, Joseph J., 44 Charme Avenue, Roslindale, Massachusetts
Doughty, Clarence H., Jr., 106 7th Street, Laurel, Maryland
Dougherty, Marshall J., 163 Lincoln Street, Uniontown, Pennsylvania
Dougherty, Raymond J., 3107 Tacker Street, Philadelphia, Pennsylvania
Dougherty, Vincen H., 720 E. 2nd Avenue, Mitchell, South Dakota
Dowell, Porter H., Russell Springs, Kentucky
Drane, Melvin E., Jr., 5718 Pearl Street, Jacksonville, Florida
Dufalo, Michael P., 3331 N. Springfield Avenue, Chicago, Illinois
Duffel, Bill R., 4803 Rusk Avenue, Houston, Texas
Dufour, Curtiss J., 3126 Allen Street, New Orleans, Louisiana
Duguid, Bruce T., 527 N. 21st Street, Coruallis, Oregon
Dunlap, John R., Route 1, Cottage Grove, Tennessee
Dutchman, George C., (Address Unavailable)
Dye, Thomas G., 7510 S. Fiqueroa, Los Angeles, California
Eaton, William T, Route 3, Woodland, Mississippi
Edenstrom, Vernon W., Christine, South Dakota
Edmonds, Harold F., 223 Clahound Street, Battle Creek, Michigan
Edsall, Richard G., Route 1, Warren, Michigan
Edwards, Charles B., 529 Whiting, El Segundo, California
Edwards, Everette, 508 E. Robert Street, Hammond, Louisiana
Edwards, James, Route 9, Wersailles Road, Frankfort, Kentucky
Egge, Edwin O., 817 N. Minnesota Avenue, Sioux Falls, South Dakota
Egrich, Nick, 607 Lewis Avenue, Columbus, Ohio
Ehlers, Karl L., Box 119, Newton Falls, New York
Emery, George H., 383 Main Street, Athol, Massachusetts
Emory, John W., Route 1, North Side, North Carolina
English, Thomas C., RFD 6, Connersville, Indiana
Engstrom, Wilbur H., 106 N. Hampton Street, Buffalo, New York
Erdin, Robert A., 142 Ryerson Avenue, Paterson, New Jersey
Erbse, Wayne O., Cuyahoga Falls, Ohio
Erskine, Robert M., 1112 W. Logan Avenue, Danville, Illinois

Esty, Milton E., 51 Goshen Street, Hartford, Connecticut
Etkins, Nathan S., 836 S. W. 6th Street, Miami Beach, Florida
Euphrat, Edward F., 290 Division Street, San Francisco, California
Evans, Henry B., 601 S. 72nd Street, Birmingham, Alabama
Evans, Robert N., 436 S. Lake Street, Phillips, Wisconsin
Everett, Lea T., 907 Buckalew Street E., Dallas, Texas
Everett, Warren W., 23-529th Avenue, South Saint Paul, Minnesota
Fain, Robert S., 907 E. Main Street, Mexia, Texas
Fairbanks, William H., RFD 2, Homer, New York
Faris, Joseph W., Hinckley, Utah
Farough, George E., 15856 Baylis, Detroit, Michigan
Faulconer, Donald E., RFD 5, Box 183, Indianapolis, Indiana
Faulkner, Edgar D., Jr., 542 K. Street, Springfield, Oregon
Ferguson, Howard A., 1212 NBC Building, Cleveland, Ohio
Fernandez, John, 501 St. S. Valverde, El Paso, Texas
Ferris, Frederick A., 109 Congress Street, Portland, Maine,
Fezio, Joseph R., 26 E. Jefferson Street, Paulsboro, New Jersey
Finkle, Edgar, W. Walnut Street, North Wales, Pennsylvania
Fiorello, Neil F., 544 N. 53rd Street, Philadelphia, Pennsylvania
Fischer, Harry, 2908 New York Avenue, Union City, New Jersey
Fisher, Julius B., Route 2, Olivet, Michigan
Fitts, Emery L., Jr., 1820 Cypress Street, San Diego, California
Flanagan, Frank R., Jr., 126 2nd Street, Richmond, Kentucky
Flanders, Charles W., 115 South Gunter, Vinita, Oklahoma
Flournoy, Raymond T., Silver Peak, Nevada
Flynn, William J., 936 Market Street, Gloucester City, New Jersey
Foble, William D., (Address Unavailable)
Foerster, Gustave E., 1716 Greenleaf Avenue, Chicago, Illinois
Foley, Peter M., 1340 N. Menard Avenue, Cchiago, Illinois
Forman, Joe, 425 Felsway, East Melrose, Massachusetts
Foster, James E., Yancyville, North Carolina
Fournier, Philip V., 6232 S. Marchfield, Chicago, Illinois
Fowler, Curtis, Route 2, Tabor City, North Carolina
Foy, George B., (Address Unavailable)
Franko, Thomas, Box 166, Yorkville, Ohio
Fratine, Dominick N., 1137 Barrett Street, Schenectady, New York
Friend, Tilden B., (Address Unavailable)
Freeman, James R., Johnson City, Texas
Freeman, Merritt E., 349 South Main Street, Adrian, Michigan
Friedman, Albert L., 1351 Grand Boulevard, Schnectady, New York
Friedman, Herbert M., 2056 79th Street, Brooklyn, New York
Frye, George F., 1430 Mann Street, Bridgeport, Connecticut
Frye, Marion C., 676 59th Street, Des Moines, Iowa
Fuentes, Candelario G., 929 Peabody Avenue, San Antonio, Texas
Fusaro, Joseph A., 14 N. High Street, Mt. Vernon, New York
Gagen, John D., 66 Lenox Avenue, East Orange, New Jersey
Gallagher, James J., 17 Walnut Street, Ashland, Pennsylvania
Gallagher, John P., 603½ Balcom Street, Eau Claire, Wisconsin
Galloway, James D., Fort Payne, Alabama
Gamble, Dean F., RFD 1, McDonald, Pennsylvania
Gardner, Delmar B., RFD 2, Croswell, Michigan
Garrett, William R., 2228 Kenmore Avenue, Charlotte, North Carolina
Gast, John J., 1357 Stowe Avenue, McKees Rocks, Pennsylvania
Gatewood, Henry, Holly Springs, Mississippi
Griffin, George C., Route 1, Nashville, North Carolina
Gentry, Robert D., 107 W. River Road, Howell, Michigan
George, Albert, 153 Welfare Avenue, Norwood, Rhode Island
Gerstein, Robert J., 3125 N. Kenneth Avenue, Chicago, Illinois
Gettel, Harlan A., Route 2, Sebewaing, Michigan
Getzendanner, J. A., 540 E. Chestnut Street, Kankakee, Illinois
Gibbons, Eldred S., Snow Hill, Maryland
Gibson, Alvin L., 109 N. Avenue, Addison, Illinois
Giese, Thomas D., (Address Unavailable)
Giultani, Quinton J., 301 Iona Avenue, Narberth, Pennsylvania
Giroux, Phillip J., 32 Bridge Street, N. Vassalboro, Maine
Glatt, James E., 138 N. Humphrey Avenue, Oak Park, Illinois
Glasby, Gren C., 20 Cronell Street, Amsterdam, New York
Glynn, Edmond B., 565 W. 215th Street, New York, New York
Golden, Yale, 11 Odell Avenue, White Plains, New York
Goldenberg, Joseph, 1136 Evergreen Avenue, Bronx, New York
Goldstein, Herman, 786 28th Avenue, San Francisco, California
Golightly, James L., Melbourne, Florida
Golt, Marion G., Queenstown, Pennsylvania
Gomes, Frank R., 3719 Brooklyn Avenue, Los Angeles, California
Gottesman, Samuel S., 1154 Stratford Avenue, Bronx, New York
Gray, James A., Sloatsburg, New York
Gredence, Louis, Box 47, Delmont, Pennsylvania
Green, Benjamin E., 203 Verne Street, Tampa, Florida
Green, Oscar E., 936 E. Pleasant Run, Indianapolis, Indiana
Green, Thomas D., Box 304, Sebring, Florida
Greenquist, Conrad E., Evansville, Minnesota
Greiner, George, 527 Main Street, Fort Lee, New Jersey
Gresens, Arthur R., 655 Linden Street, Rochester, New York
Gronewald, Jack E., 255 Yucaipa, Boulevard, California
Gruber, Charles J., 533 E. 55th Street, Brooklyn, New York
Griffin, Lawrence, 3637 Pulaski, Chicago, Illinois
Gross, Virgil L., 907 S. Chestnut Street, Aberdeen, Mississippi
Grossman, Chester A., 4213 S. Xerxes, Minneapolis, Minnesota
Grosso, Edmond V., The Springs, New Ashford, Massachusetts
Groves, Joe A., 220 Walnut Street, Clarksburg, West Virginia
Grummer, George E., (Address Unavailable)
Guinn, Lester L., 804 W. 3rd Street, North Platte, Nebraska
Haffke, Robert E., 2515 Himebaugh Avenue, Omaha, Nebraska
Hafliger, Lyle R., Wakeeney, Kansas
Haines, Dave W., Kaycee, Wyoming
Haklar, Emil S., 191 Strawberry Hill, Woodbridge, New Jersey
Haliman, Thomas D., Jr., 211 Leonard Street, Kannapolis, North Carolina
Hall, Ernest, Stamford, New York
Hall, Joseph T., 321 Brooks Avenue, Atlanta, Georgia
Hall, Robert L., 808 Orange Street, Yuba City, California
Hall, Walter J., 4 Elm Street, Jamaica Plains, Massachusetts

Haller, Paul E., Arlington, Washington
Halvorson, Wallace D., 34816 Brush Street, Wayne, Michigan
Hamblen, Robert C., 69 Haskell Street, Westbrook, Maine
Hammersborg, Goodwin H., Big Falls, Minnesota
Hamner, John T., Jr., 137 Greenlawn Drive, San Antonio, Texas
Hanesworth, James O., 725 N. Indiana Avenue, Kokomo, Indiana
Hangsleben, Harvey W., Route 1, Mascoutah, Illinois
Hannon, John T., Jr., 717 Church Street, Medina, New York
Hansen, Frank R., 185 W. Main Street, Port Jervis, New York
Hanson, Robert W., Route 1, Abbotsford, Wisconsin
Hardeman, Donald, 504 E. 5th Street, San Angelo, Texas
Harkins, Vernon J., 3922 N. 19th Street, Tacoma, Washington
Harmon, John E., Revelo, Kentucky
Harper, Russell H., Montezuma, Indiana
Harper, Wilbur W., Jr., 200 Callecita Place, Santa Fe, New Mexico
Harrah, James N., Box 23A, Caldwell, Idaho
Harris, Donald W., Box 306, Tacoma, Washington
Harris, Lloyd, 153 North A. Street, Tulare, California
Harris, William C., Route 1, Taylorsville, Georgia
Hart, Ted U., 930 S. Lyman Avenue, Oak Park, Illinois
Hartsoe, Joseph D., First Street, Weldon, North Carolina
Harvey, George A., 224 S. Front Street, Sterling, Colorado
Hasty, Donald T., Route 1, Mebane, North Carolina
Hatfield, William H., 109 McAdoo Avenue, Jersey City, New Jersey
Haubert, Jack W., 1123 Harrison, Canton, Ohio
Haught, G. E., Route 1, Farmington, West Virginia
Hauser, John F., 401 E. Marshall Street, Turlock, California
Hawkins, Henry F., Route 1, Castlewood, Virginia
Hayes, Jackson M., 270 Bellevue 2, Memphis, Tennessee
Hazelrigg, William F., 317 Dry Street, East Alton, Illinois
Health, John C., 1211 W. 9½ Street, Austin, Texas
Heavner, Earl J., RFD 3, Cumberland, Maryland
Hedenquist, Jacob E., 480 Orchard Grove Avenue, East Liverpool, Ohio
Hefner, Thomas R., 1105 Tomlinson Avenue, Moundsville, West Virginia
Heidorf, Thomas H., 46 Elm Street, Hudson Falls, New York
Heinlein, Ed J., 930 W. Compton, Compton, California
Heinzmann, Karl, 626 Stanton Avenue, Akron, Ohio
Heller, William A., 1366 Lyman Place, Bronx, New York
Helvey, Wilfred D., Box 152, Bryson, Texas
Henley, William E., 121 Spruce Street, San Francisco, California
Herbert, James A., 1914 W. Victory Boulevard, Burbank, California
Herbst, Hilbert E., 1001 First Street, Webster City, Iowa
Hermes, Richard E., Jr., 523 N. Ford Avenue, Fullerton, California
Hilbun, John C., Route 1, Soso, Mississippi
Hill, Joseph L., 722 Hackett Street, Ionia, Michigan
Hillman, Lorenzo D., Jr., 1827 W. Avenue N., San Angelo, Texas
Hirt, David O., 354 W. 28th Street, New York, New York
Hiser, Walter C., St. Paul, Indiana
Hoagland, Ralph S., Sun City, Kansas
Hodges, Charles B., Jr., 306 N. Main Street, Andover, Massachusetts
Hoefling, Richard H., 653 Jefferson Avenue, Elizabeth, New Jersey
Hogan, Francis J., 3532 Lake Avenue, Rochester, New York
Hogan, William J., 2016 N. Harston Street, Philadelphia, Pennsylvania
Holland, Donald M., Box 483, Highland, Kansas
Holland, William W., Jr., 2004 E. 14th Street, Cheyenne, Wyoming
Holmes, Harold G., Nyssa, Oregon
Holmes, Merton H., 2129 Romeo, Ferndale, Michigan
Holmes, Ross B., 317 5th Street, St. Petersburg, Florida
Holsonback, Roy L., 127 S. Bloodworth Street, Raleigh, North Carolina
Hoomis, Paul G., 343 Boston Street, Lynn, Massachusetts
Hoover, Roy M., Box 1941, Parker, Arizona
Hopkins, John M., 611 E. Benton Street, Joliet, Illinois
Horn, John D., 4410 San Jacinto, Dallas, Texas
Hornberg, Edward H., 3819 A. Hartford Avenue, St. Louis, Missouri
Houchin, Asa E., Canton, Oklahoma
Houtchens, Stanley R., 1629 12th Avenue, Greeley, Colorado
Hovater, Gary C., Box 534, Tuskegee, Alabama
Howard, Herbert G., 23 Crescent Avenue, Pittsfield, Massachusetts
Howard, Philip C., Kent, Ohio
Hrizak, Joseph, 511 Duwell Street, Johnstown, Pennsylvania
Hubbard, Henry C., Jr., 1440 S. Boston Street, Tulsa, Oklahoma
Hudson, Leslie H., 322 Bailey Street, Camden, New Jersey
Hull, Harrison N., Route 1, Box 60, Greeley, Colorado
Huntington, Charles R., 2600 Eastwood Street, Evanston, Illinois
Iacovelli, John, 645 S. 3rd Street, Camden, New Jersey
Ice, Robert D., 1054 Cecil Avenue, Louisville, Kentucky
Immekus, James F., 1401 Methyl Street, Pittsburgh, Pennsylvania
Itt, Charles L., 1418½ Broadway, Fort Wayne, Indiana
Irwin, Johnson M., Williston, Ohio
Jabour, Michel P., 1412 Webster Avenue, Pittsburgh, Pennsylvania
Jacobs, Albert, 1102 Lakeview Road, Cleveland, Ohio
Jacobson, Hilding L., 3212 Myrtle Avenue, Omaha, Nebraska
Janashak, Micheal R., 3012 5th Avenue E., Hibbing, Minnesota
Janovsky, Joseph R., 3807 W. Wisconsin Street, Los Angeles, California
Janson, Henry G., (Address Unavailable)
Jarman, Jean J., 308 Hillyer Place, Peoria, Illinois
Jarvis, Roy E., RFD 1, Martins Ferry, Ohio
Jastrzemski, John T., 14 Romney Road, Bound Brook, New Jersey
Jennings, George W., Jr., (Address Unavailable)
Jennings, Harry B., 97-13 Brisbin Street, Jamaica, New York
Jensen, Dean R., Greenfield, Iowa
Johenning, James L., 6 Westside Court, Lexington, Virginia
Johns, Harry J., Story, Wyoming
Johnson, Andrew J., 614 Selma Street, Cadillac, Michigan
Johnson, Cecil O., Box 221, Rocky Ford, Colorado
Johnson, Daniel B., 1257 E. First Street, Long Beach, California
Johnson, Edwin L., Route 4, Mount Airy, North Carolina
Johnson, Gerald W., 66 Stoneyford Avenue, San Francisco, California
Johnson, George L., Route 2, Lufkin, Texas
Johnson, James, 152 Grove Street, Haverhill, Massachusetts
Johnson, Joel F., 8306 Victor Avenue, Long Island, New York

Johnson, Robert H., Box 14, Landisville, Pennsylvania
Johnson, Wilford H., 50 Montcalm Avenue, Plattsburg, New York
Jones, Jack L., Route 1, Box 14B, Waco, Texas
Jones, James A., (Address Unavailable)
Jones, James R., Stratford Court, New Castle, Indiana
Jones, Robert E., 6019 St. John, Kansas City, Missouri
Jones, Robert F., 511 Clark Avenue, Billings, Montana
Jordan, James A., Nauvoo, Illinois
Jorgenson, Albert L., Mitchell, South Dakota
Juroshek, Mike H., Acme, Wyoming
Kaemmerling, F. M., 705 Washington Avenue, Moundsville, West Virginia
Kagels, Theodore A., Jr., 160 Delmar Street, San Francisco, California
Kahl, Curtis V., Newmanstown, Pennsylvania
Kennette, James, 5212 90th Street, Elmhurst, New York
Kasper, Joseph J., 2348 E. 22nd Street, Cleveland, Ohio
Kasten, Edmund L., Echo, Minnesota
Katrencik, John S., Route 1, Monongahela, Pennsylvania
Kaufman, Douglas, 3565 67 Eden Avenue, Cincinnati, Ohio
Keeps The Mountain, Samuel, Rosebud, South Dakota
Kelez, Steve, Meadow Park, San Rafael, California
Keller, Leonard O., Wilson Creek, Washington
Kelley, Joseph E., 235 Howard Avenue, New Haven, Connecticut
Kelly, David N., 720 Sierra Vista, Alhambra, California
Kelly, Joseph M., 122 N. Scott Avenue, Glenolden, Pennsylvania
Kelly, Milton H., 12 Union Court, New London, Connecticut
Kelly, Samuel R., 3405 Beechwood Avenue, Cleveland Heights, Ohio
Kennedy, William R., 1667 28th Avenue, St. Petersburg, Florida
Kenney, Nat M., Jr., 222 E. Poplar Street, San Antonio, Texas
Kerwan, John J., 19 W. 31st Street, New York City, New York
Kicera, Michael H., 18 S. 3rd Street, Clearfield, Pennsylvania
Kilroy, Walter D., 8426½ Long Beach Boulevard, South Gate, California
Kimbler, James H., Gregoryville, Kentucky
Kimsey, Harold R., Route 1, Jamestown, North Carolina
King, James D., Jr., Columbus, Northport, Alabama
Kirmil, John M., 28 Montgomery Street, Lawrence, Massachusetts
Klee, Kenneth G., 3676 Townsend Avenue, Detroit 14, Michigan
Klein, Robert J., Rugby, North Dakota
Klem, Michael R., 962 Lorimer Street, Brooklyn, New York
Kline, Riley K., Route 5, Bloomsburg, Pennsylvania
Kline, Steven, 169 Washington, Newburgh, New York
Klose, Paul R., 6112 E. 5th Avenue, Escondido, California
Kness, Arthur E., 210 Tyler Street, Taft, California
Knight, Ford W., Route 1, Knox, Pennsylvania
Knoll, Henry L., 710 37th Street, Oakland, California
Knowles, Ralph M., 4707 Warwick Avenue, Chicago, Illinois
Knowlden, Robert S., 5501 Nevada, Washington, D. C.
Kohler, Edward A., (Address Unavailable)
Kohout, Raymond P., 1230 S. 59th Court, Cicero, Illinois
Kolodziejski, Henry J., 119 Cotton Way, Pittsburgh, Pennsylvania
Korpela, Tauno E., Ironwood, Michigan
Kortemeyer, Henry A., Route 4, Box 444AA, Salem, Oregon
Korza, Roman J., Chestnut Street, Hatfield, Massachusetts
Kovacevich, George, 2232 Larkins Way, Pittsburgh, Pennsylvania
Kovach, Elmer G., 8610 Tompkins Avenue, Cleveland, Ohio
Krafft, Harold D., Jr., 4900 Loughboro Road, Washington, D. C.
Krakowsky, Davis, 515 McDonald Avenue, Brooklyn, New York
Krajewski, John S., Jr., 62 Rolland Street, Sloan, New York
Krall, Raymond, 3619 Hermitage Avenue, Chicago, Illinois
Kranz, Francis J., RFD 1, Box 232, Westville, Illinois
Kratz, Clarence W., 732 Otsego Avenue, Coshocton, Ohio
Kraushaar, Herbert W., 2018 Elliott Street, Alexandria, Louisiana
Krauss, Charles A., 109 Hawthorne Avenue, Neptune, New Jersey
Kress, Paul B., 126 E. High Street, Painted Post, New York
Kroll, Robert J., 202 S. Holmes, Lansing, Michigan
Kreidler, Francis W., 175 Alhambra, Apartment 301, San Francisco, California
Kucker, Thomas W., 16 Green Lane, Trenton, New Jersey
Kunkle, Ralph W., Box 27, Weissport, Pennsylvania
Kunkler, Paul E., Route 4, Logan, Ohio
Kurtiak, John, 319 Old Road, Sewaren, New Jersey
Kuss, Herman, 21 N. Hancock Street, Wilkes-Barre, Pennsylvania
Kuschell Francis T., 6330 S. Elizabeth, Chicago, Illinois
Kuta, Chester J., 1410 Bull Street, Columbia, South Carolina
Lacroix, Bob T., Havre, Montana
LaDue, Frank J., 12½ River Street, South Glen Falls, New York
Lahmsen, Jerome, 3346 58th Street, Milwaukee, Wisconsin
Lahood, George J., 434 Glen Mouton Street, Lafayette, Louisiana
Lamar, Clide H., 1219 S. Court Street, Montgomery, Alabama
Landes, Homer, 126 Thompson Street, Staunton, Virginia
Lane, William T., 717 Medaris Street, Clinton, Tennessee
Langdon, Paul E., Jr., 5675 Vine Street, Cincinnati, Ohio
Larson, Joseph A., 25 S. Broadway, White Plains, New York
Larsen, Robert D., Route 1, Box 355, Renton, Washington
Lathrop, Richard C., 8218 Gridley Avenue, Wauwatosa, Wisconsin
LaTorra, Robert A., 1714-11 Avenue, Greeley, Colorado
Lawler, Albert P., 22 Avenue Place, Malden, Massachusetts
Leask, Wallace D., 1319 N. E. Birch Street, Camas, Washington
Lee, George W., 1016 Tierney Road, Ft. Worth, Texas
Lee, John O., 1068 N. W. 26th Terrace, Miami, Florida
Lee, John T., Jr., Route 2, Box 59, Hood River, Oregon
Lee, Lynn A., Box 188, Archer City, Texas
Lee, Lester W., 1932 Gaines, Davenport, Iowa
Lee, Matthias J., 1 Walnut Street, Binghamton, New York
Legett, William G., Northfield Road, Bedford, Ohio
Lehmann, Fred, 8086 88th Avenue, Woodhaven, Long Island, New York
Leitenmeyer, F. L., 428 76th Street, N. Bergen, New Jersey
Lemeron, Harrell L., RR 3, Lawrenceville, Illinois
Lemons, William L., 314 Main Street, Wheeling, West Virginia
Lenarduzzi, Marc, 4921 Pease Street, Houston, Texas
Lenzi, Vincent J., 767½ N. Goodmen Street, Rochester, Ney York
Leville, Frederick I., 72 W. Eagle Street, East Boston, Massachusetts
Lewis, Clair E., Gay Street, Plain City, Ohio

Lewis, Paul J., General Delivery, Ocoee, Tennessee
Lewis, Thomas K., 14 Elliott Street, Portsmouth, Virginia
Lewis, Walter C., Jr., Box 545, Steubenville, Ohio
Licht, Oscar, 153 Central Avenue, Elmsford, New York
Lieberman, Isadore, 1230 W. Wyoming Avenue, Philadelphia, Pennsylvania
Lilley, David J., 5164 Norwaldo, Indianapolis, Indiana
Lingerfelt, William O., Route 2, Fyffe, Alabama
Link, Ray C., Box 326, Victoria, Virginia
Liparela, Joseph A., 208 Thomas Street, Wilkes-Barre, Pennsylvania
Lipscomb, Thomas C., 1110 Fannin Street, Houston, Texas
Lloyd, Robert H., Church Street, Lewisburg, Tennessee
Lloyd, Troy B., 123 Ohio Street, Johnstown, Pennsylvania
Lobaugh, William R., 2218 W. 17th Street, Oklahoma City, Oklahoma
Loomis, Raymond P., 612 Fonulae Avenue, Sheboygan Falls, Wisconsin
Looney, Bennie W., Gainesville, Missouri
Looper, James D., Route 2, Piedmont, South Carolina
Lorenzen, Carl A., Neligh, Nebraska
Loscombe, William J., 2970 Frink Street, Scranton, Pennsylvania
Lowman, Leonard S., 220 Third Street, Derry, Pennsylvania
Lowry, Henry J., Sr., 42 Leather Street, Atlanta, Georgia
Lufkin, Peter W., Kirby Lane, Rye, New York
Lyman, Theron U., 488 Ridgewood Road, Maplewood, New Jersey
Lyon, Donald M., (Address Unavailable)
Mackenzie, John H., 60 Highland Terrace, Middletown, Connecticut
Mackey, William C., 2200 14th Street, Troy, New York
Magyar, William A., Route 1, New Tripoli, Pennsylvania
Mallernee, John O., Glendale 8, California
Malliet, Jerome T., 66 Maplewood Avenue, West Hartford, Connecticut
Mancato, Carmine, (Address Unavailable)
Manders, John M., 1202 N. Hunter Street, Stockton, California
Marcus, John F., 48th Street, Wheeling, West Virginia
Marcus, Donald, 386 E. 38th Street, Paterson, Ney Jersey
Marean, Frank C., Jr., 1064 Pleasant Street, Worcester, Massachusetts
Marsden, Charles E., 406 May Street N, Belle Vernon, Pennsylvania
Marticorena, Steve J., 9933 Otis Street, Southgate, California
Martinez, Desiderio B., Las Cruces, New Mexico
Martinez, Jose E., 4429 Grove Avenue, Riverside, California
Masterson, Joseph F., 48 2nd Avenue, Troy, New York
Mason, Manley A., 627 Langstaff Street, Missoula, Montana
Mathews, William M., 307 North D. Street, Indianola, Iowa
Mays, Donald E., Route 1, Nelsonville, Ohio
Mauk, Walter C., (Address Unavailable)
Meisner, Fred W., Nanticoke, New York
Meinken, Diedrich J., 581 Howell Avenue, Cincinnati, Ohio
Merenda, Joseph, 17 Bradford Terrace, Everett, Massachusetts
Merkie, Charles J., 101 Myrtle Avenue, Chatham Village, Pennsylvania
Meyers, Joseph F., 71 N. Chatsworth, Larchmont, New York
Miles, Donald Lee, 682 Gladstone, Detroit, Michigan
Miller, Leonard H., 258 E. 33rd Street, New York, New York
Miller, Marion E., 1600 22nd Street, Wichita Falls, Texas
Miller, Marlin E., 10 Lincoln Apartment, Minot, North Dakota
Miller, Wilfred J., 79-24 154th Street, Flushing, New York
Miller, William A., 1664 42nd Street, Brooklyn, New York
Miller, William C., RFD 1, Hughesville, Pennsylvania
Milsovic, Ralph J., 208 Sebering Avenue, Pittsburgh, Pennsylvania
Milstead, Harold H., 1010 N. S. Street, Pensacola, Florida
Minnick, James G., Route 4, Abingdon, Virginia
Molettiere, Girad L., 601 N. Cannon Avenue, Lansdale, Pennsylvania
Monaghan, Daniel A., Jr., 400 Allen Street, Ferndale, Michigan
Monson, Alfred L., Fowler, Illinois
Montgomery, George M., 1365 S. 3rd Street, Louisville, Kentucky
Montgomery, Harry E., 805 O Street, Eureka, California
Moore, Brockman M., 1378 S. 3rd Street, Louisville, Kentucky
Moore, Gerald B., 64 Bloomfield Road, Clarksdale, Georgia
Moore, James M., Box 144, Harrisville, Ohio
Moore, Jay W., RFD, Kirkwood, Illinois
Moore, Orbry H., 403 Maple Street, Murfreesboro, Tennessee
Mordecai, George I., 371 Poplar Street, New Haven, Connecticut
Morgan, John P., Box 175, Renton, Pennsylvania
Morrison, Arnold J., Bothell, Washington
Moye, Macon, Jr., 2004 Evans Street, Morehead City, North Carolina
Mudie, Charles R., State R., Andalusia, Pennsylvania
Mularz, Alfred J., (Address Unavailable)
Mulholden, Orange L., RFD 1, Fallentimber, Pennsylvania
Mulligan, William J., Jr., 258 Post Avenue, Rochester, New York
Murphy, Gerard J., 1540 Chesterland Avenue, Lakewood, Ohio
Murphy, John J., 73-22 19th Street, Flushing, New York
Murphy, Marion K., 363 5th Street N. E., Atlanta, Georgia
Murphy, Michael A., Jr., Box 123, Belle Glade, Florida
Musket, George H., 1236 Fairview Avenue, University City, Missouri
Muttys, Joseph F., 1819 Merriman Street, Pittsburgh, Pennsylvania
Myers, Jonas E., RR 1, South Whitley, Indiana
McAlister, Dwight A., Route 2, Leavenworth, Kansas
McBay, Paul C., 123 Fellsway, West Medford, Massachusetts
McClanathan, Dempster S., Spring Arbor, Michigan
McClellan, Elmer L., 620 Elm Street, West Springfield, Massachusetts
McClure, William E., 2128 N. 15th Street, Philadelphia, Pennsylvania
McCormick, John R., Gildford, Montana
McCoy, Gregory L., 179 Goldsprings, New Haven, Connecticut
McCusker, Patrick A., (Address Unavailable)
McDaniel, Edward J. T., (Address Unavailable)
McDaniel, Herbert A., Glencoe, Missouri
McDonald, Carl D., 198 Brooks Parkway, San Antonio, Texas
McDonald, John W., Route 1, Dyersburg, Tennessee
McEwen, Emlin O., 605 Date Street, Fernandiana, Florida
McGill, Robert K., RFD Box 46, Elsinore, California
McGowan, Thomas A., 720 East Ontario Street, Philadelphia, Pennsylvania
McGowan, Wilfred J., 1400 Palm Avenue, San Mateo, California
McGrane, Arthur J., Max Meadows, Virginia
McGuire, Matthew F., RFD 1, Bergen, New York
McInnis, Wilfred J., 840 8th Street, Douglas, Arizona

McIntyre, Miles E., Jr., 208 Delaware Avenue, Ithaca, New York
McIver, Alvin G., 623 Capitol Avenue S. W., Battle Creek, Michigan
McKenney, John E., 2419 Ken Oak Road, Baltimore, Maryland
McKinney, Paul G., Lillybrook, West Virginia
McLaughlin, William T., 925 E. 17th Street, Wilmington, Delaware
McNulty, Raymond F., 264 Pleasant Street, Marblehead, Massachusetts
McQuade, John J., 2973 Harding Avenue, New York, New York
McSparin, Russell L., Stonefort, Illinois
McWilliam, Leo J., 2349 Mifflin Street, Philadelphia, Pennsylvania
Naccarato, James P., 361 S. Marshall Street, Pontiac, Michigan
Nagy, Oscar Richard, 37 Fulton Street, Bloomfield, New Jersey
Neal, James L., 2431 Cherry Street, Quincy, Illinois
Nirdlinger, Eugene, 1304 Highland Avenue, Pittsburgh, Pennsylvania
Nolan, James J., 19 Burd Street, Pennington, New Jersey
Norton, John L., 251 W. 80th Street, Chicago, Illinois
Neaville, James C., 215 W. Oklahoma Street, Tulsa, Oklahoma
Neer, Arthur T., 7½ Pine Street, Oneonta, New York
Nelson, Myles A., 3447 Goldenich Street, San Diego, California
Nelson, George S., 36 Oak Street, Ashville, North Carolina
Neumann, Kenneth E., 921 8th Street 10th Avenue West, Grand Rapids, Minnesota
Nicholls, Henry M., 1215 Main Street, Galena, Illinois
Niendorf, Clarence G., 519 Havalind Street, Laporte, Indiana
Nielson, Forrest E., Fountain Green, Utah
Nienhuis, Wyba, 37 E. 18th Street, Holland, Michigan
O'Donnel, Joseph J., 451 Old Colony Avenue, Boston, Massachusetts
Ogle, Lilburn F., Dickens, Texas
Ohnemus, Roman H., 421 N. Valencia Street, Alhambra, California
Oliver, Alfred F., 28 Oak Forest Drive, Montgomery, Alabama
Opdycke, Wendell L., Everrittstown Road, Frenchtown, New Jersey
Opitz, Charles J., 25 Upland Street, Springfield, Massachusetts
Osborn, Allen, Jr., 52 Taylor Avenue, Manasquan, New Jersey
Ostachowicz, Alphonse, 162 17th Street, Brooklyn, New York
Otto, Omer R., (Address Unavailable)
Overcash, Luther R., 155 Lane Street, Kannapolis, North Carolina
Overton, John D., Geraldina, Alabama
Owen, Arris, 4130 San Carlos, Dallas, Texas
Owen, Rex C., 50 Arden Road, Ashville, North Carolina
Owens, Benjamin V., Spavinaw, Oklahoma
Owens, Robert L., 612 Avenue D., Cisco, Texas
Oxford, Carl B., Suttle, Alabama
Pacciorini, Charles M., Route 2, Gilroy, California
Padavic, Frank J., Toluca, Illinois
Palace, Alfred R., 3752 Dickens Avenue, Chicago, Illinois
Pallotta, Rico F., 13 East Monroe Street, Bedford, Ohio
Palmer, Samuel E., Jr., 318 Hillcrest Avenue, Hinsdale, Illinois
Paredes, Alfredo P., 600 Rubio Street, Del Rio, Texas
Parker, James A., Athol, New York
Parker, William L., Route 2, Box 134-A, Tallahassee, Florida
Parker, William R., Jr., 3612 Rio Vista, Houston, Texas
Parks, Ambrose H., 306 N. 3rd Street, Steubenville, Ohio
Parrillo, Frank, 354 Broadway, Providence, Rhode Island
Payne, William H., Onton, Kentucky
Passodelis, John, 222 Station Street, Aliquippa, Pennsylvania
Pateman, Joseph C., 709 Charles Street, Perth Amboy, New Jersey
Patton, Harry O., 91-21 195th Street, Hollis, New York
Peck, Howard M., 605 W. Winona Street, Austin, Minnesota
Peek, Joseph L., 502 W. Mechanic Street, Ottumwa, Iowa
Peery, William T., Tazewell, Virginia
Peltak, Anthony T., 33 Laurel Street, Manchester, New Hampshire
Perry, R. B., Box 419, Fayetteville, Tennessee
Peters, Russell E., 730 Glenridge Drive, Palm Beach, Florida
Phelps, William E., Elsberry, Missouri
Phillip, Edward M., 1144 11th Street, Oshkosh, Wisconsin
Phillips, Chester A., 1183 Forbes Avenue, Akron, Ohio
Phillips, Elliott S., 207 Shabut Street, Mankato, Minnesota
Pianczk, Donald A., 6203 Grandy, Detroit, Michigan
Pietscher, Ronda R., RR 1, Princeton, Iowa
Pinto, William, 446 E. 85th Street, New York, New York
Pitzner, James F., 215 Ferry Street, Sewickley, Pennsylvania
Plaster, Herbert H., 105 Main Street, Hudson Falls, New York
Plock, Lowell B., 5900 Manton Avenue, Chicago, Illinois
Polcare, Arthur B., 7 Montrose Street, Everett, Massachusetts
Pridlides, James, 4904 43rd Avenue, Woodside, Long Island, New York
Provost, David E., 566 3rd Avenue, Troy, New York
Purnty, Peter F., 3524 95th Street, New York, New York
Quadrato, Louis, 148 Meriden, Waterbury, Connecticut
Quaglia, Eugene A., 344 Pleasant Avenue, New York City, New York
Quickshall, Arthur L., 715 Part Place, Austin, Texas
Quiroz, Pedro, Hebbronville, Texas
Rabold, Helmuth A., 233 16th Avenue, St. Paul, Minnesota
Rain, Cornelius, 335 E. Magnolia, Gainesville, Florida
Ramey, Robert E., Box 156, Akron, Alabama
Ramirez, Miguel A., 3858 Cottonwood Street, San Diego, California
Randall, Norman, 156 W. Brookline Street, Boston, Massachusetts
Rathkopf, Adrian M., 1680 Clay Avenue, Bronx, New York
Ratnoff, Herbert, 51 E. 90th Street, New York, New York
Raven, Henry J., 868 Fuller Avenue N. E., Grand Rapids, Michigan
Ray, George H., 37 Orchard Street, Shavertown, Pennsylvania
Reznoff, Kenneth J., Route 1, Brookfield, Ohio
Redding, Marion G., Route 3, Fort Gaines, Georgia
Redmon, Bill N., 14 Clay Street, Santa Cruz, California
Reed, Carl A., Route 2, Box 2, Silverton, Oregon
Reed, Clurin B., Jr., Route 1, Jones, Alabama
Reed, James J., 21 First Street, East Norwalk, Connecticut
Reese, Maynard M., 3-12 26th Street, Warren Point, New Jersey
Reece, Williard H., Labelville, Tennessee
Rensink, Henry C., Star Route, Deming, Washington
Reuss, Aubrey, (Address Unavailable)
Rew, Donald L., Box 123, Edwall, Washington
Rhodes, Garland S., RFD 1, Box 95, Flatrock, North Carolina
Richard, Emanuel J., 192 Franklin Street, Lynn, Massachusetts
Richard, George J., 5326 Kamering Avenue, Chicago, Illinois

Richardson, James R., Route 1, Grove City, Pennsylvania
Rider, Harry E., Cabot, Arkansas
Riggs, Thomas D., 3724 Gilpin Street, Denver, Colorado
Righettini, Reno F., 14730 Withrop, Detroit, Michigan
Riordan, Walter A., 45 Orne Street, Worcester, Massachusetts
Roach, Kenneth B., Route 3, Bentonville, Arkansas
Roberts, John D., 7942 Drexel Avenue, Chicago, Illinois
Robertson, Neil, 48 W. 53rd Street, New York City, New York
Robin, Belvin H., 303 E. Stone Avenue, Greenville, South Carolina
Robinson, Robert R., 514½ W. Palm, El Segundo, California
Rockstool, Lester A., 2605 S. Main Street, Elkhart, Indiana
Rodriguez, Louis, 59 W. 199th Street, New York, New York
Ronk, Robert E., 9315 Oakview, Plymouth, Michigan
Root, Vernon O., 524 21st Street, Bellingham, Washington
Romaine, Henry G., 132 Liberty Street, Dover, New Jersey
Rose, Frederick D., 62 Kendall Street, Framingham, Massachusetts
Ross, Hubert K., Eriline, Kentucky
Rossi, Larry, 3917 Wilkins Avenue, Baltimore, Maryland
Rountree, Thomas W., Jr., 203 W. DeSota Street, Lake City, Florida
Roy, Arthur H., 10 Woodman Street, Concord, New Hampshire
Roysdon, Richard C., 103 W. 51st Street, Kansas City, Missouri
Rundlfson, Taylor R., 2222 Sawtelle Boulevard, W. Los Angeles, California
Rush, William A., 1112 Seneca Drive, RR 3, Enid, Oklahoma
Russick, Bertram W., 651 46th Street, Des Moines, Iowa
Revels, Verlin J., Hillsboro, Wisconsin
Ryan, Donald W., 564 S. 35th Street, Apartment 3, Omaha, Nebraska
Sabinash, Harry, 423 W. Becher Street, Milwaukee, Wisconsin
Sacco, Joseph A., 417 Adams Street, Goencoe, Illinois
Safarowitz, Edward A., 756 S. Division Street, Buffalo, New York
Sager, Robert W., 1070 W. 3rd Street, Colby, Kansas
Salazar, Ramon, 2930 Love Field Drive, Dallas, Texas
Salinardo, Anthony J., 200 Chestnut Street, Fredonia, New York
Sams, James R., 1953 Walnut Street, Jacksonville, Florida
Sanborn, Lloyd D., 11 Maple Terrace, Waverly, Massachusetts
Sandberh, Arthur H., Route 2, Ravenna, Michigan
Sanders, David N., 109 Paterson Avenue, Paterson, New Jersey
Sasek, Edwin F., 712 Linden Place, Alton, Illinois
Savage, Malcolm R., (Address Unavailable)
Savicki, William, 464 Eastern Parkway, Brooklyn, New York
Scaff, Eli C., La Junta, Colorado
Scalzone, John, West Point Avenue, New Brunswick, New Jersey
Schade, Lawrence N., 592 N. Summerset Street, Salem, Oregon
Schaub, John M., 4112 Rochelle Street, Pittsburgh, Pennsylvania
Schayda, Joseph, 103 South Street, Bethel, Connecticut
Schenzel, Carl E., 408 East Street, Merrill, Wisconsin
Schiel, Fred A., Jr., 3070 Maine Avenue, Long Beach, California
Schilliaci, John J., 411 S. Washington Street, Rochester, New York
Schnier, Seymour, 535 E. 8th Street, Brooklyn, New York
Schoeffler, Dwight, 3438 85th Street, Jackson Heights, New York
Schoenfield, Walter H., 308 Myrtle Street, Montebello, California
Schultz, Durrell D., (Address Unavailable)
Schweitzer, Charles E., 37 Centre Street, Woodmere, New York
Scott, Clarence L., 1417 18th Street, Alameda, California
Scott, Robert C., (Address Unavailable)
Seale, Joseph L., (Address Unavailable)
Seaton, Howard W., Box 124, Curtis, Michigan
Seemann, Fred, 1926 Woodbine Street, Ridgewood, New York
Sellon, William A., Main Street, W. Townsend, Massachusetts
Sensenich, Michael W., 1016 Scott Street, Jeannette, Pennsylvania
Shabazain, John V., 2636 Rimpau Boulevard, Los Angeles, California
Shapiro, John J., 1361 Chandler Avenue, Far Rockway, New York
Sharp, Harry R., 7018 Vinevale Avenue, Bell, California
Shearin, Thomas R., 157 Dixon Boulevard, Uniontown, Pennsylvania
Shelley, James H., Excel, Alabama
Shelton, Charles E., c-o Mr. J. H. Sievers, Marta Bend, Missouri
Shepard, Eugene D., Greenville, South Carolina
Sheppe, Andrew J., Jr., Box 1518, Sophia, West Virginia
Shetron, Robert L., 20 Montgomery Avenue, Shippensburg, Pennsylvania
Shoemaker, Fred E., 4709 Harriet Avenue, Minneapolis, Minnesota
Shubeck, Leonard J., 2722 W. Evergreen, Chicago, Illinois
Shukalo, Francis J., 59 Sterling Street, Franklin, New Jersey
Silva, Eugene E., 1411 66th Street, Oakland, California
Simmons, Edward C., 700 N. Meridian Street, Oklahoma City, Oklahoma
Simmons, Joseph T., Jr., 1525 Locust Street, Denver, Colorado
Simpson, John E., Carrier Mills, Illinois
Simpson, Roy L., Jr., Palacios, Texas
Sims, Gerald E., Ocoee, Florida
Singerman, Adolph K., 718 E. Amherst Street, Buffalo, New York
Singleton, Leo W., Bayport, Florida
Sinrota, Martin B., 468 A. East 93rd Street, Brooklyn, New York
Sivak, Morris, 412 Blake Avenue, Brooklyn, New York
Skeba, Philip W., (Address Unavailable)
Skinner, James, 4891 Fernwood, Detroit, Michigan
Smith, Clarence W., Feed Yards, Sioux Rapids, Iowa
Smith, Odell L., Melder, Louisiana
Smith, Philip D., 313 Duncan Avenue, Jackson, Mississippi
Smith, Raymond T., 18 Gordon Street, Ridgefield Park, New Jersey
Smott, James E., 1506 S. 13th Street, St. Louis, Missouri
Snider, Aubrey D., 1707 15th Street, Lubbock, Texas
Snyder, John F., Route 6, Butler, Pennsylvania
Snyder, Robert C., Box 28, Kennydale, Washington
Sommers, Francis J., 156 Pencoyd Avenue, W. Manayank, Pennsylvania
Sorel, Clifford D., RFD 1, Plattsburg, New York
Sorensen, Everett C., 4619 N. Racine, Chicago, Illinois
Sowinski, Arthur A., 59-70 69th Street, Maspeth, Flushing, New York
Speegle, William O., c-o J. M. Speegle, Quemado, Texas
Spencer, Otho D., Star Route, Riverton, Wyoming
Sprague, William E., 2261 Iuka Avenue, Columbus, Ohio
Spulier, John L., RR 10, Ft. Wayne, Indiana
Stape, Donald N., (Address Unavailable)
Steck, Maxie E., 342 Avenue F, Newgulf, Texas
Steele, Heath C., Oxford, Indiana

Stever, Douglas B., Route 3, Stromsburg, Nebraska
Steward, Edward J., 209 9th Street, Brooklyn, New York
Stiles, Claude J., Hebert, Louisiana
Still, Oscar W., Box 114, Hutchins, Texas
Stinson, Raymond O., Route 4, Milan, Tennessee
St. John, Richard D., 804 Second Street, Jackson, Michigan
Stobe, John W., Covington, Tennessee
Stocklosa, Louis J., Route 3, Remsen, New York
Stom, Harold E., Route 3, Brookhaven, Mississippi
Stone, Jerry D., Box 95, Boaz, Alabama
Stoner, Robert R., 1317 Utah Place, Baltimore, Maryland
Stowell, Aubrey L., 943 N. Oxford Street, Indianapolis, Indiana
Strawn, Franklin T., Box 550, Smithfield, Pennsylvania
Strobel, Sidney, 1335 Morrison Avenue, Bronx, New York
Suddreth, Thomas T., Box 193, Raeford, North Carolina
Sutter, Wilbert J., 304 Karnes Avenue, Cameron, Texas
Swanzy, Malcolm O., 801 Parkway, Greenwood, Massachusetts
Swejkowski, Stanley J., 1916 N. Winchester, Chicago, Illinois
Symens, Milford H., 3271 8th, Sacramento, California
Szego, Joseph, 212 3rd Street, Passaic, New Jersey
Szkodzinski, Michael W., 423 E. 22nd Street, New York, New York
Taylor, James, Route 2, Hixson, Tennessee
Taylor, Martin H., Route 1, Hudsonville, Michigan
Tencza, Fred J., 75 Grove Street, Passaic, New Jersey
Terwilliger, Charles, Jr., c-o C. W. McSherry, Brooklyn, Iowa
Tevere, Vito, Jr., 451 E. 119th Street, New York, New York
Theriault, Raymond J., Holland, Maine
Thies, Everett W., 146 Lowell Street, Arlington, Massachusetts
Thompson, Marvin B., 300 Dowell Avenue, Powderly, Alabama
Thompson, Paul L., 410 N. 6th Street, Terre Haute, Indiana
Tirado, Jeronimo, 751 Forest Avenue, Bronx, New Jersey
Timmerman, Harold L., 2502 Cyren Street, Columbia, South Carolina
Tincher, Eugene F., Comfort, West Virginia
Tomajer, Charles R., Jefferson, New York
Topping, William P., Route 1, Box 44, Bayfield, Wisconsin
Torner, Hilmer N., 4614 Spruce Street, Philadelphia, Pennsylvania
Toth, Stephen P., 1015 Anderson Avenue, Bronx, New York
Townsley, Vernon M., 245 E. S. Temple, 24, Salt Lake City, Utah
Tripp, Donald R., 3836 Saratoga Street, Omaha, Nebraska
Trotta, Frank A., 10 Chadwick Street, Glencove, Long Island, New York
Truliman, Arthur S., 752 14th Avenue, Paterson, New Jersey
Tunze, John R., Jr., 514 W. 2nd Street, Columbia, Illinois
Tuuri, Arma A., 915 Maple Street, Negaunee, Michigan
Underwood, James W., 1346B Bayview Drive, Hermosa Beach, California
Valentine, Joseph N., 195 Broadway, Newburgh, New York
Vallery, Dean B., Route 1, Piketon, Ohio
VanDerzee, Dewitt C., 19 N. Main Avenue, Albany, New York
VanerHoeven, John, Midland Place, Newark, New Jersey
VanHise, Wilbur P., Allentown, New Jersey
VanValkenburg, Richard V. Box 117, Delevan, New York
Vargas, Martin A., 624 Meta Street, Oxnard, California
Vaughn, Paul O., 201 Ridge Street, East Pittsburgh, Pennsylvania
Vernon, Everett, N., Lakeview, Oregon
Vetter, Kenneth G., 4911 Highland, Downers Grove, Illinois
Vincent, George H., Box 91, Depew, Oklahoma
Vincent, Thomas J., Main Street, Lore City, Ohio
Vogt, Sylvester K., Lakefield, Minnesota
Volk, Jack, 17 Lark Street, Rochester, New York
Volpi, Leo U., 1275 Anderson Avenue, Palisade, New Jersey
Wagner, Bruce E., Blackduck, Minnesota
Wagner, Kenneth H., Box 403, Morro Bay, California
Waldo, James T., 11226 Fremont Avenue, Seatile, Washington
Walker, William P., Jr., 204 Peele Street, Burlington, North Carolina
Walsh, Jack R., 616 E. Line Avenue, Monrovia, California
Wanda, Howard G., RD 2, McCann Road, Olean, New York
Ward, Thomas H., Inlay City, Michigan
Warnick, Harold E., Box 844, Kermit, Texas
Washburn, Clarence J., 324 Hill Street, Oxnard, California
Waters, Duane W., 442 S. Cochran, Los Angeles, California
Watkins, Lewis P., Hixson, Texas

Watson, Edward G., 303 E. John Street, Knox, Indiana
Watt, Elbert L., 215 B Street, N. E., Washington, D. C.
Watts, Carl E., Route 3, Kokomo, Indiana
Way, Albert, Gibson, Georgia
Weathewalks, Harold W., Pompton Lakes, New Jersey
Weiner, Jack, 2041 Holland Avenue, Bronx, New York
Weinstein, Edward S., 3901 W. Van Buren, Chicago, Illinois
Welch, Raymond L., Jr., 506 S. Santa Fe Street, Salina, Kansas
Welch, William J., Jr., 127 Josephine, Somerville, Massachusetts
Wenger, Francis M., Route 1, Quarryville, Pennsylvania
Westfall, George G., 1427 N. Hamlin Avenue, Chicago, Illinois
Wharton, George C., 687 Halsey Street, Brooklyn, New York
White, Fred A., Eagle Lake, Maine
White, Richard, 96 Larkin Street, Bangor, Maine
White, Roger D., Route 1, Turner, Oklahoma
White, Walter F., 514 Oakwood Avenue, Syracuse, New York
White, William H., Jr., Box 539, College Place, Washington, D. C.
Whitlock, Lewis, 505 Waldo Street, Atlanta, Georgia
Wichmann, Delmar L., 208 West Miller Street, Bloomington, Illinois
Wilhelm, Paul R., RR 1, Covington, Ohio
Wilkinson, Earl J., 25 Birch Place, Devon, Connecticut
Willard, Walter G., 434 West Franklin Street, Hagerstown, Maryland
William, Charles L., Route 2, Mount Vernon, Mississippi
William, Curtis G., Route 2, Rocky Mount, North Carolina
Williams, James C., Erlanger Road, Erlanger, Kentucky
Williams, Lester F., Burkesville, Kentucky
Williams, Robert J., 1240 Linden Avenue, Zanesville, Ohio
Williams, William P., 504 S. Darlington, Tulsa, Oklahoma
Williamson, T. E., Jr., Route 2, Brewton, Alabama
Wilson, Arthur J., 510 3rd, Calexico, California
Wilson, Morris B., 1357 Kenwood Avenue, Beloit, Wisconsin
Wilson, Jack, 624 N. Hayworth, Los Angeles, California
Winburn, Floyd H., 1507 W. Shelex Road, Independence, Missouri
Wing, John, 61 Chrystie Street, New York, New York
Winiecki, Raymond J., Route 1, Princeton, Wisconsin
Withers, Victor C., Box 416, Sasakwa, Oklahoma
Witkowski, Jesse A., 120 E. Edison Avenue, New Castle, Pennsylvania
Witt, Edward A., 52 W. 15th Street, Chicago Heights, Illinois
Wittker, Joseph F., Saffordville, Kansas
Wood, Frank L., River Road, Box 3, Titusville, New Jersey
Wooten, Gilben G., 1028 W. Solomon Street, Griffin, Georgia
Work, Dalton L., Box 61, Rew, Pennsylvania
Worley, Frank M., 32 Nebraska Avenue, W. Asheville, North Carolina
Worsham, Lee T., 83 Adams Street, Grenada, Mississippi
Wouster, Henry J., RFD 1, Logansport, Indiana
Wreden, Henry C., 165 Mallorcaway, San Francisco, California
Wright, Weldon L., 1302 12th Street, Honey Grove, Texas
Wronka, Stephen, 9 South Street, Franklin, New Jersey
Yager, Stephen A., 423 Independence Street, Fairport Harbor, Ohio
Yambra, Joseph S., 3707 S. E. 35th Place, Portland, Oregon
Yant, Donald O., 3321 Belknap, Ft. Worth, Texas
Yates, William H., 2232 Brockway Road, Cleveland Heights, Ohio
Yeager, Harry, 400 E. Houston Street, New York, New York
Yeckley, Quenting J., 13 Buffalo Street, Pittsburgh, Pennsylvania
Yerowitz, George, 1918 Prospect Place, Brooklyn, New York
Young, Harold R., (Address Unavailable)
Youngblood, Thomas R., 113 W. Vaughn Street, Kingston, Pennsylvania
Zabawchuk, Stephen P., 1476 Wilkins Avenue, Bronx, New York
Zamborowski, Walter A., 131 Pleasant Place, Cheektowago, New York
Zeigler, Charles T., Newport, Pennsylvania
Zenesky, Mitchell W., Southwick, Massachusetts
Zinchini, William J., 318 Emerson Street, Vandergrift, Pennsylvania
Zmachinsky, John, 65 W. 192nd Street, Bronx, New York
Zola, Andrew G., 18 Welsh Way Road, Pittsburgh, Pennsylvania
Zuber, Joseph F., Turner, Michigan
Zummo, Peter, Route 3, Box 27, Hammond, Louisiana

Burhans, William F., 18 E. North Street, York, Pennsylvania
Chambers, William J., 703 Market Street, San Francisco, California
Clark, James K., Felton, Georgia

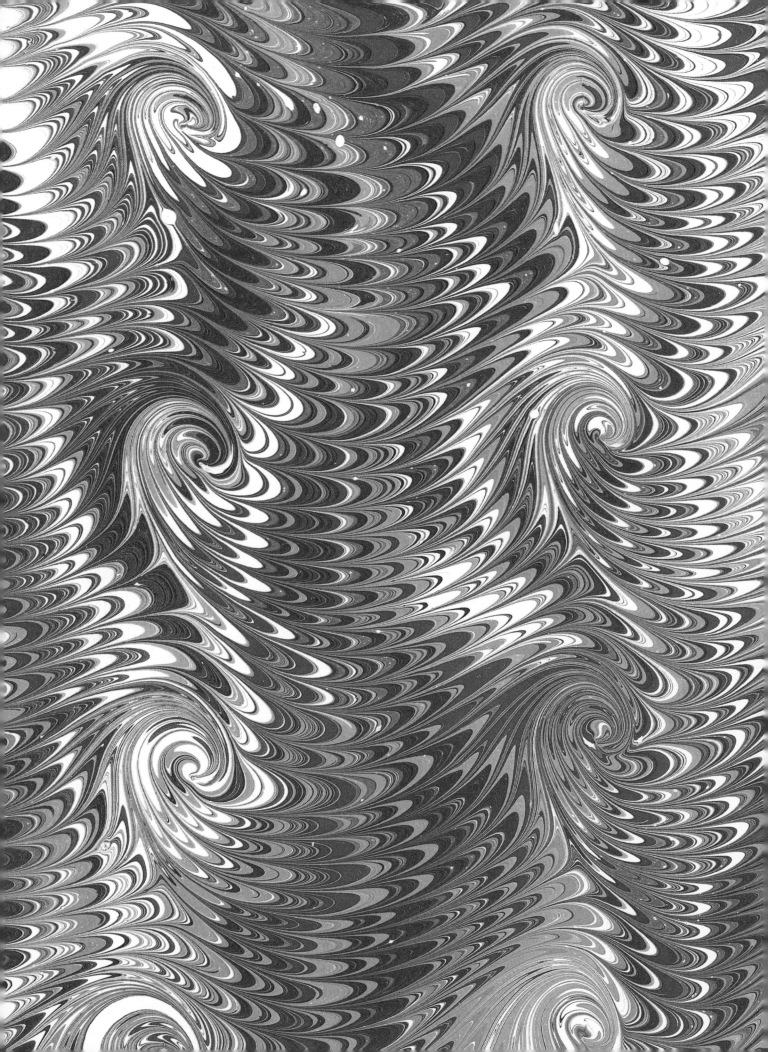